SHATTERED BONDS

The Color of
Child Welfare

―――――――――

D O R O T H Y   R O B E R T S

BASIC

CIVITAS
BOOKS

A Member of the Perseus Books Group

To my miracle,
Dessalines

Published by Basic *Civitas* Books,
A Member of the Perseus Books Group

Designed by Deborah Gayle

A cataloging-in-publication record for this book is available from the
Library of Congress.

ISBN 0-465-07058-2

02 03 04 / 10 9 8 7 6 5 4 3 2 1

Contents

INTRODUCTION

Facing the Racial Reality of Child Welfare v

PART ONE

Destroying Black Families in the Name of Child Protection 1

1. The Color of America's Child Welfare System

2. The System's Inferior Treatment of Black Children

3. Tracing the Disparity to Black Child Poverty

4. Is Racism the Cause?

5. The System's Fundamental Flaw

6. A Racist Institution?

PART TWO

The New Politics of Child Welfare 101

1. The Assault on Family Preservation

2. Why Family Preservation Fails

3. Is Adoption the Answer?

4. Welfare Reform: Ending Aid to Poor Children

5. Locking Up Parents and Children

CONTENTS

PART THREE

The System's Racial Harm 221

1. Protection of Family Rights
2. A Theory of Group-Based Harm
Conclusion: Child Welfare and Social Justice

Notes 277
Acknowledgments 317
Index 321

INTRODUCTION

Facing the Racial Reality of Child Welfare

ONE SUMMER EVENING I DROVE TO ST. STEPHEN'S CHURCH in Englewood, one of Chicago's poorest neighborhoods, to attend a meeting of Black mothers whose children had been taken by the state child protection agency. They call their organization Operation MOSES, for Mothers Organizing Systems for Equal Services. A boy playing outside directed me to the church basement where I found a half dozen women sitting around a table. The women were strategizing about a citywide campaign to call attention to the crisis of children being removed from their homes. They greeted me warmly, grateful to have the ear of a sympathetic law professor. At one end of the table was an expanding file stuffed with court papers, newspaper clippings, and letters. They sat me at the other end so that I could face everyone.

Each woman told me about her battle with the child welfare system to get her children back. Jornell, the group's founder, lost custody of her one-month-old baby when hospital staff reported her for medical abuse. This is his fourth year in foster care. Valerie relinquished custody of her three children to the child protection agency when she was living in a cold, roach-infested apartment and had no means to support them.* She had told authorities that she wanted them back in six months, but the agency moved ahead with termination of her parental rights. Devon had cared for her four nieces and nephews since they were toddlers, devoting herself to meeting their special medical and educational needs. She had seen them only twice since they were taken from her more than a year earlier because her apartment was too small.

---

*Because she is challenging the termination of her rights in court, "Valerie" asked me to use a fictitious name for her.

These women's stories reflect the color of the U.S. child welfare system today. More than a half million children taken from their parents are currently in foster care. African Americans are the most likely of any group to be disrupted in this way by government authorities. Black children make up nearly half of the foster care population, although they constitute less than one-fifth of the nation's children. In Chicago, 95 percent of children in foster care are Black. Once removed from their homes, Black children remain in foster care longer, are moved more often, receive fewer services, and are less likely to be either returned home or adopted than other children.

The child welfare system is the focus of intense public scrutiny, condemned by conservatives and liberals alike. Everyone agrees that foster care is overburdened and often damages children more than raising them in either their biological families or adoptive homes. However, the public debate has failed to examine why Black children are removed from their parents in such large numbers or what the consequences are for Black families and communities. Public sentiment and policy have chosen to focus instead on solving foster care's problems by encouraging the adoption of more children.

The number of Black children in state custody—those in foster care as well as those in juvenile detention, prisons, and other state institutions—is a startling injustice that calls for radical reform. I would call it the system's ugly secret, except that it should be obvious to anyone who has spent a day examining the statistics, visiting a child welfare office, or watching who goes in and out of juvenile court. The fact that the system supposedly designed to protect children remains one of the most segregated institutions in the country should arouse our suspicion.

In 1972, *Children of the Storm: Black Children and American Child Welfare,* by Andrew Billingsley and Jeanne M. Giovannoni, traced the history of the government's discriminatory treatment of African American children. Three decades later, racial disparities in the child welfare system have only become worse, and policy makers have rejected the concern they professed in the late 1970s and early 1980s for preserving Black families. Child protection policy has conformed to the current political climate, which embraces punitive responses to the seemingly intractable plight of America's isolated and impoverished inner cities.

The new politics of child welfare threatens to intensify state supervision of Black children. In the past several years, federal and state policy have shifted away from preserving families toward "freeing" children in foster care for adoption by terminating parental rights. Welfare reform, by throwing many families deeper into poverty, heightens the risk that some children will be removed from struggling families and placed in foster care. Black families, who are disproportionately poor, have been hit the hardest by this retraction of public assistance for needy children. And tougher treatment of juvenile offenders, imposed most harshly on African American youth, is increasing the numbers incarcerated in juvenile detention facilities and adult prisons. These political trends are shattering the bonds between poor Black children and their parents. Recent developments make it imperative to confront the racial disparity in America's child welfare system now. Only by examining the role that race plays in the child welfare system can we understand how it operates to reinforce the inferior status of Blacks in America.

Yet most contemporary critiques of the child welfare system barely acknowledge the importance of race. Scholars who deal with Black children in the child welfare system tend to focus on social work practice—how children should be treated—rather than the politics of child protection—how political relationships affect which children become involved in the system. Their primary goal is to make services more sensitive to the needs and culture of Black families, not to question the fundamental conflict between the child welfare system and the integrity of the Black family and community. Child protection authorities are taking custody of Black children at alarming rates, and in doing so, they are dismantling social networks that are critical to Black community welfare.

Most authors frame the problem with child protection as a battle between bad government and innocent parents or between bad parents and innocent children. Advocates on the side of parents argue that overzealous efforts to combat child abuse are excessively intruding on family rights. They tell horrifying stories of government agents strip-searching children and dragging them away from their parents based on false, anonymous allegations. Their effort to find common ground among parents often hides the power of race and class in directing repressive government action. For example, one author warns that we must "stop this assault on the family—before all our children become state wards." I choose to refute the myth that there is a universal system of child protection that treats all parents equally badly. Although all families risk being hurt by these arbitrary abuses of power, Black families are being *systematically* demolished. Two critical factors remain unaddressed: the system's distinct racial harm, and the role race plays in perpetuating a destructive understanding of child protection that affects all American families.

On the other side of the debate are those who tell horrifying stories of victims of parental abuse and a system that does too little to protect them. These advocates wildly exaggerate the harm inflicted by most parents monitored by child protective services as well as the good that state supervision can do. By focusing myopically on extreme cases of child abuse, these accounts deliberately ignore the damage caused by carelessly removing children from their homes. Not only do they overlook the child welfare system's devastation of Black families, but they devalue the family ties that are so important to the children they claim to support. In this book, I refute the even more dangerous myth that the child welfare system will improve children's well-being by separating more children from their parents.

This book answers three questions that correspond to its main parts. Why are so many Black children removed from their homes and placed under state supervision? How will the current politics of child welfare affect the system's racial imbalance? And why should we be concerned about the racial disparity in the child welfare system? I conclude by proposing steps that we can take to transform the system toward respecting the integrity of Black families while addressing the deprivation in many homes.

Shattered Bonds is a plea to call the child welfare system what it is: a state-run program that disrupts, restructures, and polices Black families. I hope to capture the injustice of a system that separates thousands of Black children from their parents every year and relegates them to damaging state institutions. There is little evidence that the foster care system has improved the well-being of Black children and much evidence that it supports the disadvantaged position of Black people as a whole. A recent book by a Harvard law professor advocating easier termination of parental rights is titled *Nobody's Children*—as if children in foster care have no parents who care about them. The truth is that many poor Black parents fight desperately against a wealthy and powerful system to regain their children. They are often worn down by pointless and burdensome requirements, insidious financial incentives, and racial bias. I want to provide the missing voice of Black families torn apart by discriminatory and misguided policies.

Today, the Black nationalist charge of racial genocide from the 1970s sounds hopelessly extremist, yet many of the mothers I talked to were convinced that the child welfare system is waging a war to steal Black children. Although they are right that they are the victims of a racist system, this charge tends to inflame emotions and requires careful elaboration. My goal of developing a new case for protecting Black families against state intrusion is based not only on parents' and children's rights but also on the injury to the Black community as a whole. Racial inequities in the child welfare system, I will conclude, cause serious group-based harms by reinforcing disparaging stereotypes about Black family unfitness and need for white supervision, by destroying a sense of family autonomy and self-determination among many Black Americans, and by weakening Blacks' collective ability to overcome institutionalized discrimination. By examining the evidence of racism in the child welfare system, telling the stories of disrupted families, and presenting a theory of community harm, I highlight the political role of the child welfare system in America, a role often obscured by a focus on its rescue of individual children from neglectful parents.

Some people think that the best way to help the thousands of Black children in foster care is to terminate their parents' rights and place them in adoptive homes. These people do not see themselves as racists who are bent on destroying Black families. They may even endorse stronger social support programs for America's struggling families. But they do believe child protective services must intervene immediately to save Black children from their current crisis. "These children can't wait for social programs to eliminate poverty and racism," these advocates argue. "We must act now to move them from their destructive families and neighborhoods into stable homes." I hope this book demonstrates that this new cadre of child savers are wrong.

One hundred years from now, today's child welfare system will surely be condemned as a racist institution—one that compounded the effects of discrimination on Black families by taking children from their parents, allowing them to languish in a damaging foster care system or to be adopted by more privileged people. School children will marvel that so many scholars and politicians defended this devastation of Black families in the name of protecting Black children. The color of America's child welfare system is the reason Americans have tolerated its destructiveness. It is also the most powerful reason to finally abolish what we now call child protection and replace it with a system that really promotes children's welfare.

PART ONE

Destroying Black Families in the
Name of Child Protection

JORNELL DOMINATES THE MEETINGS of the group she started for mothers whose children were taken by the child welfare department. A heavyset, lively woman, Jornell jumps into every discussion. She can barely contain her complaints about the department's actions, advice to other mothers about their cases, ideas about what the organization could do to change the system. "I live for this now. I have no other life, I have no other purpose," Jornell told me the first time we spoke. "My life is an ongoing battle to hold on to my child."

Jornell had her first son, Ronnie, twenty-five years ago, when she was a fifteen-year-old high school student. She dropped out of school and moved in with her boyfriend's mother, who took over raising the child. After getting her G.E.D. and some secretarial training at a local business institute, she worked at an assortment of temporary jobs—a receptionist at an insurance company, a clerk at the Stock Exchange, a secretary in the permit department of the Chicago Park District. But by the time she reached her thirties, Jornell was plagued with severe health problems that kept her from holding down a job. She was overweight and diabetic, and she had started drinking and smoking crack.

Jornell's involvement in the child welfare system began as soon as her second son was born in January 1998. When Jornell became pregnant with David, she was thirty-six years old, living in public housing on Social Security disability benefits, suffering from diabetes, and addicted to crack and alcohol.* She decided to get help soon after she discovered she was pregnant, when a doctor told her there was a risk that her baby "would have a defect." She joined a program called Healthy F.I.T., for Healthy Family Intervention Team, based at Mt. Sinai Hospital in Chicago, where she received prenatal care. According to the program's flyer, Healthy F.I.T. "provides drug and/or alcohol assessment, treatment, and case management services for pregnant or newly delivered women receiving care within the Sinai Health System." "I felt that I had a

* Jornell gave me permission to use her name. I am using a fictitious name for her son.

right to heal," Jornell told me. "I didn't want the drugs, I didn't want the alcohol, I didn't want to be mentally ill anymore. I followed all their recommendations. I went into long-term treatment. I did everything I was supposed to do—for myself, before the intervention. The intervention was supposed to assist me to be a family. But this is the worst entanglement anybody can become involved in."

Because she was participating in Healthy F.I.T., Jornell was known to hospital social workers even before David was born. They put the newborn on "social hold" until they could investigate her living arrangement. She wasn't allowed to bring David home until four days after she was released. When David was one month old, she brought him several times to a hospital emergency room when he had recurring digestive problems. While the baby was being treated at the hospital she gave him an enema. Jornell says she was following the advice of a doctor who had seen the baby earlier. She felt that the nurses were too busy with other children and weren't taking David's illness seriously. She now acknowledges her judgment may have been clouded; she was still recovering from a difficult pregnancy and delivery, complicated by her diabetes.

The hospital staff became alarmed at Jornell's interference and suspected that she had already overmedicated the baby at home. They called the child abuse hot line. The Illinois Department of Children and Family Services, known as DCFS, investigated. A caseworker decided that the report was "indicated"—there was credible evidence that David was at risk of physical harm—and took custody of the baby. "They said I was an overly concerned mother," is how Jornell describes the charges against her. David was placed in a foster home with four other foster children.

According to Jornell, she was so distraught by David's removal that it took her until August to fill out a child protection appeal form she received from the court clerk. A month later, an internal review team overturned the caseworker's finding of potential abuse. The decision stated that, according to a social worker who interviewed Jornell, "natural mother thinks very clearly and decisively, would not harm a child and is capable of caring for the child." It also stated that a psychiatrist who had been treating Jornell disclosed that Jornell had drug and alcohol problems in the past, but had not used either for more than a year. "Natural mother is committed to being clean," the psychiatrist reported. "NM has a problem with anger but is not aggressive (sic). In professional opinion NM is capable of parenting baby and has been consistent in interest of baby's needs over her own during pregnancy." Tests performed on David when he was born showed he was not exposed to drugs.

But DCFS did not return David. Instead, it filed a new report alleging that the baby would be at risk of harm if released to his mother because of her history of substance abuse and possible mental illness. The permanency plan had a goal of returning David to his mother after she completed the department's recommendations for her rehabilitation. Jornell had to enroll in a drug treatment program, submit monthly urine samples for drug testing, attend Alcoholics Anonymous meetings, see a parenting coach once a week, undergo a series of psychological evaluations, and meet with a psychotherapist regularly. Then she had to be evaluated by a Parenting Assessment Team, composed of a psychiatrist, psychologist, child development specialist, and social worker from a private center that contracted with DCFS. One reason Jornell had to undergo multiple evaluations was to rule out the agency's suspicion that she was suffering from Munchausen's syndrome by proxy, a mental disorder that causes mothers to deliberately make their children ill because they crave the resulting attention from medical staff.

Jornell was determined to comply with every requirement. She even had to repeat the clinical evaluations when the judge presiding over her case ruled that the first two reports were unacceptable. She successfully completed an intensive outpatient drug treatment program twice.

Despite her compliance with the DCFS plan, the Parenting Assessment Team recommended in January 1999 against immediate reunification. On the positive side, the team found that Jornell displayed no symptoms of mental illness, was constructively using all the services offered to her, and had remained substance-free for more than a year. During supervised visits, she showed a caring and responsible attitude toward David. But the team also made negative findings. It detected in Jornell's "elevated mood and accelerated speech" a "subtle" mental disorder. It criticized her answers on a parenting test as too rigid. It felt that her support network was too small. It suggested that she attend an additional rehabilitation program for relapse prevention. The team would reassess her case at the end of the year.

In the meantime, Jornell had four caseworkers, and her file was moved from the South Side of Chicago, where she lives, to a North Side DCFS office. She began to see a Black clinical psychiatrist in her community with whom she felt more comfortable. The new psychiatrist prepared several reports attesting to Jornell's ability to care for her son. When the Parenting Assessment Team issued a follow-up report in December 1999, it chastised Jornell for choosing her own therapist and spending time on social causes. She had focused her attention on organizing mothers involved in the child welfare system instead of taking full responsibility for her own parenting deficits. It recommended that DCFS refer her to the "correct service providers" for more evaluations and treatment. By this time, David had been in foster care for almost two years.

When I attended her administrative case review in August 2000, now two and a half years after David entered foster care, Jornell had done everything DCFS demanded, and she was anxious to regain custody of her son. She didn't hide her frustration with the process. The purpose of the review was to give someone from DCFS an opportunity to go over the status of reunification efforts with Jornell and her caseworker. The agency reviewer opened with a compulsory litany of procedural rules. When asked if she understood, Jornell replied, "I'm becoming a veteran at this. This is my fifth ACR." The reviewer started the session by stating, "Our first task is to schedule another review in six months." "When will I get David back?" Jornell burst out. "I just read that half the kids in foster care end up in jail. I don't want that to happen to David."

The disproportionate number of Black children in America's child welfare system is staggering. Black families are overrepresented in child maltreatment reports, case openings, and the foster care population. Spend a day at dependency court in any major city and you will see the unmistakable color of the child welfare system. Dependency court is where judges decide the fate of children who have been taken into state custody because their parents are charged with abusing or neglecting them. Nearly every family in these urban courts is Black. If you came with no preconceptions about the purpose of the child welfare system, you would have to conclude that it is an institution designed to monitor, regulate, and punish poor Black families. The racial disparity of children in protective custody mirrors the far more publicized racial disparity in our nation's prison population.

1. THE COLOR OF AMERICA'S CHILD WELFARE SYSTEM

THE CHILD WELFARE SYSTEM has always discriminated against Blacks, but its racism looked very different a century ago. Black families were virtually excluded from openly segregated child welfare services until the end of World War II.[1] Wealthy do-gooders began a charitable mission in the late nineteenth century to save poor children from parental cruelty and indigence. The orphanages they established to rescue destitute immigrant children refused to accept Blacks. The few "colored orphan asylums" were woefully inferior and overcrowded. By the time of the 1923 census, thirty-one northern states reported a total of 1,070 child-caring agencies. Of these agencies, 35 were for Black children only, 264 accepted all races, 60 took nonwhite children except Blacks, and 711 were reserved for white children.[2] Needy Black children were more likely to be labeled delinquent: "the major child caring institution for Black and other nonwhite children was the prison."[3] In the early part of the century, Black people relied primarily on extended family networks and community resources such as churches, women's clubs, and benevolent societies to take care of children whose parents were unable to meet their needs.

The child welfare system began to recognize Black children in the 1930s when services shifted from institutions to foster care and from private to public agencies.[4] Religious charities, which dominated child placements in large cities after World War II, continued to practice blatant racial discrimination. In New York City, for example, Jewish and Catholic agencies used religious preferences to close their doors to the city's predominantly Protestant Black children.[5] In 1973, the New York Civil Liberties Union filed a lawsuit challenging the city's participation in the agencies' racial discrimination. Although *Wilder* v. *Sugarman* was finally settled in 1988, the fight continued into the 1990s over the city's violations of the settlement agreement. In place of the segregated services, the city permitted an informal system that distributed children to foster care agencies based on gradations of skin shade and hair texture.[6]

The proportion of Black children in the public child welfare caseloads steadily increased in the years after World War II. The segment composed of nonwhite children almost doubled between 1945 and 1961, from 14 percent to 27 percent.[7] Twenty-four percent of the children served by public agencies in 1961 were Black. The child welfare rolls steadily filled with Black children over the next two decades. Then in the late 1980s two things happened to cement the child welfare system's current relationship to Black Americans: both the total size of the foster care population and the share of Black children exploded. The number of children in foster care has doubled in the last two decades, from 262,000 in 1982 to 568,000 in 1999.[8] The enormous growth in foster care caseloads in the late 1980s was concentrated primarily in cities, where there are sizable Black communities.[9] In 1986, Black children, who were only 15 percent of the population under age eighteen, made up about one-quarter of children entering foster care and 35 percent of children in foster care at the end of that year.[10] Today, *42 percent of all children in foster care nationwide are Black*, even though Black children constitute only 17 percent of the nation's youth.[11]

Black families are the most likely of any group to be disrupted by child protection authorities. Black children even stand out from other minorities. Latino and Asian American children are *underrepresented* in the national foster care population. Latino children make up only 15 percent of children in foster care although Latino children now outnumber Blacks in the general population. (Under U.S. Bureau of Census standards, children of "Hispanic origin" may be of any race.) Take, for instance, California, a state with a large Latino population. In 1995, 5 percent of all Black children in California were in foster care, compared to less than 1 percent of Latino children.[12] Only 1 percent of children in foster care nationwide are from Asian/Pacific Islander families.

The proportion of Black children in out-of-home care in large states such as California, Illinois, New York, and Texas ranges from three times to more than ten times as high as the proportion of white children.[13] Although only 19 percent of the child population in Illinois is Black, Black children make up more than 75 percent of the foster care population. Black children in Illinois were reported for maltreatment at a rate of 33 per 1000, compared to a rate of less than 10 per 1000 for white and Latino children.[14]

In big cities, the foster care population is almost exclusively Black, with a smaller percentage of Latino children, and only a tiny fraction of white children. More than 70 percent of foster children in San Francisco in 1994 were Black, although Blacks made up only 10 percent of the city's population.[15] Researchers found that Black children in San Diego are "markedly overrepresented" in the foster care system—at a rate of six times their proportion of the general population.[16]

In the decade between 1983 and 1993, the foster care caseloads of Chicago and New York City more than tripled in size, while the caseloads in the rest of each state remained about the same.[17] This dramatic increase was made up of Black children. In Chicago, 95 percent of the children placed in foster care are Black.[18]

The racial imbalance in New York City's foster care population is truly mind-boggling: out of 42,000 children in the system at the end of 1997, only 1,300 were white.[19] About 30 percent of the children who live in New York City are white. Yet white children make up only 3 percent of its foster care caseload. Less than 24 percent in foster care are Latino and the vast majority—73 percent—are African American. Clearly, child welfare authorities consider foster care a last resort when it comes to white families.

Black children, on the other hand, are separated from their parents with relative ease. One out of every twenty-two Black children in New York City is in foster care. The system's grasp is even tighter on poor Black neighborhoods, such as Central Harlem, where one out of ten children has been placed in foster care. This means that in every apartment building in Central Harlem, we could expect to find at least one family whose children are in state custody. This is a far cry from the more reasonable odds for white children—only one out of 385.[20] Black children are ten times more likely to be placed in foster care in New York City than white children.

Although there are larger numbers of Black children in systems like Chicago and New York, the overrepresentation of these children is even greater in cities where Blacks are more of a minority. Researchers have proposed a "visibility hypothesis" to account for this disparity. The visibility hypothesis suggests that "there is a higher probability for minority children to be placed in foster care when living in a geographic area where they are relatively less represented (i.e., more 'visible')."[21] The chances of a Black child being placed in foster care are high in cities where Blacks make up a third to half of the population, but the chances are even higher where Blacks are a tiny minority. A comparison of foster care and census data in southern California revealed that where Blacks constitute 15 percent of the census, they are placed at a rate three times greater than their census proportion. Where they constitute less than 2 percent of the census, their placement rate soars to fifteen times their proportion of the population.[22] Researchers hypothesize that visibility increases the chances of minority placement because agencies are more likely to investigate underrepresented groups or because these groups lack social supports that could ward off investigation.

In summary, the foster care system in the nation's cities operates as an apartheid institution. It is a system designed to deal with the problems of minority families—primarily Black families—whereas the problems of white families are handled by separate and less disruptive mechanisms. That so many caseworkers, judges, and lawyers work every day in the belly of this system without speaking out shows just how accustomed we have become to racial separation in America. They routinely see nothing but Black parents and children in child welfare agencies and courts. But it seems normal to many Americans that Black families are more often split apart and supervised by the state.

2. THE SYSTEM'S INFERIOR TREATMENT OF BLACK CHILDREN

THE FIRST TIME I MET DEVON at her apartment in a stable Chicago neighborhood, she was anxious to show me around. The seven-room apartment was neat and well maintained. "You see, there's plenty of space for my nieces and nephews," she pointed out as we walked down the long corridor. We passed two bedrooms—one occupied by her sixteen-year-old daughter, Ebony—on our way to the dining room, where we sat down at the table to talk. Along one wall were stacked a number of plastic bins, which Devon said held the children's clothes. On the other wall was a chest of drawers filled with papers concerning her case—DCFS reports, psychological evaluations, medical records, court documents, her diplomas from child development classes. Devon pulled out a stack of photos of four smiling children celebrating birthdays and dressed in Halloween costumes. "These are my kids," she told me proudly.

Devon calls her nieces and nephews her kids because she has cared for them since they were toddlers. She took in her brother, the father of the children, and their mother, who had a serious drug addiction. Two of the children were born while the family was staying with her. In 1994, shortly after she had given birth to her sixth child, the mother told Devon that she was going to the hairdresser—and never came back. The oldest boy, who had a different father, went to live with a stepmother. The newborn was adopted by a white family. DCFS allowed Devon to keep the remaining four children, with ages spread between one and four.

Devon devoted her life to the children. All the children have asthma and developmental problems, and Devon had to master a complicated schedule involving dispensing numerous medications, transporting the children to school, family therapy sessions, and medical appointments, and keeping up with daily loads of laundry. She took classes so that she could receive a special license for relative foster care for medically complex children. When the mother's rights were terminated in April 1999, Devon made plans to adopt the children.

"I can't remember a time when I wasn't taking care of somebody's kids," Devon told me. She grew up with ten brothers and sisters on Chicago's west side. Her abusive mother kicked her out of the house in 1976 when she was nineteen, a college student with a baby girl named Portia. The frightened young mother found herself alone in the streets clutching her seven-month-old daughter and a garbage bag filled with her belongings. Devon went to live with an older sister for the next year and a half. She juggled courses in pediatrics and nutrition at Malcolm X College while caring for Portia and earned an associate degree in 1980. Devon soon started living with Ebony's father, an older man who was nothing but trouble. "He was a loser, a gambler, and a womanizer," Devon told me. "He never beat me, but he slept around." She kicked him out when their daughter Ebony was three years old. "I was taking care of him and my daughters," Devon says. "I got tired of doing bad with a grown man. I can do bad all by myself."

Hoping to eventually get a job helping children, Devon took classes in child development, psychology, and pediatrics at local colleges as often as she could. She also volunteered for the Chicago Public Schools and worked as a counselor for a local social services agency, giving parents information about health, nutrition, and parenting skills. "I used to ride to work on the city bus dressed up like a block of cheese or a carton of milk," Devon chuckled.

But family crises kept interrupting Devon's plans for a career. She raised three children of a sister who was strung out on drugs and alcohol. Three of her brothers, all drug addicts, were sent to prison. Devon regularly visited one who was incarcerated in Illinois. Then Devon suffered a personal setback. She was diagnosed in 1991 with cervical cancer, which she blames on a sexually transmitted disease she got from Ebony's father. The cancer spread to her breast. She underwent a lumpectomy, followed by radiation and chemotherapy. She had barely recovered when another brother who had contracted AIDS arrived in Chicago from Los Angeles where he had worked as a fashion designer. While he lay dying at a respite home, Devon and another sister took turns attending to him. When her sister had a stoke, "everything fell to me," Devon says. She finally received her B.A. from Loyola University in 1994, a year after her brother's death. "He made me promise on his death bed that I would continue taking care of my nieces and nephews," Devon told me. By then, the four children Devon now hoped to adopt were already living with her.

Everything went smoothly until the private agency that supervised her case assigned a new caseworker. The caseworker told Devon her apartment wasn't large enough for the children and that she would have to move. She noted that a hospital reported to DCFS that Devon had been treated for a mouse bite. She told Devon that she would have to prove she had a source of income other than the payments she received from DCFS to care for the children. Devon made sure her landlord repaired the baseboards where the mouse had apparently entered. She began looking for a bigger apartment that she could afford. In June 1999, the caseworker and one of the children's doctors got into an argument during an appointment, and Devon reported the caseworker's unprofessional conduct to DCFS. Devon believes the caseworker then decided to retaliate. Later that month, Devon and the children were enjoying a picnic celebrating her niece's graduation from kindergarten. In the middle of the festivities, security guards surrounded the family. The caseworker grabbed the terrified children and put them in a car, handing Devon a notice that DCFS was removing them from her custody.

The children were placed in foster care with a family in a distant suburb. Devon was allowed two supervised visits with the children in the first month after they were taken. Then the caseworker informed her that she couldn't see them again because they were being transitioned to adoption by their new foster mother. The caseworker thwarted Devon's attempts to contact the children.

Devon showed me a large stuffed dog holding a heart with the inscription "I love you." "She wouldn't let me give this to the children because it's inappropriate for me to show them any affection," Devon said. "She told me it would confuse them." Once when I met with Devon she handed me a large envelope filled with cards and letters she had asked the caseworker to deliver to the children. There was a handwritten poem titled "What Is a Family?," which ended, "It's a warm and special feeling/binding heart to heart forever/in a spirit of belonging/neither time nor miles can sever." Devon signed it, "Forever Love, Mommy." She added a note at the bottom, "I haven't forgot you kids. Never will." A letter to one of the boys described her memories of his birth. "I love my kids until this Life is over. Always remember this," she wrote. "You are that precious pearl. My crown of life." Devon told me that the agency returned the package along with several gifts she had sent to the children. Her caseworker never delivered them.

Devon pursued every legal avenue she could find to regain custody of the children. At the removal hearing in juvenile court, she attempted to put on several witnesses to testify on her behalf, including a psychologist from University of Illinois at Chicago. But the judge refused to hear them. She filed an appeal of the judge's decision upholding the removal, scraping together the money to pay a private attorney to represent her. Her papers argue that DCFS failed to consider that she had successfully taken care of the children for more than seven years and that the children wanted to live with her. Devon showed me letters from her pastor, the children's teachers, a school principal, and the family's doctors praising her care for her nieces and nephews. "When I found out my rights, it became grounds for the agency to call me aggressive and confrontational," Devon says.

What seemed to trouble Devon most was that she was never given a chance to explain to the children why she disappeared. "Until my last dying breath, I'll continue to fight for my children," she told me. "All I can do is fight to let the kids know I didn't give up on them."

Not only are Black children the most likely to enter the child welfare system, but they also fare the worst under the state's supervision. Black children have the greatest odds of being removed from their homes and the smallest chance of being either reunited with their parents or adopted. They spend the most time in foster care and receive the least helpful services. The inferior treatment of Black children seems to be orchestrated at the policy level. As the child welfare caseloads have became increasingly Black, the number of out-of-home placements has risen dramatically as has the portion of funds spent on foster care as opposed to intact-family services.[23]

The System's Changing Racial Composition and Approach to Child Welfare

The child welfare crusade was conceived by early-twentieth-century progressives as a social reform movement that addressed a wide range of children's problems. Rescuing children from maltreatment by removing them from their homes was part of a broader campaign to remedy the social ills, including poverty, that harmed children. The movement also created the juvenile courts, opposed child labor, and lobbied for mandatory school attendance laws.[24] The crusaders established pensions for widows and single mothers to reduce the need for child removal. To be sure, the early reformers judged poor families by elitist standards and excluded Black children altogether. But they advocated a view of child maltreatment as an urgent *social* problem that should be addressed through various forms of *social* welfare and not just taking children from their parents. They understood that children's welfare was tied to social conditions that could only be improved by societywide reforms.

Efforts to develop a system rooted in a social vision of child welfare were squelched by the 1970s. In an attempt to secure bipartisan support for government spending on poor children, liberals such as Senator Walter Mondale abandoned their focus on poverty's harms to children. "This was part of a conscious strategy to dissociate efforts against abuse from unpopular poverty programs," writes public affairs professor Barbara Nelson in *Making an Issue of Child Abuse*. "The purpose was to describe abuse as an all-American affliction, not one found solely among low-income people."[25] Instead, Congress launched a campaign against the national problem of child abuse with the passage of the Child Abuse Prevention and Treatment Act in 1974. The government promoted, and the public came to accept, a medical model of child abuse—"a distinguishable pathological agent attacking the individual or family that could be treated in a prescribed manner and would disappear."[26] What was understood by some advocates as a social problem rooted in poverty and other societal inequities became widely interpreted as a symptom of individual parents' mental depravity.

This conception of children's problems came at great cost to poor families. For one thing, it is not at all clear that the focus on child protection has actually made children any safer. Child welfare researcher Duncan Lindsey makes a compelling case that there is no evidence that the enormous increase in child abuse reporting since the 1970s has reduced child abuse fatalities.[27]

What the new approach slashed was not child maltreatment but child welfare services. In the past several decades, the number of children receiving child welfare services has declined dramatically, while the foster care population has skyrocketed. These seemingly conflicting numbers reflect the transformation of the child welfare system from a social service system that tried to help needy families to a child protection system that investigates allegations of abuse and neglect. The number of children served by the child welfare system dropped from nearly 2 million in 1977 to 1 million in 1994.[28] The decrease reflects the dwindling number of children who received services while living at home.

At the same time, the number of white children in the system fell precipitously. The child welfare system served more than 1 million white children in 1977 but less than half that number (456,000) by 1994. As the child welfare rolls became increasingly Black, state and federal governments spent more money on out-of-home care and less on in-home services. Between 1977 and 1994, there was a 60 percent decline nationwide in the number of children receiving services in their homes.[29] For example, the percentage of children in the California system receiving family maintenance services fell from 31 percent in 1988 to 26 percent in 1995, while the foster care caseloads doubled.[30] One explanation for the shift in services is that children have more serious problems today, forcing agencies to direct a greater portion of their limited resources to crisis situations that require out-of-home care. But I don't think it's a coincidence that family services declined as the child welfare system began to serve fewer white and more Black children.

The same sort of metamorphosis occurred when the civil rights movement made the welfare system available to Black citizens.[31] Just as Blacks were once ignored by the child welfare system, Blacks were largely excluded from the

New Deal welfare programs by restrictive state eligibility requirements. Aid to Dependent Children, enacted in 1935 to prevent removal of children from their homes for financial reasons, went primarily to white mothers. In the 1960s, the welfare rights movement secured entitlements to welfare benefits. Welfare caseloads that were once almost exclusively white quickly became half nonwhite. Expanding welfare entitlements fit within President Lyndon Johnson's War on Poverty, whose federal housing and economic programs attempted to integrate more Blacks into the national political economy. But as welfare became increasingly associated with Black mothers, it became increasingly burdened with behavior modification rules, work requirements, and reduced effective benefits levels. Black welfare recipients were stigmatized as lazy, dependent, and depraved. The image of the welfare mother changed from the worthy white widow to the immoral Black welfare queen. By the mid-1990s, the American public equated welfare with Black social degeneracy and successfully demanded that the federal safety net for poor children be dismantled and that welfare recipients be put to work.

The abrogation of child welfare's social service function in the 1970s occurred as a white backlash decimated the War on Poverty programs. In *The Color of Welfare*, sociologist Jill Quadagno demonstrates that whites opposed the War on Poverty precisely because of its link to Black civil rights.[32] For example, federal housing subsidies plummeted after 1968, when white homeowners, backed by the powerful real estate lobby, resisted residential integration. White Americans rejected a social welfare solution to poverty at the same time that they rejected a social welfare solution to child maltreatment. As the welfare and child welfare systems oversaw an increasingly Black clientele, they both reduced their services to families while intensifying their punitive functions.

Black Children Are More Likely to Be Separated from Their Parents

The child protection philosophy that has reigned for the past three decades has served Black families poorly. The worst part of this punitive approach is that it unnecessarily separates Black children from their parents. Child protective agencies are far more likely to place Black children in foster care rather than offering their families less traumatic assistance. As I pointed out, the system's orientation changed along with the racial composition of its caseloads. Black children have suffered the most from this shift: agencies put Black children in out-of-home custody at dramatically higher rates than other children. According to federal statistics, 56 percent of Black children in the child welfare system have been placed in foster care—twice the percentage for white children.[33] A national study of child protective services by the U.S. Department of Health and Human Services reported that "minority children, and in particular African American children, are more likely to be in foster care placement than receive in-home services, *even when they have the same problems and characteristics as white children.*"[34]

White children who are abused or neglected are twice as likely as Black children to receive services in their own homes, avoiding the emotional damage and physical risks of foster care placement. Put another way, most white children who enter the system are permitted to stay with their families, whereas most Black children are taken away from theirs. Foster care is the main "service" that state agencies provide to Black children brought to their attention. Government authorities appear to believe that maltreatment of Black children results from pathologies intrinsic to their homes and that helping them requires dislocating them from their families. Child welfare for Black children usually means shattering the bonds with their parents.

It bears pausing a moment to visualize the consequences of the system's racially divided treatment of children. Once caseworkers determine that a report of child abuse or neglect is "indicated," or substantiated by evidence, they must next decide how to protect the child. The most critical choice they make is whether to remove the child from the home or to provide services to the family while keeping it intact. The repercussions of this decision are monumental.

Think for a moment what it means to rip children from their parents and their brothers and sisters and to place them in the care of strangers. Removing children from their homes is perhaps the most severe government intrusion into the lives of citizens. It is also one of the most terrifying experiences a child can have. Because parents involved with child protective services are so often portrayed as brutal monsters, the public usually ignores the trauma experienced by the children. But most children in foster care, who typically have been removed because of neglect, have close and loving relationships with their parents, and it is indescribably painful to be separated from them. "Children do not oblige us by hating their parents the way we may think they should," says Richard Wexler, director of the National Coalition for Child Protection Reform. "Often, neglected children love their parents just as much as our children love us. Tearing children from their parents almost always leaves emotional scars."[35]

When children are seized from helpless parents by more powerful government agents, it creates a sense of vulnerability and betrayal in children, who rely on their parents to keep them safe. It is doubly traumatic to then be dropped unexpectedly into the care of a strange adult. This is true even in the best of foster homes, never mind what befalls children in the hands of uncaring or abusive foster parents. The emotional damage increases with the length of time children spend separated from their families and with the number of moves they are required to make.

Of course, these harms of removal may be outweighed by the harm of leaving children with violent or extremely neglectful parents. In some extreme cases, it would be ludicrous to worry about harming children by rescuing them from life-threatening situations. But just as we should pay attention to the risks of child maltreatment, we should not minimize the very real pain caused by separating children from their families. The damage caused by disrupting these ties may be far greater than the harm agencies are trying to avoid.

The judge commended Devon for her extraordinary devotion to her four nieces and nephews, whom she showered with affection, tirelessly shuttled to specialists, and advocated for in social service offices. But that didn't stop him from breaking up her family because her apartment was too small. Whatever risks Devon's home posed for those children could not possibly have outweighed the certain emotional damage the caseworker caused when she abruptly sent them away from their aunt. According to psychologist Seth Farber, "only a small minority of these children have been separated from parents who are dangerous to them. The overwhelming majority have been separated from loving and responsible parents. One does not need to be a child psychologist to realize the devastating effect of removing a child from parents with whom he or she is deeply bonded."[36] And there is no justification for dismissing the pain of family breakup because of race.

There are other devastating consequences of removal, as well. When children are taken from the home, the chances for long-term state interference in the family are intensified. It becomes likely that children will spend months or years in foster care and may never make it back to their families. The racial split in in-home services versus out-of-home placements, then, has a tremendously adverse impact on Black families.

Black Children Spend More Time in Foster Care

The racial disparity in child removal is enough to indict the system. But taking children from their homes is only the beginning of the state's inferior treatment of Black families. Once Black children enter the foster care system, they remain there longer, are moved more often, and receive less desirable placements than white children. White children tend to return home quickly, whereas Black children tend to languish in foster care. Nearly half of white children who are placed in foster care return home within three months; very few Black children do.[37] This timing is especially significant because the probability of children being reunited with their parents is high immediately after placement. But the chances of reunification begin to dwindle rapidly after the first five months of placement.[38]

Numerous national and state studies have linked race to the timing of family reunification. A 1985 study found that the cumulative time in long-term foster care for Black children (62 months) was nearly double that of white children (36 months).[39] The author concluded that "regardless of the reason for referral or problem category, Black children were consistently in placement for longer periods of time than Hispanic or white children."[40]

The U.S. Department of Health and Human Services reported that in 1994 African American children were twice as likely as white children to have open cases for longer than eighteen months (64 percent versus 31 percent). African American children remained in foster care twice as long as white children, for a median length of time of seventeen and nine months, respectively.[41]

A 1997 study of the California foster care population found that 33 percent of Blacks remained in foster care after six years compared to only 11 percent of whites.

In 1994, a group of researchers reported that African American youth in Illinois spent a median of 37 months in substitute care, whereas the median for white children was 7 months.[42]

A 1999 Ohio study discovered that Black infants had slower rates of re-unification than infants from other groups. The authors concluded that, given the consistency of results from other investigations, the relationship of ethnic-ity to reunification could be generalized across many community contexts.[43] This association between race and duration of foster care involvement remains significant even when researchers control for poverty.[44] For example, in a re-cent sample of 700 foster children in rural and urban Tennessee, nonwhite chil-dren had a 42 percent lower probability of leaving state custody in three years, after controlling for all other factors, including behavioral problems, family characteristics, and services.[45]

Black Children Receive Inferior Services

Not only do Black children enter the system in disproportionate numbers and for longer periods of time, but they also receive lower-quality services once they get there. Studies show that Black children involved in the child welfare system receive inferior treatment according to every measure, including provision of both in-home and adoption services, recommended versus actual length of placement, and worker contact with the child and caregivers.[46]

Black children could be described as involuntary subjects in a govern-ment experiment in child rearing with no evidence that they have received any benefit from it. Child welfare policy makers have given little thought to study-ing the best ways to serve Black families. Instead, according to two social work scholars, "scores of minority children and their families are seen by white, mid-dle-class workers whose standards of behavior, often perceived as being the norm, have little or nothing to do with designing ways to ensure effective ther-apeutic outcomes for minority children."[47] Child welfare agencies rarely offer Black families the kind of help they need; in fact, they often subject Black chil-dren in foster care to affirmatively harmful programs, such as multiple reloca-tions to strange homes and brutal institutions, making family reunification more difficult. It is no surprise that even when African American children are eventually reunited with their families, they have the highest rate of reentry back into foster care.[48] The system has failed to remedy the underlying causes of their placement in foster care, which are related to poverty, housing problems, and lack of child care.

Inadequate housing is often part of the reason Black children are placed in substitute care or are not reunited with their parents. A national study of Black children in foster care conducted by the National Black Child Development Institute in 1989 found that more than 10 percent of children entered foster care from shelters and that inadequate housing was a factor in nearly one-third of placements.[49] A U.S. Department of Health and Human Services study found that Black children in the system are more likely to come from families with housing problems than white children.[50] Yet the study also discovered that among families with housing problems, white families are offered housing services at almost twice the rate as Black families (43 percent compared to 25 percent).

The opposite pattern emerged for parenting services, however. African American caregivers who are considered to have deficient child rearing skills are more likely to be offered "parenting services" than white caregivers with this problem. These so-called parenting services are typically parenting skills classes of varying quality. Many parents regard them more as a task they must complete to get their children back than any real assistance to their families. These classes that Black families are more likely referred to do not compare with the concrete benefits of housing services that white families are more often offered. The services offered to the Black mothers I met in Chicago matched this pattern. Their service plans focused on fixing their perceived parenting deficits with skills classes and psychological counseling. Although many did receive concrete assistance from drug treatment programs, the child welfare agency offered them few material benefits such as rent subsidies, furniture, food, clothing, and child and respite care.

Caseworkers put the least effort into keeping Black foster children in contact with their parents and into returning them home.[51] Black parents often get lousy visitation arrangements, at times and places that make it hard for them to see their children. One study discovered that Black children had fewer visits with their parents, fewer services overall, and less contact with caseworkers. The findings suggested that their parents were viewed as "less likely to profit from services designed to enhance their ability to maintain or assume responsibility for caring for their children at home."[52] A grand jury that reviewed foster care files in Contra Costa County, California, in 1995 criticized caseworkers for "ethnic insensitivity" in handling minority children in the system.[53] Records for white children were "consistently more detailed, better prepared, and oriented toward family reunification, adoption, or guardianship" than records for minority children, the grand jury said. The jurors discovered that whereas white children's files contained "well-documented" permanency plans, "records reviewed did not exhibit reasonable and consistent efforts on the part of social workers to research and document, in detail, the backgrounds of the minority child." The result was "considerable delay" in minority children's progress through the system.

The provision of mental health treatment further illustrates the racial gap in services. Two studies of children in California's foster care system, published in 1995 and 1997, found that white children were significantly more likely to receive mental health services than were African American or Mexican American youth.[54] The first study, involving 650 foster children, discovered major racial differences in mental health services even when the researchers controlled for the severity of behavioral problems, type of mistreatment, age, and gender. It was unclear, though, whether the disparity resulted from racial bias in referrals, from limited availability of "culturally sensitive" services, or from group differences in the type of help sought from caseworkers.

To better pinpoint the reason for the racial gap, the second study focused on differences in the types of services for children ordered by judges. This study confirmed a trend for white children to more frequently receive mental health services, particularly psychotherapy and counseling, even in cases of similar need. Although they acknowledged that the disparity might stem from the lack of appropriate facilities in minority communities, the researchers concluded that "the court referral system is likely a source of at least some portion of the ethnic biases in mental health service provision to children in foster care."[55] The research showed that white children benefited both from stronger legal advocacy for mental health services and from judicial preferences in favor of ordering these services for whites. In other words, Black children removed from their homes were less likely than white children to receive mental health counseling because judges and caseworkers fail to recommend it for them and because the services aren't available in their neighborhoods.

The alternative to receiving counseling for many Black children in foster care is being labeled a problem child or juvenile delinquent, with far more punitive consequences. Although Black foster children receive less mental health counseling, they are more likely to be sent to institutions.[56] A 1998 study of out-of-home care in California discovered that caseworkers more frequently placed African American children in "treatment" foster care, such as a psychiatric facility, as opposed to foster family or kinship home placement.[57] Caseworkers were likely to place children they thought had behavioral disturbances in these specialized settings as a way of addressing the perceived problem. The study's author noted that the decision to place a child in treatment foster care has a number of negative implications: it often requires moving the child a long distance from his or her family; it implies that the child is "different" from children who are placed with families; and it costs much more than foster family and kinship care.

Black Children Are More Likely to Get Stuck in Foster Care

Partly as a result of this inferior treatment, Black children are less likely than white children to be either returned home or adopted. A study of more than 8,000 children in the California foster care system from 1989 to 1992 found that race played a role in both outcomes: "Being African American was associated with a significant decrease relative to other groups in the probability of both discharge to family or guardian and adoption."[58] The researchers concluded, "The lower [chances] of favorable discharge for African American children indicate that, once in care, many of these children are likely to remain indefinitely."

Another analysis of the California data found that Black children were twice as likely to remain in foster care as to be adopted, whereas white children were twice as likely to be adopted as to remain in care. Black children's odds of being adopted are five times less than those of white children.[59] Latino children were about equally likely to experience either outcome. A similar finding was reported in a study of family reunification in Maricopa County, Arizona: Black children in this sample were half as likely as white children to return home.[60]

When children in foster care have neither biological nor adoptive homes to go to, they often become legal orphans. Courts may terminate the rights of their parents but have no new parents to give them, so the children remain in foster care, with no legal ties to any parent. Black children are the most likely to acquire this unenviable status because their odds of being reunited with their parents and of adoption are both so miserable. As a result, most of the 118,000 children nationwide whose family ties have been severed and who are waiting to be adopted are Black.[61]

A recent trend in the placement of Black children is affecting the quality of services they get. More and more Black children are placed with relatives, an arrangement known as kinship care. Between 1986 and 1990, the proportion of foster children living with relatives grew from 18 percent to 31 percent in twenty-five states.[62] In Illinois, for example, placements with relatives increased 232 percent in a five-year period.[63] By 1997, there were at least as many relative care givers as traditional foster parents in California, Illinois, and New York.[64] An exploding foster care population combined with a shortage of licensed nonrelative foster homes made relatives an attractive placement option.[65] The passage of federal law that encouraged family preservation and court decisions guaranteeing relatives the opportunity to serve as foster care providers also facilitated this development.[66] In the landmark 1979 decision *Miller v. Youakim,* for example, the United States Supreme Court held that otherwise eligible relatives could not be denied foster parent certification and the same financial support as nonkin providers.[67]

Kinship care has many advantages for Black children. It usually preserves family, community, and cultural ties. But it also has a downside. Kinship care follows a familiar pattern of discriminatory services. Black children in kinship care receive fewer services than do children in nonrelative foster care and fewer services than white children in kinship care. Agencies tend to devote fewer resources to reunification of children in kinship foster care with their parents.[68] Caseworkers have less contact with relatives and the children in their care and are less likely to offer them services.[69] In a Baltimore study, for example, twice as many foster care families received two or more services as families involved in kinship care.[70] A lawsuit filed in 1986 by the Legal Aid Society on behalf of children in kinship foster care in New York City charged that the child welfare agency delayed paying relatives their stipends and issuing children their Medicaid cards and failed to provide families with necessities such as beds, clothes, and school supplies.[71]

Of particular concern is the inferior health care received by children in kinship foster care. According to a 1995 federal report, children placed with relatives were less likely to receive health-related services than children in traditional foster care; in fact, they were three times as likely to get no routine health care at all.[72] In a study of premature, low-birth-weight infants in kinship care, only 13 percent received appropriate health care.[73] Most of the children did not receive adequate well-baby visits or immunizations, and many used emergency rooms for primary care.

It seems that some agencies view the placement of children with relatives as a way of cutting costs. Perhaps they believe that children need fewer services if they are being cared for by a grandmother or an aunt. But many kinship caregivers come from poor or low-income families like the grandchildren, nieces, and nephews placed in their homes. They are more likely to be single females and to have less income, more health problems, and more children to take care of than nonrelative foster parents.[74] A study of foster parents in Ohio found that although African American foster parents reported more satisfaction with fostering than whites, they experienced more economic barriers to providing foster care.[75] They are therefore in *greater* need of state assistance. Because Black children are the most likely to be placed with relatives, these policies systematically provide inferior financial support and services for Black children in state custody.

3. TRACING THE DISPARITY TO BLACK CHILD POVERTY

THE COLOR OF AMERICA'S CHILD WELFARE SYSTEM undeniably shows that race matters in state interventions in families. But in what sense does race matter? What are the reasons for the striking racial disparity in every aspect of child protective services?

One possibility is that Black children disproportionately enter and stay in the child welfare system because their parents are more likely to abuse and neglect them. Perhaps there are sociocultural features of Black families that predispose them to mistreat their children. In that case we would expect—we would even want—the state to intervene more often to protect Black children from the greater harm that they face.

Another possibility is that the racial disparity stems from differences in the way the system treats Black families. Even then, this racial difference might result from factors such as higher rates of poverty or unwed motherhood that make Black families more vulnerable to state intervention rather than from racial bias on the part of caseworkers and judges. Can we attribute the large numbers of Black children in the child welfare system to *racism*? Can we say that Black families are disproportionately split up *because of their race*? The answer to this question is critical to deciding what our response to the system's racial disparity should be.

Poverty and the Child Welfare System

Poverty is an obvious place to start when seeking an explanation for why children enter the child welfare system. And it is the dominant explanation of researchers in the field for the inequitable representation of Black children in foster care. The high level of Black involvement in child protective services, this theory goes, simply parallels the high level of poverty among Black families. Most children reported to the child welfare system are poor, and Black children are more likely to live in poverty than children of other groups. It is important to first describe the profound association between poverty and involvement in the child welfare system and then explain how poverty contributes to the over-inclusion of Black children.

America's child welfare system is rooted in the philosophy of child saving—rescuing children from the ills of poverty, typically by taking them away from their parents. Today's child protective services revolve around two central features of the original class-based structure. First, there are separate systems for poor and for wealthier families. Public child welfare departments that investigate child maltreatment and place children in out-of-home care handle almost exclusively the problems of poor families. Disputes over more affluent children are treated as private matters that arise primarily in the aftermath of divorce. This dual legal system based on wealth originated in the Elizabethan Poor Law. "For the poor, state intervention between parent and child was not only permitted but encouraged in order to effectuate a number of public policies, ranging from the provision of relief at minimum cost to the prevention of future crime," writes Georgetown legal scholar Judith Areen. "For all others, the state would separate children from parents only in the most extreme circumstances, and then only when private parties initiated court action."[76]

Second, the public child welfare system equates poverty with neglect. State laws in the late nineteenth century lumped together "dependent" and "neglected" children. They authorized juvenile court judges to commit children to institutions or foster homes if they were either dependent on the public for support or living without proper parental care.[77] Poverty is confused with neglect, historian Linda Gordon explains, because "it often comes packaged with depression and anger, poor nutrition and housekeeping, lack of education and medical care, leaving children alone, exposing children to improper influences."[78] Raising children in poverty also looks like parental unfitness if you believe that poor people are responsible for their own predicament and are negative role models for their children.

The contemporary child welfare system has retained the fundamental division between poor and other families, along with the confusion of poverty with neglect. To be sure, official policy has at times embraced a family-centered ideology. The federal Adoption Assistance and Child Welfare Act of 1980, for example, mandates that states make "reasonable efforts" to prevent removal of children from their homes and to reunify children in foster care with their families. The child maltreatment laws apply to rich and poor alike. But, with rare exception, the families who become involved with the child welfare system are poor.[79] Children raised in poverty are more likely to be reported to child protective services, more likely to have the report substantiated, more likely to be removed from their homes, and more likely to remain in substitute care for long periods of time.[80] Poverty—not the type or severity of maltreatment—is the single most important predictor of placement in foster care and the amount of time spent there.[81]

Why is the child welfare system filled with poor children? There are three types of associations between poverty and child maltreatment: maltreatment may be indirectly *caused* by parental poverty, *detected* because of parental poverty, or *defined* by parental poverty.

A recent criminal case arising out of the fatal starvation of a six-week-old baby in Brooklyn illustrates all three categories at work. The mother, Tatiana

Cheeks, a twenty-one-year-old Black woman on public assistance, was charged with criminally negligent homicide for failing to nourish her infant daughter.[82] Ms. Cheeks was breast-feeding the baby, who weighed only six pounds, five ounces when she died. Although relatives noticed that the baby was small and always seemed hungry after feeding, no one suspected that the baby was starving.

Poverty appears to be a causal factor in Cheeks's alleged neglect of her child. It is possible that the baby's failure to thrive resulted from Cheeks's poor nutrition or stress from trying to make ends meet. Cheeks's failure to save the baby also stemmed from her financial situation. Mothers who breast-feed often have trouble determining whether their infants are getting adequate nutrition and rely on a doctor's regular evaluations of the infant's weight. Cheeks had taken her daughter to a hospital clinic in Brooklyn several weeks before the death, but she was turned away because she did not have $25 to pay for the visit. Cheeks said that her welfare caseworker ignored her subsequent efforts to apply for Medicaid coverage for her daughter.[83] (Prosecutors were eventually persuaded by lactation experts to drop charges against Cheeks and the State Department of Health found that the hospital violated regulations when it turned Cheeks and her baby away.)

Cheeks had previously come to the attention of child welfare authorities when she left her son home alone while she shopped for cigarettes. As a result, she was referred to a social service agency for counseling. Perhaps, having already been identified as a negligent parent, Cheeks feared losing custody of her daughter if she reported the weight loss to child welfare workers. The only mechanism set up for checking the baby's progress was an accusatory system that, in effect, required Cheeks to confess to mistreating her child.

Cheeks's status as a Black woman on welfare may have influenced prosecutors' perception of the baby's death as child abuse. Was Cheeks's failure to get medical help for her baby an instance of criminal negligence or a tragic but innocent mistake? Reaching a conclusion depends not only on application of child abuse laws but also on assumptions about the fitness of different classes of women to be mothers. The dominant culture in this country has long stereotyped poor Black women like Tatiana Cheeks as incompetent, uncaring, and even pathological mothers.[84] White middle-class women, on the other hand, benefit from the presumption that they are nurturing and careful toward their children. These presumptions help to shape the public's understanding of harm to children and its attitude toward mothers who let the harm occur.

Poverty-Related Stress as a Cause of Child Maltreatment

There is a high and well-established correlation between poverty and cases of child abuse and neglect.[85] The third National Incidence Study, conducted by the U.S. Department of Health and Human Services in 1996, reports that the incidence of child abuse and neglect is more than twenty-six times higher in low-income families.[86] There were forty-seven cases of child maltreatment for every 1,000 families earning less than $15,000 per year, compared to only two incidents per 1,000 families with annual incomes above $30,000. Although child abuse occurs in families across income levels, severe violence toward children is more likely to occur in households with annual incomes below the poverty line.

Neglect is also concentrated in poor families. One study conducted in Washington State found that 75 percent of a sample of neglect cases involved families with incomes under $10,000.[87] Because of America's high rate of child poverty, we have two to three times more cases of child abuse and neglect than other industrialized countries. Most of this disparity comes from child neglect: 9 in every 1,000 children is neglected in the United States, compared to only 2 per 1,000 in Canada.[88]

The level of poverty also matters. A 1996 study of census figures and state child protective services data revealed that high-poverty zip codes had three times as many substantiated physical abuse cases as did median-poverty zip codes.[89] Children from families who receive welfare are at the greatest risk for involvement with the child welfare system, especially for neglect.[90] Researchers estimate that half of the families referred to child protective services received welfare at the time of the referral.[91]

Does this strong correlation prove that poverty *causes* child abuse and neglect? Not necessarily. Government authorities are more likely to detect child maltreatment in poor families, who are more closely supervised by social and law enforcement agencies. Welfare caseworkers may inspect recipients' refrigerators to check how benefits are being spent. Police officers may raid apartments in public housing projects to search for drugs. The disproportionate representation of poor parents in the child welfare caseload, then, may reflect a higher incidence of *reporting* of child maltreatment in poor families rather than a higher *incidence* of maltreatment itself.

It is tempting to latch onto unequal detection as the reason for the class disparity. There is an understandable reluctance to recognize a causal relationship between poverty and maltreatment. As I noted earlier, the national campaign against child abuse deliberately downplayed the connection between poverty and child maltreatment in an effort to garner wider support for federal spending on child protection. But anti-poverty advocates also fear that highlighting the higher incidence of child abuse and neglect in poor families may be misinterpreted. It might fortify the assumption that poor parents commonly abuse their children because of some character defect associated with being poor. Both parts of this assumption are false: the vast majority of poor parents do not mistreat their children, and there is no inherent psychological or cultural aspect of poverty that makes people prone to violence or neglect. The question I am addressing is whether parental indigence plays a causal role in the cases that do occur.

In "Child Abuse and Neglect: The Myth of Classlessness," social work expert Leroy Pelton challenges the belief that child maltreatment occurs without regard to class and is distributed evenly across all socioeconomic levels.[92] Pelton argues that heightened public scrutiny of poor families and class bias in reporting cannot account for most of the class disparity in child maltreatment reports for several reasons. If the class disparity were linked entirely to detection, mandatory reporting laws passed in the 1960s and 1970s should have eliminated some opportunity for bias. Yet these laws have not yielded an increased proportion of reports from wealthier families. The relationship between levels of poverty and abuse also suggests a causal relationship. Among the reported cases, the most serious injuries occur in families living in the most extreme poverty. And most homicides of children, which are difficult to conceal, are committed by very poor parents. The myth of classlessness ends up hurting poor families because it supports ineffective remedies for child abuse and neglect that focus on psychological treatments rather than eliminating hazards stemming from poverty or implementing anti-poverty policies.

Failing to acknowledge the connection between poverty and child abuse may also lead to unfair judgments about the moral culpability of abusive parents. Conservative writers, such as William Bennett and John DiIulio, who dismiss *economic* poverty as a cause of crime, blame violence instead on the "*moral* poverty" of offenders.[93] This line of thinking asserts that if economic hardships have nothing to do with child maltreatment, then poor people must abuse their children at higher rates because they are morally deficient. This view ignores the material constraints that poverty places on parents' ability to care for their children.

Many researchers point to stress to explain the association between poverty and child maltreatment.[94] The extreme stress caused by economic hardship and social isolation makes some parents more aggressive toward their children and less able to focus on their needs. We usually think of stress as the response to some cataclysmic trauma rather than to the conditions of daily existence. But, as sociologist Robert Hampton explains, "a considerable amount of stress comes not from the necessity of adjusting to sporadic change but from steady, unchanging (or slowly changing) oppressive conditions that must be endured daily."[95] Parents consumed by the effort to meet their children's most basic needs may find it difficult to address other family problems. Overcrowded and dilapidated housing exacerbate family friction and is associated with the increased use of corporal punishment.[96] Inadequate food, clothing, and health care, combined with despair that stems from stifled opportunities, are other contributing factors. "When you're overwhelmed with problems—not enough money, no job, how to feed the kids," explains Joy Byers, communications director of the National Committee to Prevent Child Abuse, "it can get so overwhelming that people sometimes lash out at the ones who are most helpless."[97] Poor mothers often experience elevated levels of psychological distress and depression.[98] These problems are even more common among welfare-recipient parents, with 48 percent of one sample of TANF recipients reporting poor mental health or poor general health.[99] Low-income parents are especially susceptible to diminished feelings of self-efficacy, self-esteem, and life satisfaction, which can negatively affect the ability to parent.[100] The combination of poverty and parental stress is associated with more punitive parenting and the use of harsher punishment.[101] A study of 241 single African American mothers found that losing a job led to "depressive symptomology [and] predicted more frequent maternal punishment of adolescents . . . and mothers' negative perception of their maternal role."[102]

Not only is stress a regular product of deprivation, but poor parents lack the financial resources that more affluent parents have to alleviate stress. Poor parents can't afford to seek counseling, hire a nanny, or take a vacation. Neglectful parents tend to have a more stressful life situation with fewer resources to cope with this stress. Most poor parents take good care of their children despite these tensions, but economic hardship has a significant impact on the most vulnerable families. "The conditions of poverty are abusive," writes Renny Golden in her book *Disposable Children,* "and some families break under the pressure."[103]

Detecting Child Abuse and Neglect

Another reason for the class disparity is that child maltreatment in poor families is more likely to be detected. I agree with Professor Pelton that bias in reporting cannot explain most of the class disparity in child abuse statistics. Nevertheless, the heightened monitoring of poor families results in the discovery of a great deal of child maltreatment—especially neglect—that would have gone unnoticed had it occurred in the privacy afforded wealthier families. Statutes passed in every state require certain professionals, such as health care workers and school employees, to report suspected child abuse or neglect to the police or state child welfare agency. Receiving social services and welfare benefits subjects poor parents to an extra layer of contact with mandatory reporters. Poor families rely on public service providers who are far more likely to report maltreatment than are private professionals who serve a more affluent, paying clientele. As Annette Appell, a law professor and former attorney at Northwestern's Children and Family Justice Center, elaborates: "Rather than visiting private doctors, poor families are likely to attend public clinics and emergency rooms for routine medical care; rather than hiring contractors to fix their homes, poor families encounter public building inspectors; rather than using their cars to run errands, poor mothers use public transportation."[104]

Middle-class parents, on the other hand, are insulated from this degree of scrutiny. It rarely crosses their minds that a lapse in judgment might lead to an investigation of their home and removal of their children. If the government subjected wealthier parents to the home inspections, drug testing, and police surveillance that takes place in poor neighborhoods, it would find more child abuse and neglect. The intensified supervision of poor families cannot account for their higher incidence of child maltreatment. Middle-class and affluent families do not have to cope with the living conditions that typically produce these harms to children. But poor parents' greater vulnerability to detection does help to explain why so many poor and so few wealthier families are involved with child protective services.

Defining Child Abuse and Neglect

In contrast to cases where poverty indirectly causes parents to mistreat their children or leads to detection, poverty may directly create harms for which parents are held responsible. Child neglect is often the result of parents' financial inability to provide for their children. Parents may be guilty of neglect because they are unable to afford adequate food, clothing, shelter, or medical care for their children. In Illinois, the state may intervene whenever a parent fails to provide "the proper or necessary support . . . for a child's well-being." In South Dakota, all that's required is a finding that the child's "environment is injurious to [his or her] welfare." Under California law, general neglect is defined as the negligent failure of a parent or caretaker "to provide food, clothing, shelter or supervision where no physical injury to the child has occurred."[105] Severe neglect occurs when "the child's health is endangered, including severe malnutrition."

Neglect is usually better classified as child maltreatment *defined* by poverty rather than maltreatment *caused* by poverty. The main reason child protection services deal primarily with poor families is because of the way child maltreatment is defined. The child welfare system is designed to detect and punish neglect on the part of poor parents and to ignore most middle-class and wealthy parents' failings. Although the meaning of child maltreatment shifted from a social to a medical model, it retained its focus on poor families. The system continues to concentrate on the effects of childhood poverty, but it treats the damage as a symptom of parental rather than societal deficits.

Newspaper headlines about grievous child beatings lead many people to believe that most of the children in the system are victims of serious physical abuse. But most cases of child maltreatment stem from parental neglect. Nationwide, there are twice as many neglected children as children who are physically abused. In 1998, just over half (54 percent) of substantiated cases involved neglect, compared to 23 percent involving physical abuse and 12 percent sexual abuse.[106] Another 8 percent of victims suffered emotional abuse or medical neglect. In New York City, for every reported case of physical abuse, there are ten cases of neglect.[107]

When child protection agencies find that children have been neglected, it usually has to do with being poor. Although the category of neglect is intended to capture only incidents where parents have the ability to provide for their children and fail to do so, neglect is usually hard to disentangle from poverty.[108] Most neglect cases involve poor parents whose behavior was a consequence of economic desperation as much as lack of caring for their children. The head of the Los Angeles child welfare department, Peter Digre, conceded before a congressional subcommittee that about half of the children in his system were removed from their homes because of poverty. "It gets down to those very specific issues about a place to live, food on the table, medical care, and things like that," he explained. A congressman bluntly summed up Digre's testimony: "Evidently, it is your department's practice to remove children from families in about fifty percent of the cases because they don't have enough money."[109]

This is not to minimize the harms to children resulting from neglect. Neglect can kill children, and the totality of its impact on the nation's children may be greater than that of abuse. But the huge role of neglect in the child welfare system is a far cry from the public perception of the problem of child maltreatment—as mainly extreme physical abuse—and has much more to do with poverty than the public is willing to acknowledge. This does not mean that we should do nothing about it. It means that we must approach child protection in a different way.

In fact, children are more likely to be taken from neglectful parents than physically abusive parents. In California, for example, there is a stark disconnect between the children who are physically and sexually abused and the children who are placed in foster care. In 1994, about half of child maltreatment reports were for physical abuse (32 percent) or sexual abuse (17 percent).[110] We would expect, then, that at least half—if not more—of the children in foster care would be there because of physical or sexual abuse. Instead, half of children in California's foster care population were removed from their homes because of severe or general neglect, and another quarter because of caretaker absence or incapacity. Child victims of sexual and physical abuse made up less than a quarter of children in foster care. Parental income is a better predictor of removal from the home than is the severity of the alleged child maltreatment or the parents' psychological makeup.[111] After reviewing numerous studies on the reasons for child removal, Duncan Lindsey concludes, "inadequacy of income, *more than any factor*, constitutes the reason that children are removed."[112] Child removal continues to relate more to saving children from poverty than protecting them from physical harm.

Inadequate housing is frequently at the center of caseworkers' decisions to place children in foster care. The U.S. Department of Health and Human Services reports that children from families with housing problems are also more likely to stay in the system longer.[113] Children are routinely kept in foster care because their parents are unable to find decent affordable housing without public assistance. The court-appointed administrator of the District of Columbia's foster care system determined that as many as half of the children in foster care could be immediately reunited with their parents if housing problems were resolved.[114]

It seemed like the size of her apartment was the only thing that kept interfering with Devon's chances of getting her nieces and nephews back. After DCFS considered returning the children, a caseworker showed up at Devon's apartment to inspect the amount of space. "First she wanted to know if I had a room for each of the children," Devon told me. "Then she said the den was too small for two children. I told her the children were fine for all the years they lived with me. Then she told me I couldn't keep the children's clothes in boxes—I had to have dressers for them. Then she asked me where I would sleep. I told her, 'Even if I sleep on the couch, what difference does it make?'"

Poverty itself creates dangers for children—poor nutrition, serious health problems, hazardous housing, inadequate heat and utilities, neighborhood crime. Children in poor families are exposed to residential fires, rat bites, windows without guardrails, and lead poisoning at higher rates than other children.[115] Children are often removed from poor parents when parental carelessness increases the likelihood that these hazards will result in actual harm.

Indigent parents simply do not have the resources to avoid the harmful effects of their negligence, so the same parental behavior and careless attitude is more likely to lead to harm to children, and state intervention, in poor families than wealthier ones.

A common ground for neglect is leaving a child unattended for long enough to endanger the child's health or welfare. It is more likely that poor children left at home or in a park with inadequate supervision will experience a calamity because their homes and neighborhoods are more dangerous. A few years ago, I rented a house across the street from an elementary school in an affluent university community. On some mornings, an apparently well-to-do white woman dropped off her son half an hour before school started on her way to work. The little boy played by himself in the lonely playground until other children and school staff began to trickle in. I doubt that it ever occurred to the mother that she risked losing custody of her son because she left him unattended. Yet many poor mothers have had their children taken away by the state when they have left them alone in the apartment, at a playground, or in the car so that they could keep their jobs.

Consider the impact on families of not having a telephone. "Every time a single parent in such a family needs to make a telephone call, she must go to a neighbor or perhaps a pay phone a block or two away," notes Richard Wexler. "That means for every call she must dress up the children to go outside and take them with her. For every call, she must hang onto the children while she talks on the phone so they don't run out into the street. Or she may risk leaving the children at home for the few minutes it takes to make that call. She is now guilty of lack of supervision."[116]

Poor parents often cannot afford to pay others to care for their children when they are unable to because they have to go to work, they are distraught, or they are high on drugs or alcohol. Nor can they afford to pay professionals to cover up their mistakes. They cannot buy services to mitigate the effects of their own neglectful behavior. Affluent substance-abusing parents, for example, can check themselves into a private residential drug treatment program and hire a nanny to care for their children during their absence. The state never has to get involved. When a famous actress enters a rehabilitation clinic to treat her addiction to alcohol, cocaine, or pain killers, no one mentions what has happened to her children. "This is a poor people's court," says Brooklyn family court judge Jody Adams. "If these people were middle class, they'd be seeing a shrink, not testifying before a judge."[117]

An Iowa case involved the child welfare department's decision to remove a six-year-old girl from her mother because of the unsanitary conditions they lived in.[118] The apartment was filthy: rooms were strewn with garbage, the sink was overflowing with dirty dishes, closets were stuffed with a combination of clutter and refuse. A majority of judges on the Iowa Court of Appeals felt that the little girl's removal from the home was justified. But a lone dissenter argued that the state had not fulfilled its obligation to make "reasonable efforts," as required by federal law, to avoid placing the child in foster care. "If this mother came from a higher economic level, she could do as many parents do who have neither the desire or ability to clean their houses," the dissenting judge pointed out. "She could hire a cleaning service." The dissenter argued that the child welfare agency should have given the mother assistance with cleaning her house. "A few hours of cleaning service would have cost the state less than the judicial time and court appointed fees spent to litigate the adequacy of this woman's housekeeping skills through the state's appellate courts," he added. "And most importantly, the child would not have suffered the trauma of removal and the insecurities that come in foster care." State child welfare agencies are often willing to incur great expense and inflict huge disruptions on poor families rather than simply provide for their material needs. Their response to this criticism is that neglectful mothers like the one in this case have a personality deficit that makes them harmful to their children. But wealthier parents who have exactly the same neglectful disposition can avoid state intervention by hiring others to mitigate the damage to their children.

Wealth insulates children from many of the potentially harmful effects of having irresponsible parents, who themselves usually avoid state scrutiny. Poverty, on the other hand, effectively raises the standard of care the government requires parents to meet. As Leroy Pelton puts it, "In middle-class families there is some *leeway* for irresponsibility, a luxury that poverty does not afford. . . . Poor people have very little margin for irresponsibility or mismanagement of either time or money."[119]

Some states acknowledge the unfairness of equating poverty with neglect by including an economic exemption in their child neglect statutes. New York law, for example, defines a neglected child as one whose parent "does not adequately supply the child with food, clothing, shelter, education, or medical or surgical care, *though financially able or offered financial means to do so.*" It has been suggested that terminating parents' rights because of neglect resulting from poverty would impermissibly infringe on their constitutional rights on the basis of wealth.

But poverty usually has just the opposite effect. Rather than operating as a *de jure* defense against neglect, it works as a *de facto* enhancement of parental culpability. Many of the indicators child welfare agencies use to assess whether a child is at risk for maltreatment are actually conditions of poverty. Caseworkers routinely check to see how much food is in the refrigerator and how many beds are in the rooms. Even children who have never been mistreated and who are in no immediate danger may be removed from their homes based on these indicators of poverty. In essence, their poverty is presumed to place them at risk of future abuse or neglect.

Poverty works in a more insidious way as well. Parental conduct or home conditions that appear innocent when the parents are affluent are often considered to be neglectful when the parents are poor. A whole host of common circumstances can trigger an investigation of poor parents. As a former caseworker in New York City's Administration for Children's Services (ACS) described her clients, "If you are poor and if you have had problems with the law, if you have ever been involved in a domestic violence dispute, if you took your child to the emergency room after an accident, if you have ever used drugs, if your children have problems in school, if you have ever been homeless, ACS has been part of your life."[120] Several studies have found that poor children are more likely to be labeled "abused" than children from more affluent homes with similar injuries.[121] For example, an investigation of suspected cases of child abuse referred by Boston hospitals discovered that "the best predictor of removal of the child from the family was not severity of abuse, but Medicaid eligibility."[122]

A 1983 Connecticut case involved a mother and her six children living in New Haven who received services from the child welfare department and were supported by Aid to Families with Dependent Children.[123] The caseworker assigned to the family noted that the children were not abused or neglected and that they were happy and enjoying a "very warm" relationship with their mother. But when nine-month-old Christopher died from an undetermined cause, the agency immediately seized custody of the mother's five remaining children. The authorities then filed a petition of neglect for each of the children. What was the evidence of neglect apart from their brother's unexplained death? The petitions alleged that "the defendant's apartment was dirty, that numerous roaches could be found there, that beer cans were to be found in the apartment, that the defendant had been observed drinking beer, that on one occasion the defendant may have been drunk, that a neighbor reported that the children once had been left alone all night, and that the two older children had occasionally come to school without having eaten breakfast." On the basis of these allegations, a juvenile court judge issued an *ex parte* order granting temporary custody of the children to child welfare authorities. The Connecticut Supreme Court eventually overturned the decision, but only after the children had been separated from their mother for three years.

It is doubtful that a judge would have perceived the same facts as child neglect if they had taken place in a middle-class home. The unexplained death of a baby would elicit sympathy for an affluent family, not draconian state intervention. The government overlooks a middle-class mother's poor housekeeping skills and occasional consumption of beer. When middle-class parents send their children to school without breakfast as they rush off to work in the morning, it is not seen as neglect requiring supervision by child welfare authorities.

The Connecticut baby's death triggered a punitive response not only because this family was already supervised by the child welfare department but also because the mother's poverty made the death seem suspicious. Her poverty also turned relatively common and innocuous parental failings into reasons to take her children away from her. Being poor, then, did more than bring the mother's inherently wrongful conduct to the attention of the authorities. It was her indigence that made the conduct seem so egregious in the first place.

In my conversations with mothers in Chicago, I soon discovered a pattern of legitimizing their long-term involvement in the system. Their children were initially removed for reasons directly related to their financial situation, ostensibly to protect the children from harm. Once under agency control, the mothers were subjected to intense scrutiny that included mandatory parenting classes, supervised visits with their children, and a battery of psychological evaluations. Any failure to attend a required class, inappropriate interaction with their children, or diagnosis of mental distress became grounds to extend their children's time in foster care. State authorities could find fault with any parent subjected to so much monitoring and examination.

The psychological evaluation, in particular, played an important role in delaying the mothers' reunification with their children. It is common for agencies to require parents to be evaluated and counseled by state-paid therapists throughout the time their children are in foster care and for therapists' reports to figure prominently in the parents' file. Psychological probing by a battery of specialists is bound to turn up some anxiety, hostility, depression, or improper attitude, especially when the subject has gone through the traumatic and frustrating experience of losing her children. The psychological evaluation also provides a surreptitious way of keeping custody of children because of poverty without saying it. In some assessments, parents' financial problems were interpreted as a symptom of a deeper psychological deficiency. A parent's willingness to raise children despite economic difficulties supposedly revealed a profound irresponsibility or delusion that was damaging to children. How could a mentally balanced person think she could raise a child without a roof over their heads or a decent source of income? Child protective authorities could justify detaining children because of this psychological weakness instead of poverty itself.

The purpose for Jornell's psychological evaluations seemed to change each year David was in foster care. Initially, the objective was to rule out Munchausen's syndrome by proxy as the reason she overmedicated David. The psychologists determined that this was an incorrect diagnosis. They also noted that her cocaine and alcohol addictions were in remission. Eight random drug tests conducted between March and July 2000 all came up negative. Her evaluations instead expressed a concern about possible bipolar disorder and "bowel preoccupation." In August 2000, a clinical evaluation prepared for the court states that Jornell "appeared reasonably well organized" and "her speech was normal." Her "thought process was essentially coherent and goal-directed," but "circumstantial." The main problem the report identified was that "her responses to questions tended to wander off the subject and she required frequent redirection in order to conduct the interview within a reasonable time frame." "Her judgment currently appeared good," the psychiatrist stated, "however, her insight was questionable." The report concluded that "a diagnosis of bipolar disorder is not justified" and that Jornell did not have "significant preoccupation with bowel functioning." Instead, Jornell's problem was that she behaved like "an unsophisticated person from a cognitive point of view."

By fall 2000, a new diagnosis appears in Jornell's records. Now the evaluators are worried about a "cognitive disorder" evidenced by Jornell's "disorganization in thinking," which puts her at risk for "poor judgment." The agency sends Jornell for a new round of thorough evaluations. This time the purpose is to assess her "cognitive functioning" to determine whether her scattered thinking is caused by "borderline intellectual functioning," a "characterological defensive style," or a mental illness apparently undetected by the numerous psychiatric evaluations she's undergone for nearly three years.

One psychological evaluation I read involved a mother I'll call June, whose five young children were removed when she left them asleep in bed for one hour (she says it was only a few minutes) to make a telephone call. There had also been past reports of suspected neglect. June's husband had a full-time job, but his income was not enough to support the family. The evaluation noted at the outset that June "expressed little interest in working because she wants to care for her children." The psychologist expressed concern that June stated she'd like to have more children "even though she does not have the financial means to support these children, and she must rely on public assistance." Because June stated that she saw mothering as "an adventure," the psychologist concluded that she failed to acknowledge "the hard-core realities and challenges" of raising five children. The psychologist discounted June's statements about the importance of communicating and spending time with her children because she "has clearly been unable to maximize her own potential in life." June's financial situation then became part of the psychologist's diagnosis. "Although [June] does not appear to meet the criteria for a specific personality disorder," the psychologist wrote, "her poor work history" and "limited psychological insight" are "suggestive of a characterological deficit."

There is also a huge potential for bias when the psychologists who perform the evaluations are selected by caseworkers and paid by the child welfare agency. Child welfare assessments provide a nice chunk of some clinics' business. This arrangement creates financial incentives for evaluators to write reports that confirm the caseworker's view of the parent. And caseworkers are apt to hire evaluators who tend to agree with them. As Jornell put it, "They make assessments favorable to the people who are paying them."

A 1990 audit of the child welfare department in Santa Clara County, California, noted the economic leverage the department has over evaluators: "A potential exists," the auditors found, "that county counsel and the social worker will select evaluators who have a history of supporting the position of the department in dependency hearings."[124] A Santa Clara grand jury that investigated these concerns heard testimony about evaluators who were "blacklisted" for failing to side with the department. Psychologists were categorized as being "anti-parent" or "pro-parent." The department used admittedly incompetent therapists to evaluate "less important" cases. Parents with enough resources and determination can obtain independent evaluations that contradict the agency-solicited report. But judges are likely to place more weight on the "official" findings.

The same scenario unfolded in a Chicago case involving a white family decided by the Illinois appellate court in 1994.[125] It began when DCFS received a report that a three-year-old girl and her baby brother were being neglected by their parents, Sandy and James. A caseworker found the family living in an unheated basement with no hot water, cooking facilities, or food and filed a neglect petition against the parents. Sandy and James agreed to an order of protection, and a judge directed them to provide their children with adequate shelter and to attend mental health counseling. At a hearing several months later, the judge found that Sandy and James had violated the order by moving to a relative's attic where there was no stove, hot water, or refrigerator and the children shared a single mattress on the floor. The judge took custody of the children and placed them with their maternal grandmother. Two years later, after Sandy and James thought they had completed the DCFS service plan, they filed a motion before Judge LaBrenda White for the return of their children.

But now their file was filled with evaluations by caseworkers, supervisors, therapists, and relatives that painted them as irresponsible and uncooperative. A DCFS caseworker noted that "housing is not the only problem here; parents volunteer [at a civil defense station] but refuse to take menial [paying] jobs." A psychiatrist described Sandy as "unkempt" and reported that she "absolutely denied that she thought there was any problem whatsoever in [her] and her husband, neither working and with no visible income, bringing up [their] children." James, the psychiatrist reported, showed a clear "underlying hostility" and a "'no care' attitude." Sandy and James were penalized for voicing their objections to DCFS taking their children. The appellate court noted that when Sandy was asked why her children were removed, she replied, "You tell me—I have NO idea." It noted as well that James "blamed DCFS" for the removal.

Judge White found Sandy and James unfit to care for their children. She put the children in "long-term placement" with their grandmother, cutting off reunification efforts and reducing visitation to once per month. On appeal, the higher court ruled that Judge White erred in eliminating reunification without first terminating the parents' rights. But it approved the judge's refusal to reunite the family. The appellate court rejected the parents' argument that their children had been improperly removed because of the family's poverty. It was clear, the court said, "when the judge ordered the parents to attend counseling, that there was more in question here than housing." The court also stated that it was legally irrelevant that the evidence showed that Sandy and James could be adequate parents. The issue was determining what was in "the best interests of the child," and "the adequacy of the natural parents is not controlling."

Sandy, James, and their children were forced into the child welfare system because of housing problems. Once under state supervision, the parents were scrutinized by a host of professionals for signs of parental unfitness, which could justify keeping their children in custody. And they were judged by a high standard—not whether they were adequate parents, but whether it was in the children's best interests to live with them. Even if Sandy and James were separated from their children for more than poverty, it was poverty that subjected them to a form of intensive inspection that very few parents must endure.

Psychological evaluations of children can also extend their time in foster care. At Jornell's administrative review, the caseworker brought up a recent psychologist's report recommending that David undergo a series of assessments for possible developmental problems. Jornell was prepared for this news. One of the therapists she'd seen mentioned that David might have Down's syndrome or some other developmental disability. Jornell took from her files a three-year-old letter from the clinic where she received prenatal care, stating the results of her amniocentesis. It showed that David was progressing normally in the womb and that there was no evidence of Down's syndrome or other genetic anomaly. "What's this for?," the agency reviewer asked. "This shows that David is normal. He wasn't born with Down's syndrome or other problems. I don't want evaluations of David to be an excuse to keep him in foster care for three more years!"

A mother recently sued the New York City system when caseworkers used this and other excuses to illegally keep her son in foster care. Joanne M. admits that when the city took her newborn son, Jeremy, in 1995, she was unable to care for him because she was homeless and addicted to drugs. She dutifully followed the reunification plan that was supposed to return Jeremy to her care. "She was so determined to win her son back," reports the *New York Times*' Nina Bernstein, "that she trudged 38 blocks from the shelter to the hospital for daily visits after her discharge, quit drugs in a residential treatment program where the baby could have joined her, completed parenting classes and job training, and eventually secured an apartment."[126]

Jeremy and Joanne should have been reunited in 1997. But the agency simply continued to shuffle Jeremy from foster home to foster home for two and a half more years. At one point, the agency mixed up Jeremy's name and birth date and couldn't tell Joanne where he was. The last straw came when agency officials told Joanne in 1999 that Jeremy, already four years old, was showing signs of behavioral problems and needed to stay in foster care. Joanne went to the national advocacy agency Children's Rights, which filed a lawsuit seeking damages for violating the family's civil rights.

Black Child Poverty

The child welfare system is designed to address mainly the problems of poor families. Because Black children are disproportionately poor, we would expect a corresponding racial disparity in the child welfare caseload. The Illinois Department of Children and Family Services prepares a multicolored map that shows the distribution of abuse and neglect cases in Chicago. Neighborhoods with the highest concentration of cases form an L-shaped pattern colored in red. There is another map of Chicago with the same color coding that shows levels of poverty across the city. The poorest neighborhoods in the city form an identical red L-shaped pattern. A third map shows the distribution of ethnic groups in Chicago. The red-colored section marking the city's segregated Black neighborhoods is virtually a perfect match. In Chicago, there is a geographical overlap of child maltreatment cases, poverty, and Black families.

There is a persistent and striking gap in the economic status of Blacks and whites that shows up in unemployment, poverty, and income.[127] True, the government has boasted about gains in Blacks' income and employment during the recent period of economic prosperity. But these rosy headlines hide the abysmal conditions of a large segment of Black children in America. The strength of the economy hasn't erased the racial gap in child poverty nor improved the situation of Black children at the very bottom. These are the children who are being separated from their families in record numbers and thrown into the dangerous world of foster care.

The statistics are dismal. Black families are three times as likely as whites to be poor. When the poverty rate among children peaked at 23 percent in 1993, white children lived in families with an average income that was about 80 percent higher than that for Blacks.[128] Despite eight years of decline, the U.S. child poverty rate is still exceptionally high by international standards, and Black children still lag far behind.[129] According to 1999 census data, 16.9 percent of American children were poor, still more than the 1979 level of 16.4 percent. One-third of Black children (33.1 percent) lived in poverty, compared to 13.5 percent of whites.[130] Especially alarming is the number of Black children raised in extreme poverty, with family incomes less than one-half of the poverty line. (In 1999, the extreme poverty line was $6,645 for a family of three.) These are the children at highest risk of being removed for severe neglect. Extreme child poverty rose sharply in 1997 to almost 3 million, an increase of 426,000 children from the previous year.[131] In 1999, more than 15 percent of Black children, versus only 5 percent of white children, lived in these dire circumstances.[132]

There are dramatic racial differences in a child's risk both of experiencing long-term poverty and of experiencing poverty at all. Poverty researcher Greg Duncan calculated that among children who turned eighteen between 1988 and 1990, nearly one-half of all Black children were poor for six or more years, while only 8 percent of white children spent so many years in poverty.[133] The chances that Black children will experience poverty increase as they grow older. Social work professor Mark Rank sums up the alarming trajectory of Black childhood poverty:

By the age of six, fifty-seven percent of black children will experience at least one year of life below the poverty line as compared with fifteen percent for white children. By age twelve the percentages rise to sixty-seven percent for black children versus twenty-one percent for white children, and by age seventeen, sixty-nine percent of black children versus twenty-six percent of white children will experience at least one year of life below the poverty line.[134]

In a sense, the economic fortunes of white and Black children are just the opposite: the percentage of Black children who *ever* lived in poverty while growing up is about the same as the percentage of white children who *never* did. While about 70 percent of Black children in Duncan's analysis had ever experienced poverty, only 30 percent of non-Black children ever had. About 70 percent of non-Black children, on the other hand, had never experienced poverty, compared to only 30 percent of Black children who were never poor.[135]

There are other features of Black child poverty that make Black families especially vulnerable to child welfare intervention. Black children are the most likely of any group to live in very poor neighborhoods. In 1990, nearly 20 percent of Black children lived in neighborhoods where at least 40 percent of the residents lived in poor families, compared to only 1 percent of white children.[136] The geographical concentration of extreme Black poverty is intensifying in some cities. Harvard sociologist William Julius Wilson found, for example, that in 1970 only one Chicago neighborhood had a poverty rate of over 40 percent. By 1980, "there were nine such areas . . . all of them neighborhoods inhabited principally by African Americans."[137] This is significant because, even after controlling for family background characteristics, researchers find that living in a low-income neighborhood can negatively affect early childhood development.[138] A group of researchers also discovered that "living in areas of localized high unemployment (particularly male) is likely to put families, otherwise vulnerable, at greater risk of child physical abuse and neglect."[139] These neighborhoods are characterized by conditions that are dangerous for children—deteriorating housing, inadequate health care facilities, and high levels of crime. Parents living in poor neighborhoods are also subject to more government surveillance.

4. IS RACISM THE CAUSE?

THE ALARMING RATES OF BLACK CHILDHOOD POVERTY are directly related to the racial disparity in the foster care population. The child welfare system is designed to detect and address neglect in poor families, and Black families are disproportionately poor. But does *racial bias* affect child welfare decision making, even controlling for economic status? In other words, are Black families unequally disrupted by child protection agencies *because they are Black*? After examining mountains of empirical studies, court decisions, newspaper articles, and interviews, I have come to the conclusion that race does influence child welfare decision making. Child welfare workers and judges find it easier to break up Black families than any other families. But even without definitive proof of racial bias on the part of these individuals, it is accurate to say that the overrepresentation of Black children in the child welfare system results from racism.

Evidence of Racial Bias

One way to approach the question of racial bias is to study whether Black children are treated differently from other children who are equally poor. Controlling for economic status, are Black families more likely to get involved with child protective services than families from other groups? The available data are inconclusive. Because race and socioeconomic status are so intimately entwined, it's hard to tell how much of what happens to Black children is related to their color as opposed to their poverty. A group of child welfare experts recently assessed the state of the research: "As families of color are overrepresented among the poor, some authors have been more successful than others in teasing out the differing effects of ethnicity and income in understanding child maltreatment rates."[140] An additional complication, even when race is found to be significant, is determining whether racial differences result from discrimination against Black families or from higher levels of abuse in these families. Reported cases of maltreatment may reflect racial differences in the actual incidence of abuse or in reporters' decision making.

Studies that have isolated race as an independent variable come to conflicting conclusions about its strength in predicting what happens in child abuse and neglect cases. For example, a study of 270 families in western New York found that African American cases were not handled any differently by child protection investigators than white cases and attributed the gross over-representation of African Americans in the county's child protection rolls to their inferior economic status.[141] Another study, funded by the National Center on Child Abuse and Neglect, examined predictors of child protective services decisions in a sample of 1,000 Baltimore families reported for child abuse and neglect during 1988.[142] "Unlike those from earlier efforts, [the findings] do not suggest that decision making is racially biased," the researchers concluded. "African-American families are no more likely to be referred to continuing services or to experience a foster care placement than white families." Also contrary to other research in this area, the Baltimore study detected no socioeconomic bias except in cases where welfare recipients were charged with recurring maltreatment. But the overwhelming weight of the evidence indicates that racial bias is at work.

A good reason to suspect that poverty cannot completely explain the system's racial disparity are the lower chances of involvement of Latino children, who are also disproportionately poor. About the same percentage of Black and Latino households earn less than $15,000, the income level most highly associated with child maltreatment.[143] In San Diego, for example, the socioeconomic status of Blacks and Latinos is about the same, and certainly closer to each other than to whites. Thirty percent of African American and 28 percent of Latino children live below the poverty line, compared to 12 percent of white children. Yet while Latino children were placed in foster care at a rate identical to their proportion of the population, African American children were overrepresented in foster care at a rate six times their census proportion.[144] As Thomas Morton, president of the Child Welfare Institute in Atlanta, asks, "How can income justify the overrepresentation of African Americans but be excused for having no impact on Hispanic families?"[145]

Nor is family structure the answer. Today most Black children are born to unwed mothers, and studies report a higher incidence of child maltreatment in female-headed households. It is tempting to see single motherhood as the reason for the racial disparity. This family characteristic might also explain the difference between Latino and African American rates of involvement, since Latino children are almost as likely as white children to live in two-parent households.[146] But the significance of family structure disappears when researchers take income into account. According to the latest National Incidence Study of Child Abuse and Neglect, rates of child maltreatment are the same for single-parent and two-parent families when income is held constant.[147]

Studies show that the actual incidence of child maltreatment among Black families is no greater than the incidence among other groups.[148] The most persuasive evidence comes from the latest National Incidence Study of Child Abuse and Neglect (NIS-3), which found a strong connection between income and child maltreatment. The report concluded that "[n]o significant or marginal racial differences in the incidence of maltreatment were found either within the NIS-3 data or in the comparison of changes since the NIS-2."[149]

If Black parents are no more likely than others to mistreat their children, how can we explain the racial disparity in the child welfare system's caseload? Although refraining from charging racial discrimination, the federal government has acknowledged that the contradiction between the incidence of maltreatment in Black families and their child welfare involvement is troubling:

> The NIS-3 findings suggest that different race/ethnicities receive differential attention somewhere during the process of referral, investigation, and service allocation, and that the differential representation of minorities in the child welfare population does not derive from inherent differences in the rates at which they are abused or neglected. The reasons for the differentiation among races/ethnicities in the child welfare system are still in need of further exploration.[150]

Let's look at the research on racism that is already available.

Some research traces the overrepresentation of Black children to racial bias in the initial reporting of maltreatment. There is strong evidence that race influences which harms to children doctors, teachers, and other mandatory reporters label as child abuse or neglect. Researchers have found that Black children are more likely to be identified as abused than white children with similar injuries.[151] For example, in a 1985 study, Hampton and Newberger conducted their own analysis of the National Incidence Survey data to determine racial differences in reporting. They discovered that African American families were more likely to be reported to child welfare authorities than white families for equally severe injuries to their children.[152] Family violence expert Richard Gelles concludes that "Blacks are more likely to be recognized and reported [but] the link between race and abuse is probably tenuous and quite limited."[153]

More recent research on the diagnosis of child abuse shows how racial prejudices creep into reporting. A study published in the 1999 *Journal of the American Medical Association* reviewed 173 cases of head trauma at a Denver children's hospital.[154] Its objective was to determine how frequently physicians missed abusive head trauma (AHT) and the factors associated with the unrecognized diagnosis. AHT is a dangerous form of child abuse, causing more deaths than any other type of injury as well as serious neurological damage to survivors. But it is difficult to diagnose in infants and toddlers because its symptoms—vomiting, fever, irritability, and lethargy—are common symptoms of other childhood conditions.

The researchers found that nearly a third of the AHT cases went undetected by physicians who examined the children. They also discovered that there was a significant racial difference in the misdiagnoses: the abuse was missed twice as often in white children as minority children. Doctors failed to diagnose AHT in 37.4 percent of abused white children, but only 19 percent of minority children. In other words, doctors were more likely to suspect that AHT symptoms indicated child abuse in the case of minority children. They were more trusting of white parents whose children presented the same symptoms.

Hospitals' handling of drug use during pregnancy provides another striking illustration of racial bias in reporting. Since the late 1980s, an increasing number of child protection cases have involved newborns exposed to drugs in the womb. In some states, infants who test positive for drugs are deemed abused and are automatically removed from their mothers' custody. As with child maltreatment reports in general, these cases disproportionately involve Black mothers.

Part of the reason for the racial disparity in removal of drug-exposed newborns is that substance abuse by indigent Black women is more likely to be detected and reported than substance abuse by other women. The government's main source of information about prenatal drug use is hospitals' reporting of positive infant toxicologies to local child welfare authorities. This testing is performed almost exclusively by public hospitals that serve poor minority communities. Private physicians who treat more affluent women tend to refrain from testing their patients for drug use and certainly would be unlikely to turn them in to child protection services.

But racial discrimination—not just poverty—plays an independent role in decisions about drug-affected infants. Research confirms that, controlling for other variables, Black women are far more likely to be reported for prenatal substance abuse and to have their newborns placed in out-of-home care. A study of pregnant women in Pinellas County, Florida, published in the 1990 *New England Journal of Medicine,* found little difference in the prevalence of substance abuse along either racial or economic lines. Yet Black women were *ten times* more likely than whites to be reported to government authorities.[155] A 1993 study of women whose newborns tested positive for cocaine in New York City hospitals discovered that Black women were 72 percent more likely than white women, and more than twice as likely as Latino women, to have their babies removed by child protective services.[156]

Additional research identifies caseworkers' substantiation of reports as the entry point for racism. A study of cases in New York found that caseworkers were more likely to substantiate reports against Black and Latino families. The researchers concluded that racial background was the only variable that could explain the way child protection workers verified allegations of neglect.[157]

There is also evidence that race affects the decision to separate reported parents from their children. As I noted earlier, a recent federal study of child welfare services investigated the racial disparity in foster care placement versus providing in-home services. The report came very close to charging that Black children are more likely to be removed because of their race. "Collectively, findings indicate that African American children in the child welfare system tend to have more problems than other children," the report noted. "It could be surmised that the circumstances of African-American children warrant removal from the home and placement in foster care more often than other children." But the report rejected this explanation:

The most telling findings in response to this issue appear when conducting analysis on the relationship of types of placement and race/ethnicity, controlling for selected case problems and characteristics. Findings from these analyses show that even when families have the same characteristics and lack of problems, African-American children, and Hispanic children to a lesser extent, are more likely than white children to be placed in foster care.[158]

Black children were more likely to be placed in foster care even when their parents were employed, drug-free, and not receiving welfare; even when they came from small families and safe neighborhoods; and even when they had no disabilities or mental health problems.

The National Child Welfare Leadership Center in Alexandria, Virginia, conducts training sessions for caseworkers on multicultural perspectives to help them relate more fairly to families from diverse ethnic backgrounds. One exercise NCWLC developed involves participants making decisions about the level of risk and agency intervention required after reading descriptions of possible child maltreatment in a series of vignettes. Half of the vignettes involve children of color, including African Americans, Native Americans, Asian Americans, and Latinos, and half involve white children. The participants aren't told until after the exercise that there are two sets of vignettes. In each set the race/ethnicity of the characters is reversed and counterbalanced to reduce experimental error.

The exercise always uncovers the participants' racial biases. "Without exception, the results of the exercise conducted in all sessions revealed that decisions about the level of risk and intervention were influenced by the race of the child and family described in the vignette, independent of all other factors," writes NCWLC's director Norma Harris.[159] Participants did not intentionally discriminate against the hypothetical minority families. Instead, notes Harris, "consistently, the participants' response to the results was one of surprise that their own decision making processes, related to risk and agency intervention, were influenced by culture."

There is evidence, then, of racial bias at every stage of the child protection process. On the other hand, there are also studies that show race is not a significant factor in predicting children's involvement in the system. Which should we believe? Two features of the system convince me that its racial disparity is indeed rooted in racism—the magnitude of the racial imbalance and the irrationality of the child protection process.

Given the evidence that Black families do not have a higher incidence of child maltreatment, the sheer enormity of the racial difference in child welfare involvement is strong evidence of racial bias. One telling set of figures is the ratio between the percentage of African American children with substantiated allegations of maltreatment compared to their representation in the state population. Because the incidence of maltreatment is equivalent across racial groups, we would expect this ratio to be 1.0. If the ratio of substantiated allegations compared to census proportion differs widely by race, we might suspect that caseworkers are biased toward finding child maltreatment in one group over another. State statistics demonstrate exactly this bias against African American families.[160] Whereas the ratios for white children are less than 1.0 and slightly higher for Latino children, the ratios for Black children range from 1.22 in Alabama, to 2.56 in Illinois, to 2.89 in New Jersey, to 3.69 in Wisconsin, to 6.94 in Minnesota. "Even if one were to agree that selected factors have a disproportionate impact on African Americans and therefore would predict a higher rate of founded allegations involving African American children, one would still need to consider what an acceptable magnitude of that effect would be," Thomas Morton argues. "Should African Americans be found 20 percent more often? Is nearly 700 percent justifiable?"[161] Such a drastic racial difference is not only unacceptable, it smacks of racial bias in the system.

Another feature of child welfare decision making persuades me that it is riddled with racism. If people who report and investigate child abuse made rational decisions that accurately identified children in need of protection, we might conclude that Black children must be entering the system for good reason. But the evidence is precisely the opposite. Numerous studies show that the decision-making process is wholly unreliable and haphazard. Something other than the neutral, scientific evaluation of evidence is guiding the influx of Black children into foster care.

When Edmund Mech reviewed the child welfare literature in 1970, he concluded that no consistent method for decision making existed.[162] Subsequent studies that examined foster care placement decisions using both hypothetical and actual case materials found substantial disagreement among judges and caseworkers. A 1972 study, for example, asked caseworkers and judges to recommend dispositions in 127 maltreatment cases.[163] The overall agreement among six judges was less than 25 percent. One judge was four times more likely to recommend removing the child than another judge. Duncan Lindsey set out to test the consequences of this low rate of reliability.[164] He analyzed the reliability rate determined by past studies within a hypothetical model that viewed decision making as a purely random process. Lindsey concluded that the child welfare system is unable to tell which children should be removed and which should be left at home. "If the level of reliability were to slip much further," he wrote, "the decision-making process would be roughly equivalent to a lottery!"[165]

Further proof of the system's irrationality is the way placement rates vary wildly from one state to another, from county to county, and from year to year without regard to rates of abuse and neglect. There is no logical reason why a child is twice as likely to be placed in foster care in Vermont as in New Hampshire. Or why one South Carolina county substantiated 89 percent of maltreatment allegations while another substantiated only 14 percent. The vagaries of child protection policy have more to do with the current political climate than with child safety.

We can trace dramatic changes in agency practice that affect the lives of thousands of children to a single case of abuse that happened to grab the headlines. The more extreme and aberrational the story, the more attention it receives. New York University law professor Martin Guggenheim describes how New York City's foster care population soared in the aftermath of the highly publicized murder of six-year-old Elisa Izquierdo by her mother in 1995: "The number of children removed from their families and placed in foster care over parental objection rose by nearly fifty percent between 1995 and 1997. During this same period, however, there was no known change in the base rate of child abuse."[166] The same chain of events has been repeated in cities across the country. For example, after three-year-old Joseph Wallace was hanged by his mentally ill mother in 1993, the Chicago foster care population rose by 30 percent in fourteen months. The avalanche of removals suggests not only that caseworkers were pressured to overreact to reports but also that "family and juvenile courts 'rubber stamp' agency recommendations to remove children from their parents, even in circumstances that do not constitute true emergencies."[167]

If caseworkers and judges have no rational method of determining which children need protection, how do they so consistently remove Black children from their homes? Such a random process for identifying maltreated children could not so effectively target one group of families without some racial input. I am not charging that these people deliberately set out to break up Black families because they dislike their race. To the contrary, they may believe that they are helping Black children by extricating them from a dangerous environment. But race negatively affects their evaluation of child maltreatment and what to do about it, whether they realize it or not.

An Invitation to Racial Bias

In fact, the child protection process is designed in a way that practically invites racial bias. Vague definitions of neglect, unbridled discretion, and lack of training form a dangerous combination in the hands of caseworkers charged with deciding the fate of families. Child neglect is sometimes defined broadly as any parental failure that presents an imminent risk of serious harm to a child.[168] This definition does not even require any showing of actual harm. Illinois child protection authorities recently removed a six-year-old boy when they learned that his mother was still breast feeding him. A juvenile court judge upheld the removal decision despite finding that the boy, described as having a "remarkably sunny disposition," had suffered no emotional harm. The agency was justified in taking the boy from his mother, the judge ruled, because he faced "enormous *potential* for emotional harm."[169] Unlike child abuse that can at least be substantiated with physical evidence, the vague definition of neglect is highly susceptible to biased evaluations of harm based on the parents' race or class or on cultural differences in child rearing.[170]

Further increasing the risk of bias, the initial decision to confirm an allegation of child maltreatment lies entirely with the caseworker. It is only after the caseworker investigates a report of child maltreatment, determines whether it is valid, and decides what to do about it that all these critical judgments face any sort of adversarial challenge or judicial review. In many states, caseworkers have the power to immediately remove children from their homes if they think the children are in imminent danger. This emergency exception to court approval is widely abused. New York City lawyers admitted in federal court that removing children on an "emergency" basis without seeking a judge's order was routine agency policy.[171] "This is akin to allowing a police officer to investigate, charge, find guilt and issue a sentence without ever appearing before a judge or jury," says Chicago attorney Diane Redleaf.[172] Caseworkers decide on their own which and how much evidence to gather. And they are free to interpret similar evidence of maltreatment in different ways, depending on a family's background. They may highlight the damaging implications of some parental behavior while ignoring other equally harmful behavior. An empty refrigerator may signal child endangerment or a career mother's hectic schedule. A bruise could be the common result of boisterous play or proof of parental abuse.

Most of the agents entrusted with the power to investigate and separate families have no special qualifications for this difficult work. Many are young college or even high school graduates who come from backgrounds foreign to those of the families they are employed to judge. A bachelor's degree in any subject will do. Less than a third of caseworkers have had any actual social work training.[173] In 1995, 90 percent of states reported difficulty recruiting and retaining caseworkers.[174] Because worker burnout and staff turnover are high, many caseworkers are inexperienced. They are typically overwhelmed with too many cases and must often make snap judgments. The Child Welfare League of America reports that some states have fifty-five children in foster care for every one caseworker. It recommends a ratio of no more than fifteen children per caseworker.[175] A grand jury monitoring the Los Angeles foster care system released a scathing report in June 2000 that blamed the "broken" system on caseworkers' high caseloads, poor training, and mismanagement. With forty-five to fifty cases to keep track of, the typical L.A. caseworker spends less than half an hour per month with each child.[176] At court hearings, it's not unusual for caseworkers to sheepishly admit to the judge that they just took over the case and don't know what's going on.

Nor do caseworkers apply any tests that have been shown to be effective at judging potential harm to children. They often rely instead on their own personal values about child rearing rather than on scientific methods of evaluation.[177] Some agencies encourage workers to act on intuition, hunches, and instinct. When a caseworker has a gut feeling that a mother might harm her child—a feeling that might be based on race—he is tempted to view the evidence in a way that confirms his inclination to protect the child.[178] These are the perfect conditions for prejudice to influence decision making.

Most states have adopted risk assessment models that have the potential to improve caseworker decision making by adding scientific standards and reducing bias. Caseworkers typically check off and weigh a list of family traits to tell the degree to which a child is likely to be abused or neglected at some point in the future. Yet a majority of these protocols have not been carefully designed or empirically validated.[179] One researcher came to the bleak conclusion that "the amount of scientifically validated research on child abuse and neglect is vanishingly small. The value of any self-styled predictive checklist is negligible."[180]

Moreover, giving risk assessment instruments to untrained caseworkers merely covers up the weaknesses in their judgments. A team of scholars that studied three types of risk systems cautioned that these systems could not replace a competently trained staff. Indeed, the models "require a staff that is trained and knowledgeable in human growth and development, parenting practices, the causes and effects of mistreatment, and family dynamics"—qualifications few caseworkers have.[181] They found further that the instruments increased caseworkers' already overwhelming workload. Two other researchers expressed concern that "many agencies are adopting risk assessment instruments in lieu of addressing fundamental problems in existing child protection systems, such as the excessive number of inexperienced or incompetent workers and the lack of adequate resources."[182] They concluded that employing these new models without needed reforms actually made a bad situation worse: "In fact, use of inadequately designed or researched risk-assessment instruments may result in poorer decisions, because workers will rely on mechanical rules and procedures instead of trying to develop greater clinical expertise."

A 1993 Unisys advertisement in a social work journal sports a technological fix to these difficulties in caseworker decision making. The ad declares in bold letters across the top, "Child abuse is a war against small, unarmed civilians. Better information is an effective defensive weapon." It goes on to describe the information system Unisys developed to aid child welfare agencies "in the battle against increasing caseloads and mountains of paper." "In Lapeer County, Michigan, Unisys has joined forces with the Department of Social Services, enabling them to handle a significant increase in caseloads with no increase in staff." In addition to helping to place children in substitute care, the system supports "an optional risk assessment model to help caseworkers assess the potential for further harm to the child." There is little comfort in the prospect of overworked and undertrained caseworkers aided by computer programs in their removal of children.

Consider a vignette from a December 1997 cover story in *People* magazine that followed caseworkers from across the country over a twenty-four-hour period as they investigated abuse and neglect reports.[183] Claudette Washington, a Maricopa County, Arizona, caseworker, decides to take custody of three children, ages three, seven, and eight, after she investigates a report that their mother, Samantha, keeps a filthy house and sometimes orders the seven-year-old boy to do a handstand in the corner for an hour when he misbehaves. The children are terrified when Washington tells Samantha they are going to foster care: "Rose and Justin, hovering nearby, are alarmed. Young Ben clings to his mother, wailing over and over, 'I want to stay with you.' After calming him, Washington takes the three kids to her car and buckles them into the backseat as Rose clutches her favorite book, one of R. L. Stine's *Goosebumps*. Washington drops them with another CPS worker, who will see that they get to a shelter that evening."[184]

Washington confesses that she doesn't like removing children because "we've disrupted their whole lives." So how does Washington justify this disruption? She lists her reasons for taking the children away from their mother as "a pattern of negligence and suspected abuse, drug use and the number of Samantha's male visitors." "She has too many guys hanging around the house," Washington explains. "Out here, molestation is one of the most common referrals I get." It is hard to judge whether Washington made the right prediction. But note that her decision was not based on any evidence that Samantha hurt her children. It was based on her intuition that they might be hurt in the future.

To be fair, the article does not reveal the children's race, and we have no way of knowing whether race played any role in Washington's deliberations. My point is not to accuse Washington of racism or erroneous decision making but to show how susceptible caseworker judgments are to error and racial bias. Black children bear the brunt of these unreliable and ill-informed decisions, which too often result in separating them from their parents.

Part of the reason for the glut of Black children in foster care is that caseworkers are taking many of them from their homes for no good reason. Instead of seizing their children, the child welfare system might have provided a visiting nurse who could have given Jornell instruction in the medical care of infants, or a housing advocate who could have helped Devon find a larger apartment. When the Child Welfare Institute in Atlanta reviewed foster care decisions in three Illinois cities in 1994, it discovered an alarming number of unnecessary removals. In fact, researchers determined that "in one-third of the cases, there was absolutely no reason for the children not to be at home with their parents," the *Chicago Tribune* reported. "The children were in foster care for the protection of their caseworkers, not for their own safety."[185]

"If only those children were placed in foster care who actually need it," writes Leroy Pelton, "we would have very few children in foster care."[186]

Cultural Prejudice

Some scholars who have investigated racial bias in child protective services believe that African American families are penalized by culturally biased interpretations of child neglect. Studies of child protection decision making show that caseworkers tend to use a model family as a frame of reference.[187] They evaluate problem behavior by the extent it deviates from this parenting ideal. The model for many caseworkers is a white, middle-class family composed of married parents and their children. As one attorney told a Minnesota task force on racial bias, caseworkers "seem to believe that unless the family meets white suburban class standards, the children are 'at risk.'"[188] From the outset, most Black families diverge from the ideal because they are headed by unmarried mothers.

Caseworkers often misinterpret Black parents' cultural traditions, demeanor, and informal means of handling family distress as neglect. The Black community's cultural traditions of sharing parenting responsibilities among kin have been mistaken as parental neglect.[189] Black women share a rich tradition of women-centered, communal child care. Black mothers who cannot afford nannies or licensed day care centers may depend on relatives and neighbors for child care. These cooperative networks may include members of the extended family (grandmothers, sisters, aunts, and cousins), as well as nonblood kin and neighbors.[190] Their relationship with children ranges from daily assistance to long-term care or informal adoption.

Carol Stack's classic research in the "Flats," for example, revealed that many children there moved back and forth between households of close female relatives.[191] Three or more women related to a child formed a cooperative domestic network, taking turns assuming parental responsibility for the child. Because these mothers do not fit the middle-class norm of a primary caregiver supported by her husband and paid child care, they are perceived as having abrogated their duty toward their children.[192] Ironically, Illinois, a state that now relies heavily on kinship care, considered children who lived with relatives other than the parents to be neglected less than a decade ago.

A similar misunderstanding has been documented in psychiatric diagnoses. A series of influential papers in the 1980s showed that mentally ill African Americans were routinely misdiagnosed.[193] Several studies found that Black patients who were admitted to a psychiatric facility with a diagnosis of schizophrenia were more likely than whites to be reclassified as depressed by research clinicians. A more recent study at a large Midwestern psychiatric hospital similarly reported that Black patients were more likely than whites to receive a diagnosis schizophrenia and less likely to be diagnosed with mood disorder. Scholars investigating the problem of misdiagnosis argue that sociocultural differences had an impact on the presentation and interpretation of psychopathology. White doctors were more likely to misinterpret Black patients' psychological symptoms because they were unfamiliar with cultural aspects of Black behavior and language patterns.

Stereotypes of Black Maternal Unfitness

Black mothers' reliance on kin networks probably has less to do with involvement in the system today than it did several decades ago. Social networks and resources have dissipated and social isolation is a more likely reason for finding child neglect. Children are more likely to be removed because they are left alone rather than because they are left with a grandmother, aunt, or neighbor. Race influences decision making through strong and deeply embedded stereotypes about Black family dysfunction.

In *Killing the Black Body: Race, Reproduction, and the Meaning of Liberty*, I described a popular mythology that portrays Black women as unfit to have children. That book exposed the explosion of rhetoric and policies that degrade Black women's reproductive decisions. The same set of stereotypes also support the removal of Black women's children. "It has been accepted that there is a fundamental problem with the black family," Megan McLaughlin, executive director of the Federation of Protestant Welfare Agencies, told *Child Welfare Watch.* "There are many people who believe that to save these children, they have to take them from their families. It is a sense that black families are already broken, and you're saving these kids from broken black families."[194] Some caseworkers and judges view Black parents as less reformable than white parents, less willing and able to respond to the treatment child protection agencies prescribe.

Three prominent images of Black mothers cast them as pathological: the careless Black mother, the matriarch, and the welfare queen. These images symbolize traits Black women are supposed to have that are detrimental to their children. It is believed that Black women neglect their children because they do not care enough about them, create a fatherless family structure that provides inadequate supervision of their children, and teach their children to be dependent on government handouts. The continuity of these derogatory stereotypes over many decades suggests that they have a real impact on the way many Americans view Black families. All of these myths about Black mothers confirm the need for the state to intervene in their homes to safeguard their children and to ensure that their children do not follow their dangerous example.

Careless Black Mothers

Charges of Black mothers' carelessness emerge from the institution of slavery. The ideal Black mother figure, Mammy, selflessly nurtured her master's children, but not her own. Mammy was both the perfect mother and the perfect slave; whites saw her as a "passive nurturer, a mother figure who gave all without expectation of return, who not only acknowledged her inferiority to whites but who loved them."[195] Mammy, however, did not reflect any virtue in Black women as mothers of their *own* children. Mammy, while caring for her master's children, remained under the constant supervision of her white mistress. She had no real authority over either the white children she raised or the Black children she bore.

In contrast, whites portrayed slave mothers as negligent and unable to care for their own children. Southern state officials commonly attributed the deaths of Black babies to accidental suffocation by their mothers in bed.[196] When a one-month-old slave girl named Harriet died in the Abbeville District of South Carolina on December 9, 1849, for example, the census marshal reported the cause of death as "[s]mothered by carelessness of [her] mother." The census marshal explained: "I wish it to be distinctly understood that nearly all the accidents occur in the negro population, which goes clearly to prove their great carelessness & total inability to take care of themselves."[197] It now appears that the true cause of the high infant mortality rate among slaves was the hard physical labor, poor nutrition, and abuse the mothers endured during pregnancy. These census reports provide an early example of the scapegoating of Black mothers for the social causes of their children's poor health.

After Emancipation, whites lamented the loss of the moral guidance that slavery provided Black mothers. For example, Eleanor Tayleur claimed that freed Black women, deprived of intimate contact with their morally superior white mistresses, displayed uncontrolled emotion and ignorance. Their purely animal passion toward their children, wrote Tayleur, led to horrible abuses: "When they are little, she indulges them blindly when she is in good humor, and beats them cruelly when she is angry; and once past their childhood her affection for them appears to be exhausted." According to Tayleur, the Black mother "exhibits none of the brooding mother-love and anxiety which the white woman sends after her children as long as they live."[198]

The view of newly emancipated Black women as unfit for motherhood was reinforced by their working lives. Whereas the virtuous white mother cared for the home and depended on her husband's wages, economic conditions forced many Black mothers to earn a living outside the home.[199] At the turn of the century, nearly all Black women worked long days as sharecroppers, laundresses, or domestic servants in white people's homes. Working in white homes undermined Black domestics' own roles as mothers and homemakers. The ideal of motherhood confined to the home and opposed to wage labor never applied to Black women and made them appear deviant and neglectful.

A contemporary icon of the careless Black mother is the pregnant crack addict. The image of the pregnant crack addict arose in the late 1980s out the urban crack-cocaine epidemic and the reporting of a surge in the numbers of newborns testing positive for drugs. Despite similar rates of substance abuse during pregnancy by white and Black women, the media erroneously suggested that the problem was most prevalent among Blacks.[200] The pregnant crack addict was portrayed as a Black woman who put her love for crack above her love for her children. News stories reported that the chemical properties of crack destroyed "maternal instinct," making women who smoked the drug incapable of nurturing their children.[201] A public health crisis that affected all communities became yet another example of Black mothers' depravity that justified harsh state intervention.

The Matriarch, Black Unwed Mothers, and Absent Black Fathers

Modern social pundits have held Black mothers responsible for the disintegration of the Black family. Stereotypes about deviant Black mothers and absent Black fathers together form a picture of dysfunctional Black families. Daniel Patrick Moynihan popularized the myth of the Black matriarch, the domineering female head of the Black family, in his 1965 report, *The Negro Family: The Case for National Action*.[202] Moynihan, then Assistant Secretary of Labor and Director of the Office of Policy Planning and Research under President Johnson, described Black culture as a "tangle of pathology" that is "capable of *perpetuating itself* without assistance from the white world." The chief cause of this pathology, Moynihan asserted, was Blacks' "matriarchal" family structure. According to Moynihan, "At the heart of the deterioration of the fabric of the Negro society is the deterioration of the Negro family. It is the fundamental cause of the weakness of the Negro community."

Black families have the highest rate of unwed motherhood, with Black families three times as likely as white families to be headed by a woman.[203] Most Black children in America are born to unmarried mothers. But the rate among whites is rising faster. Growing from 3 percent in 1965 to 25 percent today, the rate of fatherlessness among whites has reached what it was among Blacks three decades ago.[204] There are now more white babies than Black babies born to single mothers. Still, single motherhood is viewed as a *Black* cultural trait that is infiltrating white homes. Charles Murray hammered in this point in his *Wall Street Journal* editorial, "The Coming White Underclass," which warned white Americans that their rising illegitimacy rate threatened to spread to white neighborhoods the same crime, drugs, and "drop out from the labor force" that now infects Black communities.[205]

The flip side of the rebellious Black single mother is the absent Black father. Black men have a hard time fitting the ideal model of the father as married breadwinner. The stresses and dislocations caused by high rates of unemployment and low-paying jobs make sustained partnerships difficult. Harvard sociologist William Julius Wilson has linked the rise in Black female-headed households to Black male joblessness.[206] Recent interviews of poor single mothers by sociologist Kathryn Edin, coauthor of *Making Ends Meet*, reveal that these women refrain from marrying principally because of the shortage of financially attractive men in their communities.[207] Black men's unemployment rates, although decreasing, are still double those of white men. Black fathers are also separated from their families by imprisonment. Blacks make up more than half of the 2 million inmates in U.S. prisons and jails.

The dominant assumption is that Black men have little to do with their children, providing no financial support and rarely developing any emotional attachments. But there is no evidence that Black men value family relations any less than others. Stephanie Coontz reports that in one national study, "poor African-American, officially absent fathers actually had *more* contact with their children and gave them more informal support than did White, middle-class absent fathers."[208] Black fathers are often involved in their children's lives in ways child welfare agencies and the media don't recognize. However, the assumed absence of fathers from Black households has justified state intervention on the grounds that single mothers set a bad example for their children and are incapable of properly supervising their children.

The Welfare Queen

Another contemporary image of Black mothers is the welfare queen, the lazy mother who refuses to work and breeds children to fatten her monthly check from the government. This mythological character was supported by conservative writers, such as Charles Murray, who argued in the 1980s that welfare induces Black women to refrain from marriage and to have babies.[209] The claim that welfare creates a financial incentive for recipients to have more children is

refuted by empirical studies and common sense.[210] It would be completely irrational for a mother on welfare to assume the tremendous costs and burdens
of caring for an additional child given the meager increase in benefits that results. The vast majority of women on welfare have only one or two children.[211]
Yet the popular image of the welfare queen helped to drive the passage of child
exclusion laws—or "family caps"—in a number of states, denying any increase
in benefits to mothers who have children while already receiving public aid.

The public despises this mother not only because she cheats taxpayers
out of their hard-earned money but also because she uses the money selfishly.
Welfare mothers cannot be trusted to spend their benefits for the care of their
children; instead they waste them on drugs, fancy clothes, and entertainment
for themselves. Caseworkers therefore inspect the homes of poor families in
search of evidence of child maltreatment while preserving the privacy of
wealthier families. Courts assume that mothers who receive public assistance
require state supervision to ensure that benefits are devoted to their children's
welfare.[212]

The welfare queen is guilty of a more devastating injury to her children,
as well. Contemporary poverty rhetoric blames poor Black mothers for perpetuating welfare dependency by transmitting a deviant lifestyle to their children.
Part of the impetus for welfare reform was the sense that payments to Black
mothers merely encourage this transgenerational pathology. Welfare reform discourse also paid little attention to the relationship between poor Black mothers
and their children, never questioning the impact of compelling these women to
leave their young children to find low-paying jobs. This belief that poor Black
mothers have nothing beneficial to impart to their children helps to legitimate
the disproportionate disruption of their family bonds.

These images of Black maternal unfitness have been around so long that
many Americans don't even notice them. They are reincarnated so persistently
and disseminated so thoroughly that they become part of the unconscious psy-
che, part of the assumed meaning of Blackness. These stereotypes are so prevalent that even many Black caseworkers have absorbed them.

In a rare judicial acknowledgment of unconscious racism, a Missouri
federal judge explained why Congress passed a sentencing scheme that gave
(Black) crack offenders much longer sentences than (white) cocaine offenders. The court held that the racial disparity in sentencing violated the Con-

stitution's equal protection clause. Perceptions of African Americans as "dangerous, different, or subordinate," he wrote, "are lessons learned and internalized completely outside of our awareness, and are reinforced by the media-generated stereotyping."[213] The judge noted that the media helped to construct a national image of Black male youth as criminal by generating a public panic about crack and then associating Black males with the drug. These negative portrayals of Black males influenced legislators' decisions about the crack problem even though legislators did not intentionally set out to discriminate against Blacks. "The decision maker who is unaware of the selection perception that has produced his stereotype will believe that his actions are not motivated by racial prejudice," the judge explained. (On appeal, the Eighth Circuit rejected the lower court's use of unconscious racism, requiring instead proof of "discriminatory purpose.")[214] In much the same way, many caseworkers and judges are unconsciously influenced by potent stereotypes of Black mothers' unfitness when they make judgments about how to handle allegations of child maltreatment.

Friction between Black mothers and caseworkers often leads to bad outcomes for Black families. Caseworkers are instructed to treat the degree of parents' cooperation as evidence of the child's risk of harm. When reported families do not cooperate with the investigating agency, their case is more likely to be referred to court.[215] More critical than the mother's attitude toward her child is the mother's attitude toward the caseworker. Parents are expected to be remorseful and submissive. Any disagreement with the agency's proposed plan is reported as evidence of unwillingness to reform. Perceptions of cooperativeness are greatly influenced by the parent's race. Because of negative stereotyping, Black mothers are often perceived as hostile and less amenable to rehabilitation.

The mothers I talked with were constantly torn between contesting unfair decisions or complaining about their children's treatment and complacently acceding to caseworkers' demands. They legitimately feared that their outspokenness would hurt their chances of getting their children back. Evaluators labeled them "hostile," "paranoid," "grandiose," "defensive," and "reluctant to use services" if they expressed any concerns about the course of treatment the agency recommended. Even after the mothers met every requirement in their permanency plans, caseworkers were free to observe that they were not truly rehabilitated. Insufficient contrition is a sign that the prescribed treatment did not work. A number of the mothers I interviewed showed me multiple certificates marking their completion of the same drug treatment program, parent training class, or psychological evaluation. "Why did you have to go through the same class twice?" I asked one mother. "My caseworker said I didn't learn anything the first time."

White families, on the other hand, benefit from the presumption of parental fitness and valuable family ties. The white middle-class, nuclear family has long been held up as the ideal in scholarship and the media. It is questionable, as Stephanie Coontz points out in her scathing critique of traditional family mythology, *The Way We Never Were,* that this model family ever existed.[216] Nevertheless, holding up white families as the superior standard against which all other families fail is entrenched in American culture. Caseworkers are also more reluctant to intrude in white homes because white parents are better able to protect their rights. Several people in the New York City system interviewed by *Child Welfare Watch* about racial bias pointed to this reverence for white parents' authority. A former Family Court judge put it this way: "Black people often don't know their legal rights. White people may be more likely to call their attorney." Caseworkers take this into account when deciding whether to remove children from their homes. "The average feeling among caseworkers is, if you remove a white child, you stand the chance next morning of facing white parents with their lawyer," reported a former caseworker. "There's no similar fear in removing a black or Hispanic child from the home."[217]

Fighting for Their Children

One thing is certain: a growing number of Black parents who have lost their children and members of their communities believe that they are victims of a racially biased system. And they have begun to challenge child protection agencies in the courts and in the streets. Like the mothers I met in a Chicago church basement, Black parents are fighting individual and organized battles for their children.

One of the biggest lies propagated about parents involved in the foster care system is that they have all abandoned their children. Newspaper headlines decry the flood of "emotionally traumatized children," who are "products of families ruined by crack, AIDS and homelessness."[218] Titles like *Nobody's Children,* used to describe the children in foster care, reinforce this perception. Mothers of children in foster care are usually portrayed in movies and television shows as strung-out drug addicts. Fathers simply don't exist. In the motion picture *Losing Isaiah,* Halle Berry plays a crack addict who leaves her baby on a pile of trash while she gets high in a nearby abandoned building. When she kicks her habit several years later, she learns that the baby has been raised by a loving middle-class foster mother played by Jessica Lange. The biological mother wins back custody of her son but ends up returning him to the white foster family when she's unable to care for him.

A fall 2000 episode of the television show *Family Law* involved a Latino boy, Raphael, who is severely beaten and burned by his alcoholic foster father. Two of the starring attorneys decide to file a class action lawsuit on behalf of injured children to reform the city's foster care system. In one scene, the lawyers search out Raphael's drug-addicted mother so she can sign the lawsuit's complaint. They find her looking haggard and strung out in a dingy apartment. The mother begins to cry when she learns of her son's injuries. "The caseworker told me Raphael would be better off in foster care," she sobs to the female attorney. Instead of showing the mother any sympathy, the lawyer castigates her for giving up her son because she loved drugs more.

The next episode is devoted to the trial, where evidence is submitted showing the damage to children in foster care. Throughout the trial, the lawyers consistently refer to the children's parents as "crack-addicted mothers." The lawyers unethically conceal the city's settlement offer from the parents because these "crack-addicted mothers" would only spend the money on drugs instead of on their children. The audience is meant to believe that the lawyers did the right thing. Although the system is on trial for placing children in dangerous foster homes, it is ultimately the mothers who are blamed for abandoning their children to the system.

But I met a network of Black parents in Chicago who defy this image. Far from abandoning their children, they devoted every waking moment to being reunited with their children and trying to make the system better for other Black families. They made me aware that many parents who seem to have abandoned their children have just been worn down by too many agency requirements and too meager resources to complete them.

The mothers I met in the church basement were part of a grassroots organization called Operation MOSES, which stands for Mothers Organizing Systems for Equal Services. Jornell started the group after David was placed in foster care and she began to meet other Black mothers who were struggling with the child welfare department. "At first I thought this was only happening to me," Jornell told me. "I felt like I was going around in a maze. I never experienced that much helplessness in my life. Then I started approaching other mothers. I'd ask them, 'How'd they get your children?' I began to see a pattern."

MOSES got a shot in the arm when one of its members, Tina Olison, became a cause célèbre in Chicago. DCFS removed Olison's son when he was born cocaine-exposed and placed him in the care of one of Chicago's most powerful couples, a white alderman and appellate court judge. Three years later, having recovered from her addiction, found a job, and completed the permanency plan, Olison sought to regain custody of her son, known to the public as Baby T. The *Baby T* case captured front page headlines in every Chicago newspaper for more than a month. While she was in the spotlight, Olison was quoted in the papers when she spoke on behalf of MOSES about racism in the system. But when the trial ended unsuccessfully for Olison, so did the attention MOSES received from the press. The mothers continue to meet at the church to share information about the system and give each other moral support.

During the *Baby T* trial, many people from Chicago's Black community rallied around Olison and used the case to air pent-up anger about racial bias in the system. At one gathering, Reverend Anthony Williams called DCFS "the new slave master." "No other ethnic group would allow this type of holocaust to go on," Williams declared.[219] Another Black minister, Reverend Al Sampson, went on a forty-day fast outside the office of the alderman who had custody of Baby T. The Rainbow/Push Coalition held an educational forum to inform officials and community organizations about the hardships Black families confront in the child welfare system.

Other groups have sprung up around Chicago's Black neighborhoods. Madie Johnson, whose granddaughter was placed with a white foster mother even though Madie was willing to take her, founded Grandparents Helping

Grandparents. Despite Madie's five-year fight for her granddaughter, the state allowed the foster mother to adopt her. Madie contends that the adoption should not have been approved because the adoptive mother was not licensed for foster care and isn't married to her live-in boyfriend, who is only nineteen years old. Madie believes DCFS passed over her and her husband in favor of the white couple because her granddaughter, whose mother is white, appears to be a white child. "They thought she looked too white to be with a Black family," Madie says. Her organization gives advice to grandparents who want custody of grandchildren removed from their homes. Despite the increase in kinship care, Madie told me, there are still many qualified relatives who are not considered by child welfare authorities.

When a state subcommittee on DCFS reform held a hearing in Chicago, more than one hundred parents and community activists crowded the room to vent charges of racial discrimination.[220] The hearing was called by Democrat Connie Howard, who represents one of Chicago's Black districts in the state assembly. Howard introduced House Bill 1913, "The African American Child Welfare Act," seeking to give Black children protections like those Congress gave Native American children against forced removal from their communities. The hearing lasted seventeen hours. Reverend Sampson called for DCFS to declare a one-year moratorium on sending Black children out of state and to other distant white areas. "Unless the department decides to change and reform," Olison told the subcommittee, "I'm going to call it the Destruction of Children and Family Services."

Similar accusations are percolating in Black communities in other parts of the country. Speakers at community meetings in Bedford Stuyvesant and Harlem, for example, also compared New York City's Administration of Children's Services to the institution of slavery. According to *Child Welfare Watch*, parents charged that "the child welfare system separates siblings, dismantles families and terminates parental rights" and that "African-American children are a source of income for foster care agencies run by whites."[221]

Some Black families in Chicago have taken their claims of racial discrimination to federal court. In July 1999, Chicago attorney Anita Rivkin-Carothers filed a class action lawsuit against DCFS, Illinois governor George Ryan, and other state officials on behalf of all African American parents and children involved in the Cook County juvenile court system. Rivkin-Carothers represented Tina Olison in her custody trial, and Olison is the first named plaintiff on the complaint. *Olison v. Ryan* alleges that Black families have suffered systematic deprivation of their constitutional and civil rights as a result of the department's discriminatory policies. Cook County, which includes Chicago, accounts for three-quarters of the 50,000 Illinois children in substitute care. Almost all of these children are Black. The plaintiffs charge that the child welfare and court systems have targeted Black children for removal and their parents for termination of parental rights; similarly situated whites, they say, are protected from this type of family destruction.

The lawsuit alleges that DCFS is aided by the private agencies that contract with DCFS to evaluate families in the system. These agencies follow a policy of routinely supporting a change in the permanency goal for Black foster children from reunification with their parents to termination of parental rights. One of the private agencies, a defendant in the lawsuit, recommends *against* returning children home in 93 percent of assessments it conducts on Black parents and children. The sole function of these agencies, plaintiffs say, is to interrogate parents in search of damaging information that can justify permanently separating them from their children. "Whenever DCFS decides it doesn't want to return the child, it calls in certain agencies," Rivkin-Carothers says. "They are notorious for being a rubber stamp for DCFS."

Rivkin-Carothers told me she decided to sue DCFS during Olison's highly publicized custody battle. "Every night during the trial when I would get back to my office, there would be 50, 60 messages," Rivkin-Carothers said. "When I returned these parents' calls, they were in tears, telling me horror stories. Parents would say, 'I did everything I was supposed to do, I jumped through all of the hoops, and they kept raising the bar. Every time I completed one thing, they'd tell me I had to do something else.' These were Black parents, 100 percent. I realized that something had to be done."

One of the named plaintiffs, Lashonya Moffett, became involved with child protective services when police raided her building and her frightened baby-sitter ran from the apartment, leaving Moffett's two children alone. The children were placed with Moffett's mother, and DCFS assigned the case to a private child services agency. Moffett says she completed all the services the agency required, including parenting classes and counseling, and prepared to regain custody of her children. But agency officials became annoyed when Moffett moved for unsupervised visits with her children at her home. They began to move toward termination of Moffett's parental rights, starting with an outside assessment. Moffett was interviewed shortly after her mother died, and the children were moved to another foster home. The evaluation concluded that Moffett was suffering from serious depression and needed medication for her condition. As expected, Moffett charges, the agency that interviewed her recommended termination of her parental rights, and the juvenile court judge accepted its advice. The complaint contends that the court would not have terminated white parents' rights based on such flimsy grounds.

Another plaintiff, Beverly Johnson, lost custody of her three-month-old baby when she took him to Cook County Hospital for immunizations and hospital staff diagnosed him with failure to thrive. Johnson says the baby had recently lost weight from a bout of diarrhea, which was treated by a doctor. The hospital later conceded, the complaint alleges, that the baby was within normal weight range based on his premature birth. But the case was complicated by evidence of drug use in Johnson's medical records, an accusation Johnson denies. Johnson's file contains a positive result from a toxicology screen performed on the baby when he was born at the hospital. Johnson contends that the test was both unlawfully conducted without her consent and unreliable because it was never confirmed. The complaint also alleges that Cook County Hospital has a policy of testing only African American infants for signs of maternal drug use. Had Johnson been white, the complaint charges, her baby would not have been tested and removed. "When white mothers have babies who are cocaine-exposed, the hospital sends the baby home with the mother and a visiting nurse. Many times, they don't even test white mothers," Rivkin-Carothers says. "With Black families, DCFS comes in and snatches the baby."

"You have families who don't have funds to pay their light or their gas bills, families in a cold house. There are funds available for that, but DCFS doesn't give them to Black families," Rivkin-Carothers told me. "They take the children out of the home and put them in foster care and separate the family. And once you're separated, forget it—you're not going to get back together in less than a year. But if you're a white family, DCFS says we can pay for your lights and gas and keep your family together." Rivkin-Carothers contends she's seen evidence of this differential treatment during her practice in juvenile court. She pointed to one of the named plaintiffs in the lawsuit, Ernestine Davis.

Child welfare authorities investigated Davis and her four children when the city condemned the family's house because of exposed electrical wiring. Davis was required to move out of the house and obtain counseling to address her neglect of the children's safety. At a court conference with her caseworker and the judge, Davis claims, everyone agreed that the case could close if the house were made habitable. The caseworker assured Davis that DCFS would provide state funds earmarked specifically to solve housing problems like hers. Four months later, with no funds forthcoming, the court gave custody of her children to DCFS based on newly raised charges that her house was filthy and overrun with roaches. If she were white, the complaint alleges, Davis would have received housing assistance, and her children never would have entered the court system.

Rivkin-Carothers suggests a reason for this assault on Black families. "It's all about money. It's as simple as that," she remarked to me. The top-earning ten private agencies that manage cases for DCFS have contracts worth an average of $10 million. These agencies are involved in a lucrative business that depends on keeping children in the system. The more children placed in foster care and the longer they are kept there, the more money the agencies make. There is no financial incentive, on the other hand, to reunite children quickly with their parents. As Rivkin-Carothers points out, "They can't make money if the children are returned home."

"There's an easy way to solve the problem," she told me. "You don't reward these agencies for keeping children out of the home. You reward them for putting them back faster."

Why are *Black* families targeted? I asked.

"Why has there been disparity in the treatment of African Americans for the last 300 years?" Rivkin-Carothers answered. "Anytime there's a social agency that discriminates against us, they're going to claim that it's for our benefit. The funds are going to be put there with white people in charge. They make all the money and say, 'We have to service all these poor Black people.' And it's always going to happen until we can get our own agencies that are independent and will fight to do the right thing for us."

I asked Rivkin-Carothers what she hoped to accomplish by bringing the class action suit. "My clients want injunctive relief—they want DCFS to change the way it treats Black parents and children," she replied. "We want Black children to be treated like white children. We want Black families to receive the same services, and we want them to be judged by the same standards."

5. The System's Fundamental Flaw

So far I have discussed the systemic factors outside the child welfare system that make Black families more vulnerable to state intrusion, as well as evidence of racial bias on the part of actors in the system. The racial disparity is also caused by a fundamental flaw in the system's very conception. The child welfare system is designed not as a way for government to assist parents to take care of their children but as a means to punish parents for their failures by threatening to take their children away. The child *welfare* system, then, is a misnomer. The mission of state agencies is not to promote children's welfare. Rather, their purpose has become child *protection*: they try to protect children from the effects of society's colossal failure to care enough about children's welfare. The system is activated only after children have already experienced harm and puts all the blame on parents for their children's problems. This protective function falls heaviest on African American parents because they are most likely to suffer from poverty and institutional discrimination and to be blamed for the effects on their children.

The Strong Arm of Child Protection

The system's defective philosophy has poisoned the relationship between state agencies and poor minority communities. Child protective services have become an ever-present "Big Brother" in inner-city neighborhoods creating fear and mistrust among residents. Parents in these communities view caseworkers more as law enforcement agents than social service providers. They know that the job of caseworkers is not to assist families to take better care of their children. Their job is to investigate parents and to find evidence that can be used against them to gain custody of their children. Florida's child protection agency panicked after nine child abuse deaths in the fall of 1997, and the number of child removals skyrocketed. "I may be going to see one family, but six or seven others run out, grab their children, and run in the house," a Tallahassee investigator reported. "Their perception is that I'm there to snatch their children."[222] The caseworker, notes Duncan Lindsey, has been "unmistakably cast in the role of inquisitor prying into and judging the affairs of the family, with predictably adverse effects on the family."[223]

Most people in poor minority neighborhoods have either had a terrifying encounter with child protective services or know someone who has. They have a legitimate fear that it might happen to them. In their community, child protection involvement isn't a rare and secret occurrence as it is in middle-class areas. In Bushwick, Brooklyn, 20 out of every 1,000 children have been removed from their homes and placed in protective custody. That rate is ten times as high as in the affluent Upper East Side of Manhattan and seven times the rate in middle-class Bayside, Queens. There were 1,413 investigations of child abuse and neglect in Bushwick in 1998, compared to only 109 on the Upper East Side.[224] The level of child removal is even higher in Central Harlem, where 1 out of every 10 children is in foster care. In the Englewood neighborhood of Chicago, most of the families are supervised in some way by the Department of Children and Family Services. The child welfare system has a powerful, menacing presence in these communities.

And its presence has repercussions on community and family life. People sometimes use local child welfare agencies as a way of settling disputes. Several mothers I spoke with blamed their involvement in the system on a former boyfriend or relative who reported them to child protective services for some ulterior motive. Fear of involvement in the system makes others afraid to call the police or social service agencies for help with family disputes. Some mothers hold off taking their children to the doctor for accidental injuries for fear they will be reported to child protective services. "Say you take one of your kids to the hospital, the first thing they'll want to do is call Children and Family Services," one mother told me. "Even if they know it's not your fault or nothing that could be helped, they still call. If a child falls and hurt themselves or someone comes in with a sick baby, they don't care what the circumstances was or anything. That's the first thing that comes out of their mouth—'Call Children and Family Services.' That's why you find a lot of times people don't take their kids to the hospital."[225]

Others hold off reporting domestic violence. In some states it is considered neglect to permit a child to witness adults fight in the home. When a mother calls the police to report she has been beaten, she may be confessing to child neglect. "When I called 911, I was bleeding so badly I knew I needed medical attention," Sharwline Nicholson told a *New York Times* reporter. "I didn't know I'd end up down that road, that calling for help would escalate and I'd end up losing my kids."[226]

In July 2001, federal judge Jack Weinstein heard testimony in a class action lawsuit brought by twenty battered women who allege that New York City child welfare officials violated their rights by taking custody of their children. April Rodriguez told the judge that ACS put her three children, ages seven, three, and one, in foster care when she called the police to report abuse by the father of two of the children. The agency refused to return them until Rodriguez moved into the city's shelter system, forcing her to lose her job at a Manhattan video store. Although the children spent only a week in foster care, Rodriguez testified that "they weren't the same children." "My baby's shirt was filthy and her diaper was disgusting," she said. "My son, his face was bruised and bloody, and he had pus coming from his lip."[227]

A Michigan court even terminated a battered woman's parental rights based on a psychologist's prediction that the woman was at risk of entering into a relationship with another abusive man.[228] Some women decide to handle the situation themselves rather than risk intervention by child protective services.

In a recent *New York Times* article, "Child Welfare Turns Nightmare," Somini Sengupta described the impact of this fear in poor New York City neighborhoods. Cynthia Marquez, a Bushwick mother, was suspected of child abuse when her ten-year-old son with behavioral problems hit his little brother and school officials reported the bruises. A child welfare investigator inspected her apartment and questioned the children. The charges were dropped, but the encounter with the child welfare agency left its mark on the family. The next time her son threw a temper tantrum Marquez thought twice about calling the police to help her control him. Marquez's decision, Sengupta writes, reflects "a real everyday fear that a momentary crisis can become something worse. That a parental mistake can lead to an investigation. Or that in the nightmare case, a difficult child can be taken away."[229] Parents feel they are "living out every parenting move under suspicion" and routinely protect themselves against the constant threat of investigation. They carry documents clearing them of abuse and neglect charges, such as a doctor's note for school absences and food pantry receipts in case they run out of groceries.

Sengupta attributes this state of siege to the pressure on city officials to prevent another high-profile tragedy like the 1995 killing of Elisa Izquierdo by her mother. "That combustible combination of children at risk and an oversight agency under pressure not to slip up," Sengupta explains, "can create an atmosphere in which a wide range of parents—some good, some bad, some in between and stressed out—alter their conduct, color their conversations, and have the frankest of strategic conversations with their children, all because they worry about their first or next encounter with the child protective agency." As I have stressed, this adversarial relationship stems as much from systemic race and class bias as from alarm over the child abuse crisis. Children in wealthier parts of New York City also have temper tantrums, school absences, and bruises. But these signs of possible child maltreatment and delinquency appear less suspicious to reporters and caseworkers. Just as significant, parents in affluent and middle-class neighborhoods have voluntary, private resources to deal with their children's problems. Mothers on the Upper East Side and Bayside don't have to call the police or child welfare agency when they need help; they can consult with physicians, counselors, and therapists, often at the expense of their health insurance, with little fear that investigators will be alerted.

And mothers now have more to fear. Some places are cracking down on suspected child neglect in poor neighborhoods by treating it as a criminal matter. Although most child maltreatment is handled by civil child protection proceedings, it is sometimes prosecuted criminally. Many cases fall within the scope of general criminal statutes, such as those punishing assaults, homicides, sexual assaults, and incest. Many states have also passed special criminal child abuse and neglect statutes. In most states, child welfare agencies notify police about the most serious cases of abuse. But police are increasingly arresting parents even for minor instances of neglect that traditionally had been handled by child protective services.

In New York City, for example, misdemeanor arrests for endangering the welfare of a child have more than tripled in recent years. In 1998 there were more than 1,000 child endangerment arrests, compared to only 300 in 1990.[230] In the summer of 1997, Police Commissioner Howard Safir directed officers to "take action . . . when [they] see children in dangerous situations."[231] This harsh response is part of Mayor Rudolph Giuliani's assault on "quality-of-life" infractions such as panhandling and turnstile jumping, which are thought to lead to more serious crimes. The theory is that by arresting mothers on minor neglect charges, the city will prevent more serious cases of abuse. Mayor Giuliani also warned parents living in the city's homeless shelters that city agents would put their children in foster care if they didn't find a job. Sourette Alwysh, a thirty-four-year-old Haitian immigrant, was led away in handcuffs when police found her living with her five-year-old son in a foreclosed building without electricity or running water. Sidelina Zuniga, a thirty-nine-year-old Mexican immigrant, came home from grocery shopping to discover the police had taken her boys, ages ten and four, because she left them alone for an hour and a half. When she reported to the local precinct to claim them, she too was arrested.[232]

The arrest of Danish actress Annette Sorenson in Manhattan for child neglect became an international incident.[233] Sorenson and her boyfriend left their baby in a stroller on the sidewalk outside a window in the restaurant where they were dining, a practice that is common in Denmark. Passersby who noticed the seemingly unattended child notified police. The child was placed in foster care and separated from the distraught parents for several days before intervention from the Danish government. The baby's father charged that he was brutalized by the officers at the police station. While this story received attention for its clash of cultural approaches to child rearing, few commented that the baby's father is African American and that the baby appears Black by American standards. The child's race, then, may explain why the people who reported the episode and the police took such extreme measures to protect the child.

Although New York City's policy is extreme, it is not unique. Carole Taylor was charged with misdemeanor child endangerment for allowing her six children to live in a messy apartment in Chicago's Cabrini-Green housing projects without food or furniture except some soiled mattresses.[234] Geraldine Jeffers, a thirty-eight-year-old Cincinnati mother, was convicted of child endangerment when she went to the hospital because of complications with her pregnancy, leaving her fifteen-year-old daughter in charge of her four younger children.[235] Neighbors called the police to report that the children were left alone overnight. The prosecutor noted that Jeffers's home was filthy and in disarray.

Even when charges are dropped or thrown out by a judge, the children have been scarred by their mother's arrest and their time in foster care. Laura Venegas was arrested when police found her two sons playing alone in front of their aunt's East Harlem apartment. Prosecutors agreed to drop child-endangerment charges, but Venegas had already spent a night in jail, and one of her sons got a black eye while in foster care. "Keep your eyes on your children," Venegas warns her friends. "You never know when the police might arrest you."[236]

It seems Orwellian to call what the child welfare system does "serving" families, when the vast majority of its clients are "served" against their will.[237] The agency's "service plan" usually has little to do with *services* for the family. It is typically a list of requirements parents must fulfill in order to keep their children or get them back. Rarely are parents asked what services they need. The plans remind me of probation orders that list requirements and restrictions judges impose on criminals. Violation of a single provision lands the offender back in jail. In the child welfare system, parents who fail to comply risk never seeing their children again.

In 1997, outside specialists issued a report evaluating New York City's Administration for Children's Services. The report recommended that ACS improve its accountability by measuring "client satisfaction." "We saw customer satisfaction as an important issue," one task force member told *Child Welfare Watch*. "Because if you're working toward returning a child, you have to engage the parent. If the parent is having a problem with the system, that's an obstacle to getting the child home."[238] In their study, the specialists found that parental input did not play a significant role in ACS's system for evaluating the agencies that provide foster care services.

Amy Sinden, a poverty lawyer in Philadelphia, once represented a Black woman whose three-year-old daughter was removed when she left her too long at the shelter where they were living.[239] The client had recently moved from Virginia to Philadelphia to try to kick her crack habit. She had been clean until the day she left her daughter with another shelter resident to run errands. She visited one of her cousins hoping to borrow some money and ended up using crack with him. When she returned to the shelter after midnight, she discovered that the shelter had called the child welfare agency and a social worker had taken her daughter into custody.

Three days later, Sinden met her client in court and was presented with the social worker's reunification plan. The social worker told the mother that to get her daughter back she had to send the child to live with her mother-in-law in Virginia while she completed six months of inpatient drug treatment in Philadelphia. When Sinden asked the mother whether she agreed with the plan, she stared at her blankly. "Pretend the worker didn't tell you what you have to do," Sinden told her. "How would you want to deal with this problem if it was entirely up to you?" Apparently this was the first time anyone proposed that the mother have some input in the decision.

> She looks confused and startled, as if she's so used to thinking within the confines of what she has been told is permissible that the concept of thinking about what she wants is entirely foreign. Eventually, she expressed to me that she's terrified of leaving her daughter for six months—terrified that her daughter will feel abandoned, terrified that her mother-in-law won't treat her daughter well, terrified that her mother-in-law will try to get permanent custody, terrified that being separated from her daughter will make it harder to give up the habit. It is seeing her daughter's face every morning that gives her the resolve to keep fighting her addiction.[240]

Afraid of contradicting the social worker, the mother isn't sure what to do when her lawyer suggests a drug treatment program where she could live with her daughter.

The agency's plan soon takes on outlandish proportions. The family's fate becomes focused on a list of tasks a caseworker has typed or scribbled on a form. Compliance overshadows the child's needs or parent's ability to care for the child or even the truth of the original charges of maltreatment. The issue is no longer whether the child may be safely returned home, but whether the mother has attended every parenting class, made every urine drop, participated in every therapy session, shown up for every scheduled visitation, arrived at every appointment on time, and always maintained a contrite and cooperative disposition. Caseworkers use foster care as leverage to coerce compliance with their demands instead of a refuge for children who are truly in danger. Many courts apply a rule that failure to complete the permanency plan is prima facie evidence that children should not be reunited with their parents. As incredible as it sounds, parents' ties to their children are routinely severed because the parent failed to fulfill some provision on a caseworker's list.

Sometimes permanency plans are so complicated or onerous that they seem designed to ensure failure. A grand jury investigating child protective services in San Diego heard testimony about plans that ordered parents to devote more than forty hours per week to various rehabilitation programs. Defense attorneys testified that they advised their clients to quit their jobs so they could keep up with reunification requirements. Parents typically rely on public transportation to get to all these appointments. They are often suffering from health problems or contending with some other crisis. "Obviously, there is no time to earn a living or otherwise live a life," the grand jury concluded. "A parent often becomes a slave to the reunification plan."

One mother from a poverty-stricken town near St. Louis described to me how her caseworker was pressuring her to pay an electricity bill. "I don't care what you got to do, if you don't have the receipt in my office soon, I will be out there to take your kids," he told her. "That's how he talks to me every time I call," the mother says. "He'll tell me to have something done and when I call back to let him know it's done, he'll say, 'I don't think you're really trying.' I just told him one day, 'I work five days a week, just like you do. What you want me to do—quit my job?'"

Vernon Bush is a plaintiff in the Chicago race discrimination lawsuit who became involved in the system when his four children were born drug exposed. He says that DCFS required him to perform the following tasks to be reunited with his children. Many of them require travel to the far Chicago suburbs where the children were placed, and he has no car.

1. Participate in substance abuse treatment
2. Attend Alcoholics Anonymous and Narcotics Anonymous meetings
3. Make random urine drops to test for unlawful drugs and alcohol
4. Participate in individual counseling
5. Participate in family counseling

6. Attend instructions on treating asthma
7. Learn sign language
8. Learn CPR
9. Attend speech therapy, sensory integration therapy, developmental play group therapy, occupational therapy, and physical therapy for the children
10. Attend educational classes
11. Attend all medical appointments scheduled by the foster parents
12. Attend all court dates and administrative reviews
13. Make scheduled visitations with all children, who are spread among four placements
14. Maintain employment to support his family
15. Contact each case manager once per week
16. Complete a psychological exam

Bush says caseworkers pressured him from the very beginning to relinquish his rights to two of his sons. He believes the agency required such a backbreaking plan so that he would become overwhelmed and give up.

"Voluntary" Placements:
The Price of Help for Poor Children

Valerie wasn't reported to DCFS. She called child protective services for help with her two girls, ages three and five, and her baby boy. In the winter of 1998, Valerie and the children were living in a cold, dilapidated apartment infested with roaches. All of the children were sick. One girl was suffering from lead poisoning, and the baby, who was born two months premature, was recovering from a hernia operation. Her son's father, a recovering drug addict, had just relapsed and was back in a drug treatment program. Valerie turned to alcohol. "It was overwhelming," Valerie told me. "And I had no one to help me."

Valerie and the children ended up in her aunt's apartment. But the situation there was worse: the aunt's utilities were cut off, and they had no lights or hot water. Valerie and the children had to sleep on the floor. "I hit rock bottom. I had to call DCFS," Valerie says. "I told them I just needed time to heal.

I figured in six months I would get my children back." Valerie relinquished custody of the children, and they were placed in foster care.

I asked Valerie how she reached a point of such desperation. Valerie traced her problems to an incident that happened when she was seven years old. Until that summer, she led a happy childhood in a house full of relatives on Chicago's South Side. She had been playing outside her house with a group of friends when she went inside a house down the block to ask a teenage neighbor to join them. The older girl sexually assaulted her. Too traumatized to tell anyone, Valerie kept the secret until her life fell apart at age fifteen. Valerie was hospitalized for two weeks when she began experiencing severe depression, headaches, and seizures and was diagnosed with manic depression, now known as bipolar disorder. For the next four years, she went in and out of psychiatric institutions as doctors clumsily experimented with therapies for her mental illness.

"They kept me chained up every night," Valerie remembers. "One night they strapped me down so tight, I woke up bleeding. They once gave me a drug that had me paralyzed for two days. Then they gave me medication that was so strong, I couldn't bathe myself or feed myself. I was like an infant. I was that way for months. I don't think jail could have been any worse."

Finally the doctors discovered that lithium worked to relieve Valerie's symptoms. At nineteen, she was released from the hospital and received outpatient services. A year later, Valerie's bipolar disorder went into remission. "When I got my freedom back, I made up for lost time," she told me. "I started going out and going shopping." Her mother was transferred to an office in Denver, Colorado, and Valerie moved with her. She enrolled in a trade school and studied fashion design for two years. She fell in love with a kind, responsible man named Donald, who lived in her apartment building.* After dating for five years, they were engaged to be married. Donald joined the Navy, and the two spent three glorious months in San Diego together before Donald went out to sea. In 1991, Valerie was shaken by another crushing tragedy. The Navy notified her that Donald had been killed in the Persian Gulf War. Valerie moved back to Chicago. "I started drinking heavily, looking for a reason to live. The pain was so great." She started seeing another man and found the motivation to stop drinking when she became pregnant with her first daughter in 1993.

---

*At Valerie's request, the names of individuals in her story are fictitious.

Her second daughter was born two years later. Valerie had already broken up with the father, and never even told him she was pregnant. The next year she met another boyfriend, a recovering drug addict, and was soon expecting her third child. But that relationship, too, was short-lived. Not long after the birth of her son, her boyfriend left to enter a drug treatment program, and Valerie placed the children in foster care.

"My first caseworker was good," Valerie recalls. "She promised to help me and told me DCFS would return the children in six months like I wanted." Valerie says that at her first administrative case review, the reviewer told her this was the official permanency goal. Valerie was given a service plan that provided for weekly visits with the children and required psychological counseling, parenting classes, substance abuse treatment, urine drops, and evaluation by a Parenting Assessment Team.

But at the end of six months, Valerie wasn't reunited with her children. Instead she got a new caseworker from a private agency that contracted with DCFS. "When I met her for the first time in court, she looked away and wouldn't shake my hand," Valerie told me. "The second time I saw her was during a visit with my children. She said to me, 'This is all your fault, you're not a good mother. I'm going to make sure you lose your kids. The foster parents are going to adopt them.'" Valerie and the caseworker were constantly at odds. "Whatever I did was wrong. She said I didn't know how to talk to children with special needs. She said I was holding them wrong. She even followed me to the bathroom." Valerie says the caseworker accused her of dropping out of counseling after Valerie received a letter stating her appointments were discontinued until she was assigned a new counselor. Valerie also says the caseworker deliberately delayed getting her into services. Valerie wasn't able to attend a parenting class scheduled for May until the following September, thwarting her plans to take a college course. When Valerie successfully completed "Introduction to Parenting Skills," the caseworker directed her to take another parenting class in December. Because of the delays, the Parenting Assessment Team's evaluation was postponed for another six months.

The setbacks and stress of the reunification process took its toll. In March 2000, Valerie began to experience symptoms of her bipolar disorder that had been in remission for twenty years. She began losing weight, crying inconsolably, shopping hysterically. The judge ordered a psychiatric evaluation, and Valerie was placed on medication. Because of her mental distress, Valerie found it harder to make all the appointments the caseworker scheduled. At her administrative case review in August, Valerie learned that DCFS had changed the permanency goal from returning the children to terminating her parental rights and putting the children up for adoption.

One especially tragic consequence of the child protection approach is that parents must often confess to unfitness to get help for their children. In many poor communities, there are no public services to ensure children's welfare apart from the child protection agency. Social work professors Sheila Kamerman and Alfred Kahn note that child protection has "absorbed virtually all of the system's resources," leaving nothing for families who simply need help.[241] "It increasingly seems that only abused or severely neglected, delinquent, or runaway children can hope to receive public services in most jurisdictions." The only option for many parents desperately seeking counseling for a troubled teenager or decent shelter or respite from a family crisis is to present their problem as a case of child abuse or neglect. Child welfare agencies tell parents they must sign papers admitting they are neglectful. Community workers advocating for poor families are advised to report their clients to child protective authorities if they want to get services for them. One of my students took in a teenaged boy from a low-income Black family who had become trapped in a bitter fight between his estranged parents. The family needed counseling—the kind of mediation wealthier families pay for or have covered by their health insurance policies. When my student called various state agencies looking for help for the teen, she was told to call the child abuse hot line.

In the most difficult cases, parents voluntarily place their children in foster care. These agreements may entail a temporary stay away from home or the transfer of legal custody to the state. In New York City, the share of voluntary placements among all children in foster care has increased in recent years. The number of parents giving up their children rose 41 percent in 1997.[242] One in ten children admitted to the city's foster care system in 1999 was voluntarily placed.[243] A growing number of these cases involve rebellious or emotionally disturbed adolescents whose parents can no longer handle them. Many troubled children live in group homes for months while they wait for scarce residential treatment center beds.

When a parent turns a child over to foster care, it is rarely truly voluntary. In some cases, desperate parents reluctantly approach the child welfare agency only when they can find no other source of government support. The parents may be too ill or stressed to care for their children, or their children may need services they cannot afford. The AIDS epidemic has caused an explosion of poor minority mothers who need state assistance for both reasons. A few states have passed statutes that allow disabled parents to share custody of their children with a "standby guardian" who helps with child raising without usurping all parental authority. Unfortunately, most families coping with AIDS or other serious illness do not have this option. The West Virginia Supreme Court of Appeals reversed a judge's decision to sever the bonds between a mother, Ada R., who was dying from AIDS and her HIV-positive son, Micah.[244] Leaving Micah in foster care, the court lamented the mother's "heartbreaking struggle to deal with her disease, while, at the same time, not turning her back on her child." "By doing what she felt was best and voluntarily placing Micah with the Department," the court said, "Ada R. has ended up not only fighting to remain alive, but also fighting to remain a parent."

The shortage of mental health care for children is especially acute. Limits in private health care plans and lack of access to public services make it tough for even middle-class parents to get treatment for their children. Although Medicaid-eligible children are entitled to mental health care, this provision is not consistently enforced. In some states, residential treatment centers refuse to accept children on Medicaid unless they are wards of the state. Many state and local officials mistakenly believe that federal reimbursement for out-of-home care is available only if the state has legal custody of children. For many children, then, the only way to qualify for publicly funded mental health services is to enter the child welfare system

A report by the Bazelon Center for Mental Health Law in Washington, D.C., describes the dilemma faced by the parents of a girl with a serious emotional disturbance and developmental disabilities. The only treatment center in their area refused to accept Medicaid. The parents could not afford to pay its private fee of $99.25 per day. The child welfare agency told the mother that she should file a "willful neglect and abandonment" petition in juvenile court so the state could place her daughter in a mental health facility.[245] According to the Bazelon Center, in half of the states almost one-quarter of families seeking mental health care for a child must choose between treatment and retaining legal custody of the child.[246] Only eleven states prohibit the child welfare agency from requiring parents to relinquish custody to gain access to mental health services.[247] One family advocate sums up the choices of parents seeking help for their children's mental health problems as "beat 'em up, lock 'em up, or give 'em up."[248]

Other parents agree to short-term placement or surrender custody as a way of avoiding abuse or neglect proceedings. Some parents decide that it's better to voluntarily place their child in foster care for a brief period than to risk child protective authorities taking the child for a long time. Giving up custody to the state has become the price of public support for poor and low-income children. The state then provides to foster parents the very services it denied to the parents. Respite care, for example, is often subsidized by the state for foster parents—but not for parents—of children with serious mental health problems.[249]

Voluntary placements are also a way for agencies to remove children from "unsuitable" homes without having to prove their parents abused or neglected them. Parents being investigated by child protective services are sometimes intimidated into agreeing to place their children in foster care. Caseworkers demand an immediate decision from terrified and unsophisticated parents while withholding information about the process and the consequences of placement.[250] They threaten parents with permanently losing their children if they don't agree to a temporary separation. A survey conducted by Legal Services of New Jersey on voluntary placements suggests that this practice is common in that state. Parents reported that they were coerced to sign placement agreements by threats that the court would take their children if they did not cooperate. Many parents did not realize that they were waiving their rights to appointment of an attorney and prompt judicial review. "Unaware of any other options," the report concluded, "parents often feel they have no choice but to sign a placement agreement."[251]

The *New York Daily News* recently reported that New York City's child welfare agency pressured teen mothers in its custody to give up their babies in an effort to relieve the shortage of foster homes.[252] Teen girls who became pregnant while in foster care spent months in maternity wards with their newborn babies because the city couldn't find enough homes that would take both mother and child. Social workers told fifteen-year-old Anisha Henry that if she didn't relinquish custody of her baby boy, they would take him away from her—with frightening consequences. "And if they take him away from me I wouldn't get no visitation," Anisha said. "I was hurt; I was in tears. I told them I didn't go through nine months for no reason, just so they could take him away."

Parents often buckle under the pressure to relinquish custody because of the power imbalance in legal contests with child protection authorities. Parents come into the child welfare system at a huge disadvantage. Most start out from a disenfranchised status—Black, female, poor, uneducated. Like criminal defendants, they are pitted against the tremendous might and resources of the government. They are unfamiliar with the way bureaucracies and the courts operate. They don't know their legal rights. And, worst of all, they know that if they don't cooperate, they risk losing their children. When they appear in court, they are confronted by a battalion of state-paid attorneys and advocates, all trying to prove that they are bad mothers. The mother, perhaps accompanied by a public defender, stands on one side of the courtroom. On the other side arrayed against her are a state's attorney, a guardian ad litem, and a caseworker. The state may have also called witnesses to testify against her. "When I got in the courtroom, I felt a wall," Jornell told me. "The judge and the attorneys were on one side and I was on the other side. They were moving things along without me. All they wanted to do was get rid of the mother." Philadelphia attorney Amy Sinden reported that her clients feel overwhelming pressure to acquiesce in the caseworkers' plans for them. "Even where coercion is not intentional on the part of the social worker, parents are often too quick to accede to the agency social worker's suggested resolution of their case, resulting in false agreements."253

Parents who turn to child protective services for help often find themselves in an adversarial relationship. Once agencies have custody of children, they take control of child rearing and place conditions on parents' involvement with their children. Parents have no say over where their children are placed or important decisions about their children's health, education, and religious and cultural upbringing or even how often they can see them. The child welfare agency may require parents to complete training courses and therapy sessions as a condition of reunification. And, most devastating, it may refuse to return children when parents are ready to take them back. Parents who "voluntarily" step into the maze of child protective services usually have a hard time getting their children out.

Avoiding Responsibility for Children's Welfare

The child welfare system's strong-arm tactics stem from its underlying philosophy. The child welfare system is built upon the presumption that children's basic needs for sustenance and development must and can be met solely by parents.[254] The state intervenes to provide special institutionalized services—primarily placing children in foster care—only when parents fail to fulfill their child-rearing obligations. The child protection approach is inextricably tied to our society's refusal to see a collective responsibility for children's welfare. It is a society willing to pay billions of dollars a year on maintaining poor children outside their homes, but begrudges spending a fraction of that on supporting families.

This approach to child welfare is defective in three related ways. First, it places all responsibility for taking care of children on their parents, without taking into account the economic, political, and social constraints that prevent many parents from doing so. Most single mothers, for example, face numerous barriers to providing for their children, including a segregated job market, inadequate wages, and a dearth of affordable child care.[255] Thousands of poor families in this country lack the income to meet their children's basic needs of food, clothing, and shelter and live in a deprived environment that is dangerous for children. The child welfare system hides the systemic reasons for families' hardships by laying the blame on individual parents' failings. "The underlying philosophy of the present child welfare system is that *all* families *should* be able to function adequately without the assistance of society," explain Billingsley and Giovannoni, "and that failure to perform the parental role without such assistance is indicative of individual pathology."[256]

Recall Tatiana Cheeks, the mother who was charged with homicide for failing to nourish her baby. Punishing her for the death of her child covers up the social causes of the tragedy—inaccessible medical care, inadequate education, and poor nutrition in inner-city neighborhoods. Some people reading news reports of her arrest may believe that making poor Black mothers criminally liable is a solution to poor infant health in these communities. Holding parents accountable for poverty-related harm to children replaces efforts to relieve children's poverty.

A second defect is that child protection is activated only when families are already in crisis. The role of government is limited to rescuing children who have been mistreated by deficient parents, rather than ensuring the health and welfare of all families. Duncan Lindsey calls this the "residual approach" to child welfare because state intervention is treated as a last resort to be invoked only after the family has exhausted all resources at its disposal. "The child welfare agency becomes the site of triage where casualties are sorted, and only the most seriously wounded receive attention," Lindsey writes. "But because the damage to children is so great by the time they enter the system, the number who survive and benefit is minimal."[257] This is a fitting analogy to describe what happens to Black children in the child welfare system: Black families over-rely on hospital emergency rooms because of inadequate access to regular medical care.

Under this approach, caseworkers perceive families' problems as those amenable to social work intervention; they have at their disposal only limited tools to treat the immediate crisis. Caseworkers are discouraged from dealing with the systemic problems many must realize are the causes of child neglect. At one of her case reviews, Jornell wanted to talk about how her case related to the removal of other Black children in Chicago and the institutional barriers she faced in being reunited with David. A court-appointed advocate literally put her hands over her ears. "I don't want to hear about the system," she told Jornell. "I'm only here to help you get David back." Ann Hartman, a University of Michigan professor of social work, honestly confesses caseworkers' reluctance to confront systemic inequities: "The minute we turn around to attempt to address the system that is victimizing people, rather than making the victimization palatable, which is what our profession has done, we will have our heads in a noose."[258] It is inevitable that agencies' solutions for family problems will be inadequate, if not damaging to families.

Finally, because the system perceives the resulting harm to children as parental rather than societal failures, state intervention to protect children is punitive in nature. The state's solutions to children's deprivation involve intrusive meddling by social workers, behavioral requirements, and temporary or permanent removal of children from their homes. Child protection proceedings are more akin to criminal trials than most civil adjudications because they pit individuals against the state and issue moral condemnation of parents.[259]

The child welfare system, then, embodies a cruel paradox. At the same time that it brutally intrudes upon too many Black families, it also ignores the devastating impact of poverty and racism on even more children. For every child placed in foster care because she was malnourished or unsupervised, there are hundreds more who suffer the same deprivations. The National Incidence Study discovered that 75 percent of children known to be neglected in the community have not been investigated by child protective services.[260] The state is guilty of both overintervention and underintervention when it comes to Black families. The system haphazardly picks out a fraction of families to bludgeon, while it leaves untouched the conditions that are really most damaging to children. *All* the children in the neighborhoods where child protective services operate are at risk for poor nutrition, inadequate health care, run-down housing, violence, and inferior education. The babies in Tatiana Cheeks's community die at a rate that is three times higher than that of babies in affluent parts of New York City. Should child protection authorities take all these children away from their parents? Instead the government sacrifices some unlucky families to perpetrate the hoax that it is protecting poor Black children from harm. The child welfare system reinforces the inferior status of poor Blacks in America both by destroying the families who come within its reach and by failing the families who don't.

This narrow concept of child welfare hurts all families in America, but it hurts Black families the most. The color of today's child welfare system results from the relationship between its flawed philosophy and the realities of institutional racism. The very design of the systems that deal with families—both the market approach to family well-being and the punitive approach of child protective services—operates in a racist society to dismantle families at the bottom of the social ladder. It fosters the widespread assumption that "the Black child's problems stem from his negatively valued family and disorganized community, and that his solutions lie in the institutions of the larger white society."[261] Child welfare interventions become a way both to punish Black parents for their perceived psycho-moral depravity and to place Black children in the state's superior care. As I explain in the last chapter of this book, ending racial discrimination in the child welfare system requires addressing both its racial bias and its structural flaws.

Experts have posited a number of reasons for the explosion in the foster care population since the 1960s—the discovery of "battered child syndrome," the crusade to bring child abuse to national attention, the passage of mandatory child abuse reporting laws, federal funding incentives for states to spend more dollars on out-of-home care, and more recently, the crack and AIDS epidemics that have left thousands of children without parents. All of these developments have played a part in expanding the foster care rolls. But none can explain why policy makers have so tenaciously pursued the path of child removal, why there hasn't been an equally effective campaign against the travesty of family breakup, or why the nation hasn't embraced instead a program of family supports.

As significant as these forces was the darkening of the foster care population. As the foster care caseloads increased, so did the share of Black children. The financial and philosophical support for dismantling families instead of providing them services was tied to this racial transformation. Racism operates to prop up a defective system whose damage falls unequally on Black people. Can anyone honestly doubt that the modern acceptance of child removal as the system's chief function depends on the disproportionate demolition of Black families? If the rate of white children entering foster care began to approach the present rate of Blacks, we would certainly see more moral outrage over the level of state interference in families. One anonymous observer put it bluntly, "If more white kids were going into the child welfare system, it would change. The fact that [more] white people don't go into the system says to me it is a bad place to be."[262]

6. A Racist Institution?

DESPITE ALL THIS EVIDENCE, it is still hard to find direct proof of racially biased decisions on the part of reporters, caseworkers, and judges. Racial motives are rarely articulated and may even be unconscious. Anyone interviewed knows better than to say, "I thought that mother was unfit because she's Black" or "I put the children in foster care because of their race." The way race affects child welfare decision making is more complicated than that. Stereotypes about Black family dysfunction often work subconsciously. People in the system find that their options are limited by forces outside their control. They are likely to bristle at the charge of racial discrimination: "It's not our fault that the most deprived children we see are Black and that the law requires us to intervene to protect them from harm."

Some people will say that the racial disparity in the child welfare system does not constitute racial discrimination without a showing of racial motivation. The system is racist only if Black children are pulled out of their homes by bigoted caseworkers or as part of a deliberate government scheme to subjugate Black people. Any other explanation—such as higher rates of Black poverty—negates the significance of race. This is the position conservative pundit Lawrence Mead took in responding to a conference paper I presented on this topic. He argued that the racial imbalance in today's child welfare system was different from official segregationist policies of the Jim Crow era. He wanted to see clear evidence of official racial animus, like the signs that read "FOR WHITES ONLY" at Southern drinking fountains. "There's no smoking gun!" he protested. Agency officials also hide behind Black poverty as an excuse for the racial inequality in their services. The commissioner of New York City's Administration for Children's Services, Nicholas Scoppetta, defended New York City's outrageous statistics by saying, "I don't really think it's a question of racism, but of economic circumstances people find themselves in and drugs."[263]

As an initial matter, race need not be the *only* reason a child is removed from the home for the decision to be racially biased. State agents may be primarily motivated by the desire to protect children, but race may be a factor in their deliberations about which course of action to take. Harvard Law School professor Randall Kennedy refutes a related argument that racial profiling is a defensible technique when police officers use other factors along with race to identify criminal suspects.[264] The fact that race is only a marginal factor, Kennedy argues, "cannot logically negate the *existence* of racial discrimination." He concludes, "Taking race into account at all means engaging in racial discrimination."[265]

Without proof that child protective authorities are actually "taking race into account," can we call the disparate treatment of Black children a pattern of racial discrimination? After reviewing studies on race and child welfare services, a group of researchers concluded that this characterization would be misleading "because evidence about the needs of the children and families prior to service receipt cannot be used to argue that these less favorable outcomes result from worse child welfare services for African American children than Caucasians rather than from worse initial circumstances of African American families."[266] In other words, the child welfare system can't be blamed for discriminating against Black children because Black children are already worse off than whites when they enter the system.

The disparate initial circumstances of Black and white children doesn't negate the existence of racial discrimination, either. Even if equally poor or equally wealthy families had precisely the same risk of intervention regardless of race, this would not discount the far greater risk to Black families. When some researchers conclude that race is not a significant predictor of involvement in the child welfare system, they mean that race by itself—without accounting for income, single parenting, neighborhood, and other relevant factors—cannot explain why certain families are disrupted by child protection agencies. Black children are no more likely to be removed from their parents *all else being equal.*

But all else is not equal. And all else is not equal because of a continuing legacy of racial discrimination. Racism allows us to predict with absolute certainty the color of families you will see if you walk into any urban juvenile court or child welfare agency.

The high level of Black childhood poverty reflects systemic biases against Black Americans. Being Black in America means having a huge risk of being poor and little chance of ever being wealthy. "The odds of black Americans experiencing affluence versus poverty are approximately one to twenty-five versus the one to one odds of all Americans," notes Mark Rank.[267] Numerous scholars, including most notably William Julius Wilson, have documented the profound impediments to Black economic equality.[268] The effects of racist institutions established over centuries combined with persistent discrimination in employment, lending, housing, education, law enforcement and social services place Blacks of all classes at a disadvantage and have produced concentrations of extreme poverty and isolation in the inner cities. Because of past systemic discrimination, each generation of Blacks has had limited wealth, and all the advantages wealth bestows, to pass on to the next. Sociologist Dalton Conley explains: "While young African Americans may have the *opportunity* to obtain the same education, income, and wealth as whites, in actuality they are on a slippery slope, for the discrimination their parents faced in the housing and credit markets sets the stage for perpetual economic disadvantage."[269] Or as economics professor William Darity Jr. puts it, "there is a cumulative racial transmission process at work perpetuating economic disparity across generations."[270] Black males still suffer 12–15 percent losses in earnings as a result of continuing discrimination at all stages of employment.

State disruption of families is one symptom of this institutionalized discrimination. It reflects the persistent gulf between the material welfare of Black and white children in America. The racial disparity in the child welfare system—even if related directly to economic inequality—ultimately results from racial injustice.

Even if the racial disparity could be explained by higher Black poverty rates and not intentional discrimination, this would not negate the racist impact of the system or the racist reasons for its inequities. Racism often involves but does not require prejudice against Blacks. Racism is "a *structural* relationship based on the subordination of one racial group by another."[271] In America, racism is a system of white privilege that is maintained by ideologies, institutions, and practices that place white people in a superior position and people of color in an inferior position economically, socially and politically. This definition of racism describes perfectly the differential treatment of white and Black children by the child welfare system.

My answer to critics who demand to see evidence of ill will against Black families, then, is that racial motivation is not necessary to show that the system discriminates. We should not ignore, though, the considerable evidence that race and not poverty alone affects decision making at every step of the child protection process. Racism in reporting illustrates how racial bias combines with broader inequities to push disparate numbers of Black children into the system. Earlier I cited studies that show racial differences in doctors' interpretations of child abuse and neglect. But this kind of racial bias on the part of mandated reporters does not provide the whole picture. Many Black children are in the system not because their parents were turned in by white outsiders but because of reports by members of their own community. Social isolation and economic deprivation have left many Black families without the resources necessary to raise healthy children. When parents, relatives, and neighbors become desperate, they often feel they have no recourse but to call on a system they view with suspicion.

Researchers who traced the reason for the overrepresentation of Black families in child protective services in a western New York county found no evidence of bias in reporting by mandated reporters.[272] In fact, almost half of all reports of child maltreatment came from nonmandated sources. African American families were almost twice as likely to be reported by other relatives as white families. Nationwide, almost half (47 percent) of abuse and neglect reports are submitted by nonprofessionals.[273]

Another study comparing the reporting behavior of nonmandated and mandated reporters found that the chances of community members reporting neglectful situations were significantly greater than the propensity of mandated reporters to do so.[274] The inclination of community members to report child maltreatment was confirmed by research that surveyed the opinions of a diverse group of mothers as well as child welfare workers.[275] The researchers asked the mothers and workers about the seriousness of harm to a six-year-old child subjected to various neglectful behaviors described in a set of vignettes. The mothers saw a more serious threat to the child in each dimension of neglect than did the caseworkers. African American and Hispanic mothers rated a number of dangers in the stories as more serious than the white mothers. A follow-up study of primarily white, middle-class child welfare workers and African American mothers also found that the mothers perceived all categories of neglect as more serious than the workers.[276]

Jeanne Giovannoni and William Meezan note that these studies "contradict assertions that mandated reporting requirements impose child rearing values on lay communities. Rather, these studies suggest that there may be a lack of responsiveness to community concerns, particularly around issues of neglect."[277] This does not mean that Black families want more of the kind of response that child welfare departments have made to child neglect in their communities. It does mean that Black communities may be even more concerned about child maltreatment than government authorities but have only inadequate and even harmful ways to deal with it.

Refining the precise reason for the system's racial disparity—Black child poverty, caseworkers' cultural misconceptions and racist stereotypes, policy makers' insensitivity to Black families, or the structure of the system itself—might help to develop targeted programs for reducing the imbalance. But trying to isolate a single overriding source of the system's inferior treatment of Black children fails to capture the way institutional racism works. Black children are overrepresented in child protective services because of the interplay of societal, structural, and individual factors that feed into each other to determine which families fall under state scrutiny and supervision.[278] To address the systemic discrimination against Black families, then, it is most helpful to attribute the disparity to a web of racial injustice that includes all of these causes.

Pointing out these injuries to Black families in the child welfare system is not to condemn all caseworkers, judges, or foster parents. Many caseworkers are dedicated to serving their clients without the resources they need. Many judges see the system's injustice but feel powerless to effect any meaningful change. Many foster parents are generously doing what they can to care for children already harmed by social deprivation. My condemnation is directed at the structural features of child welfare that result in racially disparate harms to families. As Leroy Pelton points out, "foster care is a *social system* and as such it has its own inherent characteristics quite apart from the qualities of the people—the staff and foster parents—who operate within that system."[279]

It would be a mistake to obscure the system's racial origins and impact by focusing solely on economic inequality. To begin with, poverty and race are so interrelated in America that it makes little sense to try to separate them in bringing attention to the racial injustice of the child welfare system. Downplaying the role of race also gravely mischaracterizes the problem. It has become fashionable to search for sources of Blacks' disadvantaged position apart from contemporary racism. Black people's poverty, family structure, welfare dependency, and lack of intelligence are all popular explanations for the persistent racial gap in power and well-being. Melvin Thomas, a sociologist at North Carolina State University, calls these theories "anything but race" perspectives. He argues that "anything but race" perspectives are refuted by empirical studies that show the continuing impact of racial discrimination: "They ignore race when key racist practices such as segregated neighborhoods, culturally destructive educational practices or employer discrimination are forgotten in the rush to focus on something—anything other than race."[280]

But "anything but race" theories are even more pernicious in the way they permit whites to ignore their social advantages based on race. "They defend the advantaged position of whites by claiming they have 'superior' characteristics such as: higher cognitive ability, stronger work ethic, better morals, stronger families, more human capital or skills, etc.," writes Professor Thomas. "Because they see whites as somehow 'better' than blacks in some important way, their superordinate position in society is deserved. . . . If discrimination—the inequitable allocation of resources based on race—is left out of the analysis, there could be no other conclusion: black disadvantage is a result of deficiencies within blacks themselves."

Social scientists, government bureaucrats, and policy pundits are all scrambling to explain the racial disparity in the child welfare system as "anything but race." Black children are pouring into foster care in grossly disproportionate numbers, they argue, not because of their race but because of some problem with their families. Ignoring the role of race in child protective services allows people to believe that the system is fair and that they are actually helping poor Black children by placing them in state custody. Ignoring race also avoids the ugly reality that the system treats white families better not because they are somehow superior to Black families but because they benefit from racial privilege.

So far I have considered whether the child welfare system is guilty of racism because of the reasons families become involved in it. Some people might still believe that the system is a good—or at least racially neutral—way of dealing with the problems Black families experience as a consequence of racial discrimination. They may still see racism only on the outside of child protective services, with people on the inside left to handle the aftermath of discrimination as best they can. This is probably what it *feels* like to most of the reporters, caseworkers, administrators, and judges who make decisions everyday about Black families in the system. They see themselves more at the mercy of racism than as perpetrators of racism. It is important to ask, then, does the system produce its own racial harms? What is the impact of targeting a minority group for family destruction? I take up these questions in Part Three of this book. There I argue that the child welfare system's racism lies not only in its disparate treatment of Black children but also in its injury to Black people as a group.

The opening passage of *Children of the Storm* still rings true today: "The racism that characterizes American society has had tragic effects upon Black children. It has given the Black child a history, a situation, and a set of problems that are qualitatively different from those of the white child. In a narrower context, American racism has placed Black children in an especially disadvantaged position in relation to American institutions, including the institution of child welfare."[281] In the three decades since the book's publication, the position of Black children in the child welfare system has not improved. In fact, child protective services have become even more segregated and more destructive. As the child welfare rolls have darkened, family-preserving services have dried up, and child removal has stepped up. Child welfare reflects the political choice to address dire child poverty in Black communities by punishing parents instead of confronting the structural reasons for racial and economic inequality. It is time to face the inescapable reality: America's child welfare system is a racist institution.

PART TWO

The New Politics of Child Welfare

CLICK ONTO *www.mnadopt.org/search.asp.* Or *www.state.il.us/dcfs/adlink. htm.* Or *www.tdprs.state.tx.us/adoption/tare.html.* You will find on these and other state web sites hundreds of photographs of children in foster care who are available for adoption. Public child welfare agencies call them the "waiting" children. Adoption web sites are states' high-tech means of advertising foster children to potential adoptive parents. In most cases, the rights of their parents have been permanently terminated by the state. But some foster children broadcast on the Internet are not yet legally free for adoption. In some states, like Illinois, almost all the photos display Black faces. The U.S. Department of Health and Human Services plans to collect all the nation's adoptable foster children into one megasite—"a gargantuan, searchable Virtual Orphanage that would likely scare the dickens even out of Dickens," writes journalist Peggy Farber.[1] This is the web image of the Black family—children destined to be permanently separated from their irreparable parents, whose only salvation is to be adopted into new families.

Instead of working to eliminate racism in the child welfare system, federal and state governments have recently implemented policies that will increase the system's racial disparity. The past five years have witnessed the passage of critical legislation that weakens family bonds. Three political trends in particular threaten to make the child welfare system even worse for Black families. First, both federal and state laws began to abandon family preservation as an important focus of child welfare practice. In its place, a new orientation emphasizes "freeing" children in foster care for adoption by speeding up termination of parental rights. Second, welfare reform measures aimed at pushing more mothers into the workforce make it harder for the most desperate recipients, who are disproportionately Black, to take care of their children. Child welfare policy is cracking down on neglectful parents precisely at a time when welfare policy eliminated guaranteed support for poor children. Finally, tougher criminal penalties are locking up growing numbers of Black parents and children. The children of many incarcerated parents end up in foster care, and under accelerated termination time lines, long jail terms are increasingly seen as a reason to permanently sever parental rights. Juvenile detention and imprisonment are an alternative route for children to enter state custody. Combining the numbers of Black children in the foster care and criminal justice systems produces a disturbing level of state supervision of children. These major shifts in federal and state policy on child protection, welfare reform, and criminal justice are converging to proclaim a dangerous message: the solution to the problems of poor Black children is either to dissolve their family ties so that they can be adopted by more privileged parents or to lock them up in the nation's expanding prison system.

1. THE ASSAULT ON FAMILY PRESERVATION

The New Federal Adoption Law

It is often said that American child welfare policy operates like a pendulum. It swings from expressing the predominant objective of keeping troubled families together to making protection of children from parental harm its top priority. Family preservation and child safety are treated as two opposing ends of the spectrum of child welfare concerns. These shifts have not been based on any real changes in rates of child maltreatment. They are often responses to highly publicized incidents of abuse by parents or by the system and to the political currents surrounding child welfare debates. "Watching federal policy develop in the field of child abuse and neglect over the past two decades has been like watching the sunrise in Barrow, Alaska in late November!" proclaimed one expert. "Federal and state political action over the last several decades could be characterized as being symbolic rather than substantive, reactive and punitive rather than proactive and supportive (of either children or adults)."[2]

In reality, child welfare policy in the past century has never swung entirely to the side of family preservation or child protection. Federal and state policies have reflected to varying degrees both a family-centered and a child-saving philosophy. Programs designed to maintain poor children in their homes have existed alongside the practice of placing poor children in substitute care since the early 1900s. Although child welfare agencies abandoned an official policy of removing children on grounds of poverty alone, they never fully embraced the policy of supporting poor families. Their professed concern for family preservation serves more as a justification for their continued reliance on child removals for parents who are deemed unreformable. For most Black children in the system, the reality has consistently been foster care placement.

In the 1970s Congress began to examine the toll that foster care was taking on children and their families. Leading scholars criticized the child welfare system for unnecessarily removing children from their homes and leaving them to languish in foster care.[3] Hearings on Capitol Hill revealed that federal policy created financial incentives for state child welfare authorities to prefer placing children in foster care over keeping families in tact.[4] The federal government reimbursed states for the costs of out-of-home placements but not for services provided to families within the home. Stanford law professor Michael Wald noted in 1976 that, although state child welfare agencies received federal funds for each child in their custody, "the agency loses this money when the child is returned home, even though the agency must still provide services to the child."[5] Congress attempted to correct the overemphasis on foster care by passing legislation that tied federal funding to reforms in states' approaches to child welfare. The Adoption Assistance and Child Welfare Act of 1980 encouraged states to replace costly and disruptive out-of-home placements with preventive and reunification programs. The law, which is still in effect today, requires that before placing children in foster care, state agencies must make "reasonable efforts" to enable them to remain safely at home. It also mandates that states make reasonable efforts to safely return children in foster care to their parents.

In the past several years, the pendulum of child welfare philosophy has swung decisively in the opposite direction. Congress has abandoned the focus on preventive and reunification programs it once expressed. Leading the way is the Adoption and Safe Families Act enacted by Congress in 1997 to amend the 1980 Child Welfare Act.[6] President Clinton signed the law within a year of directing the federal government to take steps to double the number of foster children adopted annually to 54,000 by 2002.[7] The new federal adoption law—known as "ASFA"—represents a dramatic change in the way the federal government deals with the overloaded foster care system. Its orientation has shifted from emphasizing the reunification of children in foster care with their biological families toward support for the adoption of these children into new families.

Both ASFA and the 1980 Child Welfare Act reflect the prevailing wisdom that children in foster care should be quickly placed in permanent homes because the instability of foster care damages children's psychological and social development. The goal of permanency stands as a pillar of current child welfare philosophy. Two books were particularly influential in convincing policy makers that permanent homes are essential to healthy child development.[8] Mass and Engler's *Children in Need of Parents*, published in 1959, was the first book to document foster care drift and the psychological harms that stem from multiple placements. The 1973 classic, *Beyond the Best Interests of the Child*, asserted that continuity in children's relationships with a caregiver is essential to normal psychological development. Its authors, Joseph Goldstein, Anna Freud, and Albert Solnit, argued that children separated from their parents can form bonds of attachment with other adults who fulfill the role of parent. The longer children are away from their biological parents, the more likely they will bond with their new "psychological parents." According to "psychological parent" theory, moving children after these bonds have formed causes serious emotional damage. Critics have soundly denounced this perspective for discounting the connections children maintain with their parents even while in substitute care, as well as children's ability to develop relationships with more than one "psychological parent."[9] Empirical studies show, for example, that children in foster care suffer psychological harm when they are cut off from their family and that they benefit from contact with their parents during placement. Policy makers and judges nevertheless hold fast to the preeminence that Goldstein, Freud, and Solnit accorded permanency.[10]

Concern for permanency places a limit on the federal mandate that state agencies make reasonable efforts to reunify children in foster care with their parents. Returning children home quickly satisfies their need for permanency, but what happens if parents are not ready to take back the child? How long can reunification efforts take before the damage of unstable custody arrangements occurs? At what point should agencies give up on parents for the sake of placing children in a permanent home? Judges are not willing to wait forever for parents to become fit enough to regain custody of their children. Most states have enacted statutes that make the length of time a child remains out of the legal custody of the parent a ground for terminating the parent's rights. In fact, the most common reason courts use for termination is a finding that the child has been in foster care longer than the law allows.[11] Although the 1980 federal law encouraged reuniting children with their biological parents, it also provided for termination of parental rights as an avenue for permanency. The 1997 amendment intensifies the tension between permanency planning and family reunification by putting added pressure on states to expeditiously free children for adoption. In cases of conflict between reunification and permanency efforts, permanency must prevail.

Proponents of the policy change framed their critique of family preservation philosophy as a defense of children's rights. They argued that keeping families together often sacrifices children's interests for the sake of parental rights. Representative Deborah Pryce argued that ASFA "will elevate children's rights so that a child's health and safety will be of paramount concern under the law. . . . Let us do it for the children."[12] The *Washington Post* praised the law for putting "a new and welcome emphasis on the children,"[13] and a Milwaukee columnist declared that ASFA was "to the abused and neglected children in our nation's foster care system what the Voting Rights Act was to black Americans in 1965."[14]

Advocates drummed up support for ASFA by pointing to cases where family preservation failed miserably. They recounted tragic stories of children who were killed after caseworkers returned them to blatantly dangerous parents. They passed around photographs of abused children to members of Congress. Perhaps the most effective rallying tool was *The Book of David: How Preserving Families Can Cost Children's Lives* by prominent family violence scholar Richard Gelles. *The Book of David* reported the events surrounding the suffocation of a little boy by his abusive mother after caseworkers sent him home from foster care. Gelles attributed this tragic lapse in judgment to the priority policy makers placed on families, rather than children. According to Gelles, caseworkers were interpreting the requirement to use "reasonable efforts" to preserve families to dictate reunification at all costs. Family preservation policies were a license to risk children's safety. Gelles argued that "the basic flaw of the child protection system is that it has two inherently contradictory goals: protecting children and preserving families." He advocated reinventing the child welfare system "so that it places children first."[15]

Numerous newspaper articles at the time also blamed cases of deadly child abuse on family reunification policies. In "The Little Boy Who Didn't

Have to Die," *McCall's* claimed that a boy who was returned home from foster care "appears to have been doomed by a decade-old national policy determined to patch up troubled parents and preserve families."[16] *New York Newsday* made the same point in an article explosively titled "Family Preservation—It Can Kill."[17] Members of Congress waved these stories about tragic child abuse cases as evidence that federal policy should abandon its emphasis on family unity. "Every one of us in this body can turn to and refer to headlines in their papers," Representative Barbara Kennelly, one of the bill's sponsors, stated during the House debate, "the terrible, heartbreaking case with little Emily in Michigan, other cases across the United States, headlines telling us the very worst can happen."[18] Senator John Chafee, the law's coauthor, recalled the child abuse death of Sabrina Green. "Now, Mr. President," he said, "we cannot bring Sabrina Green back to life, but we can take action to prevent such deaths in the future."[19] In short, ASFA supporters placed children's right to be safe in opposition to parents' right to custody of their children.

These statements follow a very common habit of contrasting parents' rights and children's rights. This way of framing the issue assumes that parents and children's interests are in opposition to each other. And it assumes that only parents—and not children—have an interest in family integrity. ASFA is said to be "child centered" because it focuses on safety, whereas the prior law was "parent centered" because it focused on keeping families together. But many child welfare scholars and activists have refuted this opposition of children's to families' rights.[20] As Bruce Boyer, a clinical professor in the Children and Family Justice Center of Northwestern University Law School, put it, "in family preservation, to my mind, there's a commonality of interests."[21] Typically, furthering a family's interests will also benefit the children who belong to that family. Children also have an interest in maintaining a bond with their parents and other family members. The reason for limiting state intrusion in the home, therefore, is not only a concern for *parental* interests but also the recognition that children suffer when separated from their parents and community.

ASFA places limits on the reasonable efforts mandate that was blamed for caseworkers' deadly mistakes. It generally narrows the requirement by directing state authorities to make the health and safety of children in foster care their "paramount concern." It also exempts states from using reasonable efforts to return children who are abandoned, tortured, or repeatedly or severely abused. Most people would agree that children have an interest in, if not a right to, government protection from this sort of violence. Yale law professor Akhil Amar has argued that the Thirteenth Amendment requires states to protect children from the domination of an abusive parent just as they protect citizens from enslavement.[22]

But the new law's reform goes far beyond ensuring the safety of children who have been removed from violent homes. Victims of severe abuse covered by these provisions are a tiny minority of children in foster care and represented "easy cases" for termination even before the law was amended.[23] Most children in foster care, who were removed from their homes because of poverty-related neglect, will be affected more by Washington's major policy initiative—the emphasis on terminating parental rights to make children available for adoption. The federal adoption law and the rhetoric promoting it weaken the government's commitment to family preservation and establish a preference for adoption as the means of reducing the exploding foster care population. Congressional sponsors declared that ASFA "is putting children on a fast track from foster care to safe and loving and permanent homes."[24] Most of the children referred to in this statement are Black. And the homes the law supports are adoptive, not biological, ones.

Congress implemented its preference for adoption through a set of mandates and incentives to state child welfare departments. The new law establishes swifter timetables for terminating biological parents' rights to "free" children for adoption. Termination of parental rights is the most extreme measure judges can impose in abuse and neglect cases. It permanently severs the legal ties between parent and child, ending the parent's physical custody, "as well as the rights ever to visit, communicate with, or regain custody of the child."[25] The laws of every state permit juvenile or family court judges to terminate the rights of parents found to be unfit to care for their children. Judges frequently terminate the rights of parents whose children have been in foster care beyond a statutory deadline. These deadlines have little to do with child abuse; they instead concern the length of time a child has spent out of the parents' custody. Provisions like this affect parents whose children have been in foster care for too long but whose rights could not be terminated on other grounds.

Termination of biological parents' rights is a necessary prerequisite for children to be adopted by new parents. ASFA accelerates this process. The law requires a permanency hearing to be held within a year of a child's entry into foster care. If the child is still in foster care three months later, the child welfare agency may have to start termination proceedings. The law mandates that states file a petition to terminate the rights of parents whose child has been in foster care for fifteen of the previous twenty-two months. (The law allows states to exempt cases where a relative is caring for the child, where a compelling reason exists that termination would not be in the best interests of the child, or where the agency did not make reasonable efforts for reunification.) By 1999, all fifty states had passed legislation that mirrored or was tougher than the federal law.[26] Some states imposed even shorter deadlines and expanded the grounds for severing biological ties. In Nevada, for example, a parent's failure to comply with the terms of the reunification plan within six months can trigger a hearing on termination of parental rights. The American Bar Association initiated the "Termination Barriers Project" to develop guidelines for state legislation promoting early termination of parental rights.[27]

Some child welfare experts have criticized the imposition of accelerated time clocks on parents who are trying to regain custody of their children. In testimony on the proposed federal adoption law, the Children's Welfare League of America expressed concern that the bill's deadline for initiating termination proceedings might "disrupt good and timely progress toward reunification."[28] Jess McDonald, Director of the Illinois Department of Children and Family Services, charged that the time frame to initiate termination of parental rights proceedings "is an overly prescriptive mandate . . . [that] does not allow states the flexibility to decide on a case by case basis what is in the best interests of the child." These experts in the field recognized that it can be harmful to children to place a deadline on agencies' efforts to reunite them with their parents.

ASFA also offers financial incentives to states to get more children adopted. The federal government pays states a bonus for foster child adoptions during the fiscal year that exceed a baseline of the average annual number of children adopted in the state between 1995 and 1997. States receive $4,000 for each child adopted above the baseline. The bonus goes up to $6,000 for each adoption of a special needs child. There is also technical assistance to states to increase the number of adoptions. The law provides for the Secretary of Health and Human Services to help states in developing guidelines for expediting termination of parental rights, specialized units for moving children toward adoption as a permanency goal, and models to encourage fast-tracking of infants into pre-adoptive placements. These federal enticements are spurring states, in turn, to put pressure on agencies to move more children into adoptive homes. Children's Services of Roxbury, a private social service agency in inner-city Boston, was given a quota.[29] The state told the agency to double the number of children it usually placed for adoption. The Illinois Department of Children and Family Services circulates a list of agencies ranked by the percentage of children they move into adoptive homes. "It's embarrassing to get a low ranking," says the director of a Chicago agency.[30]

The incentives appear to be working. There were 46,000 adoptions of foster children in 1999, a 28 percent increase from the previous year. The number of adoptions doubled in Illinois, and they went up 75 percent in Texas and 57 percent in Florida. Forty-two states earned $20 million in federal adoption bonuses.[31] The federal incentives to move children out of foster care steer states in one direction. They encourage states to get more children adopted. But the new law doesn't provide comparable financial incentives or technical help to states to improve their family preservation programs.

Another key component of the move toward adoption is "concurrent permanency planning." This policy places foster children on two tracks at the same time—one track focuses on reuniting them with their parents; the other seeks to find them a permanent home with another family. Caseworkers must pursue both goals simultaneously. The point of this policy is to ensure that there will be a permanent home waiting for children in the event that reunification efforts fail. Concurrent permanency planning is supposed to keep children from being stranded in foster care. But this policy puts caseworkers in a schizophrenic position. It intensifies the conflict already inherent in child welfare practice between preserving families and seeking adoptive homes. Caseworkers' conflicting duties reflect a more fundamental "dual-role" structure of public child welfare agencies. Agencies combine helping impoverished families to overcome their problems with coercing them to conform to agency standards through the threat of removing their children.[32]

Although federal law still requires that states make reasonable efforts to reunify children with their families, it now encourages states to make concurrent efforts to place these children with adoptive parents. A number of states have already instituted concurrent planning policies. Jornell's latest permanency plan lists ten recommendations. The first recommendation reads, "We are not presently moving to change the goal Return Home as other information is needed to make this determination." The last one reads, "Concurrent planning to occur in the event that parent's rights are terminated."

Giving agencies the conflicting missions of reuniting foster children with their families while preparing them for adoption is likely to dilute agencies' efforts at family preservation. When children enter the child welfare system they become candidates for adoption. By offering bonuses for adoption, the new federal law weakens even more caseworkers' incentive to keep families together. "Can unbiased decisions be made with regard to the risk to a child in an atmosphere where adoptive placements are being encouraged and financially rewarded?" asks one social work professor.[33] The scales are weighted toward ending children's ties with their parents and moving them into adoptive homes.

As part of concurrent planning, children are increasingly placed for foster care in a potential adoptive home. The new terms for these arrangements are "fost-adopt" or "pre-adoptive" placements. There is new federal money available to assist states in developing programs that place children in pre-adoptive families without waiting for termination of parental rights. Turning foster homes into adoptive ones avoids uprooting the child if reunification fails and adoption occurs. Ideally, the child's birth parents will get to know the foster/adoptive parents during the concurrent planning process and can feel more comfortable about the adoption. But these benefits occur only in cases where adoption is inevitable or mutually agreed upon. Placing foster children in pre-adoptive homes while parents are still struggling to reunify the family preordains the outcome. Seeing foster parents as adoptive parents, moreover, gives them a vested interest in the breakdown of preservation efforts. Foster parents have a great deal of influence over the children in their care and their visitation schedules. They are instructed to report negative incidents between biological parents and children. When both caseworkers and foster parents team up to pursue adoption, it is easy to sabotage biological parents' efforts to maintain ties with their children.

Parents are already at a disadvantage in a match with foster parents. Foster parents usually have better incomes and less chaotic lives. Courts and agencies tend to overlook their deficiencies while highlighting the parents' flaws. If reunification has been delayed, the foster parents have had time to develop a relationship with the children. As one family court judge observed, "One wonders if any natural parents of children in foster care could pass muster if the superior capabilities of the foster parents are the measure of 'best interests.'"[34] Agencies that view foster children as candidates for adoption and foster parents as potential adopters are likely to lose sight of preserving biological families.

The new law's supporters argue that these measures are critical for the more than 100,000 foster children who are awaiting adoption.[35] Of course, states should often facilitate adoption of children who have been abandoned by their parents or who cannot be returned safely to their families. But there is a big difference between removing barriers to the adoption of children who are already available to be adopted and viewing the legal relationship between children in foster care and their parents as a barrier to adoption. ASFA threatens to permanently separate children from families, families that might have been preserved with the right incentives, adequate state resources, or creative custody arrangements. Family preservation efforts often fail because they are inadequate: children are returned to troubled homes without focusing on the right problems and without providing the level or continuity of services required to solve them. Having never delivered on its promise to support poor families, Congress is now using the alleged failure of family preservation programs to justify permanently separating more Black children from their parents.

Disparaging Biological Bonds

One of the most disturbing aspects of the new focus on adoption is the message it sends about the families whose children have been placed in foster care. Throughout congressional testimony on the proposed legislation, adoption was portrayed as better for children than reunification with their biological families. Virtually every mention of biological families was negative, whereas adoptive homes were referred to as loving and stable. Foster parents were described as "loving caregivers" who are unfairly prevented by biological parents' rights from developing stable relationships with the children they take in.[36] Congress assumed that permanence and safety came from adoption, not from reunifying children with their parents. "Terminating parental rights is the critical first step in moving children into permanent placements," declared Senator Chafee.[37]

The debate overlooked children's interest in living with their parents. To the contrary, the congressional record as well as the public discussion were saturated with stories about parents who were permitted to brutally torture and murder their children because of caseworkers' insistence on family reunification. All the blame for the problems with foster care were heaped on family preservation policies. Representative Dave Camp of Michigan accused the family preservation philosophy of "creat[ing] a system where nearly half a million children currently reside in foster care."[38] After describing the "sufferings of the abused, abandoned, and neglected; infants who have been burned at an open fire; children raped and assaulted," an article in the *Washington Post* claimed that "the Family Reunification and Preservation Act is the cause of these grotesque practices."[39]

Even Ray Suarez, the host of National Public Radio's *Talk of the Nation* opened a show on the eve of ASFA's enactment in these terms. "Talk to anyone who's involved with children, families, and the law, and before long the horror stories start," Suarez told the audience. "Children removed from a home for their safety then returned only to be killed; children who bounce from home to home for years because a parent won't surrender legal rights to the child so he can't be adopted; families collapsing under the weight of dysfunction, drugs, poverty; where children are raped by mom's boyfriend or scalded, or starved, or beaten."[40]

The message from all these quarters was clear: preserving families endangers children; placing children in adoptive homes protects them.

With this backdrop of vilifying foster children's families, adoption has leapt to unprecedented popularity. Adoption is now embraced across the political spectrum as the solution to the foster care crisis. As First Lady, Hillary Rodham Clinton made adoption a centerpiece of her children's rights platform. She was a vocal supporter of the federal adoption legislation. "For the thousands of American children who wait for a stable, loving home that will always be there, it is not a moment too soon," she stated on the day her husband signed it into law.[41] Mrs. Clinton told reporters that adoption reform was a personal priority and that she was thinking about adopting a second child.[42] The enthusiasm for adoption is by no means limited to Democrats. During his campaign, President George W. Bush declared that "foster care ought to be a bridge to adoption."[43] Surrounded by Black children in a Detroit center, he announced a plan to promote adoptions, including $1 billion to expand the adoption tax credit from $5,000 to $7,500. He boasted that by expediting termination of parental rights, Texas had increased adoptions by 50 percent in one year. Bush established the Governor's Committee to Promote Adoption to put Texas at the forefront of adoption reform. Although the Bush proposal also included funds for preventive services, newspaper headlines focused on its goal of "getting more foster kids adopted."

Discussions in the media about what's best for children in foster care increasingly revolve around adoption. I recently listened to a program about social services on my local public radio station. At one point, the conversation among the guests turned to government and charitable programs designed to ensure permanence for children in foster care. The guests focused on how states would meet federal targets for adoption. No one mentioned fulfilling states' duty to try to return foster children to their families. They even used "adoption" interchangeably with "permanence." Like ASFA's supporters in Congress, these commentators were equating permanence for children with adoption, ignoring reunification with parents as an important option.

In *Nobody's Children: Abuse and Neglect, Foster Drift, and the Adoption Alternative*, Harvard law professor Elizabeth Bartholet calls on liberals to join the historically conservative campaign to increase adoptions. She advocates intensifying government inspection of homes, limiting family preservation programs, and escalating termination of parental rights. Bartholet sees "blood bias," the assumption that biological ties are central to the definition of family, as an impediment to moving more children into caring homes. Her mission, in a nutshell, is to break down biological and racial barriers to state intervention in poor Black families so that more children can be removed from "nonfunctioning" parents and their communities and adopted by more nurturing ones.

Unsurprisingly, Bartholet believes that new federal policy signals a positive move away from maintaining biological parents' ties to their children. Indeed, she says the federal adoption law does not go far enough to limit family preservation efforts and eliminate barriers to termination of parental rights. To Bartholet, ASFA's requirement that agencies show they provided timely reunification services is a "loophole" that threatens to swallow the new deadlines for termination. This prerequisite is understandable, she concedes, because "it seems unfair to take children away from parents who might be able to function as adequate parents if only they received certain services from the state."[44] So why shouldn't states be required to try to reunite families before they permanently tear them apart? "The problem is that the state typically does *not* provide adequate and timely reunification services," Bartholet answers. Bartholet views delaying termination in these cases as "punishing children for the sins of the state" because she doesn't see that unnecessarily breaking up families hurts children.

Most telling, Bartholet even considers the exemption from speedy termination when it is in the best interests of the child to be a loophole.[45] But there are many times when it serves children best to retain their bonds with their parents, and it is a good thing that ASFA allows caseworkers and judges to take children's interest in family relationships into account. The danger is not that caseworkers opposed to terminating parental rights will exploit this provision. The danger is that the law's other incentives to free children for adoption will overwhelm consideration of their family bonds.

The popularity of adoption can be seen in other academic circles. Take, for instance, recent proposals to renew civil society. In the past decade, a group of prominent scholars has advocated reviving social ties outside of government, such as families and voluntary associations, to address a perceived decline in morality, political participation, and communal engagement. Robert Putnam's celebrated book *Bowling Alone* is an example of the revivalists' claim that Americans have lost the sense of community they once shared. Two documents published in 1998—*A Call to Civil Society: Why Democracy Needs Moral Truths*, by the Council on Civil Society, and *A Nation of Spectators: How Civic Disengagement Weakens America and What We Can Do About It*, by the National Council on Civil Renewal—set forth an agenda for restoring moral decency and civic engagement. These appeals were endorsed by public academics across the political spectrum, including Jean Bethke Elshtain at the University of Chicago's Divinity School, William Bennett, who served as secretary of education under President Ronald Reagan, and University of Maryland professor William Galston, a former Clinton policy advisor. Their proposals to revive civil society, then, constitute a significant bellwether of contemporary thought on family policy.

The revivalists' proposals center on strengthening the family, which they see as the most important institution of civil society, by supporting marriage and reducing divorce and single parenting. They advocate measures that will "enhance parental authority in the upbringing of children."[46] But whose parental authority? The revivalists seem oblivious to the racial disparity in state supervision of children and the trends converging to further weaken Black family bonds.

The revivalists' only recommendation related to the child welfare system is to strengthen and expand the institution of adoption, including transracial adoption.[47] Adoption is an important part of civil society, the scholars argue, because it ensures that more children will grow up with two married parents. They claim inaccurately that adoption has been "significantly weakened in recent years" and advocate "sweeping away impediments to adoption." To the contrary, what has been weakened by recent state and federal legislation is government efforts to preserve ties between poor parents and their children. The civil society revivalists' policy recommendations endorse the existing consensus to reject any national effort to address the systemic causes of children's deprivation and to pursue instead the private remedies of marriage and adoption. By choosing to bolster adoption without mentioning programs that preserve the families of children in foster care, the revivalists favor the more privileged adoptive parents. Apparently, parents whose children have been removed by the state are less deserving of social support because they are less likely to be married.

It seems odd that scholars who stress family freedom and integrity would focus unilaterally on adoption when it comes to child welfare policy. They are right that the government should usually facilitate the adoption of children whose family ties have been irremediably fractured. But shouldn't a civil society promote children's welfare by supporting impoverished families? At the very least, scholars interested in protecting families from state domination should acknowledge that foster care constitutes a form of state supervision of poor children and that adoption often involves government disruption of their relationship with their parents. A civil society should be wary of state solutions to social problems that rely on terminating parents' rights, rather than on reducing poverty or building stronger supports for families. The revivalists' turn to adoption as the *only* strategy for improving the child welfare system is further illustration of how popular this approach has become.

The support for adoption as the solution to the foster care crisis presents a fascinating reversal of the typical comparison of adoptive and biological bonds. Dominant American culture has always revered the genetic connection between parents and children and treated adoption as a second-best and unnatural alternative.[48] The fortunes spent on fertility treatment and high-tech means of conception such as in vitro fertilization are a powerful reflection of the value Americans place on genetic relatedness. Yet in supporting the federal adoption law, speaker after speaker referred to adoptive families as real and biological families as false. Representative Pryce urged her colleagues to support the legislation "in the interest of thousands of children who need a *true* family to love and protect them."[49] Representative Shaw of Florida predicted that the law "is going to bring about the joy of adoption and the bonding of a *real* family to so many kids."[50] Senator Mike DeWine, on the other hand, referred to the homes of abused children as "households that look like families but are not."[51] Erasing the stigma of adoption is an important step in expanding our notions of family. But it seems that this preference for adoption over biology is reserved for the poor Black children who are the majority of "waiting" foster children.

Brooklyn law professor Marsha Garrison insightfully observes that the perceived conflict between children in foster care and their parents is a striking departure from "the general emphasis on relationship protection that has characterized advocacy on behalf of children."[52] The preference for permanence at the expense of family ties in the context of foster care stands in stark contrast to the treatment of this issue in the context of divorce. The belief that divorce inflicts emotional damage on children is regaining popularity. *The Unexpected Legacy of Divorce: A 25-Year Landmark Study,* by Judith Wallerstein, Julia Lewis, and Sandra Blakeslee, made the *New York Times* bestseller list and the talk show circuit. Based on a study that followed ninety-three children whose parents had divorced over the past quarter century, Wallerstein and her colleagues argue that family breakup causes long-term harm to children. She advises couples to stay together for the sake of the children. When parents do divorce, child advocates generally emphasize the importance of protecting the children's relationships with their parents—even parents who lose custody.

Family law recognizes a strong emotional attachment between children of divorce and their noncustodial parents and views interference with this relationship as an awful injury to the child. Judges typically issue orders that permit visitation by the noncustodial parent and that often impose a great deal of inconvenience, instability, and trauma on parents and children alike. If the mother gets custody, she has to arrange her schedule to give time to the non-custodial father to see the child. Some children bounce between two homes so that they can stay close to both parents. When custodial parents remarry, the stepmother or stepfather is rarely treated as a substitute for a biological parent. Children who acquire a stepmother usually still regard their biological mother as their "real" mother, and courts protect this biological relationship despite changes in the family's composition. "In divorce, the child's relationship with a noncustodial parent is almost invariably described as a positive factor in her development that should be encouraged and facilitated," Professor Garrison notes. "In foster care, however, the noncustodial parent is typically seen as a threat to the child's relationship with her foster parent or her opportunity to obtain adoptive parents." Judges terminate relationships with divorced parents "only in extreme cases where the parent threatens the child's health or safety." But terminating the rights of parents with children in foster care "is urged whenever the child's return home cannot be accomplished quickly."[53]

The deference to noncustodial relationships after divorce raises additional questions about the new emphasis on terminating parental rights. Why do so many children's rights advocates appreciate the importance of preserving the parent-child bond in the case of divorce, but not in the case of foster care? For some, the reason may be economic. Preserving children's ties to noncustodial middle-class fathers helps to guarantee that these children will not be added to the welfare rolls. In contrast, terminating the rights of poor parents so that their children can be adopted by wealthier ones yields a financial gain for the state. As Garrison notes, "If the child is adopted by parents who can afford to pay his keep, he costs the state nothing, and even subsidized adoption is cheaper than foster care."[54]

For others, the critical distinction may be the parental maltreatment that resulted in foster care placement. But divorced parents may also lose custody because they are unfit. In an earlier study on divorce's impact on children, Judith Wallerstein found that 15 percent of middle-class divorced fathers suffered from severe psychiatric illness, 40 percent of father-child relationships were "profoundly troubled," and 25 percent of surveyed children moderately or intensely feared their fathers.[55] Yet judges resolutely protect divorced fathers' relationships with their children, even when the fathers are not suitable caretakers. Courts understand, at least in the case of divorce, that parental unfitness does not necessarily negate children's bonds with their parents.

I believe that the main reason for preferring extinction of parental ties in foster care is society's depreciation of the relationship between poor parents and their children, especially those who are Black. Most Americans can grasp a white middle-class child's emotional attachment to her biological father even though she is being raised by a stepfather. No one doubts the family ties of a wealthy child who spends a year away from home at a distant boarding school. The public has a harder time, though, imagining a strong emotional bond between Black parents and their children. Jacquelynn Moffett, Executive Director of Homes for Black Children, discovered that the white participants in a workshop on Black adoption she conducted in Charleston, West Virginia, "really did not have a concept of Black families."[56] "They really did not believe that Black families exist," Moffett explains, "so they had no concept of Blacks being caring toward children." When parents of children in foster care are portrayed as deranged and violent monsters, it becomes even more difficult for the public to believe that their children would want to maintain a relationship with them.

The new federal policy further disparages biological parents by stacking the deck against them in contests with foster and pre-adoptive parents. For the first time, the federal law gives foster and pre-adoptive parents an opportunity to be heard in custody proceedings. Courts used to exclude these potential parents until they determined that the biological parents were unfit. Only then would it be fair to compare the biological parents with others in determining what's best for the child. Senator Grassley defended the new measure on the grounds that foster and pre-adoptive parents "are the ones in the *best* position to . . . represent the children's concerns. It is an important change to make as we seek to better represent the children's best interests."[57] He seemed to be saying that Congress chose foster and pre-adoptive parents over biological parents to represent the interests of children in foster care.

The Clinton administration opposed this provision out of concern that it gives foster parents standing that is "incongruent with their role as temporary caregivers of children" and "could result in the creation of unnecessary adversarial relationships between foster parents and biological parents and/or between foster parents and the State child welfare agency."[58] Allowing pre-adoptive parents to intervene in unfitness hearings also intensifies the class and race conflicts often inherent in these adjudications. Deciding the best interests of children in this setting might conjure up the question, Would this child be better off in the comfortable home of this white, well-to-do couple or struggling on public assistance with that neglectful Black mother? Some pre-adoptive parents can afford to hire high-powered lawyers, whereas biological parents typically have inadequate representation. The law also places pre-adoptive parents in a better position than relatives who may want to permanently care for children but not adopt them. Relatives who aren't already providing care and aren't interested in adopting need not be notified at all.

Biased Against Whom?

How do the law's supporters justify its departure from the traditional protections of family integrity? The new priority placed on child safety and adoption is defended as a correction of bias in child welfare practice. Advocates of the policy charge that caseworkers and judges are biased against children's interests, in favor of parental rights. They claim that caseworkers coddle abusive parents and that judges bend over backward to avoid interfering in their authority over the children they mistreated. This favoritism, they argue, led caseworkers to interpret the reasonable efforts language to require returning foster children to violent homes. It also made judges unwilling to terminate parental rights. "Child welfare has grown into an enormous bureaucratic system that is biased toward preserving the family at any cost," stated Republican Representative Dan Burton of Indiana on behalf of ASFA.[59] "We will not continue the current system of always putting the needs and rights of biological parents first," Senator Chafee described as the purpose of the law.[60] The new child welfare philosophy reflects the judgment that, given this bias, the risk of wrongful reunification outweighs the risk of wrongful disruption of families.

To support her call for more coercive measures, Professor Bartholet paints a picture of extreme reluctance to intervene in child maltreatment. She tells the story of a fictitious drug-addicted mother named Linda who she says "is made up from bits and pieces of thousands on thousands of real people's stories."[61] Although child protection authorities twice find that Linda's older child has been abused so severely that he is hospitalized, they decide against removing him from the home and close the case. Linda subsequently gives birth to a premature drug-exposed baby with medical and developmental problems. Caseworkers still refuse to remove the children and fail to notice when Linda drops out of the drug treatment program they arrange for her. An overwhelmed Linda eventually slams the baby down in his crib to calm his incessant crying, causing internal injuries.

According to Bartholet, this unwillingness to remove children even in the face of repeated and grievous abuse is common: "Agencies are likely to investigate only on the basis of fairly serious allegations, and even then they are likely to do little more than investigate," Bartholet writes. "Even if they find that severe maltreatment occurred they are unlikely to remove the child except as a last resort or in the most extreme cases."[62] This suggests to the reader that most children in foster care must be victims of horrible abuse who were placed in state custody only after their parents were given every chance to reform. One would never suspect from Bartholet's account that families become involved with foster care because they are homeless, that children are taken from parents who left them unattended for a few hours, that thousands of newborns have been detained in hospitals based on a single positive drug test, or that half of Black children under supervision of child protective services are placed in foster care. Linda's story does not comport with the experiences of real Black families I have described in Part One. Besides, coercive removal of children from their parents *should* be "a last resort," used sparingly when efforts to keep the family together would be dangerous or have proven futile.

Contrary to this tale of reverence for family ties, there is tremendous pressure on judges, caseworkers, and administrators to remove children reported for maltreatment and to keep them in foster care. Risk-averse authorities are more afraid of making the wrong decision to return a child to an abusive home than of making the wrong decision to keep a child in state custody.[63] The former error may generate scathing headlines and public outcry, whereas the latter will probably go unnoticed. State officials rarely receive negative feedback as a result of mistaken decisions to intervene in poor Black families. This fear restrains caseworkers and agencies from being too bold or innovative in their family preservation efforts.

The pressure to remove children mounts after the death of a child by parents known to the system, and foster care caseloads skyrocket accordingly.

When Kayla McKean was beaten to death by her father despite repeated reports of abuse, the Florida legislature passed what was formerly known as the 1999 Kayla McKean Child Protection Act. (Kayla's grandfather demanded that Kayla's name be removed from the law.) The law has provisions for prosecuting caseworkers if they fail to remove a child who is later abused. Fearing criminal liability, caseworkers began to take children from parents based on the slightest indication of harm. It is no surprise that the foster care population has quadrupled in some Florida counties since the law went into effect.[64]

There are also financial incentives to keep children in foster care. State child welfare departments frequently contract with private agencies to provide foster care services. These agencies, in turn, hire caseworkers who place children referred to them in foster homes and implement plans for reunification. The agencies are then reimbursed by the state for each day that children remain in foster care. They lose this payment when a child returns home. "States and private agencies now have financial incentives to keep children in foster care and financial incentives to place them for adoption," notes the National Coalition for Child Protection Reform, "but no financial incentives to keep them in their homes or return them there."[65]

Moreover, public sympathies tend to side with foster parents who have selflessly cared for children mistreated by their own flesh and blood. It seems cruel to remove children from their new nurturing homes to return them to the very people who once hurt them. "Claims of birth parents tend to be discounted as rigid formalities—mere procedural rights of adults that should not be allowed to interfere with the obvious and unarguable interests of the children," maintain Northwestern law professors Bruce Boyer and Steven Lubet.[66] The public feels the pain of children when they are ripped from the arms of foster parents but not when they are taken from their families in the first place. Judges tend to think this way, too. Peggy Cooper Davis, a professor at New York University Law School, analyzed 193 judicial opinions issued over twenty years that employed the "psychological parent" theory espoused by Goldstein, Freud, and Solnit in their landmark book, *Beyond the Best Interests of the Child.* Professor Davis found many cases that denied the rights of biological families based on evidence of the need for continuity of care by foster parents. "There were very few cases in which those rights were bolstered by evidence concerning the need for continuity of relationships with biological families," asserts Davis.[67]

A critical part of typical caseworker training is to erase any empathy toward parents to enable ruthless child removals. Being "objective" means, first, to see the parent and child as having opposing interests and, second, being blind to the parent's point of view. "I tend to err on the side of the child," says David Weinrich, a Los Angeles child welfare worker. "If I'm wrong, and I have been, then I'm wrong, but at least I took precautions."[68] Caseworkers are instructed not to relate to parents or to be "sentimental" about taking their children away.[69] Weinrich found it difficult at first to remove children from their parents: "It was something I had to learn, and I needed supervision in the beginning . . . to do it without getting emotionally entangled. I did get better at it."

A recent account by a former caseworker of her experience in New York City's Administration for Children's Services reveals how the bias against parents causes unnecessary pain and trauma to children.[70] Akka Gordon—a pseudonym—worked in emergency services for just over one year before she quit, disillusioned by the suffering she was expected to inflict on her poor Black and Latino clients by separating the children from their parents. Her description of how removal decisions are made sheds light on the pressures operating in today's child welfare practice:

> Caseworkers and their supervisors are accountable for each case; the days when cases piled up on desks without anyone contacting a family are long over. But accountability at ACS is a one-way street. A manager or supervisor has no one to answer to if a child who shouldn't be in foster care is removed from home anyway. There is no penalty for the wrongful taking of a child. And the pressures to remove are intense. I was trained to do removals in cases that did not necessarily qualify as abuse or neglect because, as one of my supervisors reminded me, "prevention is better than a cure." When I was resistant to doing a removal on a case, that same supervisor's advice was, "It's better to be safe than sorry." And at moments of uncertainty, the mantra was "Cover your ass"—a phrase heard often around the office. It was backed up by a pervasive fear—among caseworkers, supervisors, managers, and attorneys—of seeing our photograph in the *Daily News* as the person who made an error that was literally fatal.

Gordon explains that any inclination to keep families together was routinely thwarted by case managers who had the final word. Caseworker actions in support of family unity were met with swift recrimination. Caseworkers had to file electronic reports in which they had to choose whether a home was "safe" or "unsafe." "But my manager accepted only one," writes Gordon. "Any time I determined a child to be 'safe,' my manager rejected it and returned it to me. The first step to protect yourself, I quickly discovered, is to determine that a child is 'unsafe' from the outset of an investigation." If an investigator could find no evidence to substantiate abuse allegations from a mandated reporter, such as a teacher or doctor, the manager simply refused to sign off on the case. One of Gordon's coworkers who made the mistake of honestly telling a judge she thought the children were not in danger was demoted for "failing to protect the children of the City of New York."

There are other kinds of incentives to remove children as well. Caseworkers in New York City can earn time-and-a-half for removing children at night, so it is simple to find someone in the office who will step in to take children without knowing the circumstances of the case. Placing children in foster care is also easier than working with an intact family. "Keeping a case obligates a worker to do regular home visits and follow-ups to make sure a family is getting preventive services," Gordon explains. "It also means dealing with anything that may go wrong and continuing to be responsible for the children's safety."

New York City Mayor Rudolph Giuliani praised ACS's success in reducing the number of child deaths in the city and presented the agency as a model for the rest of the country. But Gordon asks, "what kind of model is an agency whose success continues to depend on routinely causing unnecessary pain to children and the parents who want to take care of them?"

The bias against parents follows them into the courtroom. In hearings to adjudicate parents' right to get their children back, parents are at a significant disadvantage. As we saw in Part One, parents must defend themselves against a veritable army of opponents seeking to keep them separated from their children. Parents, who are almost always indigent, often stand alone before the judge. At best, they are represented by a public defender or pro bono attorney assigned by the court. Only rarely can parents threatened with termination afford to hire a private attorney of their choice. The child welfare agency, represented by a state's attorney, typically joins sides with the guardian ad litem who is supposed to speak on behalf of the child. Although guardians should not be adversaries of the parents, they tend to take on this role. For example, Patrick Murphy, the Public Guardian of Cook County, has built a reputation for tending to oppose reunification of children in foster care with their parents. He once attacked family preservation programs on the op-ed page of the *New York Times,* writing that "in most cases, giving services and money to parents who have abused and neglected their children can do nothing but reward irresponsible and even criminal behavior."[71] Judges, in turn, tend to follow the recommendations of the guardian.

There is also usually an imbalance in the quality of representation. Whereas state's attorneys and guardians ad litem make a career at litigating child abuse and neglect cases, public defenders often view family court as a training ground for criminal trials. Cathryn Stewart, an assistant clinical professor at Northwestern University Law School, told me that most parents receive inadequate legal representation. "Parents should be represented by a special group of lawyers who specialize in family law and who are committed to making abuse and neglect work their career," she said. A University of Chicago study of the Public Defender's Office, which represents 90 percent of parents in most Illinois counties, found that the office needed more staff and better training to properly advocate for its clients.[72] Matthew Johnson, a professor of clinical psychiatry in Newark who serves as an expert in child welfare cares, echoes that pro bono attorneys who represent indigent parents in New Jersey are inexperienced in trying abuse and neglect cases and have little incentive to build any expertise in this area of law.[73]

In New York City, on the other hand, lawyers appointed by the family court to represent parents are drawn from a panel of lawyers that make this work a major part of their practice.[74] But the state legislature set their hourly fees more than a decade ago at a meager $40 for work in court and $25 for work outside court. Frustrated when their appeals for a raise went unanswered, panel attorneys in most of the city refused to accept new cases starting in January 2001. Jody Adams, a Manhattan Family Court judge, called the impasse "a daily disaster in the lives of many of New York City's children." "Small children remain in foster care; adolescents remain in pretrial detention, their cases unreviewed past the statutory deadline, while their mothers weep in court," Judge Adams wrote to the *New York Times.* "But only if they're poor."[75]

The state can also afford to hire psychological experts to testify about parents' inadequacies. According to Dr. Johnson, their negative assessments of parental ability are "often scientifically questionable and at times irresponsible."[76] It is common for psychologists to offer "bonding evaluations" in which they measure how estranged children have become from their parents and how attached they have become to their substitute caregivers. Their predictions that children would be forever scarred if they were reunited with their parents are not supported by current scientific knowledge.[77] I observed a hearing in Cook County Juvenile Court where the judge couldn't find the bonding evaluation in the file, and everyone simply agreed without any evidence at all that the children had bonded with the foster mother.

Psychologists sometimes testify against parents without ever having examined them, basing their conclusions entirely on caseworker reports.[78] Others ignore tests that find nothing troubling in the parent's personality, while focusing on a single evaluation that uncovered a pathological tendency. The judge in Jornell's case, for example, rejected the positive reports prepared by an African American psychiatrist in Jornell's community. Instead, he relied on the evaluations submitted by DCFS that at one point speculated that Jornell might suffer from Munchausen's syndrome by proxy because she overmedicated her baby. Jornell's mistaken medical judgment was transformed into a rare psychosis that leads mothers to deliberately send their children to the hospital because they crave the attention from medical staff. This possible diagnosis sent her on a three-year saga of psychiatric evaluations and therapy sessions that produced a variety of revised assessments. The psychologists who prepare evaluations for court typically have a long-running contractual relationship with the child welfare agency that is petitioning to terminate the parent's rights and therefore have a vested interest in supporting the agency's determination. To add to the unfairness, public defenders or pro bono attorneys representing parents routinely find experts for trial from a list of the very same psychologists who have a financial relationship with the state agency.

Whereas courts scrutinize the psychological flaws of biological parents, they are less likely to require corresponding evaluations of the foster parents. Dr. Johnson challenged this oversight in a 1992 New Jersey case, *In re J.C.*, that overturned a trial judge's decision to terminate a Latina mother's rights three years after she voluntarily placed her two daughters in foster care.[79] The judge ruled that the woman's daughters had bonded with their pre-adoptive families. The mother obtained a better lawyer for her appeal, who secured a new hearing and more extensive evaluations. The foster parents for the older daughter gave up custody because of her behavior problems, which they linked to the girl's desire to stay with her mother. The agency still refused to return the girl to her mother until the appellate court ordered it to focus on reunification.

The mother's new attorney retained Dr. Johnson to examine the mother, the younger daughter, and the proposed adoptive mother. The expert hired by the child welfare agency wrote explicitly in her report that she had not evaluated the pre-adoptive mother. Johnson's examination revealed serious deficits. Despite evidence in school records that the girl was frequently tardy and in danger of failing, the foster mother denied knowledge of her educational difficulties and did not know the names of the girl's teachers. The foster mother also harbored hostility toward the birth mother, which she expressed to the child. The girl reported that the foster mother chastised her for talking about her mother. Moreover, the foster mother was caring for more children than agency policy recommended. Johnson informed the court of "multiple risks associated with the child's continued placement at the proposed adoptive home," risks that the child welfare agency and the trial judge had originally overlooked.

Some states have compounded the hurdles parents must face in court by shifting the burden of proof to them instead of child welfare agencies. In implementing ASFA, states have begun to pass laws that make it easier for agencies to win petitions to terminate parental rights.[80] In Arkansas, for example, parents must prove that they made a "genuine, sustainable investment" in completing the reunification plan. Illinois law puts a time-limited burden on parents to challenge the state's reunification efforts. Parents must file a motion requesting the court to find that the state made no reasonable efforts toward reunification within sixty days of the state's deadline for making these efforts. In North Dakota, parents who fail "to make substantial, meaningful efforts to secure treatment" for an addiction are deemed to have abandoned their children.

The bias in the media and the courts against keeping families together has had a profound impact on the public's perception of the foster care problem. Led to believe that families involved in the system are dangerous, many people automatically reject returning children home as a viable option. *Time* ran an investigative cover story in November 2000 on "The Crisis of Foster Care."[81] It began with a grisly account of the death of six-year-old Terrell Peterson in his Atlanta kinship foster home. Terrell, who weighed only twenty-nine pounds when he died, had been tortured, burned, and battered. During his stay in foster care, he was kept tied to a banister and fed only oatmeal and grits. The caseworker never checked to see whether he was being cared for properly. The article goes on to document case after case of children killed, maimed, or forgotten while under the care of state protection agencies. Two-year-old Gilbreania Wallace died from brain injuries inflicted by a foster mother with a questionable record. She was placed there by a private agency under contract with the California child welfare department that was plagued with corruption and mismanagement. Homer Bennett drifted among fourteen different Chicago foster homes during his fifteen years in state custody where he thought it was within the rules to be beaten with belts. "Nobody preserved his family unit," the *Time* reporter notes.

One question that logically arises from foster care fatalities is whether the victims might have been safer remaining with their parents. You would expect that readers would contemplate as a solution to the crisis sending fewer children into this "foster hell," as the author describes it. Yet not a single letter that *Time* published responding to the article raised this possibility. Instead readers accepted the foster care system while calling for its improvement. They proposed spending more money on "the resources, training, and support that foster care agencies need," on "researching potential foster parents," on "attracting some of our nation's best social workers, administrators, and resource families to this difficult field," and on adoption.[82] Others objected to criticism of the foster care system, arguing that the abuses *Time* described "would be happening at an even more alarming rate if foster care did not exist." What would happen if we devoted more resources to supporting families instead of foster care? No one asked that question.

Newspaper headlines about a child killed by her parents sends child welfare authorities into a panic, driving up the numbers of children needlessly taken from their homes. Headlines about a child killed by foster parents never leads to a dramatic *reduction* in children placed in foster care. The public believes that removing more children from their homes will diminish the chances for deadly mistakes. But overloading the system with children who could remain safely with their parents means that caseworkers have less time and money to find and follow the minority of children who really are in danger. The escalating costs of foster care drain the system of funds that could be used to support families, only worsening the conditions that lead to serious abuse. Overzealous child protective authorities scare away families who might have sought help for their problems before they spiral into violent situations. This is why tragic cases of child abuse continue to appear even under the watch of the toughest child protection regimes. Children fall through the cracks not because child welfare agencies are devoting too much to family preservation. Children fall through the cracks because agencies are devoting too much to child removal.

A recent front-page story of child abuse illustrates how the child protection philosophy can backfire. In February 2001, *New York Times* reporter Nina Bernstein recounted the odyssey of two boys from Brooklyn whose mother, Linda Harley, slashed and battered their faces before taking them on a 3,000-mile train trip from California back to New York.[83] New York City's Administration for Children's Services returned the boys from foster care to the mother's custody in 1998 after she served time for stabbing the boys' father. The agency closed the case after monitoring the family for a year. But Ms. Harley, a former prostitute and drug addict, began to neglect the boys when she returned to abusing drugs and alcohol. By December 2000, she had asked her family to take legal custody of the boys because she could no longer handle them. Instead, she took the boys by bus to California and attacked them in a motel room with a knife, metal pipe, and high-heeled shoe.

People are quick to place the blame for cases like this on child welfare authorities too dedicated to keeping families together. But New York City's ACS is the very agency that was created in response to the Elisa Izquierdo murder to make sure that a similar tragedy didn't happen again. It is the very agency that increased the number of children placed in foster care by nearly 50 percent in two years. It is the very agency that already had custody of 40,000 of the city's minority children. Is the solution to take even more children from their parents? Bernstein's follow-up headline—"Family Loyalty and Distrust of System Helped Hide Abuse of 2 Boys"—suggests a different answer.[84] Bernstein explains that Ms. Harley's mother and sisters refused to report earlier evidence of

Harley's mistreatment of the boys because they didn't trust child protective services. "Rather than betray a wayward sister and daughter struggling to overcome years of drug addiction, violence, and prostitution," Bernstein reported, "they wanted to handle her problems and her sons' needs privately." Had ACS paid more attention to supporting families, Harley and her family might have been more comfortable turning to the agency for help. The agency might have taken more effective steps to assist Harley in the years after the children were returned to her. And, if truly supportive programs failed, caseworkers assigned to the family would have had more time to investigate signs that the children were in danger.

What about the argument that the prior law dangerously favored parents? The new orientation toward child safety and adoption, say its proponents, fixes the law's invitation to ignore children's well-being. But the reasonable efforts requirement was itself enacted in response to evidence that caseworkers offered families minimal assistance and even obstructed parents' attempts to reunite with their children. Even under the reasonable efforts requirement, state agencies continued to make anemic efforts to prevent out-of-home placements and to reunify families. The Department of Health and Human Services under the Reagan administration superficially monitored states' compliance.[85] A major hindrance was that there was no legislative guidance as to what reasonable efforts must minimally include. In *Suter v. Artist M,* the United States Supreme Court recognized this failure when foster children brought a federal lawsuit against the Illinois Department of Children and Family Services seeking to enforce the reasonable efforts provision.[86] The Court rejected their right to sue, finding that "how the State was to comply with this directive . . . was, within broad limits, left up to the State." The Court concluded, in other words, that the term was too ambiguous to be enforced by the federal courts.

Far from leading invariably to risky reunifications, the law's vagueness allows judges to terminate parental rights without any serious inquiry into the agency's activities. Although many agencies recognize the importance of documenting reunification services before petitioning for termination, many others successfully seek termination after doing practically nothing. A Minnesota child welfare official conceded to Congress that "our efforts are reasonable in relation to funding available, but not in relation to our knowledge of effective programming."[87] Judges often rubber stamp agencies' own determination that they took sufficient steps to reunite the family. One study of the provision's implementation found that "many judges simply ignore the reasonable efforts requirement or else make positive findings based on inaccurate or incomplete information."[88] A guardian in Illinois abuse and neglect proceedings testified before Congress that "judges are finding the reasonable efforts requirement satisfied simply because services are unavailable."[89] Some states have statutes permitting termination of parental rights based solely on the length of time children are in state custody without even considering the extent of agencies' efforts to reunite the family.[90] This means that child protection authorities can remove children from their parents, do nothing to facilitate their return—or even make it difficult for parents to contact them—and then petition for termination of parental rights on the grounds that the parents and children have been separated for too long.

Most of the time, the reasonable efforts mandate did not lead either to strenuous attempts to reunify families or to termination of parental rights. Instead, according to Children's Rights Director Marcia Lowery, the requirement "was really used as an excuse to do nothing."[91] Lowery says caseworkers interpreted it to mean "you do not have to move toward adoption because you have to preserve the family, and then nobody makes you do anything to actually provide services." This state of inertia meant that children—especially Black children—entered foster care in record numbers and remained there longer.

The shift in policy, then, is unjustifiably weighted against keeping families together. The new federal law clarified the definition of reasonable efforts by making child safety a priority, but not by establishing specific guidelines governing the services that agencies should provide to families. This could easily be regarded by some agencies as a license to ignore the reasonable efforts requirement altogether by claiming that making them would jeopardize a child's "health and safety." When the U.S. General Accounting Office investigated how a Florida county was implementing ASFA, it found that "child welfare agency attorneys have begun to more proactively identify cases for which efforts to prevent removal from home or to return a child home may not be warranted."[92] A Florida child abuse investigator told Richard Wexler, Director of the National Coalition for Child Protection Reform, that caseworkers easily get judges to approve removal without reasonable efforts: "We usually just put on the petition that the level of abuse was too severe or the risk was deemed too high to offer services."[93] It is now more likely than ever that the law's vague terms will support unnecessary placements of children in foster care. Moreover, Congress poured money into adoption incentives but not into incentives to improve family preservation programs. It shines the spotlight on the paltry number of adoptions but not on the excessive removal of children from their parents.

2. WHY FAMILY PRESERVATION FAILS

THE FINAL ARGUMENT made for expediting termination of parental rights is that family preservation doesn't work. Instead of spending more time and money on futile programs to salvage dysfunctional families, agencies should act quickly to put children in better homes. The problem with the argument that family preservation has failed is that it was never given a chance to succeed.

The term "family preservation" has two general meanings. Broadly speaking, family preservation is a philosophy about the goals of child welfare practice. "Family preservation as a philosophy," writes Marianne Berry, a leading expert in the field, "emphasizes the importance of families to children and to society and the value of strengthening families as a first strategy in crisis."[94] This approach holds that agencies should take steps to prevent the need to remove maltreated children from their homes and to reunite children in foster care with their families. Family preservation acknowledges the tremendous power government has to disrupt families and its corresponding obligation to provide support to minimize its destructive impact.

Family preservation also refers to a variety of specific social work practices designed to avert the need to place children in foster care.[95] Child welfare experts most frequently use the term to describe an intensive, home-based, crisis-oriented model that serves families at imminent risk of having children removed. (The Child Welfare League of America labeled this model "Intensive Family-Centered Crisis Services" to distinguish it from other types of family preservation programs.) Caseworkers make themselves available around the clock to two or three families for several weeks. They spend long hours in the family's home on a daily basis, counseling parents, coordinating services, and monitoring children's safety. They try to build on the family's strengths while meeting needs identified by the family itself. All the caseworkers in a study of Michigan's Families First program, for example, reported being available twenty-four hours a day, compared to only 40 percent of caseworkers with clients in foster care. While most Families First caseworkers had hours of face-to-face interaction with families over the weekend, only one caseworker involved with foster care families had any weekend contact at all.[96]

There is also a dramatic difference in services offered. Family preservation programs typically offer concrete assistance with emergency needs, such as money to buy furniture, repair a car or appliance, or restore electricity or telephone service to the home. A caseworker offered Kendra Fillmore a wide variety of resources after the twenty-two-year-old mother was referred to Illinois Family First for leaving her three young children alone in their apartment: "transportation for medical appointments, groceries, formula, diapers, cockroach treatment, and cash assistance for overdue rent."[97] The caseworker also resolved paperwork problems that had stalled Kendra's application for Social Security Insurance benefits and kept her oldest child from entering a Head Start program. "Ultimately, one of the most successful interventions," write researchers who studied the program, "was to convince the public housing authority to move Kendra up on the waiting list for subsidized housing."[98] About 80 percent of Michigan Families First caseworkers spent an average of $345 in flexible funds for this kind of emergency help. Only 7 percent of caseworkers spent any flexible funds on families involved in foster care, and they spent a total of less than $60.[99]

If family preservation efforts are successful, they avoid the emotional trauma of separating children from their parents. Some advocates argue that these programs save states the far more expensive costs of keeping a child in foster care. For example, a 1998 Michigan Auditor General report found that the average cost for family preservation services was $4,367 per family, compared to the annual cost per child of $12,384 for foster care and $56,206 for institutional care.[100] They also avoid the physical dangers of foster care. Placing maltreated children in foster care doesn't necessarily protect them better than leaving them with their parents. Foster children are neglected and abused at alarming rates. For example, a Baltimore study found that the rate of sexual abuse in foster care was more than four times higher than the rate in the general population.[101] According to federal statistics, children are twice as likely to die of abuse in foster care than in the care of parents.[102] Of course, in many cases children are safer in foster care than left at home with abusive parents. But family preservation programs can avert harm to children at home without the need to expose them to the perils of substitute placements.

Unfortunately, many studies evaluate family preservation programs only according to rates of subsequent out-of-home placement. By this standard, a successful program is one that results in fewer children placed in foster care. Although this probably reflects a reduction in maltreatment, a better measure of success would include the rate of repeated child abuse or neglect, whether or not it resulted in foster care placement. Social work professor Kristine Nelson points to her 1992 study of nine family preservation programs, which found that 22 percent of the families were reported again for child abuse and neglect while their cases were open.[103] This result compares favorably to the 30 to 47 percent recidivism rate reported in traditional child welfare programs. This is evidence, concludes Nelson, that "children are being protected at least as well in family preservation services as in other child welfare services."[104]

An added benefit is that caseworkers who work closely with a small number of families are better able to tell when children are at risk than the typical overwhelmed caseworker who has infrequent contact with families. Huge caseloads make it harder to judge whether it's safe to reunite children with their parents and to monitor children's safety after reunification. Under these conditions, caseworkers both err on the side of unnecessary out-of-home placements and miss signs of real danger. Caseworkers engaged in family preservation programs have a much better sense of families' strengths and weaknesses.

Why haven't family preservation programs been more successful at preventing maltreatment and the need for foster care? The biggest problem is that states have not invested enough in making these programs available. Despite their asserted family orientation, child welfare agencies do not provide suitable prevention and reunification services to most families. A wealth of research now confirms, according to a recent review of the literature, that "services to maltreated children and their families are increasingly nonexistent, inaccessible, or inappropriate."[105] A 1997 report issued by the General Accounting Office stated that more than half of the family support programs it surveyed "were not able to serve all families who needed services primarily due to the lack of funds and staff."[106] University of Chicago social work professor Mark Courtney surveyed children entering foster care in California between 1988 and 1991 and found that 70 percent received only emergency response services, only 10 percent received extensive services, and 20 percent received no services at all.[107] Social work researchers Richard Barth and Marianne Berry conclude, "family preservation services are still not available for the vast majority of families in need."[108]

Here is how Elizabeth Bartholet describes the quality of family preservation efforts: "The state typically does *not* provide adequate and timely reunification services. Child welfare agencies are notoriously underfunded and overburdened. Appropriate services are often unavailable or, if available, they are costly and agencies have not been given the funds to pay for them. . . . States still fail on a systematic and widespread basis to provide the services they are supposed to provide."[109] For Bartholet, though, this is reason enough to permanently sever the bonds of these disadvantaged families and move their children into more privileged homes. Detractors charge that the government never adequately implemented family preservation programs and then blame these programs for harming children because they preserved their families!

Existing services often fail at prevention or reunification because they do not address the needs of families, are inadequately funded, and do not last long enough. What most agencies offer does not even qualify as a family preservation program.[110] When *Child Welfare Watch* surveyed administrators of New York City foster care agencies, it found that "next to staff trainings, caseworkers spent the *fewest* hours working with birth parents."[111] They devoted the bulk of their time to paperwork. As I described in Part One, "services" means a list of requirements parents must fulfill to be reunited with their children. Although some terms, such as completing a drug treatment program, can provide concrete benefits, the service plans rarely address the families' economic problems. The Child Welfare League of America found that although the most urgent need of more than half the New York families it studied was for day care or baby-sitting, the most common service provided was foster care.[112]

A recent study of the factors that prevented successful reunification efforts in San Diego discovered that inadequate housing and reliance on welfare predicted re-entry into foster care.[113] "The findings suggest providing economic and housing assistance to poor families might increase reunification rates," the author concludes. Research on the impact of concrete services confirms this hunch. A New Jersey emergency fund that gave cash grants of a few hundred dollars or less to families involved with child protection prevented foster care placement.[114] Families in an intensive family preservation program who received concrete services were more likely to avoid child removal, and the children performed better in school.[115] Marianne Berry similarly found that "families were more likely to remain intact when services were concrete, such as teaching of family care, supplemental parenting, medical care, help in securing food, and financial services."[116]

Family preservation programs must include not only counseling and training for parents but also financial remedies for poor families' material needs. How can the state's efforts be considered reasonable if they don't address the cause of the family's involvement in the system? In a recent state court lawsuit the Washington State Coalition for the Homeless successfully argued that the child welfare department had to provide families with housing assistance if homelessness was the main reason for foster care placement.[117]

Another deficiency is programs' short duration. What is available is typically "short-term, crisis-oriented, and stopgap."[118] Based on early successes and strong foundation support, intensive family preservation services "essentially became oversold as *the* model of service for high-risk families."[119] Services for families in California, for example, are permitted to continue for a maximum of six months and, on average, end after only half this time.[120] Some programs have been decreased to only four weeks.[121] But brief, intensive intervention to avert imminent placement must be followed up with longer-lasting support. As social work scholar Ann Hartman reminds agencies, "family preservation can be only one part of a continuum of child welfare services."[122]

Although the intensive family preservation model can often halt a crisis, it cannot cure the long-term difficulties faced by poor families. Most families in the child welfare system are mired in a constellation of deplorable social conditions—chronic poverty, racial discrimination, violent neighborhoods, inferior education, shoddy housing, poor health, drug addiction, profound depression, lack of child care. How can agencies expect to address, let alone solve, these problems with a generic parenting class or ephemeral crisis intervention? What happens to families after the caseworkers leave and the emergency support disappears? "Reunifying these children with families who are not adequately prepared or supported," writes Marianne Berry, "is equal to setting the family up for yet another crisis, possibly resulting in further abuse, neglect, or even death."[123] The ideology of family preservation is then blamed when inadequate efforts end in repeated maltreatment.

Caseworkers are reporting that a large portion of families in the system have substance abuse problems. The short-term, crisis-oriented approach simply does not fit drug addiction, which is often a chronic, relapsing problem. Worse still, there are not enough treatment facilities to serve the numbers of parents seeking help, and parents must surmount imposing barriers to enter those that exist. A 1997 survey of state child welfare agencies by the National Center on Addiction and Substance Abuse at Columbia University (CASA) found that they could provide appropriate substance abuse services to only 31 percent of all parents and 20 percent of pregnant women who needed them.[124] A year later, the Child Welfare League of America reported that only 10 percent of agencies could locate treatment programs for their clients within thirty days.[125] Nearly all of the CASA survey respondents reported that parents who need residential substance abuse treatment must wait; only 5.8 percent said treatment was immediately available.[126]

Even those services that are available are rarely appropriate for mothers because most treatment programs are based on a male-oriented model. Most outpatient clinics do not provide child care, and most residential treatment programs don't admit children. Treatment programs fail to provide the comprehensive services that women need, such as prenatal and gynecological care, contraceptive counseling, appropriate job training, and counseling for sexual and physical abuse. Predominantly male staff and clients are often hostile to female clients and employ a confrontational style of therapy that makes many women uncomfortable. The typical focus on individual pathology tends to exclude social forces that are critical to understanding women's substance abuse. When all of these obstacles converge to sabotage participation in the program, mothers are blamed for failing to complete treatment and threatened with termination of their parental rights.

Government officials have largely ignored the burgeoning need for comprehensive, long-term treatment for women. While shortening the time frame for parents to recover in ASFA, Congress rejected proposals to expand drug treatment services for families involved with child protection agencies. Half of the states spend no child welfare funds on substance abuse treatment, relying instead on Medicaid coverage. But Medicaid excludes some residential treatment facilities and may run out before clients have recovered. As I elaborate later, welfare reform adds another set of timetables that increase the pressure on many substance-abusing parents. Under welfare reform, poor mothers must meet new training and work requirements to retain their benefits that may conflict with participation in a drug treatment program. The two-year cut-off for receiving Temporary Assistance to Needy Families benefits may clash with both the time needed for treatment and the deadline for termination of parental rights. Most states either limit or deny altogether welfare benefits to people who have been convicted of some drug-related crimes. Few welfare workers are trained to perform the screening needed to refer their clients to drug treatment services.

Studies show that longer periods in treatment may increase chances for recovery.[127] A 1998 study by the Mathematica Policy Research Group found that treatment programs for pregnant women in five states that adopted existing 28-day programs did not result in higher-birth-weight infants, but outcomes were better for babies born to mothers who received more intensive and longer-term treatment.[128] Similarly, a study of comprehensive programs for mothers who abused crack and alcohol found that 77.8 percent remained sober and drug-free after nine months of completing treatment.[129] Successful treatment programs include comprehensive services that address the complexity of problems that substance abusers typically have—"mental and physical health services for women, child care assistance (some allow women to bring children with them to treatment), pediatric services for children, individual and single-sex group therapy, marital or family counseling, parenting education, literacy programs, and job training."[130]

Substance abuse interferes with parenting and can make parents dangerous to children. In many cases, though, keeping children with their parents while offering intensive family preservation services and drug treatment is safer, more stable, and less traumatic for children than placing them in the care of strangers in the foster care system.[131] For example, a University of Florida study compared the development of a group of drug-exposed newborns who were placed in foster care with a group allowed to remain with birth mothers who were able to care for them. It found that at six months the infants who stayed with their mothers fared much better on such tests as rolling over, sitting up, and reaching out.[132]

As we saw in Part One, agencies dispense limited family preservation services on a racially biased basis. Black families charged with child maltreatment are more likely to have their children placed in foster care than to receive services in their homes. They also receive services that are inferior to those offered other groups. Social work expert Sandra Stehno points out that the reliance on brief, intensive services to families already at risk of foster care placement is especially troubling in the case of minority families.[133] This model often excludes families with the most serious and chronic problems, such as homeless families and families with an addicted parent, because they are not considered amenable to short-term treatment. Black families are the most likely to fall into this excluded category. In addition, most of the original programs that serve as models were implemented in rural areas with white populations. The most popular prototype for intensive, in-home crisis intervention, the Homebuilders program, began in Tacoma, Washington, in 1974. These models have not been adequately tested in the inner-city Black communities that are disproportionately involved with child protection agencies. "Policy makers have done little as yet to support the development of minority-defined, minority-based models of family preservation," Stehno argues.[134]

Sometimes agencies not only fail to provide services that might help families to avoid foster care but affirmatively interfere with family reunification. Caseworkers caught in the dual role of supporting families while recruiting foster and adoptive parents sometimes sabotage parents' quest to reunite with their children. As one researcher summarized, "caseworkers have been known to fail to assist parents in obtaining housing, to unreasonably oppose visitation of the child by the parent, to place children in homes that are not easily accessible to the parent, to fail to tailor the reasonable efforts to the specific problems facing the family, and, in some instances, to not do much of anything at all."[135] A mother's chances of being reunified with her children depends largely on the agency's commitment to that goal. In a survey of the heads of a dozen agencies that handle most of New York City's foster care cases, *Child Welfare Watch* found "huge variations in agency performance—based on size, leadership, caseworker quality, access to services, and even in their capacity to supplement their government funding with outside money."[136] Agencies place some children on an adoption "track" and gear their resources toward moving the children into adoptive homes instead of returning them to their parents. Luis Medina, executive director of St. Christopher's, Inc., in the Bronx, reported that "how well a parent does has everything to do with an agency's efforts to get the family reunified." He says that St. Christopher's made a concerted effort to reduce the numbers of children it designated for adoption instead of reunification. By improving services to families, the agency has been able to lower the adoption track rate from 40 to 14 percent in the past five years. On average, foster care agencies in New York City plan on putting up about one-third of their foster children for adoption, but some have adoption track rates close to one-half.

Sporadic visitation of children in foster care is a common reason for delaying reunification or even terminating parental rights. Although parents miss their children, visiting them in a stranger's home or a government office can be a deeply humiliating experience. Visitation rubs in the fact that the parent has lost authority over her child. As one mother explained, "the fact that you are visiting your child in a foster home is a reminder you are, at least for the time being, a failure as a parent."[137] Agencies often make it difficult for parents to maintain contact with their children. Judges issue visitation orders, but agencies wield considerable control over how they are carried out. They treat visitation as a perk that parents must earn and that can be revoked for parental infractions. They schedule visits at inconvenient times and places, limit the frequency of visits and the length of time parents can spend with their children, and fail to provide needed transportation.[138] In New York, for example, the law requires only visits every two weeks between parents and children. And a 1997 analysis found that more than half of the children studied saw their parents even less than the state-mandated minimum.[139] "Visitation requires a lot of time and effort on the part of social workers because they have to arrange for everybody to be in the same place at once," Boston College social work professor Anthony Maluccio explained to *Child Welfare Watch*. "A lot of caseworkers don't have the time." When children react adversely to brief encounters with their estranged parents, caseworkers often respond by decreasing visitation instead of giving families more time to deal with the hardships of foster care. Requiring caseworkers to supervise visits can also unnecessarily interfere with parents' interaction with their children.

The allocation of federal child welfare funding is largely responsible for the inadequacy of family preservation services. States depend heavily on federal monies, both in the form of fixed grants and reimbursements of expenditures, to operate their child welfare systems. Under the 1980 Child Welfare Act, federal spending for all child welfare services increased more than threefold in a decade, from $0.5 billion in 1981 to $1.6 billion in 1990. By 1995 it had reached $4.1 billion. But most of this money was allocated to maintaining children outside their homes. In fact, the percentage spent on foster care and adoption steadily increased during this period, while the share for family preservation efforts shrank.[140] The 1980 law established a separate funding stream for state foster care expenses. Whereas federal foster care spending is open-ended, funds for preventive and reunification services are fixed. Under Title IV-E of the Social Security Act, the federal government reimburses states for the maintenance of all foster children who fall below certain income standards, regardless of the amount spent. Title IV-B of the Social Security Act, on the other hand, provides capped annual appropriations for child welfare services. Funding for services was so inadequate that Congress passed the Family Preservation and Support Services Program in 1993 to provide states an additional $930 million over five years.

Federal reimbursements for foster care totaled $3.6 billion in 1995, compared to less than $500 million spent on child welfare services.[141] (Mark Courtney estimates that federal, state, and local governments spent a whopping $11.2 billion directly on child welfare programs that year.)[142] A 1995 General Accounting Office report calculated that "the federal government spent about $.12 on child welfare services in 1993 for every $1 spent on foster care."[143] That was down from $.40 spent on child welfare services in 1983. Foster care still eats up most of the federal child welfare budget.

States stretch a growing share of their limited child welfare resources to pay for abuse and neglect investigations and cannot tap into the larger pot of federal foster care funds for services that support families. "The effect," concludes the GAO report, "has been to further constrain resources for preventive and rehabilitative child welfare services that offer some promise of containing growth in foster care caseloads."[144] Funding shortages combine with other institutional limitations to dilute agencies' family preservation efforts. The realities of overburdened child welfare systems—"high caseloads, mandated worker deadlines, reduced qualifications of staff, staff turnover, and inflexible organizational boundaries and funding streams"—are antithetical to providing intensive, tailor-made services to families.[145]

The government's puny investment in family preservation was reflected in the growth of the foster care population after the 1980 Child Welfare Act was passed. Despite the reasonable efforts mandate, the number of children in foster care doubled over the next decade. In the years between 1987 and 1992 alone, the foster care population shot from 280,000 to more than 460,000.[146] Moreover, the average length of stay in foster care remained about two years.[147] Part of the reason for the rise in foster care caseloads was that the 1980 law came on the heels of the Child Abuse Prevention and Treatment Act of 1974, which strengthened mandated reporting of child abuse. Marianne Berry argues that the foster care figures stem from an inundation of maltreatment reports, not an unwillingness to follow the new family preservation approach. "Child-welfare workers and administrators shifted to a new philosophy toward placement prevention at the same time that they were faced with steadily increasing child-abuse caseloads," Berry explains.[148] But this reason simply shows that federal child welfare policy is fraught with contradictory objectives that weaken its commitment to supporting families.

Congress missed another opportunity to adequately fund state family preservation efforts when it passed ASFA in 1997. While giving states bonuses for moving more children into adoptive homes, the law provides no incentives for agencies to return children safely to their parents. While giving parents less time to meet reunification requirements, Congress did nothing to strengthen state reunification services. In fact, Congress considered and rejected proposals to expand both reunification and drug treatment services for families involved with foster care. Although the law is praised as a bipartisan achievement, there were splits over the issue of new spending for family services. Proposed legislation would have given priority in federally funded drug treatment programs to parents referred by child protection agencies and would have reimbursed states for one year of reunification services. But Congress adopted ASFA instead—without enough assistance to parents whose children are in foster care. "It was more important to pass the fundamental adoption reforms that enjoyed overwhelming support," explains the Associated Press.[149] By 1997, lack of funding, a media backlash against poor Black families, and a waning commitment to the underlying philosophy had converged to decimate family preservation as a child welfare strategy.[150]

There is solid evidence that family preservation programs can work. To begin with, let's examine the statistics used as proof of failure. About one-third of maltreated children who are kept or returned home will be maltreated again.[151] This means that in two-thirds of cases children stay safely with their parents. Many instances of repeated abuse or neglect would have been avoided by more intensive, longer-lasting, or appropriate services. If even underfunded and scarce family preservation efforts succeed most of the time, why should we declare family preservation a failure?

The record of family preservation programs is the subject of intense debate among social work researchers.[152] As with so many aspects of child welfare policy, studies measuring the effectiveness of these programs reach conflicting results. One problem with the record is that some studies of family preservation services were plagued with methodological flaws.[153] As I mentioned, most measure success using placement-prevention rates instead of rates of repeated maltreatment. It's possible, though unlikely, that some children in family preservation programs are maltreated again but not placed in foster care. Some show success at preventing foster care placement during the period of service, leaving the long-term effects a mystery. Some used small samples and failed to include a control group receiving more traditional services so that outcomes could be compared.

Critics also charge that caseworkers are unwilling to refer the riskiest families to these programs, so the children studied may have avoided foster care even without family preservation services. Caseworkers may erroneously claim that children are at imminent risk of placement to make their families eligible for intensive services. Chapin Hall Center for Children at the University of Chicago conducted an experiment assessing the effectiveness of the Illinois Family First program during its first four years. The study concluded that "most of the children served by the program would not have been placed in substitute care in the absence of the program."[154] The researchers dispute the program's success because "it is not meaningful to talk about preventing an event if the event wouldn't have happened anyway."[155] This and some other controlled studies found no substantial difference between comparison-group placement rates and those produced by the family preservation program. If programs do not avoid foster care placement because the children they serve were not really at risk of removal, they cannot be credited with saving foster care expenditures and may actually increase the costs of child welfare services. But the Chapin Hall study itself has been criticized for "failures of representativeness, reliable measures, intervention integrity, comparable groups, attrition, and protection from research bias."[156]

A number of compelling studies, on the other hand, show that good family preservation initiatives are better than traditional approaches at preventing child maltreatment and foster care placement. In *Protecting Children and Supporting Families*, Gary Cameron and Jim Vanderwoerd reviewed eleven studies of comprehensive support programs that states began to implement in the 1970s.[157] This multifaceted model provided packages of support services to risky families that addressed family members' personal and environmental problems. The package might include services to improve family interactions, such as parent training classes and family counseling, as well as more concrete help with the family's material needs, such as child care, medical services, and housing assistance. Many programs provided supports for at least one year. According to Cameron and Vanderwoerd, "the research evidence suggested that participants in comprehensive support programs often had lower reported rates of child maltreatment and out-of-home placement than baseline or comparison groups."[158] Added benefits of comprehensive programs were significant state savings because of averted foster care costs and positive changes in parent-child relations.

One study in the review assessed Special Services for Children, a demonstration project offered to disadvantaged families in the Bronx in the late 1970s.[159] The researchers compared a group of sixty families randomly assigned to an enriched program with a group of sixty families who received the normal array of services. Three additional services were available to the SSC families, but not to the comparison group—a 24-hour hot line, emergency financial assistance, and family assistants or special friends. First, the study found that the experimental families made heavy use of the three enrichment services. About half of the families tapped the financial assistance, one-third requested a family assistant, and one-quarter phoned the hot line. The SSC families also had more contact with workers and were involved in the program for longer periods than the comparison group. Second, the study found that "significantly fewer experimental children (4%) than comparison children (17%) were placed into care during the intervention period."[160] Moreover, the children in the enriched program ended up with better physical and emotional living arrangements. Finally, the researchers calculated that the enriched services saved New York $61,625 in foster care expenditures over the three-year project and projected $404,225 in savings over the next four and a half years.

A more recent and frequently cited study of the Michigan Families First program compared a group of 225 children at risk of placement who received intensive services at home with a similar group of 225 children who had recently exited foster care.[161] The study found that children who participated in Families First were less likely to be removed from their homes months later. A year after the beginning of the study, 24 percent of the Families First children had been placed in foster care, compared to 35 percent of the children in the control group. This research shows that intensive family preservation programs that offer a variety of concrete supports to families can make a difference. It also shows that caseworkers involved in these programs do not invariably keep children with their parents regardless of the risk to their safety.

Research also proves that intensive programs can safely speed reunification of children in foster care with their families. In their review of these studies, Chapin Hall researchers Julia Littell and John Schuerman reported that reunification rates ranged from 25 percent to 100 percent across several programs.[162] One well-designed study assessed the effects of the Utah Family Reunification Services project, an intensive, in-home program implemented in 1989. Caseworkers served no more than six families at a time and spent an average of three hours per week with each family for three months. The study followed 110 families with children in foster care who were randomly assigned either to the preservation project or to a control group that received services from regular caseworkers with caseloads averaging twenty-two families.

The difference in reunification rates of the two groups was significant. At the end of the treatment period, 93 percent of the children in the project group had returned home, compared with only 28 percent of the control children. The families who received intensive services also experienced lower rates of reentry into foster care. Six months later, most of the children in the project (70 percent) were still at home, whereas most of the children in the control group (58 percent) were in substitute care. When researchers followed up at the end of a year, they discovered that 75 percent of the children whose families received preservation services were living at home. Less than half of the children in the control group were at home.[163] Other studies have similarly concluded that "relatively brief and intensive family-centered services can significantly affect reunification rates" both at the end of treatment and throughout a one-year follow-up period.[164]

In sum, although some studies dampen the enthusiasm for family preservation programs, many others confirm that these programs can safely reduce the need for putting children in foster care. This is grounds for states to work harder at improving these programs to reach more families and to decrease the need to place children in substitute care. Evidence that a particular model is not as effective as people hoped is no reason to scrap family preservation as a goal of the child welfare system. None of the studies weaken in the slightest the benefits of supporting families. Although critics question the strength of studies proving the success of these programs, they have not shown that family preservation programs *increase* rates of child abuse and neglect. Nor have they shown that foster care is safer. Instead, the shift in policy was based on tragic but sensationalized cases that resulted from overwhelmed agencies—not intensive family preservation services.

Others might argue that adoption is even safer still. Experts estimate that adoptive parents are responsible for only 1 percent of abuse and neglect reports although they represent 3 percent of the population.[165] But we have to weigh the advantages of adoptive homes against the disadvantages of needlessly separating children from their families. There is no basis in the empirical research or history of family preservation efforts to abandon them in favor of terminating parental rights. Even the Chapin Hall researchers conclude that although the Illinois program didn't serve the target group of riskiest families, it "did provide many needed services to many families, services that would not have been available otherwise."[166] The message of their study, they say, "is one of caution, but not despair."[167]

In fact, the subsequent demise of family preservation in Illinois led to an *increase* in child abuse deaths.[168] Illinois officials abruptly abandoned its Family First program in 1993 when three-year-old Joseph Wallace was killed by his mentally ill mother after he was returned from foster care. (Although a Family First caseworker warned against Joseph's return home, a judge in a different county who was unfamiliar with the case approved reunification.) In typical fashion, the child welfare agency intensified child removals, and the foster care population jumped by 30 percent in a year. Ending family preservation was dangerous for children. Child abuse deaths spiked from seventy-eight under the program to ninety-one in 1997. Five children were killed in foster care, more than ever before.[169]

Still, we cannot expect even the most intensive and comprehensive programs to fix the fundamental flaws in the child welfare system. Even the best programs cannot be expected "to solve major social problems one case at a time."[170] Family preservation programs as they are currently conceived work on an emergency basis, trying to minimize the damage to children after family problems have already reached a crisis stage. They focus on the family's immediate needs, with little attention to the social conditions that contributed to them. These programs are better at providing material resources than routine child welfare services. But because they adopt the predominant view that child maltreatment stems from personality deficits, some rely too heavily on psychological therapies. These programs are superimposed on a child welfare system that discriminates against families on the basis of race and wealth and that makes no provision for supporting families before they are charged with abuse and neglect. Why aren't the concrete resources some programs provide made available to all families that need them? Caseworkers trying to preserve families must depend on other social service systems, such as those providing welfare, child care, education, substance abuse treatment, and medical care, that are themselves inadequate.

Family preservation programs function within a structure that inherently conflicts with the goal of preserving families. The child welfare system's primary mandate remains to investigate parents to see whether they should be blamed for their children's harmful environment and whether their children should be removed from it. Social work professor Leroy Pelton emphasizes the barrier to family integrity created by the system's dual role to coerce parents while trying to help them. "The investigative/coercive/child-removal role diminishes, hampers, and overwhelms the helping role within the dual-role structure of public child-welfare agencies," writes Pelton, "as huge and increasingly larger portions of their budgets are devoted to investigation and foster care, with little money left over for preventive and supportive services to combat the impermanency of children's living arrangements."[171] For family preservation efforts to truly work they must be incorporated into a radically reformed child welfare system whose paramount goal is to support families, not break them apart.

3. Is Adoption the Answer?

FEDERAL AND STATE LAWS now place foster children on a "fast track" to adoption by imposing swifter timetables for severing their ties to their parents and by allowing concurrent planning for adoption. Despite its failure ever to fully support family preservation, government has turned to adoption as the solution to the nation's disastrous foster care system. A recent letter to the *New York Times* gives an idea of the intense momentum building around the campaign to move more foster children into adoptive homes. "Over the last five years, the New York City Family Court has begun a fast-track agency adoption system. This intensive push by the court to speed up the adoption process for children in foster care has resulted in the completion of several thousand agency adoptions each year," wrote Administrative Judge Joseph Lauria in March 2001. "Last November 18, the Family Court participated in Adoption Saturday, a national endeavor to expedite the adoption of children in foster care. The New York City Family Court completed more than 200 adoptions in one day. Adoption Saturday is just one example of the court's commitment to achieving permanency for children in foster care expeditiously."[172]

At first glance, policies promoting adoption of foster children seem unobjectionable. In fact, adoption is one of the few priorities that both socially minded liberals and compassionate conservatives can agree on. Everyone, it seems, has jumped on the adoption bandwagon. What could be wrong, after all, with placing children destined to drift in foster care into loving and stable homes? And what politician would dare oppose this happy ending?

But the plan to use adoption to cure the ills of foster care suffers from serious flaws. Its most basic defect is that the adoption strategy will not accomplish its main objective to reduce significantly the enormous foster care population. This is because the strategy includes terminating more biological parents' rights, and not all of the "legal orphans" produced will be adopted.

Their numbers will be added to the long-term foster care caseloads. Even more damaging is the adoption strategy's failure to address the child welfare system's most glaring injustice—the racially biased removal of too many children from their homes. In fact, the new emphasis on adoption only makes the system's racial disparity worse.

In a fairer system, policies promoting adoption would be commendable. There are more foster children who should be adopted than are presently finding adoptive homes. States need to attract more adoptive parents and support them better, and they need to expedite the process for moving children available for adoption out of foster care. But the campaign to increase adoptions took an ominous turn when it made the devaluation of foster children's families and the rejection of family preservation efforts its central components. Black children's family bonds are portrayed as a barrier to adoption, and extinguishing them is seen as the critical first step in the adoption process. Adoption is no longer presented as a remedy for a minority of unsalvageable families but as a viable option—indeed, the preferred option—for *all* children in foster care. The *Seattle Post-Intelligencer,* for example, called the half million children in foster care "orphans of the living."[173]

Rushing to Terminate Parental Rights

Foster children's ties to their parents have become a nuisance. Under the new policy, parents' rights are treated as the chief impediment to permanency (read as adoption) for children in foster care. Terminating parental rights is seen, in the words of Senator Chafee, as "the critical first step in moving children into permanent placements." Mandatory time lines speed up this determination. Although the federal adoption law doesn't set a hard and fast deadline to terminate parental rights, it effectively shifts the presumption in favor of termination when children have spent a long time in state custody. Agencies are now under pressure to move children out of foster care into adoptive homes as fast as possible.

State child welfare systems are starting to feel the law's reverberations. The American Bar Association's "Termination Barriers Project" trains lawyers, judges, and caseworkers to expedite termination of parents' rights. Terminations have more than doubled in Oklahoma, California, and Illinois since

1995.[174] Florida's child welfare department planned to add 125 new attorneys and staff to handle the anticipated deluge of termination petitions.[175] In the year after ASFA was implemented, the number of termination petitions against birth parents in New York City shot up by a third, from 3,209 in 1998 to 4,201 in 1999.[176] In Cook County, Illinois, the state filed 5,990 termination petitions in 1997—up nearly five times from 1993. According to the *Chicago Reporter*, "terminations grew from 958 to 3,743 in that period, meaning that three out of every five cases ended with parents losing custody."[177] Remember, Black children make up 95 percent of child welfare cases in Chicago, the main segment of Cook County.

Proponents of the expedited approach say it's unfair to children to make them waste away in foster care waiting for their parents to reform. But sometimes children spend too long in foster care because of unreasonable demands placed on their parents or delays caused by the child welfare agency. Agencies remove children from their homes, make reunification nearly impossible, and then petition to terminate the parents' rights because reunification is taking too long. In these cases, the state destroys a family for no good reason.

Does it violate the rights of both parents and children to sever family ties solely on grounds that the child has spent too much time in foster care? Courts have reached divergent answers to this question. In recent years, Minnesota's appellate courts have become increasingly receptive to terminating parental rights. Whereas appellate judges used to reverse termination orders, finding that parents' rights were violated, they are now upholding these orders and even mandating that family court judges terminate parents' rights to their children. The Supreme Court of Minnesota rejected a mother's argument that complying with a statutory limit on long-term foster care, despite a therapist's testimony that the children would be better off psychologically if they maintained contact with their mother, was not in her children's best interests.[178] The court upheld termination of the mother's rights, ruling that the best interests inquiry was satisfied by determining that the statutory time limit had passed.

Fortunately, some judges have scrutinized agencies' efforts to reunite families before rushing to terminate parental rights. A case recently decided by a Brooklyn family court judge illustrates how agencies can thwart parents' efforts to get their children back and then rely on their successful interference to end the family relationship. In *Matter of S. Children*, Angel Guardian Home, a private agency hired by New York City's Administration for Children's Services, petitioned to free five children for adoption on the grounds that their mother, Gladys S., had abandoned them in foster care for more than a year.[179] The state initially removed the children from Gladys in January 1997 for reasons related to poverty: there was not enough food in the home, one child had ringworm, and another had diaper rash and a cut over the right eye. What happened next is typical of the system's utter failure to match "services" to families' needs. Instead of attending to the children's economic and medical needs, Angel Guardian Home directed Gladys to a pointless battery of psychological therapies. The agency also falsely accused Gladys of using drugs and required her to submit to three random drug tests—all with negative results. It was undisputed that Gladys was dedicated to being reunited with her children. She spoke regularly with caseworkers, attended every service plan review, was present for all home visits, and visited her children every two weeks without fail.

On what basis, then, could Angel Guardian Home claim that Gladys had "permanently neglected" her children? The agency worker assigned to the case, D. J. Norwood, determined that Gladys had failed to comply with his demand that she attend psychological therapy. Norwood testified that Gladys began missing scheduled appointments in March 1998 and was dropped from the program because she stopped attending. He told the court that he warned Gladys that if she didn't complete the program, "the agency would have no choice but to change the plan to adoption."

But the judge's review of the agency and clinic records disclosed a different story. First, the judge found that the clinic stopped treating Gladys in March because her Medicaid coverage was discontinued. The files showed that the clinic notified Norwood about the Medicaid lapse in April, but Norwood failed to take any steps to restore coverage until July. Norwood had the nerve to claim at the trial that his belated attempt to reactivate Gladys's insurance constituted "diligent efforts" to reunify the family.

The judge also found that the agency's requirement that Gladys undergo psychological therapy was nonsensical in the first place. The initial service plan called for Gladys to get a psychological evaluation to "rule out" the need for therapy. But the agency changed the plan to require therapy without waiting for the evaluation to take place. Case notes showed that Norwood "warned birth mother that she must be in an outpatient psychiatric clinic in order to have her children returned to her" and that "if she is not at clinic it could be interpreted as permanent neglect"—*before* he received any psychiatric assessment. To make matters worse, two evaluations in the agency's files showed that Gladys had no mental illness requiring psychological treatment. Instead, she was diagnosed as having "borderline intellectual functioning"—the same as Jornell's latest diagnosis after three years of psychiatric evaluation and therapy. The court noted, however, that Gladys was never offered any services designed to assist a parent with limited cognition. So what was the clinic treating Gladys for before her Medicaid coverage ran out? The psychologist saw the purpose for treating Gladys as "to reduce anxiety as she works toward reuniting with (her) children." In other words, the main service Gladys received was therapy for the trauma the agency inflicted on her by taking her children away!

When the case was finally decided in February 2001, Gladys's children had spent four years in foster care while the agency put their mother through a baseless ritual that did nothing to address the family's needs. The judge noted that new federal policy makes it imperative that agencies provide appropriate reunification services. "Especially in light of the Adoption and Safe Families Act, which strictly limits the period that children may remain in foster care," the judge stated, "a child protection agency's efforts may not be formulaic, but must relate meaningfully to the cause of the separation between the parent and the child." The judge found insufficient evidence of permanent neglect and dismissed the petition to terminate Gladys's parental rights. This court's close inspection of the agency's actions and carefully reasoned opinion are remarkable. Most termination petitions in New York City are granted with little notice. And even though the judge refused to terminate Gladys's rights, he kept her children in foster care.

In a more far-reaching decision, an Illinois judge recently considered the constitutionality of the fifteen-month deadline for termination of parental rights.[180] In *In the Interest of H.G.*, the child welfare department petitioned to terminate a mother's rights under the provision of the Illinois Adoption Act that defined as unfit any parent whose child had been in foster care for fifteen out of twenty-two months. In implementing the federal adoption law, the Illinois legislature transformed Congress's permanency time line into an independent grounds for declaring a parent unfit. The parent's rights are terminated under the Illinois law unless the *parent* can prove that it is in the child's best interests to be returned home within six months. The mother's attorney pointed out that the deadline had expired only because a hearing in the case had been delayed three times—each time at the *state's* request.

Judge Judith Brawka held that the statutory deadline was unconstitutional. The judge found that the provision infringed on the mother's fundamental right to a relationship with her daughter. Although the government has a compelling interest in giving children a permanent home, it must narrowly tailor the termination statute to further that interest. "The problem is inherent in that this particular statute, unlike all of the other provisions for findings of unfitness," Judge Brawka reasoned, "relates not to conduct of a parent or an internal flaw of character or behavior or mental illness or physical infirmity, but rather the mere passage of time." That test, the judge said, is arbitrary. It says nothing about the parent's ability to care for the child. The state had a constitutional duty to prove that the mother was unfit before ending her parental rights, so requiring the mother to prove her fitness also violated the Constitution. The state's appeal is pending before the Illinois Supreme Court.

Losing Patience with Substance-Abusing Parents

Efforts to reunify substance-abusing parents with their children are on a collision course with new termination deadlines. It is usually difficult for parents with drug or alcohol problems to successfully complete a treatment program and conform to other agency requirements within the established time limit. As Illinois DCFS Director Jess McDonald stated at a recent government hearing, "the 12-month permanency clock for children ignores the clock of treatment for addiction, which at best is 24 months."[181] The conflict between recovery from substance abuse and statutory deadlines is frequently the reason for termination of parental rights.[182] In this contest, judges typically give top priority to children's interest in permanency. Children's need for permanency, they reason, supersedes their need to maintain ties to parents with addiction problems. "After six months, parents' rights should be terminated," stated one caseworker. "I have some cases where the children have been in foster care for 2 to 3 years because parents continued to relapse. I feel if parents can't get their priorities straight in six months then they probably never will, and why make the children suffer. Haven't they suffered enough?"[183]

Those who favor expediting termination of parental rights refer to a different set of conflicting clocks. They argue that the conflict between the clock of child development and the clock of parental recovery from substance abuse means that agencies should quickly abandon unsuccessful efforts to reunite addicted parents with their children. According to Joseph Califano, president of the National Center on Addiction and Substance Abuse, "there is an irreconcilable clash between the rapidly ticking clock of physical, intellectual, emotional and spiritual development for the abused and neglected child and the slow-motion clock of recovery for the parent addicted to alcohol or drugs."[184] CASA warns that "the child welfare system, which must attend to the urgent developmental needs of children, cannot have the patience with the recovery process that should be accorded to addicts in public health arenas."[185] According to this view, children in foster care experiencing a rapid rate of development are quickly injured while waiting for their substance-abusing parents to recover.

In addition to giving substance-abusing mothers less time for treatment, some states are moving to terminate their rights immediately after they give birth.[186] Alabama's child welfare law exempts states from making reasonable efforts to preserve families when the parent abuses drugs. Florida defines child abuse and neglect to include using a controlled substance or alcohol during pregnancy. The Illinois child maltreatment law includes a rebuttable presumption that a mother is unfit if she gives birth to a baby who tests positive for a controlled substance. In a case involving the conviction of a Black woman who smoked crack while pregnant, the Supreme Court of South Carolina held that a viable fetus is a child for purposes of the state's child abuse law.[187] Like abuse and neglect laws generally, statutes making prenatal substance abuse proof of child abuse or parental unfitness have a disparate impact on Black mothers and their children. In fact, these statutes seem almost targeted at poor Black mothers. As I discussed in Part One, the media's obsessive concentration on crack babies has created the impression that all pregnant drug addicts are Black. Moreover, there is overwhelming evidence that hospitals test and report Black mothers and newborns at far higher rates than their white counterparts. Child protection agencies' removals of infants who test positive for drugs has therefore been grossly racially imbalanced.

As noted earlier, numerous obstacles to receiving appropriate treatment make it difficult for many substance-abusing parents to recover within the time frame imposed by the new permanency policies. There is evidence, though, that given adequate time and services, many of these parents could be reunited with their children. Does the emphasis on permanency unwisely short-circuit substance-abusing parents' efforts to keep their families together?

The priority given to permanency is often misplaced. Courts sometimes misjudge the importance to children of speedy resolution of placement compared to preserving the relationship with their parents. Even where experts find a continuing emotional bond between addicted parents and their children, accompanied by the promise of successful drug treatment, some judges are unwilling to wait for parents to recover. In *In the Interest of N.F. and C.H.*, the mother, Janet, argued that the closeness of her relationship with her two children should preclude termination.[188] The court explained that a strong bond between parent and child is a mitigating but not overriding factor in considering whether to terminate the parent's rights. It concluded, "We do not believe we should exercise more patience with Janet because of the nature of her problem. The rights and needs of a child for permanency are not dependent upon the type of disability which saddles the parent."

Courts sometimes base the decision to terminate parents' rights on an erroneous understanding of addiction and the recovery process. They view a substance-abusing parent's relapse as evidence of immutable parental unfitness and the futility of state reunification efforts. For example, in *Andrea L. v. Superior Court*, the judge refused to extend family reunification services beyond the statutory limit because the mother relapsed.[189] The mother had been in complete compliance with the child protection agency's plan except for one instance of a positive drug test. She even tested negative for drugs on four subsequent occasions. The drug treatment center's progress report stated that she had made "great changes in her decision making skills, communication skills and [had] a much more positive outlook" and recommended that the reunification process continue.

The exchange among the county counsel, mother's attorney, and the juvenile court judge about the significance of the mother's sole relapse illustrates the destructive impact that uninformed perceptions of addiction can have on family bonds. The county counsel took the position that the mother's relapse completely negated the great progress she had made in the drug treatment program: "It doesn't matter how many programs mother completed before she relapsed. The relapse takes her back to square one. All the intervention has not been successful, so I don't see that there is a sufficient offer of proof that the children can be safely returned to her care given a dirty test for cocaine." A representative of the drug treatment program was prepared to testify that she was confident in the mother's chances for success. But the judge had little patience with the mother. "At this point I am very frustrated," the judge stated. "I mean, this mother had been stepping forward. She had been doing what she was supposed to do. She had been testing clean. Somebody explain to me the lure of cocaine such that a mother will jeopardize being able to have her children back with her. It's beyond me to understand." The judge cut off reunification services, virtually guaranteeing termination of the mother's rights. The appellate court upheld the judge's exercise of discretion, holding that the judge could reasonably conclude that the mother's relapse justified not extending the service deadline. Judges sometimes fail to understand that relapse is a common aspect of the recovery process and doesn't necessarily negate a determined addict's chances for successfully completing treatment.

Parents so deep into drugs or alcohol that they have abandoned their children should not be permitted to stall state efforts to place the children with adoptive families. But these cases appear to represent a minority of parents who have lost custody of their children because of substance abuse. Child welfare policy should be aimed at keeping these hopeless cases to a minimum.

Creating More "Legal Orphans"

Proponents of the shift away from family preservation claim that increasing adoptions is the best way to reduce the foster care population. Their calculations are based on a faulty premise: they assume that the foster care problem stems from barriers to adoption, especially family preservation policies that make it difficult to terminate parental rights. This contention implies that if states remove these barriers—if courts terminate parental rights faster—the foster care problem will dissipate and even disappear.

This is a false hope. There are not enough people wishing to adopt to absorb the high volume of children already pouring into foster care. As New York

City's child welfare commissioner Nicholas Scoppetta recently acknowledged, "I think the message is, we will need more adoptive parents if children are freed for adoption and parents' rights are terminated under ASFA."[190] As I mentioned earlier, the federal incentives for adoption have been effective. The number of adoptions nationwide has almost doubled, from 28,000 in 1996 to 46,000 in 1999.[191] By 1998, thirteen states had adoptions rates that had increased more than 50 percent over the average of the three previous years.[192] But even this surge in adoptions is not enough to find homes for the growing number of foster children. This is especially true because the adoption strategy hinges on termination of parental rights. Because many of the children whose family ties are severed won't be adopted, the policy may actually result in a net increase in the foster care population.

Data on the foster care system over the past twenty years show that the number of parental rights terminations far outpaces the number of adoptions. Martin Guggenheim's analysis of statistics gathered from Michigan and New York over the period from 1987 to 1993 shows a dramatic increase in the number of children who become "legal orphans"—children of parents whose rights have been terminated and who are waiting in foster care to be adopted.[193] Although the number of adopted state wards also increased, it lagged behind the number of children becoming state wards as a result of termination of their parents' rights. Both states, in short, experienced "a dramatic increase in the number of children who are freed for adoption but not adopted." Indeed, in New York the number of unadopted state wards jumped 225 percent in four years, from 648 in 1987 to 2,383 in 1991. Guggenheim concludes: "Five years of aggressively terminating parents' rights has produced a clear pattern: The number of children freed for adoption goes up every year; the number of children adopted fails to keep pace with the number of adoption-eligible children; and the total number of orphaned children not adopted continues to increase fastest of all."[194]

True, Guggenheim's figures date from a period before federal incentives for adoption were implemented. But they also date from a period when the Child Welfare Act was supposed to encourage states to preserve families and to prefer reunification over adoption. Despite this emphasis on avoiding termination, Guggenheim noted, child welfare policy "resulted in creating the highest number of unnatural orphans in the history of the United States." Other aspects of foster care make the crisis even more dire today. The foster care population grew from 520,000 children in 1996 to 568,000 children in 1999. In 1996, 11 percent of these children had been in foster care for three to four years, and 10 percent had been there for more than five years. By 1999, 15 percent had been in foster care for three to four years and 18 percent for more than five years. And the number of children waiting for adoptive homes doubled during this period, reaching 117,000 children.[195]

The federal law's accelerated deadlines for termination of parental rights will probably increase the population of "legal orphans." There will be more parentless children stuck in foster care without any legal ties to a family. Federal adoption incentives, on the other hand, even if they achieve congressional goals, will fail to provide enough new homes for all of these children. This shortfall is exacerbated by the fact that the children most likely to be affected by the expedited termination process are the very ones least likely to be adopted—Black children. Black parents' rights are already terminated sooner than those of white parents, yet Black children are less likely than white children to be adopted. This is why most of the children waiting to be adopted are Black.

The Costs of Adoption

There are additional costs to the adoption strategy, even when states are successful at finding adoptive homes. Research demonstrates that most children in foster care continue to value ties to their parents despite the physical separation and despite the reasons for removal. "It's hard for me to tell you how bad foster care is," twelve-year-old Boyd told a congressional committee. Boyd spent five years in foster care after his mother was hospitalized from a severe beating by his father. "My mother used to come visit me a lot when I was in care, and when she left, it felt like the whole world was leaving me."[196] Researchers who have actually listened to *children's* opinions about their placement discover that foster children, especially older ones, want to keep connected to their parents. One study interviewed 95 children ages eleven to fourteen who had been in foster care between six months and two years about their feelings about their parents.[197] More than half of the children said they missed their parents *most of the time.*

Another project interviewed 111 foster children between ages nine and eighteen who were unlikely to return home. Forty-one percent said they would like to be adopted if they could choose their new parents. But half of the children "were adamant that they did not want to be adopted under any condition."[198] Why wouldn't a "legal orphan" want to find an adoptive home? Some of the children "still regarded their natural parents as their real family and still derived considerable strength from this relationship," the researchers explained. "They regarded adoption as destructive of that relationship, and their agreement to adoption as a betrayal of their families." Legally severing these children's ties with their parents will not erase their emotional connection, nor will adoption make their biological parents disappear from their hearts and minds.

We can agree that many children are better off in safer, more nurturing adoptive homes. But this does not mean that termination of parental rights automatically produces a stable adoption.[199] Unlike adoption of babies voluntarily relinquished or abandoned by their mothers, adoption resulting from coercive termination of parental rights carries added risks for children. A 1981 study comparing the effects of voluntary and involuntary termination of parental rights on children freed for adoption suggests a relationship between coercive termination and the instability of subsequent adoptions.[200] The study found that children whose mothers contested termination of parental rights were more likely to resent being adopted, especially if their mothers appeared competent. The adversarial nature of the proceedings left the children "in a limbo of anxiety and heightened loyalty conflicts in relation to the parents, grief about losing them, and hostility toward the agency seeking termination." "Many felt that acceptance of adoption would be an expression of disloyalty toward the biological family," the study's author reported. Some of the children resisted adoption so stubbornly that their adoptions were disrupted and they returned to foster care. "Involuntary terminations of parental rights by court order," the study concluded, "seemed to create more serious problems for children than it solved."[201] Caseworkers under pressure to turn foster care placements into adoptions when neither the foster parents nor the children are prepared for it express concern that the resulting adoptions might fail. Officials in several states estimate that the rate of disrupted adoptions—when the adoptive parents change their minds—has reached between 15 and 25 percent.[202]

The interests of unadopted children in foster care are not automatically furthered by the extinction of their legal connection to their parents—even if they should not be returned home. Termination weakens family stability for many foster children by disrupting their relationship with their parents, while failing to result in a permanent placement. "State governments appear to be destroying family ties of a large, and continually increasing number of children," charges Martin Guggenheim, "with no concomitant benefit to children."[203] In fact, research shows that children who end up staying in foster care fare better as adults if they maintain ties to their families than if they are cut off from their families.[204] Some experts argue that parental rights should never be terminated unless there is already a prospective adoptive parent available for the child. Nor should the state cut off a close parent-child relationship just because the child has been in foster care past a statutory deadline.[205]

The focus on severing biological ties to make room for adoptive ones assumes that adoption is the right answer for every foster child who can't be reunited with her parents. Although most experts now agree that children flourish best in stable homes, there is disagreement about the range of ways to achieve stability. Current policy is based on the assumption that there are only two routes to permanency for children in foster care—either speedy reunification with their parents or adoption into a new family. The conviction that children in the system who cannot return home must be immediately adopted is especially harmful to Black children. Because Black children have poor odds at being adopted, this view leads to pointless terminations of their parents' rights. Black children are also more likely to be placed in the care of relatives, who often do not wish to adopt them. The limited view of permanency, then, can result not only in needlessly destroying their ties with their parents but also in moving them from the homes of loving relatives. Black children's lives are frequently disrupted in the name of permanency.

Before petitioning for termination of parental rights, agencies should consider the strength of the attachment between parent and child, the likelihood of adoption, and the child's wishes, all of which are probably related to the child's age. Some adolescents and teens object to termination because they don't want to lose their relationship with their parents.

Law professor Susan Brooks was once the guardian ad litem of an eight-year-old boy named Lee who was placed in foster care when police found him wandering one night in a public housing project. He and his mother were homeless, and she was addicted to crack and alcohol. The court terminated the mother's rights when she didn't "get her act together" fast enough, and Lee remained in an overcrowded and neglectful foster home. The bright spot in Lee's life was staying in touch with his half-sister who lived with her father and paternal grandmother. The agency took a different stance on Lee's continuing ties to his family: "One day, Lee was speaking with his sister on the telephone and learned that his mother was present in the room with her. Lee's mother was sober and was visiting his sister, with whom the mother's rights had not been severed. Lee wanted to talk to his mother and to see her. Instantly, all the agency professionals involved were up in arms. They bemoaned how they would deal with the child's mother, meaning how they could disengage her from Lee's life."[206]

Lee, now ten-years-old, has been placed with another foster mother who is unwilling to adopt him, and he doesn't want to be adopted if it means never seeing his family again. Permanency plans that hinge on terminating parental rights "may make adults more comfortable, particularly adults who want to adopt children in the traditional, closed sense," writes Brooks, "but they will create undue suffering for children."[207] Although these drastic measures are enforced in the name of children's rights, they often have more to do with punishing neglectful parents and smoothing the way for adoptive parents.

There are alternatives to adoption that could ensure family stability while preserving the parent-child relationship. In a 1994 survey of children in Illinois state custody who had been living with a relative for more than one year, 85 percent of relatives reported that the best plan for the children was to remain with them until the children were grown.[208] Many of these relatives shun adoption, however, because it violates kinship norms and creates an adversarial relationship with the parents.[209] Eighty-five percent of one sample of kinship foster parents did not want to adopt.[210] After all, they are already part of the child's family. Long-term care of foster children by relatives can provide a stable home while avoiding the unnecessary tension of adoption proceedings. Children can often remain safely with kin while maintaining contact with their parents, leaving open the possibility of reunification if circumstances improve. "Children are sometimes happy living with an aunt or someone else, without seeing the need to end the legal relationship with a parent," says Stacy Platt, a

Chicago clinical professor and guardian ad litem. "These are their parents, they want to love their parents, there is a bond."[211]

Several states are experimenting with subsidized guardianship programs for kin caregivers. Guardians have more legal rights than foster parents and greater authority to make parenting decisions. But, unlike adoption, guardianship does not require termination of parental rights. Guardianship, then, adds legal permanence to the relationship between children and kin caregivers without the disruption caused by adoption.[212] Professor Garrison correctly asserts that any "justification for a policy favoring adoption over those alternatives must be based on evidence demonstrating that severance of parental ties better serves children's interests than does preservation."[213] ASFA's effect, however, may be to encourage courts to mechanically abide by statutory deadlines even when there is evidence that termination would not be in the child's best interests. And because the federal law prefers adoption to guardianship, agencies may favor nonrelative adopters over relatives who are reluctant to adopt the children in their care. Kin caregivers in Chicago charge that caseworkers are pressuring them to adopt or they risk losing the children they are raising.[214]

Terminating parental rights to free children for adoption, then, is not a win-win situation. Termination often imposes costs on children even when they are adopted. We should not let the joyful image of adoption cover up the extinction of family ties and related costs that these adoptions entail. This is not to say that it is never worth the costs of termination to enable children to grow up in more stable and caring families. This is the best course of action for many children in foster care. But we should take the toll of terminating parental rights into account in deciding individual cases and in figuring out the best strategies for reducing the foster care population.

Misidentifying the Problem with Foster Care

The pragmatic problems with the new emphasis on adoption are related to a more fundamental philosophical flaw. Congress has misidentified the foster care problem. The injustice of the American foster care system does not stem from too few children being adopted. It stems from too many children being removed from their homes. Even if all of the thousands of Black children in foster care were adopted tomorrow, the problem would not be solved. Acquiring new homes for all these children would do nothing to stem the tide of family destruction. And it would not cure the racism in the child welfare system. It would only make these injustices worse. Relying on adoption to fix the foster care system not only ignores the racial disparity in child removals but also makes the disruption of Black families permanent. When Congress stated that its aim was "to make sure that every child has the opportunity to live in a safe, stable, loving and permanent home,"[215] it had in mind terminating the rights of Black parents, not reducing poverty or building stronger supports for families.

By promoting adoption so myopically, some advocates forget that our ultimate goal should be to *reduce* the need for adoptions. In an ideal society, we would expect nearly all children to be raised by their biological families in a healthy, safe, and nurturing environment. Adoption would be a well-accepted but rare alternative for children whose parents are unable to take care of them. Although adoption is as valuable as biology as a basis for forming parent-child relationships, it typically occurs because of unfortunate circumstances—the death of parents, an unplanned pregnancy, child abuse or neglect. Most often, it results from society's inequitable distribution of the resources needed to raise children. We should therefore support adoption while working to curtail its causes. By combating poverty and its dangers to children, a more equitable society would radically decrease its need for adoption.

Professor Larry May, a philosopher at Washington University and an adoptive father, believes that my proposition that there would be fewer adoptions in an ideal society reflects a bias against adoptive parents.[216] Professor Bartholet similarly argues that government has been biased against adoption, treating it as "involving risks to be protected against, rather than benefits to be sought after." Regulators have "focused on preventing adoption from happening inappropriately," writes Bartholet. "On preventing, for example, children from being improperly separated from birth parents, or placed with unfit adoptive parents."[217]

I believe that adoptive families should have the same legal and social status as biological families once the adoption takes place. Several years ago, I wrote an article called "The Genetic Tie," which criticized the importance Americans place on genetic relatedness.[218] I called for a reconception of the genetic tie as a nonexclusive bond that forms the basis for a more important social relationship between parents and children. But I cautioned that the value we place on genetic relatedness "should be guided by a particular concern for the relational bond between less powerful parents and their children, remaining especially vigilant for policies that value the genetic tie on the basis of race." My criticism of current adoption policy is directed at the system that produces children in need of adoptive homes, not at adoption itself or at the people who adopt. Moreover, the fact that adoption is often a happy solution for adults who want to be parents does not erase the unjust circumstances that make thousands of Black children available for adoption.

It is true that government has not done enough in the past to promote adoptions of children in need of homes. It is a good idea to help state agencies find and attract potential adoptive parents and to reward people who decide to adopt. We should also work to eliminate the stigma that drives infertile couples to expensive reproductive technologies instead of adoption of children who are not genetically related to them. Adoption tax credit legislation, for example, gives some adopters needed assistance with the costs of adoption. These laws increase the odds that children with no legal parents who want to be adopted will be placed in stable and nurturing homes. But laws that divert state resources away from family preservation and that disrupt family ties as a means of facilitating adoption are another matter.

Tying Termination to Transracial Adoption

The shift in federal policy from family preservation toward adoption corresponded with the change in the federal position on transracial adoption. The relationship between these two trends was more than a coincidence of timing. The new adoption law was tied to the growing movement to remove barriers to adoption of Black children by white middle-class couples. White adoptive families are seen as a major source for reducing the large numbers of Black children in foster care. At the same time, family preservation policies are seen as a hindrance to white families' ability to adopt them. Although the federal adoption law is racially neutral on its face, its connection to transracial adoption reveals the racial politics that undergirds its popularity. Most of the biological families whose bonds the law disparages are Black, whereas most of the adoptive parents whom the law favors are white.

For decades, the federal government permitted public adoption agencies to enforce race-matching policies that sought to place Black children exclusively with Black adoptive families. But in the 1990s, after aggressive lobbying by supporters of transracial adoption, Congress took steps to remove barriers to whites willing to adopt children of other races. Transracial adoption was championed as a critical step in increasing the numbers of adoptions of Black children, the population with the lowest rate of exit from foster care. Advocates argued that race-matching policies forced Black children to languish in foster care awaiting scarce Black adoptive parents when they could have been adopted by whites. The Multiethnic Placement Act of 1994, known as MEPA, provided that agencies receiving federal funding cannot delay or deny the placement of children for adoption or in foster care solely on the basis of race. Federal guidelines still allowed agencies to consider the capacity of prospective foster or adoptive parents to meet the needs of minority children. Dissatisfied, transracial adoption advocates renewed their lobbying for an absolute elimination of racial considerations. Two years later, Congress strengthened MEPA to effectively prohibit agencies from using race at all as a factor in placement decisions.

Adoption policy has historically tracked the market for children, serving the interests of adults seeking to adopt more than the interests of children needing stable homes. Foster care and adoption have a supply and demand relationship. While the foster care system provides a source of children for adopters, adoption provides a source of homes for children in foster care. For example, in the early 1900s, child welfare officials softened the child rescue philosophy of the nineteenth century and refrained from terminating parental rights when the supply of newborns available for adoption exceeded demand.[219] In more recent decades, however, the growing demand for adoptable older children as babies became scarce helped to generate policies that free children for adoption by terminating parental rights quickly. The modern retreat from family preservation programs, much like the abolition of race-matching rules, can be seen as an effort to increase the supply of children for whites who want to adopt. The current interest of white couples in adopting Black children stems from the shortage of adoptable white babies, whose soaring price tag reflects their market value. *Roe v. Wade*'s protection of women's right to abortion and the diminished social stigma attached to single motherhood have drastically cut the numbers of white women who give up their babies for adoption, creating what has been called the "White Baby Famine." Until recently, the number of adoptions in the United States steadily declined since reaching a peak of 175,000 in 1970.[220]

All of the literature advocating the elimination of racial considerations in child placements focuses on making it easier for white people to adopt Black children. For example, a leading book on the subject states that "in the case of transracial adoption the children are non-white and the adoptive parents are white."[221] Transracial adoption advocates don't mention the possibility of Blacks adopting white children. Nor do they acknowledge that most race-matching in adoption involves matching white adoptive parents with white children. Child welfare agencies routinely allow whites to choose the white foster children they prefer. Stanford law professor Richard Banks argues that it is this facilitation of whites' preferences for white children—not barriers to transracial adoption—that is mainly responsible for low Black adoption rates.[222] White people's demand for white children isn't seen as a race-based claim, whereas the position that Black children belong with Black adoptive parents is. Banks contends that both types of racial classification are unconstitutional: when government agencies fulfill adoptive parents' racial preferences they are engaging in racial discrimination. Although the end of race-matching was defended as serving the interests of Black foster children, it has helped to create a system that protects the rights of white adults to have access to the children of their choice.[223]

Congressional and media discussions of ASFA linked family preservation policies to white middle-class couples' difficulties in adopting Black children in foster care. For example, a *U.S. News and World Report* article titled "Adoption Gridlock" began with the story of a white North Carolina physician and his wife who resorted to adopting two Romanian orphans after several American agencies rejected their offer to adopt a Black child.[224] This article and others implied that the emphasis on reunifying Black children with their biological families unfairly prevented white couples from adopting American children. The rhetoric supporting ASFA praised reforms in federal child welfare policy for removing the twin barriers to adoption—race-matching restrictions and prolonged family preservation efforts. Terminating parents' rights faster and abolishing race-matching policies were linked as a strategy for increasing adoptions of Black children by white families. Connecting these two issues—family preservation and transracial adoption—allowed commentators to claim that the foster care problem could be solved by moving more Black children from their families into white adoptive homes.

Professor Bartholet, one of the most outspoken and influential advocates of transracial adoption, also explicitly makes this connection. Her book, *Nobody's Children*, provides the most thorough articulation of the rationale that links the assault on family preservation to the promotion of transracial adoption. Her arguments were instrumental in the passage of the recent federal legislation abolishing race-matching policies. Bartholet contends that because there are so many Black children in foster care, it will be "very hard to find qualified and interested same-race families for all the children in need of foster or adoptive homes."[225] She proposes a vision of child welfare that would permit more poor Black children to be removed from their communities and adopted by white middle-class families.

Bartholet assails just about every protection of Black children's ties to family, community, and culture as harmful to children and an impediment to adoption by more privileged people. She ridicules the interest in preserving Black cultural heritage as "romantic" by pointing out that most children in state custody come from "neighborhoods which are the least supportive environments for children and families."[226] According to Bartholet, entire communities breed child abuse and neglect and should be treated as inferior venues to raise children. "We should be willing to face up to the fact that child maltreatment is only rarely aberrational," Bartholet argues. "It ordinarily grows out of a family and community context. Keeping the child in that same family and community will often serve the child no better than keeping him or her with the maltreating parent."[227]

The idea of transplanting disadvantaged children is not new. Charles Loring Brace, founder of the New York Children's Aid Society in 1853, espoused a similar philosophy when he sent destitute city children to work on farms in the Midwest. "More and more, Brace became convinced of the futility of helping dependent and delinquent children save by transplanting them (while still saplings) to new environments," writes historian Walter Trattner.[228] For several decades, the New York Children's Aid Society's "orphan trains" transported more than 110,000 needy children of Irish, Italian, and Eastern European descent to be raised in rural Protestant homes.[229]

Bartholet therefore denounces kinship care. She characterizes placement with relatives as a devious way of avoiding federal prohibitions against race-matching. "Private foundations and nonprofit child welfare groups have joined forces with public agencies to promote kinship care," she claims, "in part to help ensure that children in need of homes remain within their racial group."230 Because she sees entire poor Black communities as unfit, she doubts the qualifications of relative caretakers. "Often the blood kin are plagued by the same problems and victims of the same circumstances as the child's parents," Bartholet writes. "The extended kinship group has to be seen as a high risk group for parenting purposes."231

Bartholet opposes not only policies that reserve Black children for Black foster and adoptive families but any attention to race at all in making placement decisions. Using race as a factor in any aspect of placement might interfere with a white person's chances of adopting a Black child. She objects to demands for social work practice to be more sensitive to cultural differences as a "euphemistic cover" for race-matching. "'Cultural competence' is one of the code phrases in the post-MEPA era," Bartholet charges, "for assessing whether agencies remain sufficiently committed to same-race matching and are doing enough to recruit families of color to make same-race placement possible."232 Similarly, MEPA's requirement that state agencies recruit prospective foster and adoptive parents reflecting the racial diversity of children needing homes, says Bartholet, is also used to undermine the law's central goal of promoting transracial adoption. She sees state efforts to attract more Black foster and adoptive families as hindering opportunities for whites to adopt.

Transracial adoption becomes especially explosive in the context of terminating parental rights to free children for adoption. Tensions between biological parents and pre-adoptive parents increasingly take on a racial cast. Cities across the country have been riveted by contests between Black biological mothers and white foster parents who want to adopt their children. The *Baby T* case, mentioned in Part One, was a hot news item in Chicago for several months. The case pitted a thirty-seven-year-old Black mother, Tina Olison, who lost custody of her son when he was born cocaine-exposed, against one of Chicago's most powerful white couples, Alderman Edward Burke and Appellate Court Judge Anne Burke, who had been his foster parents for nearly three years. Having complied with the child welfare agency's permanency plan,

Olison sought to regain custody of her son. She successfully completed parenting classes and drug treatment programs, earned a certified nursing assistant certificate, found an apartment, and held down two jobs. But the Illinois Department of Children and Family Services abandoned its goal of returning Baby T to his mother when an independent agency questioned Olison's parenting abilities. The agency reported that Olison displayed an "intense and menacing anger" toward clinicians. As evidence of Olison's poor parenting skills, a caseworker testified that Olison once fed Baby T a Cheeto at thirteen months. Instead, DCFS petitioned to terminate Olison's parental rights to permit the Burkes to adopt the boy.

The case sparked alarm among Blacks that the Burkes had benefited from both political clout and racial privilege. It resurrected arguments over whether a white couple could truly love a Black baby, especially since Ed Burke had been the nemesis of Chicago's first Black mayor, Harold Washington. The spectacle included a vigil by a South Side minister and his parishioners, who marched in front of Burke's home, pushing an empty baby stroller, and vowed to fast until the Burkes returned Baby T. Members of the African American community held fund-raisers to help Olison defray her legal costs.

Others, however, argued that the Burkes should be commended for caring for the baby and that the bond between them superseded Baby T's biological tie to his mother. Public Guardian Patrick Murphy, Cook County's chief advocate for children, sided with Olison at first, blasting DCFS for predetermining that the Burkes should adopt Baby T regardless of his mother's efforts to regain custody. He called the case "the worst social worker/legal lynching I've ever seen." Murphy later reversed his position when Olison became more combative in her fight for custody. Whereas DCFS emphasized the amount of time the child had spent with his foster parents, Olison's advocates noted that she had been drug free since her son was only six weeks old—why hadn't the family been reunited sooner? Was Olison forced to jump over extra hurdles just to facilitate Baby T's adoption by a more privileged couple? And was she being punished for showing justifiable resistance to official destruction of her relationship with her child?

The *Chicago Tribune* closely covered the parental fitness hearing in juvenile court for three weeks, including detailed descriptions of testimony, moving color photographs of the parties, interviews with experts, and explanations of the state procedures for terminating parental rights.[233] It was an unusual display of attention to the kind of custody hearing concerning a Black child that takes place in Chicago juvenile court every day. The Baby T case became a cause célèbre not only because of the notoriety of the foster parents but also because of their race. The case was transferred to Kane County judge Judith Brawka because Olison feared she could not get a fair hearing in Cook County, where Anne Burke presides. After a nineteen-day trial costing an estimated $3 million, Judge Brawka decided not to terminate Olison's rights but ruled that Olison was not ready to regain custody of Baby T. Baby T continues to live with the Burkes, with court-monitored visitation with his mother.

These contests bring to the surface a theme that runs more subtly through some of the discourse supporting transracial adoption—the belief that Black children fare better if raised by white adoptive families than if returned home. Advocates of transracial adoption frequently assert the benefits of racial assimilation that Black children and white parents experience by living together. In her previous book, *Family Bonds,* Bartholet rejects the claim that Black children belong with Black parents not only because "there is no evidence that black parents do a better job than white parents of raising black children with a sense of pride in their racial background," but also because black children reap substantial advantages from a white environment.[234] Unlike Black children "living in a state of relative isolation or exclusion from the white world," Bartholet contends, "black children raised in white homes are comfortable with their blackness and also uniquely comfortable in dealing with whites." As in the rhetoric promoting ASFA, the rhetoric promoting transracial adoption supports the dissolution of poor Black families by depicting adoptive homes as superior to children's existing family relationships.

The picture painted by the media and advocates of transracial adoption as a panacea for the foster care crisis bears little connection to the real world adoption market. The transracial adoption issue is a red herring. It diverts attention from the main harms the child welfare system inflicts on Black families. The white couples the public envisions as adoptive parents are typically not interested in the poor Black children who make up the bulk of the foster care population. The vast majority of white adoptive parents are only willing to take a white child. Wealthier couples prefer to use private agencies or lawyers and are willing to pay $10,000 to $30,000—even as much as $100,000—in fees to arrange the adoption of a white baby.[235] In fact, private domestic adoptions account for more than one-third of U.S. adoptions, while only 16 percent of adopted children come from public agencies. The balance are stepparent, kinship, and overseas adoptions. Infertile whites have even started "adopting" the embryos left over from other white couples' attempts to conceive through in vitro fertilization. In 1993, only 1 to 4 percent of adoptions were adoptions of Black children by white parents.[236] The abolition of race-matching policies has not led to a surge in these numbers. Most of the people who adopt Black foster children are middle-aged Black women who often are relatives or foster parents.[237]

Even when they adopt outside their race, whites generally prefer non-Black children of Asian or Latin American heritage. Many travel to distant countries to avoid the American foster care system. There are about 20,000 children adopted from abroad each year—about 15 percent of the total number of adoptions.[238] Congress recently changed the immigration laws to permit these children to automatically become United States citizens, removing a significant hassle involved in foreign adoptions. "It's at long last a recognition that a child of American parents, whether born here or adopted overseas, is an American, and there's no distinction between the two," announced the bill's sponsor, Representative Bill Delahunt.[239] When *ABC Evening News* reported the gala in Boston's Faneuil Hall in February 2001 celebrating the new citizenship of 75,000 adoptees, the cameras panned a sea of white parents holding Asian and Eastern European children. "Of dozens of white adopting parents I have interviewed in three years," reported Mary Jo McConahay in the *Los Angeles Times,* "almost all said they would consider adopting a Latino child abroad before a black child at home."[240] Gloria Hochman of the National Adoption Center, a federally funded adoption registry, agrees. If these adoptive parents "could have adopted a healthy white infant in this country, they would not have gone overseas."[241] The notion that state agencies are turning away thousands of white parents anxious to adopt Black foster children is ludicrous. Yet this mirage is held out as a reason for opposing policies that preserve Black families.

4. Welfare Reform:
Ending Aid to Poor Children

THE PASSAGE OF THE FEDERAL ADOPTION LAW corresponded with the growing disparagement of mothers receiving public assistance and welfare reform's retraction of the federal safety net for poor children. In the public's mind, these undeserving mothers—just like the unfit mothers in the child welfare system—are Black. The rejection of public aid to poor families in favor of private solutions to poverty—low-wage work, marriage, and child support—mirrored the appeal to adoption to fix the public foster care system. This intersection of welfare and adoption reform is only the latest chapter in a long history of intimately related policies addressing children's poverty. Public assistance to poor families and programs dealing with neglected children are two sides of the same coin. Yet Americans' compassion toward poor children has always existed in tension with the impulse to blame their parents. The reason that child welfare's problems seem so intractable, writes Nina Bernstein in her book about reforming foster care, lies in "the unacknowledged contradictions between policies that punish the 'undeserving poor' and pledges to help all needy children."[242] Racism has consistently led to a resolution of this tension that refuses adequate social support for families and hurts Black families the most.

The Adoption and Safe Families Act was passed on the heels of the overhaul of federal welfare policy. The Personal Responsibility and Work Opportunity Reconciliation Act of 1996 ended the federal guarantee of cash assistance to America's children and allowed states to implement extensive welfare reform programs. The federal entitlement program, Aid to Families with Dependent Children (AFDC), was replaced by Temporary Assistance to Needy Families (TANF), which provides benefits for a limited time while recipients look for work. The overlap of these two laws marked the first time in U.S. history that "states have a federal mandate to protect children from abuse and neglect but no corresponding mandate to provide basic economic support to poor families."[243] Welfare-to-work programs have helped some poor mothers find jobs and improve their ability to support their children. But state welfare reform measures hinder the ability of many others to care for their children: they reduce cash assistance to families, eliminate payments to some families altogether, and require mothers, often without adequate child care, to work and participate in job training, counseling, and other programs.[244]

What will happen to the children of mothers who fail to meet new work rules because of child care or transportation problems, who are unable to find work within the two-year time limit, or who leave their children at home without adequate care while they participate in required work programs? It is likely that some of them will be removed from their mother's custody and placed in foster care. "Whatever its limitation, the AFDC program complemented the child welfare services system," writes social work professor Mark Courtney. "It provided a base of financial support to poor families regardless of whether parents chose or were able to work."[245] With that base kicked out from under families, the child welfare system is bound to catch some of the falling children.

The Connected Roots of
Public Aid and Child Welfare

During the Progressive Era, women successfully exploited the ideology of motherhood to win public relief for unmarried and widowed mothers living in poverty.[246] The logic that propelled this welfare policy was precisely the opposite of that backing welfare reform today: widowed and single mothers needed government aid so that they would not have to relinquish their maternal duties in the home to join the wage labor force. The rationale for mothers' pensions was also directly related to child welfare policy. Offering destitute mothers public assistance prevented the need to place their children in orphanages and asylums. The nation's leading child welfare experts declared welfare's mission at the first White House Conference on Children, convened in 1909: "Children of reasonably efficient and deserving mothers who are without the support of the normal breadwinner should, as a rule, be kept with their parents, such aid being given as may be necessary to maintain suitable homes for the rearing of children." This maternalist rhetoric was powerful enough to mobilize disenfranchised women, defeat conservative opponents, and convince American legislatures to embark on social welfare programs far ahead of those of most European countries. Mothers' aid, initially provided through state and local programs, laid the groundwork for the modern federal welfare system.

In some respects, the Progressive women's crusade achieved a remarkable transformation of Americans' understanding of public welfare. Until then, local asylums or poorhouses doled out paltry relief to the "worthy" poor alone. Only those stricken by natural calamity, such as the blind, deaf, or insane, and orphaned children, were deemed deserving of any public assistance. The mothers' aid programs not only rejected the prevailing laissez-faire approach to poverty but also "sought to remove relief from the stigma of pauperism and the poorhouse," writes historian Linda Gordon in *Pitied But Not Entitled: Single Mothers and the History of Welfare.*[247] Nonetheless, the benefits fell far short of meeting the needs of female-headed families. Part of the problem was the reformers' adherence to the traditional notion that wives should rely on their husband's wages to support the family.

Just as important were the reformers' prejudices about the poor women they were trying to help. The Progressive welfare movement was marred by the elitism of the privileged, white activist network that led it. A defining aspect of its welfare vision was the social control of poor immigrant families and the total neglect of Black women.[248] The reformers feared that welfare might provide an incentive for state dependency, moral degeneracy, and family breakdown. So reformers reached a compromise. "Benefits that would have been set higher if based solely on the worthiness of children had to be tempered by the suspect worthiness of their parents," explains social work scholar Leroy Pelton. "Thus, benefits would fall at some in-between value."[249] This is why the public has always been willing "to support needy children more generously in institutions or foster homes than with their own parents."

Immigrant women were the primary objects of Progressives' moral concern. Worried about urban immigrants' threat to the social order, the reformers treated welfare as a means of supervising and disciplining recipients as much as a means of providing charity. According to this social work perspective, the cure for mothers' poverty lay in socializing foreign relief recipients to conform to "American" family standards. Aid generally was conditioned on compliance with "suitable home" provisions and often administered by juvenile court judges who specialized in punitive and rehabilitative judgments.

Black single mothers, on the other hand, were simply excluded. The first maternalist welfare legislation was meant for white mothers only. Whereas European immigrants could be assimilated through cultural reform efforts, Blacks stood outside the bounds of redemption. Administrators either failed to establish programs in locations with large Black populations or distributed benefits according to standards, such as suitable home tests, that disqualified Black mothers. In 1931, the first national survey of mothers' pensions broken down by race found that only 3 percent of recipients were Black.[250]

The New Deal solidified welfare's stratification along racial as well as gender lines. Social insurance (Social Security and unemployment insurance) provided a dignified entitlement primarily to white, male wage earners and their wives. Aid to Dependent Children, the precursor to Aid to Families with Dependent Children, was created primarily for white mothers, who were not expected to work. ADC handed out paltry, discretionary relief to mothers who met not only means standards but also degrading morals tests. The New Deal regime, then, incorporated the most limiting aspects of the early reformers' view of poor relief—the reliance on male wages to meet the needs of families and the moral supervision of mothers receiving aid. It also continued the racist exclusion of Black mothers based on discretionary standards. Southern states notoriously expelled thousands of Black children from their welfare rolls in the 1950s because their mothers weren't married.[251] Moreover, Black recipients received smaller stipends, on the grounds that "blacks needed less to live on than whites."[252]

It took three decades for the civil rights movement to open the welfare system to Blacks. A federal directive requiring states to abandon suitable home standards for eligibility eliminated one of the chief barriers to Black mothers' inclusion. At the same time, the federal government inserted itself into state policy regarding the removal of neglected children from homes receiving welfare. With federal encouragement, state ADC eligibility workers began taking Black children away from mothers deemed unsuitable instead of simply denying benefits. Congress amended Title IV of the Social Security Act in 1961 to provide federal funds to maintain these children in foster homes.[253] Federal foster care funding was first provided under ADC and later AFDC, until it got its own program under Title IV-E in 1980—another example of the close connection between public aid and child welfare programs. With the growing numbers of Blacks in the welfare caseloads came the stigma of "welfare dependency," work requirements, and reduced effective benefit levels. The image of the welfare mother transmuted from the worthy white widow to the immoral Black "welfare queen."

Just as the origins of the public aid and child welfare systems were linked at the beginning of the twentieth century, so their fates were linked at the century's end. If welfare was created to avoid the removal of needy children from their mothers, then eliminating welfare must have implications for child welfare policy. A number of conservatives explicitly voiced this connection in the welfare reform debate. They anticipated that abolishing guaranteed federal aid to poor families would increase the child welfare caseloads. In fact, depriving poor women of parental rights appeared to be the goal of some pundits and politicians. Charles Murray, whose writings about "welfare dependency" undergirded the overhaul, proposed back in 1993 sending recipients' children to orphanages.[254] "Those who prattle about the importance of keeping children with their biological mothers," he wrote, "may wish to spend some time in a patrol car or with a social worker seeing what the reality of life with welfare-dependent biological mothers can be like." Republican Speaker of the House Newt Gingrich ran with the idea. In promoting his "Contract with America," the precursor to the welfare reform law, he argued that government funds supporting poor mothers should be diverted to programs that would put their babies up for adoption or place them in orphanages.[255] Welfare reform, observes Nina Bernstein, resurrected the conviction that "parents who cannot rear their children without public aid are almost by definition unfit to bring up the next generation."[256]

Images from *Oliver Twist* made orphanages unseemly to many people. But Republicans adopted the basic concept in other welfare reform policies. Governor Pete Wilson used his administrative powers to add information about relinquishing children for adoption to the packet given to mothers registering for welfare in California. When families exhaust public assistance, "I think you're looking at a situation where the county is going to have to take custody of the child and do one of two things: either find a foster parent or find an adoptive parent," Wilson explained at a press conference. "The child's well-being has to come first."[257]

New York City Mayor Rudolph Giuliani implemented a policy in fall 1999 that required the homeless to work as a condition of shelter.[258] Those who failed to comply, he announced, would be expelled from shelters and their children placed in foster care. When twenty-two-year-old Eve Engesser violated the rule, child welfare authorities seized her two sons, ages eight and four, from a Suffolk County shelter and placed them in foster care. A state court overturned the shelter rule within a few months for violating a court decree that guaranteed homeless people the right to shelter.

Congress also incorporated the idea of taking children from destitute mothers. Children meeting AFDC eligibility standards are no longer guaranteed federal aid in their parents' home, but they are still entitled to federal foster care assistance in a stranger's home. Leroy Pelton cuts to the heart of the relationship between welfare reform and child removal: "If we cannot defend the societal neglect of innocent children, let us separate them in a manner that they can be treated differently than their mothers."[259] The public tries to absolve itself of the obligation to support poor families by calling the negative consequences of welfare reform "child neglect" and holding mothers responsible.

Welfare reform in the 1990s is diametrically opposed to the welfare philosophy of the Progressive reformers. We seem to have regressed in our thinking about poor families to the time of asylums and orphan trains. What caused so much erosion of Americans' sense of social responsibility for poor children? The modern welfare state has increasingly degraded the caregiving work all women perform. As growing numbers of women join the workforce, society decreasingly rewards mothers' labor in the home. An individual's entitlement to government assistance now depends on his or her relationship to the market. Former workers are entitled to compensation by social insurance programs for their prior participation in the wage labor force.[260] As unpaid caregivers with no connection to a male breadwinner, single mothers are considered undeserving clients of the welfare system. The main objective of welfare reform is to push single mothers to replace the welfare checks they use to support their children with a salary or a husband.

Feminists have long decried this devaluation of mothers' work in the home and campaigned for some form of public compensation for it. Economics journalist Ann Crittenden recently popularized this campaign in *The Price of Motherhood: Why the Most Important Job in the World Is Still the Least Valued*.[261] Crittenden decided to write the book when she had a baby. She calculated that by leaving her job at the *New York Times* so that she could spend more time with her son, she sacrificed more than half of her lifetime earnings. Crittenden argues that the reduced earnings of mothers constitute a "mommy tax" that can easily run college-educated women more than $1 million. "For working-class women," she writes, "there is increasing evidence both in the United States and worldwide that mothers' differential responsibility for children, rather than classic sex discrimination, is the most important factor disposing women to poverty."[262] Yet the tremendous contributions that these mothers make go unrecognized and unrewarded.

The devaluation of caregiving does not fall evenly on all mothers. Maternalist thinking no longer justifies public aid because the public views this aid as benefiting primarily Black mothers. The public devalues Black mothers' work in particular because it sees these mothers as inherently unfit and even affirmatively harmful to their children. There is little reason, then, to support their caregiving work at home. To the contrary, contemporary poverty discourse blames Black single mothers for perpetuating poverty by transmitting a deviant lifestyle to their children. Far from helping children, this view holds, payments to Black single mothers merely encourage this transgenerational pathology.

This disrespect was once tied to guaranteeing a supply of poor Black mothers to do menial chores in white people's homes. New Deal Democrats from the North struck a deal with their Southern brethren that systematically denied Blacks eligibility for social insurance benefits.[263] Federal programs allowed states to define eligibility standards and excluded agricultural workers and domestic servants in a deliberate effort to maintain a Black menial labor caste in the South. Whites feared that Social Security would make both recipients and those freed from the burden of supporting dependents less willing to accept low wages.[264]

During the 1960s, congressional debate over adding mandatory work provisions to the welfare laws included white people's interest in keeping poor Black mothers available for cheap domestic service. As Senator Russell Long argued in 1967, "Either I do the housework or Mrs. Long does the housework, or we get somebody to come in and help us, but someone has to do it, and it does seem to me that if we can qualify these people to accept any employment doing something constructive, that is better than simply having them sitting at home drawing welfare money."[265] Five years later, Southern white politicians similarly helped to defeat the Family Assistance Plan, which would have provided for a guaranteed income, by arguing, "There's not going to be anybody left to roll these wheelbarrows and press these shirts."[266]

Welfare reform resuscitates this view of Black mothers' work. New policies devalue poor Black women's caregiving in their own homes while pushing them into menial housework for others. A cartoon by Wasserman in the *Boston Globe* on the eve of welfare reform suggests this motivation behind work requirements. It shows a politician holding a document labeled "Welfare Reform" while talking to a woman accompanied by her two young children:

> Politician: "You are a bad mother."
> Welfare mother: "Why?"
> Politician: "You hang around the house taking care of the kids. We'll cut you off if you don't take a job."
> Welfare mother: "Doing what?"
> Politician: "Taking care of someone else's kids."[267]

From the Welfare Rolls to the Child Welfare Rolls?

The welfare law's key provisions all affect poor parents' ability to care for their children. The law eliminates the federal safety net for poor children established as part of the New Deal more than sixty years ago. It replaces the federal guarantee of cash assistance for single mothers and their children, AFDC, with the TANF block grant. States now have wide discretion in deciding how they want to spend these funds. AFDC benefits were already set so low that they left families in poverty. Parents had to supplement their welfare checks with unreported income just to survive.

Sociologists Kathryn Edin and Laura Lein set out to uncover how single welfare mothers could possibly raise their children on such meager amounts. They found that poor mothers use welfare benefits to supplement low wages and other sources of income and to tide them over during bouts of unemployment. "Neither welfare nor work provided enough income for families to live on," Edin and Lein report in *Making Ends Meet: How Single Mothers Survive Welfare and Low-Wage Work*.[268] "Because of this, all but one of the 379 mothers we spoke with engaged in other income-generating strategies to supplement their income and ensure their economic survival." The sole mother who relied exclusively on welfare, they note, failed to give her child adequate food and clothing and risked losing custody on grounds of neglect.

Under the TANF block grant, states are free to make benefits even lower than under AFDC. The federal law also places strict limits on mothers' receipt of benefits. The centerpiece of welfare reform is the mandate that all able parents must work in return for the government's financial support. Instead of an entitlement, welfare is now conceived as short-term assistance to families until parents find a job. The general guideline is that parents must start working within two years of their initial receipt of federal aid. But states can require recipients to find jobs even faster.

To foster compliance, states require recipients to engage in work-related activities or to participate in specific work programs. The federal law also establishes a five-year lifetime limit for parents to receive TANF benefits. Once again, states have the option of setting a shorter time limit. They may exempt up to 20 percent of their average monthly caseload from these work requirements and deadlines in cases of extreme hardship or domestic violence, but implementation is left to state discretion. Parents who don't comply with the new rules are "sanctioned"—punished with reductions in their benefits or even elimination of their benefits altogether. Most states impose "full-family sanctions," which eliminate the entire family's cash grant, for continued noncompliance with work requirements. Families can also lose food stamps and medical insurance for adults. Recipients can be sanctioned for declining an undesirable work assignment, failing to attend a class, missing an appointment, or not submitting required paperwork.

Welfare reform's impact on child welfare hinges largely on whether work mandates are actually pulling families out of poverty. On the one hand, work requirements combined with skills training and other employment-related services have helped many mothers to find jobs. Those who are earning decent salaries can probably take better care of their children. Many mothers, on the other hand, are being forced off the welfare rolls into low-paying jobs or unemployment, leaving them with fewer resources to support their children. These desperate parents, who may be unable to afford basic food, shelter, and medical care for their children, are at greater risk of entering the child welfare system.

There is already a striking overlap between families receiving welfare and families involved with the child welfare system. Children of welfare recipients are at the greatest risk for referral to child protection services because of their families' extreme poverty.[269] Researchers estimate that about half of all families referred to state child welfare authorities were receiving welfare at the time.[270] In Illinois, for example, the families of 40 percent of the children in foster care received AFDC in the month they were reported to the child welfare department. An additional 20 percent of foster children came from families that had some active association with AFDC but were not receiving cash benefits.[271] Any reduction in the resources these families have to support their children, then, is likely to have an impact on child welfare caseloads. During the debate on welfare reform, the Children's Defense Fund estimated that for every 1 percent increase in the number of children who lost cash assistance, there would be a 22 percent increase in the foster care population.

Is there any evidence that welfare reform has increased the rate of involvement in the child welfare system? The jury is still out on welfare reform's impact on children. State officials are congratulating themselves for painlessly reducing their welfare caseloads. By the end of 2000, work requirements had slashed the nation's welfare rolls in half.[272] Every state posted substantial declines in the number of recipients. A recent study examining the effects of welfare reform failed to detect any major fallout on the child welfare system.[273] In Illinois, in fact, child welfare caseloads have fallen since the federal welfare law was passed. Cook County Public Guardian Patrick Murphy attributes this decline to the elimination of welfare incentives for poor teen girls to have babies.[274]

But it is too soon to declare welfare reform a victory for children's welfare. There are signs that the glowing figures hide the true story of family suffering. What has happened to the millions of families that exited welfare? Amazingly, there are no national surveys that track them carefully. Studies indicate that only about one-third of mothers who left the welfare rolls are working full-time. The rest are working part-time or not at all. Those who found jobs earn extremely low wages, on average only $6.75 an hour.[275] Many take home less than what they received on welfare. In New York, for example, 28 percent of former recipients work an average of thirty hours a week but can't lift their families out of poverty.[276] Barbara Ehrenreich confirmed for herself that even holding two low-wage jobs with no children to support barely brings in enough to pay the rent. She spent three months in Florida, Maine, and Minnesota passing herself off as an unskilled worker and found it was impossible to earn a living wage at the low end of the labor market. In contrast to the U.S. welfare system, Ehrenreich writes in *Nickel and Dimed: On (Not) Getting By in America*, "most civilized nations compensate for the inadequacy of wages by providing relatively generous public services such as health insurance, free or subsidized child care, subsidized housing, and effective public transportation."[277] Welfare reform expects families to get by on poverty wages with the puniest social support system in the industrialized world. One welfare-to-work program advised recipients to make ends meet by rummaging for food in trash dumpsters.

A sizable number of mothers were thrown off state welfare rolls because they were sanctioned, not because they found work. Shortly after welfare reform was implemented in the Mississippi Delta, Jason DeParle reported in the *New York Times*, "the families dropped for violating the new work rules outnumbered those placed in jobs by a margin of nearly two to one." After reviewing the available evidence, three public health researchers conclude: "The handful of methodologically acceptable studies of women leaving TANF indicate that although many are indeed finding employment, job retention and persistent poverty appear to be significant problems."[278]

Cities across the country are showing signs of family deprivation. Take, for instance, the state of poor families in Milwaukee since former Wisconsin governor Tommy Thompson (now Secretary of Health and Human Services in the Bush administration) replaced cash assistance with strict work requirements. Demand for food assistance has increased by 30 percent. Homeless shelters have reached capacity. Infant mortality has increased almost 40 percent in the Black community.[279] In February 2001, the number of homeless people sleeping in New York City's shelters rose above 25,000 for the first time since the 1980s.[280] Women and children accounted for the largest increases. The U.S. Conference of Mayors reported in 1999 that, despite the economic boom, visits to soup kitchens and food banks climbed by almost 20 percent.[281]

How can it be that welfare reform has moved so many mothers into jobs while increasing despair among poor families at the same time? The answer has to do with the effects of tough work requirements on families with varying life situations. Although recipients with good skills, health, and support networks have been able to take advantage of state work programs, the most disadvantaged families have sunken deeper into poverty. This is why child poverty rates have declined to their lowest level in decades but *extreme* poverty—income below 50 percent of the poverty line—has been growing.[282] Even Ron Haskins, a Republican who helped draft the welfare reform law, concedes that "there is a group of mothers at the bottom who are worse off as a result of welfare reform."[283]

Black single mothers are faring the worst of all. "Despite the long period of economic growth," notes welfare scholar Joel Handler, "the labor market has deteriorated for women, mostly with children, mostly black, and mostly without a high school diploma."[284] Not only are Black mothers less equipped for jobs, but they confront racial discrimination when they apply. They are also more likely to live in areas of concentrated poverty where jobs are scarce. In most states, whites are leaving welfare for employment faster than Blacks.[285] The *Chicago Reporter*'s analysis of data from the Illinois Department of Human Services revealed that "a higher percentage of white aid recipients leave the system with jobs, while many more minority recipients are removed because they fail to comply with state rules."[286] Less than a third of all recipients who left the Illinois welfare rolls in 1998 and 1999 earned enough money to no longer qualify for benefits. Half of the closed cases involved recipients who were dropped for failing to comply with the TANF rules. There was a stark racial disparity in these two categories. Forty percent of white leavers had sufficient income, compared to 27 percent of minorities. And whereas 39 percent of white leavers were sanctioned, 54 percent of minorities fell in this category. The greater difficulty that Black recipients face in finding jobs is reflected in the changing demographics of the welfare population. The proportion of Blacks and other minorities has grown under welfare reform.[287] In some states, Blacks on welfare now outnumber whites for the first time.

Moreover, the successes of welfare-to-work programs may be reversed if the economy slides into recession. Most experts agree that the triumph of welfare reform depended on the unprecedented prosperity America enjoyed in the years after it went into effect. The economy already looked gloomier when President George W. Bush took office at the beginning of 2001. Recession is bad for all workers, but mothers who have recently left the welfare rolls are the most vulnerable. Because they lack seniority and may only work part-time, they are likely to be the first ones fired. Welfare reform facilitates the transition to work but makes no provision for recipients who lose their jobs. "The two big safety nets they could turn to for support in earlier recessions—unemployment and welfare benefits—have become markedly shredded," notes *New York Times* reporter Peter Kilborn.[288] Former recipients working part-time or sporadically at low-wage jobs may not qualify for unemployment benefits, which are tied to prior earnings, and they may be excluded by time limits from collecting welfare again.

In the event of an economic downturn, there won't be enough jobs for welfare recipients who need them. "There are not enough relevant, geographically accessible jobs available to employ the 3 million-plus people who have to find work," observes Peter Edelman, who resigned from the Clinton administration in protest over welfare reform.[289] This is already the case in some economically depressed parts of the country. Frank Howell, a researcher at Mississippi State University, projected the development of only one new job in the Mississippi Delta for every 254 families exiting welfare.[290] In Milwaukee, there are six job seekers for every opening.[291] As more and more families start hitting the five-year lifetime limit for receiving public assistance, they will be competing for fewer and fewer low-wage jobs. New York State is bracing for the end of 2001, when 71,400 families—nearly a third of the state's welfare recipients—exhaust their lifetime benefits.[292] State officials opted to institute a local program known as Safety Net to absorb families permanently denied federal aid.

We can predict what will happen to child maltreatment rates by examining past experiences with welfare reductions. One study found that child abuse and neglect referrals in Los Angeles County rose 12 percent following AFDC grant reductions of 2.7 percent. An additional 5.8 percent cut in benefits resulted in a 20 percent increase in maltreatment reports and 10 percent increase in children entering the child welfare system.[293] Families who leave welfare without finding employment are three times more likely to become involved with the child protection system than unemployed families who receive welfare benefits.[294] It is *income insecurity*, not welfare receipt, that is the best predictor of foster care placement.[295] Children are better off with parents who at least have the stability of a welfare check than parents who have no source of income at all. Parents without stable income may feel greater stress, a risk factor in child maltreatment. "Welfare reforms that increase parental stress or cause parents to be more harsh and punitive may have negative consequences for children," warn Ann Collins and J. Lawrence Aber of the National Center for Children in Poverty.[296]

Increasing the income of welfare recipients, on the other hand, has been shown to reduce rates of child abuse and neglect.[297] One study found that Texas counties with higher average monthly AFDC expenditures per child had lower reporting of child abuse and neglect. A Washington State study discovered that providing AFDC families with child care income deductions, allowing them to retain more disposable income, lowered child neglect reporting rates. A January 2001 evaluation of welfare-to-work policies in six states compared various program features in terms of their effects on children's school performance, behavior, and health.[298] The researchers found that the programs that included earnings supplements had positive effects on elementary school-aged children. Programs that offered financial rewards—either by providing families with cash supplements or increasing the amount parents could keep when they worked—benefited children more than mandatory employment services. "Welfare reforms and antipoverty programs can have a positive impact on children's development," the study concluded, "*if they increase employment and income.*"

Although welfare reform has not yet led to a general swelling of child welfare caseloads, the hardest hit families have lost children to foster care. A recent *New York Times* article on Wisconsin's welfare plan reports that 5 percent of mothers removed from public assistance have been forced to "abandon their children."[299] One California county imposes "full family" sanctions for a recipient's failure to comply with program requirements, cutting off payments for parents and children. The termination of benefits, in turn, triggers a mandatory home visit by a welfare caseworker, who may then notify child protective services.[300]

Welfare-to-work programs may not rescue enough families from poverty to offset the numbers forced into the child welfare system by time limits, sanctions, and working conditions. States have the option of giving child-only grants to these families. They can also consider families with children at risk of entering foster care as meeting the hardship test and exempt them from the time limit. But the federal law leaves these determinations to state discretion. According to poverty lawyer Martha Matthews, "welfare to work program successes seem unlikely to decrease significantly the demand for child welfare services, or even offset the impact on child welfare systems of families whose economic circumstances are worsened by time limits and sanctions."[301] In short, welfare reform may cause a net increase in the number of children entering foster care.

A recent study by child welfare researchers Christina Paxson and Jane Waldfogel suggests that the most punitive aspects of welfare reform have already caused an increase in child maltreatment and foster care placement.[302] Examining state-level child welfare data spanning 1990 to 1998, Paxson and Waldfogel controlled for other changes that were occurring at the same time as welfare initiatives. They found evidence that strict lifetime limits and tougher sanctions for noncompliance are related to higher maltreatment rates. All else being equal, states that have adopted full family sanctions have experienced a 21 percent increase in the number of substantiated cases of maltreatment. The imposition of immediate work requirements is associated with a 9 percent increase in foster care placement. The study found the strongest link between lowering benefits and increases in the numbers of children entering out-of-home care. Conversely, a 10 percent increase in benefit levels reduced neglect by 32 percent and out-of-home placements by 8 percent. These negative effects on child welfare are especially troubling, they argue, given that welfare reform was instituted in a strong economy only a short time ago.

Losing Other Supports for Children

Who watches the children of welfare recipients who leave home for mandated paid employment? Welfare programs typically do not provide adequate child care services for mothers who move off welfare by taking jobs. Many former recipients are unaware that they are eligible for child care assistance. The only work available to unskilled women on welfare is often the night shift at faraway locations, compounding the difficulty of finding child care. Sociologist Harriet Presser discovered that a high school diploma or less qualified women for only the female-dominated service sector as cashiers, nurses aides, waitresses, and housekeepers—jobs characterized by irregular and round-the-clock hours.[303] Many subsidized programs for preschool children, such as Head Start, operate only on a part-time basis.

In fact, the new welfare law affirmatively made finding affordable child care more difficult for many poor women. It eliminated the federal statutory guarantee for three important child care programs—entitlement programs that had ensured child care assistance to AFDC recipients participating in work programs, to employed parents transitioning off AFDC, and to low-income working parents at risk of becoming dependent on AFDC if child care were not subsidized.[304] Federal funds for child care are now capped, and states have broad discretion to determine which families qualify for child care benefits under the federal block grant. The increase in federal spending on child care will not match the influx of poor mothers entering the workforce. The Congressional Budget Office projects a shortfall of more than $1.8 billion in child care funds for low-income working families by 2002.[305] Many working mothers who cannot find affordable child care will either quit their jobs or leave their children with inadequate supervision while they're at work. Either way, the lack of child care places them at risk of intervention by child protection authorities.

Putting welfare mothers to work in day care centers was proposed as the new welfare law was debated. A 1995 *Washington Times* editorial suggested that welfare mothers with small children "can work in day care centers, tending their own children while caring for the children of other working mothers."[306] The National Governors Association's policy statement on welfare reform recommended that welfare recipients work in child care facilities as one of several transitional jobs used to move these women into private, unsubsidized work.[307] Mothers receiving TANF benefits may meet their work requirements by caring for the children of other TANF mothers who are participating in community service activities. So many states have adopted the idea of using welfare reform to fill child care needs that a third of child care centers surveyed in five cities now employ welfare recipients who are satisfying work requirements. Eighty percent of the for-profit chains, which pay the lowest wages, employed welfare recipients.[308]

Of course, child care is an important and potentially fulfilling job. But there are several troubling aspects of the transition of mothers from welfare into paid caregiving work. Child care workers are one of the lowest-paid professions in the nation. In 1998, family day care providers earned an average of $13,000 per year, and the mean annual salary for child care workers was only

$12,058.[309] Entry-level child care jobs paid an even lower rate of $6.00 per hour, or $ 10,500 per year. A third of child care programs, moreover, offer no health insurance to their employees. Unskilled women receiving welfare are typically hired as the lowest-paid assistants at day care centers offering the lowest wages. Most centers that hire welfare recipients do not provide any on-site training. The more prestigious and well-paid teaching positions are reserved for women with college degrees and professional training. Welfare mothers are the clients of child care chains that hire other untrained, low-paid women as workers with high turnover rates. Underlying this arrangement is the assumption that children from poor families, unlike those of affluent parents, do not need supervision by child care providers who are trained in early childhood education or who have chosen child care as their vocation.

Families that leave welfare because they have found work or have been sanctioned can lose a whole host of services critical to children's well-being. Welfare carries with it health care coverage under Medicaid, food stamps, and public housing. Although states are supposed to preserve Medicaid and food stamps for families dropped from the welfare rolls, millions of eligible children and parents have fallen through the cracks of state bureaucracies.[310] Why don't the working poor who qualify simply apply for these services? Some don't know they are eligible. Others are too embarrassed by the stigma attached to public assistance to ask for help. A recent federal investigation of state and city Medicaid programs found that many eligible families were uninsured because welfare offices discouraged would-be applicants for Medicaid and improperly denied benefits based on welfare workers' misinterpretation of the eligibility requirements.[311] But this is the wrong question, argues a writer to the *New York Times* editorial page. "We should be asking the question: 'How in this time of unprecedented prosperity are people working full time and not earning enough to feed their families?'"[312]

Breaking Up Families

In addition to throwing many children deeper into poverty, the federal welfare law contains a number of features that appear calculated to separate poor children from their families. Under the TANF block grant, states are no longer required to give cash assistance to relatives who care for poor children. Like parents, relatives are subject to work requirements and lose their benefits if they fail to find a job within time limits. Relatives can be required to participate in work, community service, and training programs even if it is unlikely they will ever return to the job market because they are too old or too sick. Those who are not working at the end of the two-year time limit could lose TANF cash assistance and related benefits. Relatives also run the risk of depleting their lifetime TANF allotment to receive aid for children in their care. "For example," writes Faith Mullen, "absent a hardship waiver, a 64-year-old grandmother who assumed care of her three-year-old grandson because of his mother's death will receive aid at most until the child reaches age eight. At that time, the grandmother will be in the impossible position of finding work, living on an inadequate income, or giving up custody of the child."[313] Kinship caregivers may qualify for federal or state foster care benefits and may receive a "child only" TANF grant that does not require compliance with welfare-to-work requirements. But many relatives who don't have a foster care license and need public assistance must rely on TANF benefits.

Some recipients caring for a relative's child may return the child to foster care rather than undergo the added burdens of job requirements or community service. Curley Brown was forced to send her niece and nephew back to foster care when she refused to participate in a mandatory work program and lost the $435 in cash payments and food stamps Mississippi had paid her.[314] Brown's care for her ailing mother and brother, in addition to the children she took in, made it impossible to perform the thirty-five hours of weekly service the state demanded. Mississippi now spends more money—$510 a month—to support the children in foster care. Agencies may now be more reluctant to place children with relatives who are not economically self-sufficient. As a result, warns Mark Hardin, director of the Center on Children and the Law, "relatives may no longer be financially in a position to become a custodian or guardian."[315]

The federal welfare law contains funding provisions that are more likely to disrupt than strengthen poor families. It leaves federal funds for foster care and adoption assistance as an uncapped entitlement while reducing and capping federal funds for cash assistance to families and for child welfare services that support families.[316] Congress also made a tiny change in the wording of the foster care funding law that gives an unprecedented boost to the expansion of foster care. By deleting the term "nonprofit," the law allows federal foster care matching funds to be used for the first time to pay for the care of children living in for-profit institutions.[317]

The availability of federal matching funds for foster care may provide a financial incentive for state agencies to move children into foster care. "If an economic downturn caused more families to seek welfare, federal funds might run out," Jean Tepperman of the Action Alliance for Children cautions. "Then putting a child in foster care would be the only way the state could get money for the child's support."[318] A child welfare agency faced with a family whose TANF benefits have expired may choose to place the children in out-of-home care rather than find the funds needed to preserve the family.

Consider the effect of this funding scheme on welfare offices' treatment of teen mothers who need public assistance. TANF denies aid to teen mothers not living with parents, adult relatives, or legal guardians. When these homes present a danger to the child, child protective services must move the mother into another adult-supervised arrangement. Federal matching funds may tempt agencies to place these teen mothers in foster care.[319] The TANF provision also increased the need for agencies to investigate teen mothers' homes.

The law also preserves the historical difference in the generosity of public aid and foster care payments. The median monthly TANF benefit is only about half of the median foster home maintenance stipend. In California, in 1996, the monthly stipend for two foster children aged eight and sixteen totaled $859, whereas AFDC benefits for the same children were only $479.[320] The difference is even greater in states with lower welfare benefits. And while the family's total welfare check increases only marginally for each additional child, foster parents receive a full stipend for each child in their care. This differential results in a huge gap between federal spending on foster care and on cash assistance. It costs the federal government *eleven times* as much per child to provide foster care as to provide public aid to families.[321]

In addition, the welfare law changed the criteria making children eligible to receive Social Security Income (SSI), the federal means-tested disability program that provides cash assistance and Medicaid to qualified individuals. As more and more families are pushed below the poverty line, many rely on the SSI system as the only source of financial and medical assistance for themselves and their disabled children.[322] But the SSI children's program came under increasing attack by the same forces that opposed AFDC. Suspicious of the poor families entitled to disability checks, conservatives accused the program of being riddled with fraud. For example, Christopher Wright of the Cato Institute charged that "gaming the childhood disability system has become an epidemic" and that "fraud appears to be deeply rooted within the culture of the program."[323] Despite the lack of concrete support for these allegations, Congress tightened eligibility standards. The Congressional Budget Office estimates that as a result, 267,000 children will lose SSI coverage over six years.[324] Some of these children will no longer qualify for Medicaid. Families who lose SSI benefits for their disabled children may no longer be able to care for them at home and will be forced to relinquish custody to child welfare authorities.

Welfare reform also makes it more difficult for parents whose children had been removed to regain custody. The federal welfare law cuts off aid to parents for children who are away from home for forty-five days or more. (States may elect to extend this limit up to six months and may exempt families working toward reunification.) This hardly gives parents time to correct the conditions that led to the removal. The loss of benefits may cause parents to be evicted from their homes, run out of food, and lose other resources needed for reunification with their children. The new accelerated time lines for terminating parental rights intensify the time pressures these parents face. Welfare reform and changes in child welfare policy are crushing poor parents from both ends.

When Two Systems Converge

The 1996 welfare reform law executed welfare's new social role. Government aid to poor mothers is no longer seen as charity but as a means of modifying their character and lifestyle. The current regime rejects the supportive ends of welfare, concentrating instead on its disciplinary function. Underlying this transformation is the age-old conviction that children's poverty is caused by their mothers' moral shortcomings. "Both Democrats and Republicans emphasized the wrongs of mothers—their 'unwillingness to work,' their failure to marry (or stay married), their irresponsible sexuality and childbearing," writes welfare historian Gwendolyn Mink.[325] Like the old suitable home criteria, the new TANF rules impose a set of behavioral stipulations as a condition of public assistance. They are designed to pressure women on welfare into conforming to the proper marital, childbearing, and parental standards.[326] There are penalties that encourage recipients to make sure their children are immunized and attend school regularly. Others discourage recipients from becoming pregnant as teens or outside of marriage. Still others are meant to deter drug use by recipients and to coerce cooperation with child support enforcement. The purpose of welfare, then, is to reform poor mothers' behavior.

Of course, this is also a chief aim of child welfare laws. Child protection agencies regulate poor mothers' behavior through permanency plans that mothers must complete to keep their children or get them back from foster care. Mothers receiving TANF who have children in the child welfare system, then, are subject to two behavior modification programs. Two government agencies—the public aid and the child protection departments—supervise them for the purpose of making them better mothers. Unfortunately, the convergence of two sets of competing requirements can make it harder to take care of their children.

One of the goals of welfare reformers is to discourage women receiving public assistance from having any children at all. Welfare handouts gave women a financial incentive to have children out-of-wedlock, argued conservative pundits like Charles Murray. Research showed that public assistance never had this impact on women's childbearing and marital decisions. During the 1990s, state legislators nonetheless proposed a number of avenues to pressure women on welfare to have fewer children.[327] The most benign measure was to make Norplant and other long-acting contraceptives available to poor women in every state through Medicaid. Some lawmakers proposed adding extra incentives to prevent welfare mothers from conceiving. Several introduced bills that would offer women on welfare a financial bonus to use Norplant. Some even proposed mandating Norplant insertion as a condition of receiving future benefits. Many states passed laws, popularly known as "family caps," denying any increase in payments for children born to women who are already receiving public assistance. Ordinarily, states determine a standard of family need according to the number of family members, sources of income, and other factors. Under the family cap, a family's standard of need is not adjusted upward to accommodate the new child. When the threat of insufficient benefits doesn't work to deter childbearing, mothers on welfare will have to take care of the extra children with the same monthly amount.

In addition to discouraging childbirth, the second central tenet of welfare reform is that mothers should leave home for paid employment. Work requirements flow from the premise that mothers' welfare dependency is harmful to children. Relying on welfare to support children, this theory goes, reflects maternal irresponsibility and an unwillingness to work. Children who see this bad example in their mothers learn to depend on government handouts instead of becoming self-sufficient. Reformers claimed that a "culture of dependency" was passed down from generation to generation.

The powerful myth of the shiftless "welfare queen" helped to garner popular support for both aspects of welfare reform. Americans' image of a welfare recipient is a poor Black woman who deliberately gets pregnant to fatten her monthly grant and then squanders it on drugs. According to University of Connecticut sociologists Noel Cazenave and Kenneth Neubeck, "Clinton and other politicians were able to successfully play the welfare 'race card' by exploiting popular welfare racist attitudes that were well documented by polling and other data."[328] For example, three-quarters of white respondents to a National Opinion Research Center Survey rated African Americans as less likely that whites to prefer to be self-supporting. The Black welfare queen embodies all of the character defects welfare dependency was supposed to promote—laziness, chicanery, maternal neglect—and legitimizes welfare's new behavior-modifying function.

The federal welfare law established work requirements in an attempt to put an end to the cycle of dependency. Welfare-to-work programs focus on improving recipients' attitude about work. A four-week job readiness class held at a Southside branch of the Chicago Public Library teaches welfare mothers self-esteem, interview techniques, and "what to wear—even how to fix their hair and apply their makeup."[329] At a week-long "job club" in Southern California, a job search specialist teaches recipients how to "dress for success" and leads motivational exercises.[330] These programs typically overlook the reason most single mothers rely on welfare—the market offers them no better alternative. "The problem is not work ethics," says Denver law professor Julie Nice. "It is the lack of jobs."[331] In *Making Ends Meet*, Kathryn Edin and Laura Lein report that virtually all of the mothers they interviewed supplemented their welfare checks by working. Lack of skills and education gave the mothers they interviewed very limited options for side work. Most refused to engage in more lucrative criminal activity, opting instead for "cleaning houses, maintaining apartment buildings, mowing lawns, baby-sitting, collecting bottles and aluminum cans, or other poorly paid work." The perception that welfare recipients don't have jobs because they refuse to work is wrong on two counts. Most mothers on welfare have to work to provide for their children. And the reason they don't leave welfare for paying jobs is because it would only make their children worse off.

Forcing low-skilled mothers into the workforce regardless of the conditions they confront assumes that *any* job is more beneficial to their families than the care they provide at home. "The Personal Responsibility Act does not make work pay, or even make work available," notes Gwendolyn Mink. "Yet it insists that single mothers are worth more outside their homes than inside them."[332] While family caps devalue the childbearing decisions of women receiving public assistance, work requirements devalue these women's relationships with their children.

The depreciation of welfare mothers' caregiving contradicts attitudes toward middle-class mothers. Whereas single welfare recipients must take paid jobs, more affluent mothers are expected to stay home full-time to care for their children. Middle-class mothers are supposed to depend on their husband's income to meet their financial needs. Katherine Teghtsoonian's textual analysis of child care policy debates in the late 1980s reveals the stark disparity in the value placed on different mothers' caregiving.[333] Teghtsoonian found that conservative opponents of the Act for Better Child Care Services (the ABC bill), which extended public support for out-of-home child care, "articulated a strongly held belief that full-time care by mothers is the best arrangement for children and that government policy ought to be facilitating it." They expressed their preference for full-time motherhood by criticizing child care centers as well as women with children who worked outside the home. Even some Democratic supporters of the ABC bill conceded that full-time maternal care was best for children, but that out-of-home child care services were critical for women forced into paid employment by economic necessity.

But this support for full-time motherhood was reserved for middle-class women alone. The conservative congressmen excluded mothers receiving AFDC benefits from their support of full-time caregiving. According to Teghtsoonian, "the prescription for these women who are poor, without husbands, and racially coded black in American public discourse was *not* full-time motherhood, but mandatory labor force participation, with their children placed in out-of-home child care contexts while they are at work." Advocates of the ABC bill took advantage of the devaluation of welfare recipients' mothering to garner support for child care funding. Because child care was viewed as a service for needy mothers rather than a universal social program, it failed to attract adequate federal support.

Women involved in both welfare and child welfare systems are receiving contradictory messages about what it means to be a good mother. While child welfare laws punish poor mothers for neglecting their children, welfare reform pushes these same mothers into paid employment without the supports needed to care properly for them. "The goals of welfare reform, which is focused on adult self-sufficiency," warns Mark Courtney, "compete with the goals of the child welfare system, which focuses on safe, nurturant child rearing."[334]

Welfare-to-work programs send a message to recipients that contradicts the importance they themselves place on mothering. When Stephanie Limoncelli, a sociology graduate student at UCLA, observed a Southern California welfare-to-work program, she was struck by the tension between the staff's emphasis on paid work and the participants' emphasis on caring for their children that marked the interactions she observed.[335] One of the main lessons the mostly Black and Latina participants received was not to let their children get in the way of finding a job. Staff either stressed that maternal responsibilities were secondary to paid work or ignored them altogether. The trainers admonished the mothers not to interrupt their job search to tend to sick children and never to mention their children during interviews. The program also attempted to reform the participants' view of their role as mothers. Staff tried to convince the women that taking care of their children meant providing financial support, not nurturing and spending time with them. One trainer suggested that participants impress potential employers by boasting, "I'm a workaholic. I often stay so late that I neglect my family!"

Participants "countered the program's 'workfirst' focus by articulating a 'childfirst' philosophy," writes Limoncelli. Whereas the program materials assumed that employment was the only source of self-esteem, the participants insisted that motherhood was the most positive and fulfilling part of their lives.

A job specialist advised participants not to discuss their families when telling employers what they like to do in their spare time. "Don't your children stress you out?" the specialist asked. "Therefore you wouldn't want to go home to more stress." "But I go home and take care of my kids," one of the participants protested. "I teach them. I have patience with that." "But there are times when you want to be without your kids," the specialist persisted. "Not really," was the response.

The participants frequently asserted the futility of trying to combine mothering with low-wage work. Even before welfare reform, poor single mothers had a tough time providing for their children economically while doing a good job at being a mother. We usually read about the trade-offs professional women make in juggling the demands of their busy careers with raising their children. These privileged mothers can afford full-time child care, sometimes provided by live-in nannies, but agonize over the time they spend away from their children.

It is even harder for poor mothers to be both good providers and good mothers. For them, working can interfere with keeping their children out of danger—"off the streets, off drugs, out of gangs, not pregnant, and in school."[336] "The regular jobs open to unskilled and semi-skilled women were precisely those jobs that are least compatible with mothering," write Kathryn Edin and Laura Lein in *Making Ends Meet*. Because these jobs rarely provide health insurance, mothers must often delay medical care for their children. They require mothers to work irregular hours and don't provide paid vacations, sick days, or personal time. This makes it hard for mothers who can't afford child care to spend time with their children or check on children left home alone. "Because virtually all the women we interviewed were at least as concerned with parenting as with providing," Edin and Lein explain, "many chose not to work for a time."

What will happen when TANF rules force these mothers to leave home for paid employment despite the hazards it poses for their children? In subsequent interviews in 1997 and 1998, Edin and her colleagues discovered a deep ambivalence among mothers contemplating leaving welfare for work. These women felt optimistic about the potential for employment to improve their children's well-being and self-esteem. But the mothers were also concerned about the price their children might pay: "The women worried about finding adequate and affordable child care; where their children would go after school; who would help them with their homework; who would mentor them through the trials of childhood; and who would be there, generally, to keep them safe and on track."[337] Edin and Lein believe the answer depends on whether they can find jobs and public support services that minimize the tension between working and protecting their children.

Mothers who aren't that fortunate may soon find themselves out of work. Soon after welfare reform was implemented, Jason DeParle described the harsh consequences for Black mothers in the "hard-luck" counties of the Mississippi Delta.[338] Nearly half of the women from the welfare-to-work program in Greenville, Mississippi, who were placed in jobs went to the Springwater Farms catfish plant in Eudora, Arkansas. The women caught a school bus that left Greenville at 6:30 A.M. each morning for the hour-long commute to work. Patricia Watson arranged for a teen-age relative to take her adopted six-year-old niece, Jasmine, to school and watch her afterward. When Ms. Watson returned home, she discovered that the teenager had misplaced the little girl. She conducted a house-to-house search until she found Jasmine playing with a friend in the neighborhood. "She quit the plant, lost her welfare benefits, and is relying on her mother for now," DeParle reports.

Parents involved in both systems may also be required to comply with conflicting requirements from two state agencies. Welfare agencies in most states require recipients to sign documents called Individual Responsibility Agreements, or IRAs, which list parental obligations they must fulfill.[339] IRAs are very similar to the permanency or reunification plans that child welfare agencies impose on parents. Georgia's Personal Responsibility Plan, for example, requires that recipients ensure that minor children go to school, attend parent-teacher conferences, and participate in parenting skills classes and family planning counseling. Recall how complicated and time consuming child welfare permanency plans can be. Now imagine trying to comply with a permanency plan in order to hold on to your child while complying with an IRA and work-related requirements in order to hold on to welfare benefits. Mothers involved in both systems may be simultaneously attending parenting classes, completing a drug treatment program, and finding safer housing under a permanency plan while attending job readiness classes and searching for a job under a welfare-to-work plan. There are reports that TANF rules sometimes prohibit mothers from taking time off from work to visit their children in foster care, appear in court for a custody hearing, or attend an administrative review at the child welfare office.[340]

Yet state officials place high expectations on welfare recipients to be good mothers. Despite welfare reform's interference with their ability to supervise their children, mothers are sanctioned if their children aren't good students. For example, under Wyoming's Individual Responsibility Plan, mothers must ensure that their teenagers attend school full-time, maintain a "C" average, and graduate on time. But how are mothers supposed to supervise their children's school attendance and homework if they work long and irregular hours or travel long distances to get to the job? It's impossible for middle-class parents to guarantee their children's performance in school. Imagine how much tougher it is for poor mothers whose children attend inferior schools and engage in a daily battle with dangerous neighborhood pressures. Poor mothers have fewer material resources to supplement their children's schooling or to offer their children as incentives for good grades.

Another legal development is likely to further penalize poor mothers pushed into paid work with inadequate support. In the past decade, a number of states and cities have enacted criminal statutes that punish parents for failing to prevent their children from becoming delinquent.[341] The first of these laws, passed by California in 1988 as part of a campaign against gang violence, imposes criminal liability on parents who fail to exercise "reasonable care, supervision, protection, and control over their minor child." Some jurisdictions hold parents strictly liable for their children's delinquency. As I will soon discuss, profound race and class biases make poor minority children more vulnerable to criminal sanctions than youth from white, middle-class families. Parental liability laws lay the blame on the single mothers who are raising them under difficult circumstances. These are the very mothers whom welfare reform prevents from spending time with their children and from guarding against the hazards that often plague poverty-stricken communities.

Has a state made reasonable efforts to prevent a child from entering foster care if it refuses to give the family cash assistance needed for basic subsistence? If child welfare agencies are removing children from parents who lost welfare benefits, aren't they finding neglect based on "poverty alone?"[342] And if the reasonable efforts language requires states to provide grants to families at risk of losing a child to foster care, why not impose a duty on states to provide these grants to all families that need them? Of course, this duty would effectively create an entitlement to welfare benefits, which would defeat the purpose of welfare reform! These questions point out the profound contradiction that welfare reform poses for child welfare policy, a contradiction that stems from the profoundly flawed definition of child welfare. American child welfare policy rejected the view of child maltreatment as a social problem that had to be addressed with societal remedies. The provision of cash assistance to needy families, although not enough to lift them out of poverty, allows child welfare agencies to claim that children's problems are caused mostly by parental deficits that can be treated with psychological therapies. When government aid to poor families ceases altogether, it becomes clear that children are going without food, shelter, and medical care because their parents cannot afford them. Welfare reform makes it harder to pretend that child maltreatment is unrelated to poverty.

5. Locking Up Parents and Children

THE COLOR OF CHILD WELFARE is related to the fate of parents and children in the criminal justice system, another predominantly Black institution. A major cause of family disruption is the high incarceration rate among young Black fathers and a growing number of Black mothers. Many of the children left behind are placed in foster care. The criminal justice system itself also takes custody of large numbers of Black children, committing them to juvenile detention centers and adult prisons. There is an overlap between the poor Black children who make up foster care and juvenile justice caseloads. Children who "act out" in foster or group homes are often punished by transferring them to juvenile detention facilities. And many of the teens who "age out" of the foster care system end up spending time in prison. The trend toward imposing long mandatory prison sentences for drug offenses and treating juvenile offenders as adults is escalating this family breakup. Adding the effects of prisons and juvenile detention to that of foster care produces an astounding level of state supervision of Black children.

The Relationship Between the
Criminal Justice and Child Welfare Systems

Considering the impact of incarceration on Black families reveals a relationship between the child welfare system and the criminal justice system. The most direct connection is that imprisoning parents throws many children into foster care. But there are less obvious and more profound systemic associations between criminal justice and child welfare. Demographically, the two institutions are remarkably similar. They are both populated almost exclusively by poor people and by grossly disproportionate numbers of Blacks.

The United States has the largest prison population in the world, and over half of it is Black.[343] With only 5 percent of the global population, the United States houses 25 percent of the world's prisoners. The number of incarcerated Americans increased sixfold—from fewer than 200,000 inmates to 1.2 million—between 1972 and 1997. The prison population has continued to soar despite recent declines in the crime rate. Today, 2 million Americans are incarcerated in local jails or state or federal prisons.[344] Because of tough mandatory sentencing laws enacted in the 1980s, the number of prisoners grew at a faster rate during the Clinton administration than under either Ronald Reagan or George Bush. The bulk of this explosion stemmed from locking up young Black men. Black male inmates now number about 800,000, the most in U.S. history. Black men ages 25 to 29 are almost ten times as likely as young white men to be incarcerated. Twelve states and the District of Columbia imprison Blacks at a rate more than ten times that of whites.[345] The racial disparity in incarceration rates has become worse in recent decades: the racial imbalance increased in thirty-eight states and the District of Columbia between 1988 and 1994.

As alarming as these racial differences is the huge proportion of Black men behind bars. By the early 1990s, almost one in ten of all Black men were in prison on any given day and almost one-third of Black males could expect to be incarcerated during their lifetime. In stark contrast, a white boy stood only a 4 percent chance of ever being imprisoned. A 1991 study found that nearly one-third of all young Black men living in Los Angeles County had been jailed at least once that year.[346] Calls by conservative politicians to stop crime by doubling the current prison population would mean locking up nearly a quarter of all young African American men.[347]

This pattern of overrepresentation is replicated in the juvenile justice system. Although in 1997 the juvenile population was 79 percent white and 15 percent Black, Black youth accounted for 31 percent and white youth for 66 percent of delinquency cases handled by juvenile courts.[348] More than one in four adjudicated delinquency cases ended in placing children outside their homes—in residential treatment centers, juvenile corrections facilities, foster homes, or group homes.[349] As with foster care, Black children are sent to out-of-home placements at the highest rates. That same year, 32 percent of cases involving Black youth resulted in out-of-home placements, compared to 26 percent of cases involving white youth. The racial disparity is even starker in confinement to juvenile detention facilities. Between 1988 and 1997, the increase in Black youth detention (52 percent) was more than double the increase for whites (25 percent).[350] In 1997, judges sent 27 percent of Black delinquents to juvenile detention centers, compared to only 15 percent of white delinquents.

There is also a great deal of overlap between the very individuals involved in the criminal or juvenile justice and child welfare systems. In Chicago, the juvenile courthouse is divided into two sections. On one side, judges decide juvenile delinquency cases involving children charged with offenses. On the other, judges decide dependency cases involving children whose parents are charged with abusing or neglecting them. The poor Black teens who have spent time in foster care often turn out to be the same ones who are sent to juvenile detention. Participants at a recent conference at the Justice Department's Office of Juvenile Justice and Delinquency Prevention observed that "child welfare and juvenile justice professionals end up working with many of the same kids."[351]

Studies show that maltreated children are more likely to be involved in juvenile delinquency. There is also evidence that children's experience in the child welfare system affects their chances of arrest. A Justice Department study, *The Cycle of Violence*, compared the juvenile delinquency records of a group of children who had been maltreated and a group that had not.[352] It found that maltreatment increased the likelihood of arrest by 53 percent. Among the maltreated group, those who had three or more foster care placements had arrest rates almost double that of children who had fewer placements.

These findings don't prove a *causal* connection between maltreatment or foster care drift and delinquency. It may be that foster children with behavior problems are moved more often. Perhaps the same disadvantages of poverty and discrimination that push children into the child welfare system also make them vulnerable to arrest. Researchers have discovered a correlation between the race of victims of maltreatment and the likelihood of juvenile delinquency. One study of arrests for violent offenses found that whereas maltreatment did not increase the likelihood of arrest for white children, maltreated Black children did have higher arrest rates.[353] This racial disparity probably has more to do with the *state's treatment* of abused and neglected children than with the maltreatment itself. It appears that when child welfare authorities take custody of Black children, it increases their chances of becoming involved in the juvenile justice system.

Why do Black children move from the child welfare system to the juvenile justice system? The main reason is that the child welfare system doesn't stick by Black children when they get in trouble. When teenagers have problems with the law, it is critical that their parents advocate on their behalf and offer to provide private alternatives to detention in a state facility. Black teens in the foster care system rarely get this kind of attention. The Vera Institute of Justice collaborated with New York City's Administration for Children's Services (ACS) to investigate why so many teenagers were entering the child welfare system through juvenile justice.[354] The analysis revealed a large number of teens moving between the two systems, but not in the patterns ACS expected. The Vera Institute estimates that more than 1,000 teenagers were involved with both ACS and juvenile justice in 1997. Most of the adolescents ACS received from the juvenile justice system had actually been in the agency's care at the time of their arrest and were being returned to ACS. It also found that foster children were overrepresented in juvenile detention centers. Although foster children constituted less than 2 percent of the general population, they made up 15 percent of the children in detention.

In *Adolescent Pathways,* the Vera Institute notes that parental involvement is critical to what happens to children at every stage of the juvenile justice process. If a parent comes to the precinct within a few hours, teens arrested for minor offenses are usually released. Probation officers interview parents in considering whether to divert the case from prosecution. Judges notice the presence or absence of parents in court and consult with those who appear in deciding how to rule. Children in the foster care system routinely receive detention because no adult shows up. The Vera Institute found that "there is no system to notify ACS when a teenager in foster care is arrested." Foster parents do nothing, deferring to unreachable caseworkers to intervene. Moreover, according to the report, "as children age, foster homes are a declining resource." One-third of adolescents over age thirteen in ACS's custody live in group homes or institutions, known as congregate care. These facilities discharge teens who are arrested instead of sending someone to take responsibility for them.

The child welfare system also plays an affirmative role in foster children's involvement in juvenile justice. The Vera Institute found that ACS teenagers are much more likely to be arrested in their homes than other teenagers in juvenile detention. Whereas only 4 percent of the non-ACS teens surveyed were arrested at home, 36 percent of the teens in foster care and 55 percent of the teens in congregate care were. In other words, the teens in the child welfare system were being arrested for incidents related to their placements. Some foster parents and group homes are quick to call the police to handle misbehavior by the teens in their custody. In fact, one facility called the police almost forty times over an eleven-month period.

Child welfare authorities deal with teenagers who rebel against placement in group or foster homes by treating them as juvenile delinquents. It is not surprising that teens sent to group homes frequently run away. Many of these institutions literally terrorize children on a daily basis. Children in group homes in Indiana are ten times more likely to be physically abused and twenty-eight times more likely to be sexually abused than children in their own homes.[355] Relying on a 1997 grand jury report, the *Los Angeles Times* related that "many of the nearly 5,000 foster children housed in Los Angeles County group homes are physically abused and drugged excessively while being forced to live without proper food, clothing, education and counseling."[356] Adolescents at a New York group home "described a pattern of incidents in which longer-term residents raped, robbed, or assaulted newcomers while night-shift staff slept on the job."[357]

Teens who escape these horrible conditions risk being labeled "runners" by caseworkers who soon lose patience with them. Because of the shortage of foster homes for adolescents, judges sometimes confine chronic runaways picked up by the police in juvenile detention centers. "Judges are in a bind because they know it's not safe on the streets," a Seattle social worker reported.

"These kids end up in detention."[358] She cited the example of a seventeen-year-old girl with serious mental health and substance abuse problems who originally entered foster care under a voluntary placement. When the girl ran away from several foster homes, the child welfare department refused to place her in more structured treatment. The only alternative was commitment to a detention facility under a succession of thirty-day orders for probation violations. The social worker says she advises teens to stick out foster care no matter how hellish the conditions because their future may be even bleaker if they enter the juvenile justice system.

A high percentage of teens leaving foster care end up in prison. Foster care benefits end abruptly when children reach the age of majority—eighteen or twenty-one, depending on state law.[359] These young adults must "exit" the system, usually leaving the foster homes or institutions where they are living to reunite with their families or make it on their own. Congress estimates that about 20,000 young people "age out" of foster care each year.[360] The vast majority of these abandoned teens are Black. In 1999 Congress passed the Foster Care Independence Act to increase funding to states to assist youth in moving from foster care to independent living, but state support is still inadequate. For most of these youth, who typically have spent years in state custody, the transition is rough. Studies show alarming correlations between aging out of foster care and dropping out of high school, unemployment, and homelessness. A national evaluation by Westat, Inc., for example, found that 46 percent of 810 former foster children studied had not completed high school, 51 percent were unemployed 2.5 to 4 years after leaving care, and 25 percent had been homeless at least one night.[361]

These dire circumstances often lead to criminal involvement. Berkeley researcher Richard Barth discovered that more than a third of the fifty-five youths he studied spent time in jail or prison.[362] A Connecticut study found that 75 percent of the youths in the state's criminal justice system were once in foster care.[363] Eighty percent of Illinois inmates spent time in foster care as children.[364] The prison system supplies children to the child welfare system when it incarcerates their parents. The child welfare system supplies young adults to the prison system when it abandons them after years in foster care.

There is a disturbing overlap, then, between Black teens who are involved in both the child welfare and the criminal justice systems, moving from foster care to juvenile detention and prison. Just as destructive is the combined impact of these two systems that regulate essentially the same population. Independently, each system enforces the inequitable state supervision of Black children. Taken together, the level of Black children in state custody has reached crisis proportions. It is hard to calculate the precise number because no one keeps track of the children who are counted in two systems at once. But we know that the nation's foster homes, juvenile detention centers, and prisons house far too many children, and we know that most of them are Black.

The racial disparity in the criminal justice and child welfare systems is no coincidence. These institutions serve a similar social function. Both use blame and punishment to address the problems of the populations under their control. The explosions in both the prison and foster care populations during the 1980s occurred at a time of rising income inequality. Expanding the foster care and penal systems are substitutes for implementing social policies that address poverty and racial inequality. "We were, in effect, using the prisons to contain a growing social crisis concentrated in the bottom quarter of our population," writes Berkeley legal studies scholar Elliot Currie.[365] "The prison *became* our employment policy, our drug policy, our mental health policy, in the vacuum left by the absence of more constructive efforts."

The monumental investment in prisons comes at the cost of disinvestment in other social institutions that serve the communities that produce the inmate population. The tens of billions of dollars spent each year on building the prison industrial complex were taken from other social systems that educate, house, and heal poor children. Tough-on-crime policies are now politically expedient, and prisons are an accepted source of economic growth. Prison expansion is so ingrained in American politics and market economy that we have seen "the virtual institutionalization of a societal commitment to the use of a massive prison system," writes Marc Mauer of the Sentencing Project.[366] This misdirection of funds is similar to child welfare policies that spend far more on foster care than on preserving families. The foster care industry is also firmly entrenched, with current reforms directed at moving foster children into adoptive homes.

As a result of the political choice to fund punitive instead of supportive programs, criminal justice and child welfare supervision is pervasive in poor Black communities. On any given day, nearly one in three Black males in their twenties is under the control of the criminal justice system—either in jail or on probation or parole.[367] The extent of criminal justice supervision in some inner cities is even greater. In Baltimore, for example, half of young African American men are in the system. This oversight by prison wardens and probation officers is probably the most familiar exposure to government institutions for most inner-city Black men.[368] For Black women, child protective services play a similar supervisory role.

In the same way that the penal system buries the systemic reasons for crime, the child welfare system hides the systemic reasons for child maltreatment. The simultaneous expansion of the foster care and prison populations reflects the public's abandonment of poor Black families. Instead of devoting adequate resources to support these families, the state increasingly shuffles them into the punitive machinery of law enforcement and child protection. Stereotypes about Black criminality and irresponsibility legitimate the massive disruption that both systems inflict on Black families and communities.

Incarceration of Black Parents

Social scientists are beginning to investigate the impact of America's unparalleled rate of incarcerating its citizens. Keeping so much of the population behind bars surely inflicts collateral damage on society. As Marc Mauer asks, "What does it do to the fabric of the family and community to have such a substantial proportion of its young men enmeshed in the criminal justice system?"[369] The repercussions of prison policy extend to the labor market, the stability of neighborhoods, and the workings of democracy. Among the most serious effects of mass imprisonment are the negative consequences for children with parents in prison. Given the huge racial disparity in the prison population, most of this harm befalls Black families.

A special report recently issued by the Bureau of Justice Statistics on "Incarcerated Parents and Their Children" reveals the startling dimensions of this crisis.[370] In 1999, most state and federal prisoners reported having a child under age eighteen. About 2 percent of the nation's children—close to 1.5 million children—had a parent in prison that year. This represents an increase of a half-million children in less than a decade. About half of incarcerated parents lived with their children prior to imprisonment. Black children are the most likely to have an incarcerated parent. Seven percent of Black children had a parent in prison in 1999, making them nearly nine times more likely to have an incarcerated parent than white children. Having a parent behind bars is mainly a problem for Black children.

Even if incarcerated parents are able to maintain contact with their children, imprisonment has a disrupting effect. Inmates can no longer take care of their children either physically or financially, placing extra economic and emotional burdens on the remaining family members.[371] Children are deprived of the emotional support and guidance parents provide. Losing a parent to prison has serious psychological consequences for children, including depression, anxiety, and problems in school.[372] One study of children of incarcerated mothers found that they experienced a trauma from the separation so profound that they displayed symptoms of posttraumatic stress disorder.[373] The stigma of having a mother or father in jail can also cause children to feel angry and defiant.

Incarcerated parents face enormous barriers to staying in touch with their children. Most prisons are located in remote areas far away from the cities where many inmates' families live. This distance may force families to lose contact with the parent or to move closer to the prison to visit the parent regularly. Their efforts may be frustrated at any time if administrators decide to transfer the parent to another facility. Although most inmates keep in regular contact with their children through letters and telephone calls, the distance of prisons usually thwarts personal visits. A majority of both mothers and fathers report that they have never been visited by their children since entering prison.[374]

Incarceration of mothers and fathers inflict different kinds of harms on children. More than half of men in prison are fathers.[375] About half of these fathers lived with their children before they were incarcerated. Studies show that many incarcerated fathers contributed to their children's financial well-being before entering prison.[376] Mass incarceration, then, deprives thousands of children of important economic and social support from their fathers. It depletes poor Black communities of their workforce and income, damaging their already precarious economic stability.

Incarceration also ruins Black men's chances for employment after they are released.[377] Welfare reform's cutbacks put more pressure on these fathers to help support their children, but serving time diminishes the employability of men who already lack the education and skills needed to compete in the labor market. Many employers refuse to hire anyone with a criminal record. Those that make exceptions offer only low-paying, menial work. Black men released from prison earn 10 to 30 percent less than Black dropouts without criminal records. Children who are incarcerated have virtually no chance of stable employment when they grow up.[378] The staggering barriers to finding a job make ex-convicts the "untouchables of the workforce," writes *New York Times* reporter Peter Kilborn.[379]

Along with reducing the opportunities inmates have for legal work, imprisonment strengthens their connections to criminal networks.[380] Returning to crime is a tempting alternative to their dismal prospects for employment. Incarceration often leads to a vicious cycle of unemployment, crime, and more incarceration. According to Princeton sociologist Bruce Western, while only 29 percent of Black male high school dropouts in their twenties were employed in 1999, 41 percent were in prison.[381] "To the extent that incarceration aggravates the already severe labor-market problems of their mostly low-income, poorly educated inmates," warns Elliot Currie, "it will increase the costs to the public sector of dealing with them on the outside." It also makes it nearly impossible for inmates to support their families after they are released.

Kilborn interviewed a Black, twenty-five-year-old ex-inmate named Bobby Eubanks who was struggling to support his three children by working odd jobs as a common laborer for $6 an hour. His fiancée, a home health aide, was expecting his fourth child. Eubanks was sent to juvenile detention during his senior year in high school for selling cocaine. He was later imprisoned for thirty-four months on a second drug offense. He told Kilborn that he couldn't find a steady job after he was paroled in May 2000. "I've been all over New Orleans filling out applications," Eubanks said. "But they don't call. All the applications ask if you have ever been convicted of a crime, and that kills the whole thing right there." Two days after the interview, Kilborn reports, Eubanks was shot and killed at a nightclub in a botched attempt to rob the owner.

Although only a small fraction of incarcerated parents are mothers, their numbers are rising rapidly.[382] The skyrocketing rate of female incarceration signals increasing disruption of families. Although judges used to show mothers leniency, they are now often compelled by mandatory sentencing laws to give mothers long prison terms. As a result, the number of children with a mother in prison nearly doubled in the past decade. The incarceration rate of Black women is growing faster than that of Black men or the overall prison population. From 1985 to 1995, the number of Black women in state and federal prisons increased by more than 200 percent.[383] Black women represent over 45 percent of women in federal prisons. Most are locked up for nonviolent property and drug crimes.

Children's lives are disrupted more by women's incarceration than by men's. Incarcerated mothers are far more likely than incarcerated fathers to have lived with their children before going to prison. Female inmates were usually the primary caretakers of their children, often providing their sole economic and emotional support.[384] One-third of mothers in prison had been living alone with their children when they were arrested compared to only 4 percent of incarcerated fathers. Black women in prison are even more likely to be unwed mothers. When fathers are imprisoned, the mother almost always continues taking care of the children. When mothers are imprisoned, children must usually leave home. A single mother must find a relative—usually her mother—who will keep her child while she is in jail. Relative caregivers who fill in for incarcerated mothers receive inadequate government support, and most cannot meet the increased child care expenses.[385] They must also deal with the difficult task of developing their own relationship with the child while helping to maintain the child's ties to the mother. Children sometimes end up in foster care and risk permanent severing of their family ties.[386] One in ten mothers in state prison reported that their children were in foster care or state institutions.[387] Like incarcerated fathers, mothers have a hard time finding employment when they return home.

Of course, some crimes make the perpetrators unfit parents. For example, a conviction for extreme acts of domestic violence against the child or the other parent might be grounds for terminating parental rights. Some scholars have theorized that removing criminal parents may benefit children by relieving the family of problems caused by the parents' antisocial behavior. But in most cases, incarcerated parents and children both have an interest in preserving the bond between them. The United States Supreme Court's recognition in *Santosky v. Kramer* of parents' constitutionally protected interest in maintaining a relationship with their children applies to incarcerated mothers and fathers. "The fundamental liberty interest of natural parents in the care, custody, and management of their child does not evaporate simply because they have not been model parents or have lost temporary custody of their child to the state," the Court declared.[388]

Prior to the *Santosky* decision, states routinely allowed the adoption of inmates' children without parental consent. After *Santosky*, states have taken divergent positions on the strength of inmates' rights and the degree of assistance the state will provide to keep families together. For example, in 1983, the New York state legislature abolished incarceration as a sufficient basis for termination of parental rights. Under New York law, the state must make "diligent efforts" to help incarcerated parents and their children to maintain a meaningful relationship. The state provides transportation for children to correctional facilities to visit their parents. Mothers can keep their infants with them in prison. Some states have diversion programs that allow young children to live with their mothers in community-based facilities. Imprisoned parents must comply with the child welfare agency's permanency plans if their children are state wards. Inmates who have no relatives to rely on and whose children are sent to foster care may be powerless to prevent termination of their parental rights and their children's adoption. Other states are far less sympathetic to inmates' parental rights. Some courts have ruled that a lengthy jail term is enough to permanently sever the bond between imprisoned parents and their children. Incarceration itself constitutes statutory grounds for termination of parental rights in some states.

Some people believe that deprivation of family contact is part of the deserved punishment for committing a crime. When parents decide to break the law, they reason, they take the risk of losing their children. But the unequal imprisonment of Black parents results from rampant racial discrimination at all levels of the criminal justice system, from the identification of suspects to sentencing of convicted offenders. There is now overwhelming evidence that the criminal laws are enforced unfairly against Blacks.[389] Recent exposés of "racial profiling" provide a good example. Police officers routinely stop motorists on the basis of race for minor traffic infractions as a pretext to search for drugs.[390] A 1992 *Orlando Sentinel* study of police videotapes discovered that although Blacks and Latinos represented only 5 percent of drivers on the Florida interstate highway, they made up nearly 70 percent of drivers stopped by police and more than 80 percent of drivers whose cars were searched.[391] As New Jersey governor, Christine Todd Whitman conceded that state troopers singled out

Black and Latino motorists and were three times more likely to search them than whites.[392] The experience of being stopped by police on account of race is so common that it is widely known in the Black community as "DWB"— driving while Black.

These race-based stops may amount to an inconvenience or a citation— or they may be an excuse to search for evidence of a more serious crime. Racially biased searches lead to racial disparities in arrests and convictions. Boston federal judge Nancy Gertner acknowledged this pattern by reducing a Black defendant's sentence on grounds that his lengthy prior record was probably skewed by discriminatory traffic stops.[393] She reasoned that by taking racially biased traffic convictions into account, the federal sentencing guidelines overestimate the defendant's culpability and perpetuate racial disparities in the state system.

Judge Gertner's conscious effort to avoid racial discrimination in applying the federal sentencing guidelines is apparently an aberration. In a recent study of close to 80,000 offenders sentenced under the federal guidelines, University of Georgia professor David Mustard discovered gigantic racial gaps.[394] After controlling for crime-related, demographic, and socioeconomic variables, Professor Mustard found that Black males with low education and income received substantially longer sentences, especially for drug trafficking. Black males were also less likely to avoid prison when judges had that option available.

Police officers also enforce the drug laws in a racially biased way. Although whites use drugs in far greater numbers than Blacks, Blacks are far more likely to be arrested for drug offenses. Blacks represent only 15 percent of the nation's illegal drug users but make up three-quarters of those imprisoned for drug possession.[395] This gross racial disparity results in part from the conscious decision of police departments to target their drug enforcement efforts on urban and inner-city neighborhoods where minorities live. "Common sense, then, dictates that if the police conducted pretext stops on the campus of U.C.L.A. with the same frequency as they do in South Central, a lot of whites would be arrested for drug possession," notes journalist Jeffrey Goldberg.[396]

Regardless of prisoners' guilt or innocence, the damaging consequences for children must be added to the social costs of pursuing a policy of massive incarceration. In addition to the financial and emotional strain it causes individual families, imprisoning parents increases the total amount of state supervision of Black children.

Detention of Juveniles

In March 2001, a Broward County, Florida, judge sentenced fourteen-year-old Lionel Tate to spend the rest of his life in prison for a crime he committed when he was only twelve. Lionel was convicted of first-degree murder for killing six-year-old Tiffany Eunick, a family friend, while they were playing at his home. Prosecutors convinced the judge that Lionel deliberately pummeled the little girl to death in an act the judge called "cold, callous and indescribably cruel." But Lionel testified that he killed her accidentally while imitating professional wrestling moves he had seen on television. Lionel's mother was so convinced of her son's innocence of murder that she rejected a plea bargain offered by prosecutors that would have carried only a three-year prison term and ten years on probation. Lionel's conviction shows the extremes of the states' increasingly punitive attitude toward children who commit crimes.

Juvenile justice also inflicts a disproportionate amount of collateral damage on Black families. Although the juvenile justice system treats youthful offenders more leniently than adults, it has the power to take children into custody and place them in secure confinement. These children are removed from their homes and from their parents' care. Like incarceration of parents, detention of juveniles is marked by enormous racial inequity.

Black children are detained by the state at higher rates than any other children in the nation.[397] Since the 1970s, the percentage of white children held in public detention centers and reform schools has declined precipitously while the percentage of Black children in state facilities has mushroomed. In 1977, 57 percent of youth in public detention facilities were white, 30 percent Black, and 11 percent Latino.[398] By 1987, about half of the detained population was Black. Sociologists Katherine Hunt Federle and Meda Chesney Lind reject violent crime rates as an explanation for this disparity: only 15 percent of juveniles locked in these facilities had been arrested for serious violence. "The growth of the institutionalized minority population in the juvenile justice system," they conclude, "can be explained only in terms of a pervasive, systemic racism."

Juvenile justice statistics from three states in 1996 show the gross over-representation of minority youth in state custody. In California, the state with the highest number of juveniles in custody, minorities made up 53.4 percent of the youth population, but 59 percent of juveniles arrested, almost 64 percent of juveniles held in detention, and 70 percent of juveniles placed in secure corrections.[399] Although minorities made up only 14.3 percent of the youth population in Ohio, they represented 30 percent of the juvenile arrests and 43 percent of children in prison. In Texas, while minorities made up half the state's youth, they accounted for 65 percent of juveniles in detention and 80 percent of juveniles in secure corrections. All of the children held in Texas adult jails were Black or Hispanic.

Researchers have reached divergent conclusions about the impact of race on juvenile detention decisions. Some suggest that so many Black children are confined to detention facilities not because of their race but because of the seriousness of their crimes, because of their poverty, or because of their uncooperative behavior. On the other hand, numerous studies demonstrate that, even after taking severity of present offense and prior record into account, juvenile court judges hand down more severe sanctions on Black juveniles in delinquency dispositions.[400] A recent, well-designed study found that race had an independent and significant influence on detention.[401] Using data on felony offenses in five counties of one state, the researchers controlled for factors other than race, such as site, socioeconomic status, and offense characteristics, that might explain differences in confinement rates. Race was directly responsible for higher rates of detention at three stages in the juvenile justice process—police contact, juvenile court intake, and the preliminary hearing.

After reviewing research on racial bias, University of Missouri criminologist Kimberly L. Kempf similarly concluded that race predicts the fate of children in the juvenile justice system, even when factors such as prior record and severity of offense were taken into account.[402] Kempf highlights the need for a process-oriented approach that examines the interdependence of decisions at multiple stages of juvenile justice and recognizes that decisions made early in the process—by police officers and prosecutors, for example—affect how judges ultimately dispose of cases. In her own study of juvenile justice cases in Pennsylvania, Kempf found that racial disparities in the early stages built on each other to produce worse outcomes for Black children.

Jerome Miller writes that his experience as head of the Massachusetts juvenile correction system confirmed these findings of cumulative racial bias. His account gives a vivid picture of the way discrimination creeps into every stage of juvenile justice processing to lock up more Black children who are not guilty of serious offenses and the way white children are sheltered from such harsh treatment.

> I learned very early on that when we got a black youth, virtually everything—from arrest summaries, to family history, to rap sheets, to psychiatric exams, to "waiver" hearings as to whether or not he would be tried as an adult, to final sentencing—was skewed. If a middle-class white youth was sent to us as "dangerous," he was more likely actually to be so than the black teenager given the same label. The white teenager was more likely to have been afforded competent legal counsel and appropriate psychiatric and psychological testing, tried in a variety of privately funded options, and dealt with more sensitively and individually at every stage of the juvenile justice processing. By contrast, the black teenager was more likely to be dealt with as a stereotype from the moment the handcuffs were first put on—easily and quickly relegated to the "more dangerous" end of the "violent-nonviolent" spectrum, albeit accompanied by an official record meant to validate each of a biased series of decisions.[403]

Children may be detained before they even go to trial, either by a police officer or by a judge. Like every step in the juvenile justice process, this decision is subject to unfettered discretion. As a result, detention rates vary widely among different parts the same county or state. For example, in the three police departments in the largest county of one state, detention rates ranged from 5 percent to 43 percent. When the police pick up a child, they must decide whether to put the child in secure custody or return him to his parents. Both police and judges are more likely to hold Black children than white children in pretrial detention. Once detained at the intake level, children are more likely to be detained at a preliminary hearing. Detained juveniles, in turn, receive harsher sentences than those who are home with their parents when their case is adjudicated. It is not surprising that racial disparities increase at each successive stage of processing.[404] As juveniles proceed through the system, from arrest to intake and eventually to detention or incarceration, the percentage of nonwhites grows larger and larger.

Black children also end up in state custody because they are more likely to be tried as adults. A much-publicized report on the California system released in 2000, *The Color of Justice,* concluded that "transfer from juvenile to adult court appears to exacerbate already large racial disparities in sentencing." From the time of its creation at the end of the nineteenth century, the juvenile court has relinquished its jurisdiction in the case of very serious offenses. In the 1960s and 1970s, the United States Supreme Court formalized the procedures for transferring juveniles to adult criminal court. Every state has enacted legislation that allows for the transfer of some juvenile offenders to criminal courts for prosecution as adults. Political pressure to treat juvenile offenders more harshly has led to a sharp escalation of these transfers in the past decade. The number of children serving time in adult prisons more than doubled between 1985 and 1997.[405]

A juvenile may be tried as an adult through judicial waiver, prosecutorial choice, or statutory exclusion of certain offenses. The most common means of transferring a child to criminal court is a juvenile court judge's waiver of jurisdiction. When judges make waiver decisions they are choosing between punishing the juvenile in adult criminal court or rehabilitating him in juvenile court. There is little statutory guidance for judges who must decide between these two options. Statutes simply give judges broad discretion to determine a child's "amenability to treatment" or threat to public safety. This may be based on the youth's age and prior record, the seriousness of the offense, and clinical evaluations. The nearly unlimited discretion afforded juvenile court judges and the subjective nature of the waiver criteria lead to rampant discrimination in transfer decisions. Professor Frank Zimring calls waiver of jurisdiction the "capital punishment of juvenile justice" and compares judges' wide discretion to the standardless death penalty laws that the Supreme Court overturned in *Furman v. Georgia*.[406] The only change in recent years has been the passage of even tougher laws requiring judges to try children as adults for certain crimes. Some juvenile justice experts believe that the trend for state legislatures to tie judges' hands is even worse for children than unmitigated judicial discretion. At least judges used to have the option of showing leniency toward children. Now they must treat children as adults for a growing list of offenses, including many drug-related crimes.

Numerous studies have uncovered gross variations in the reasons for and rates of waivers among states and within counties of the same state.[407] Indeed, the location of the waiver hearing appears to have as much effect on the outcome as the juvenile's dangerousness. Judges also decide to transfer juveniles to adult court according to their race.[408] A report by the General Accounting Office found that Black juveniles were two to three times more likely to have their cases waived than whites for violent offenses.[409] The campaign to prosecute juvenile offenders as adults has affected Black children the most. Between 1988 and 1997, the number of waived cases involving Black youth rose by 35 percent, compared with a 14 percent increase for whites.[410]

Dissenting from a decision to keep a sixteen-year-old white boy in juvenile court, Minnesota Supreme Court Justice Alan Page issued a scathing condemnation of the judicial system's racial favoritism.[411] M.E.P. was charged in a delinquency petition with first degree murder for shooting a man in the head to settle a drug debt. The juvenile court judge denied the prosecutor's petition to try M.E.P. as an adult, finding that the boy's drug addiction was amenable to treatment. On appeal, a majority of Supreme Court justices held that the judge did not abuse his discretion. Justice Page disagreed. He argued that there was ample evidence of M.E.P.'s dangerousness, including the callous and cold-blooded nature of the shooting at point-blank range and M.E.P.'s long criminal history. Justice Page also drew the court's attention to a case decided the year before involving a sixteen-year-old Black boy, M.R.G., who was also charged with first-degree murder for shooting a man to death. M.R.G. was attending a party with his mother and girlfriend when the man flashed rival gang symbols at them and threatened to rape M.R.G.'s mother. M.R.G. responded by pulling out a gun and shooting the man from four feet away. M.R.G. had no history of violence; his only prior record was for truancy. Yet the juvenile judge transferred M.R.G. to be tried as an adult, and the appellate court upheld the decision. "The only significant distinction between M.E.P. and M.R.G. is that M.E.P. is white and M.R.G. is black," Justice Page stated. "This case presents a striking example of why people of color . . . believe the judicial system is biased against them."

The Color of Justice, an analysis of juvenile transfers to criminal court in Los Angeles County, discovered huge racial disparities. The study reports that

"Hispanic youth are 6 times more likely, African American youth are 12 times more likely, and Asian/other youth 3 times more likely than white youths to be found unfit for juvenile court and transferred to adult court in Los Angeles County."[412] Higher rates of arrest for violent offenses did not account for these racial differences. The transfer rate to adult court for minority violent arrestees was still double that for white violent arrestees.

The Color of Justice reiterates the cumulative impact of racial disparities at each stage of juvenile justice processing. "Compared to white youths," the study calculated, "minority youths are 2.8 times as likely to be arrested for a violent crime, 6.2 times as likely to wind up in adult court, and 7 times as likely to be sent to prison by adult courts." At each step, minority youths' odds of ultimate imprisonment increase. Looking at statewide data, the authors discovered even greater disparities. Whereas African American youths were 6.7 times as likely to be arrested for a violent offense than whites, they were an astounding *18.4 times more likely than white offenders to be sentenced by an adult court to prison.*

Researchers have found another connection between juvenile detention and family disruption. While juvenile detention disrupts Black families, family disruption increases the likelihood that a child will be detained. The racial disparity in detention is related to policies that focus on family support and cooperation in determining the disposition of delinquency cases. Recall the Vera Institute's finding that foster children are detained at such high rates because no adult takes responsibility for them at the precinct or juvenile court. A study of Florida's detention system discovered a related explanation for high detention rates of Black children. Florida's Department of Health and Rehabilitative Services, DHRS, which initially reviews all juvenile arrests, refuses to recommend delinquent youth for diversion programs if their parents cannot be contacted or are unable to attend an intake interview. Department supervisors conceded that Black parents are often single mothers working at low-wage jobs who cannot take off from work to be interviewed. Others are single mothers on welfare with small children at home who cannot afford child care, do not have telephones, or must rely on inconvenient public transportation to get to the DHRS office. When these mothers don't show up to meet with DHRS caseworkers, their children are recommended for detention.

"Our manual told us to interview the child and the parent prior to making a recommendation to the state's attorney," a delinquency intake supervisor explained. "We are less able to reach poor and minority clients. They are less responsive to attempts to reach them. They don't show. They don't have transportation. Then they are more likely to be recommended for formal processing. Without access to a client's family, the less severe options are closed. Once it gets to court, the case is likely to be adjudicated because it got there. It's a self-fulfilling prophesy."[413] Caseworkers often interpret Black parents' distrust of the juvenile justice system as an uncooperative attitude. This, too, can lead to parents losing custody of their delinquent children.

White parents, on the other hand, are more likely to hold professional and managerial positions that give them the flexibility and resources to cooperate with caseworkers. They also have greater access to private treatment options, such as psychological counseling and drug treatment, which enables them to keep their children out of formal processing. Most Black children in trouble have access to these sorts of services only by being adjudicated delinquent and then committed to residential facilities. Like Black families' experience in the child welfare system, the price of services for children is relinquishing custody to the state.

These early decisions by intake officers to recommend formal prosecution and detention, based on a child's family situation, throw Black children into a process that too often ends in their incarceration. Black juveniles are punished more severely than whites, in essence, for being members of poor, struggling families. The Florida caseworkers and supervisors realized that these policies ultimately worked against Black children. But they felt that their hands were tied by agency rules.

Another reason juvenile justice authorities refer Black children to court instead of informal alternatives is that they hold stereotypes about Black families. Many think that Black children come from female-headed households that are ill equipped to handle a troubled child. Because they perceive single mothers as incapable of providing adequate supervision for their children, they believe they are justified in placing these children under state control. Judges rely heavily on predisposition reports that disparage Black juveniles' family situations, often resulting in detention decisions. Florida officials interviewed by professors Donna Bishop and Charles Frazier felt that this bias against Black children was justified. "Inadequate family correlates with race and ethnicity. It makes sense to put delinquent kids from these circumstances in residential facilities," a juvenile court judge told them. "Detention decisions are decided on the basis of whether the home can control and supervise a child," explained a prosecutor. "So minorities don't go home because, unfortunately, their families are less able to control the kids. I think the way the system sets up programs shows some institutional bias. If family stability was not a prerequisite to admission to less severe program options, race differences would be less."

Another prosecutor's racial views would almost be comical if they didn't have such a destructive impact on Black children's lives. "In black families who the dad is, is unknown, while in white families—even when divorced—dad is married or something else," he said. (I wonder whether by "something else" he meant "white.") "The choices are limited because the black family is a multi-generational non-fathered family. You can't send the kid off to live with dad." So, in the mind of this prosecutor, you have to send Black kids off to live in detention centers and prisons.

The ease with which Black children are formally processed because of racial bias or their family situation has a domino effect. Having a prior record is one of the principal grounds for severe sanctions, including transfer to criminal court and sentencing to adult prison. When Black children are initially sent to formal processing, instead of the alternatives whites are more likely to get, they also have a greater chance of being incarcerated if they get into trouble again. The cumulative impact of racial bias at each stage of the juvenile justice process sends more and more Black children into state custody—the likely result of adoption and welfare reform, as well.

PART THREE

The System's Racial Harm

IF A CHILD SURVIVES FOSTER CARE, says Jennifer Toth, author of *Orphans of the Living*, "it's not because of the system, it's despite the system."[1] The American public is well aware of the damage suffered by children who grow up in foster care. If there is one thing that child welfare experts and politicians across the spectrum can agree on, it's that the foster care system is in crisis. The instability of foster care contradicts the centerpiece of contemporary child welfare policy—the importance of permanency to the healthy development of children. Children who enter foster care spend too long in the state's custody, they move too many times from home to home, and they are too often hurt or killed while in the care of strangers. Those who "age out" of foster care commonly end up without work, sleeping in homeless shelters, or serving time in prison.

Disturbing headlines reveal a system that is too overwhelmed to care properly for the children it takes from their parents. In March 2001, Chicago police found six-year-old Allen Kalfus lying lifeless in a tub of ice-cold water at his foster home. The Department of Children and Family Services was aware that Allen's foster mother punished him by forcing him to take cold showers. She had also been reported by neighbors and parents for neglecting the children in her care. DCFS initiated proceedings against her but didn't remove Allen from her custody. The summer before, two caseworkers from a Chicago-area facility asphyxiated an eleven-year-old state ward, Tina Winston, when they pinned her to the floor to calm a temper tantrum. "It's tragedy enough when a parent kills a child," wrote the editor of the *Chicago Tribune*. "It's an outrage when the state rescues a child only to place him in harm's way, when the state recognizes that a child might be in danger in foster care, but lets the rules be the rules and fails to rescue him again."[2]

Americans are also beginning to realize that the harms inflicted by the foster care system fall disproportionately on Black children. Popular accounts of foster care's problems, presented in the past as a color-blind issue, are examining the plight of Black children in the system. In *The Lost Children of Wilder*, journalist Nina Bernstein recounts the twenty-year legal battle to dismantle the dominance of private religious agencies over New York City's foster-care beds. Under the guise of religious preference, Catholic and Jewish charities blatantly excluded Black Protestant children, who were relegated to inhuman state institutions. Hollywood screenwriter Antwone Quenton Fisher tells the miraculous story of his triumph over a childhood spent in orphanages and foster homes. His best-selling memoir, *Finding Fish,* describes the emotional and physical abuse he suffered for thirteen years at the hands of Mizz Pickett, a mean woman fond of berating him with, "Nigga, I'll take ya back where I gotcha from." After moving him briefly to a boys' reform school, the state abandons Fisher as an emancipated minor at a YMCA men's shelter. Although Fisher ultimately turns his life around, we are left to imagine the fate of most Black children subjected to such degrading treatment.

It is plain to see that the child welfare system hurts Black children. But what is the nature of this harm? What is wrong with the huge racial imbalance in the foster care population? This is a critical question because our understanding of what is wrong with the system will determine what steps we take to fix it. The *Wilder* lawsuit was intended to end the deliberate classification of children in foster care according to race and religion. But by the time the plaintiffs won, the nature of discrimination against Black children had already changed. The *Wilder* settlement does nothing to address the astounding racial disparity in New York City's current child welfare system. The main problem is no longer that minority children in foster care are treated differently than white children in foster care. The problem is that just about all the children in foster care are minorities. "Discrimination is no longer the issue," Marcia Lowery, the attorney who brought the case, acknowledged. "This is a system that serves almost exclusively minority kids, and serves them badly."[3]

Today's child welfare discourse is marked by an abysmal failure to grasp the child welfare system's racial harm. This misunderstanding has led to proposals to reform the system that will only make it worse for Black children and their families. The damage inflicted by foster care is, in fact, being used to justify intensified destruction of Black families. If Black children are harmed in state custody, these reformers contend, then the solution is to sever their ties to their parents and move them into adoptive homes. Others see the harm in excessive state intrusion in families but don't see the significance of race. Surely parents and children who are wrongfully separated from each other suffer a terrible injury, they acknowledge. But why is it helpful to explain this injury in terms of race?

Both aspects of the child welfare system's racial disparity—the state's intrusion in families and its racial bias—are essential to explaining its injustice. First, the overrepresentation of Black children in the child welfare system, especially foster care, represents massive state supervision and dissolution of families. Second, this interference with families helps to maintain the disadvantaged status of Black people in the United States. Not only does the child welfare system inflict general harms disproportionately on Black families, but it also inflicts a particular harm—a racial harm—on Black people as a group.

1. Protection of Family Rights

American constitutional jurisprudence defines the harm caused by unwarranted state interference in families in terms of individual rights. Wrongfully removing children from the custody of their parents violates parents' due process right to liberty. The U.S. Constitution doesn't mention families. But the U.S. Supreme Court has found protection of family rights in the Fourteenth Amendment's provision that "no state shall deprive any person of life, liberty, or property without due process of law." The earliest cases interpreting this prohibition to protect citizens against government interference in their substantive liberty involved parental rights. The United States Supreme Court first suggested the constitutional stature of parents' interest in raising their children in *Meyer v. Nebraska*, a 1923 case challenging a ban on foreign language instruction in public schools before the eighth grade.[4] The plaintiff was a teacher who argued that his conviction for teaching German to a ten-year-old student violated his liberty to pursue his profession. In overturning the teacher's conviction, the Court noted that the statute interfered with "the power of the parents to control the education of their own."

Two years later, the Court elaborated the reason for protecting parents' ability "to direct the upbringing and education of children under their control."[5] In *Pierce v. Society of Sisters*, the Court invalidated an Oregon law that required parents to send their children to public school. The Court explained that parents serve a special role of preparing children for participation in society. Taking over this role gives the state too much power over citizens because it standardizes children according to an official model. "The child is not a mere creature of the state," the Court reasoned. "Those who nurture him and direct his destiny have the right, coupled with the high duty, to recognize and prepare him for additional obligations."

Although the Court framed its decisions in *Meyer* and *Pierce* as a vindication of individual rights, closer inspection reveals that the families in these cases were at the center of bitter political contests.[6] The Nebraska statute, like other state prohibitions of foreign-language teaching that proliferated after World War I, enforced a nativist distrust of immigrants, especially from Germany. The motivation behind these laws is reminiscent of the contemporary English-only campaigns that express an anti-immigrant sentiment. Nebraska's counsel argued before the Court that the law's purpose "was to create an enlightened American citizenship in sympathy with the principles and ideals of this country." Oregon's prohibition of private schools was similarly born out of animosity toward the Catholic faith and a desire to teach American children "along standardized lines, which will enable them to acquire a uniform outlook on all national and patriotic questions."

The Court's recognition of parents' rights, then, can be seen a way of protecting the ability of minority groups to socialize their children according to their own standards. The Court has inconsistently adhered to this philosophy, however. The Court has upheld the state's power to limit the liberty of minority parents when it disapproves of the group's doctrines. *Prince v. Massachusetts* involved, as the Court put it, "another episode in the conflict between Jehovah's Witnesses and state authority."[7] The Court upheld the conviction of a Jehovah's Witness under child labor laws for bringing her nine-year-old niece along with her to preach and distribute religious leaflets on the street. The Court held that the state's interest in guarding the girl's well-being overrode her guardian's parental and religious rights. "Parents may be free to become martyrs themselves," the Court stated. "But it does not follow that they are free, in identical circumstances, to make martyrs of their children."

To add another historical layer to these cases, family law scholar Barbara Bennett Woodhouse argues that the real political challenge to state compulsory education laws came from anticommunist opposition to universal public schooling.[8] She notes that the plaintiffs' chief advocate in both *Meyer* and *Pierce* was William Dameron Guthrie, an ultraconservative law professor at Columbia University who was dedicated to the defeat of social welfare legislation. Perhaps the Court wasn't concerned with minority parents' rights, after all. Still, the Court's language established an important rationale for protecting parents' interest in raising their children according to their own values, rather than a state-imposed regime.

The constitutional protection of parents' rights doesn't enforce parental domination over children, akin to the protection of owners' interests in controlling their property. It protects the function parents serve in training and socializing children, which in a free society is better left to families than to the state. University of Maryland professor William Galston argues that these cases recognize the "'expressive interest' of parents in raising children in a manner consistent with their understanding of what gives meaning and value to life."[9] The ability parents have to rear their children is an expression of their freedom of conscience; it one of the most significant ways individuals convey their values. For most people, the freedom to conduct their family life according to their personal beliefs is as meaningful and precious as the freedom to organize with others for political ends. The state interferes with parents' authority to educate their children when it removes them from the home and places them in the care of others.

In its 1982 landmark decision *Santosky v. Kramer,* the Court applied the "fundamental liberty interest of natural parents in the care, custody, and management of their child" to determine the test for terminating parental rights. "Even when the blood relationships are strained," the Court stated, "parents retain a vital interest in preventing the irretrievable destruction of their family life."[10] *Santosky* established a bifurcated process in which judges first decide the fitness of the parent before determining what is in the best interest of the child. The Court set a high standard: before it can sever the bond between a parent and child, the state must prove by "clear and convincing evidence" that the parent is unfit. Just as crucial to safeguarding family ties was the Court's ruling that consideration of the best interest of the child does not belong in this first stage of the hearing. "*Santosky* thus stands for the critical principle that before the state may sanction interference in the relationship between a parent and a child," explain Northwestern law professors Bruce Boyer and Steven Lubet, "there must be some threshold showing—independent of what may be in the best interest of the child—that the parent's conduct falls beneath some minimum acceptable threshold."[11]

The best interest of the child is an open-ended inquiry that encompasses all of the child's circumstances. Focusing first on the best interest of the child would allow the judge to compare the biological parents with foster parents or people who want to adopt the child. Although we want judges to act in the interest of children, this standard would permit courts to take children from capable parents just because the court disapproves of them. Most recently, in *Troxel v. Granville*, the Court reaffirmed the importance of parental control over their children's upbringing when it struck down a Washington statute that gave liberal discretion to judges to grant visitation with children against their parents' wishes. The Court reiterated the rule in *Santosky* that judges can't override the authority of parents who haven't been found unfit just because they think the children would be better off.

Unwarranted government intervention in families also has an adverse impact on children. It is psychologically damaging for children to be ripped from the relationships of intimacy and support on which they depend. When the state seeks to protect children, it must decide not only whether intervention is necessary for children's safety but also whether "it is destructive, both of the bonds upon which the child depends for healthy nurturance and of the child's right to grow in a community that is open, flexible, and self-defining, rather than state-controlled."[12] Slighting parents' rights can hurt children because it makes families vulnerable to state intrusion for the wrong reasons. The constitutional rules for termination of parental rights ensure that children are not separated from their families for reasons that have more to do with the racial, religious, or cultural biases of judges than with protecting the child's physical and emotional well-being.[13] Undue state intervention in families violates the individual interests of both parents and children.

2. A Theory of Group-Based Harm

These explanations of harm do not account for the particular injury inflicted by racially disparate state intervention. Without considering race, we do not capture the full scope of the harm caused by taking large numbers of Black children from their families. Indeed, without considering race, we might not see any harm at all. Focusing solely on individual cases, many of which are difficult to judge, obscures the impact on the Black community of state interventions taken as a whole. High rates of removal of Black children from their homes harm Black people *as a group,* as well as individual parents and children. This is the child welfare system's *racial* harm.

I argued in Part One that the racial disparity is a group-based harm in terms of the *reasons* for racial differences in child welfare interventions. The overrepresentation of Black children in foster care is not simply an accident. All those displaced children do not "just happen to be Black," as adherents to a color-blind approach would say. The disproportionate number of Black children under state supervision results from discriminatory decision making within the system as well as racist institutions in the broader society. High rates of poverty among Black families, bolstered by stereotypes about Black parental unfitness, create the system's racial disparity. Black children suffer a racial harm because their chances of being taken from their parents are far greater than those of white children. Even without proving deliberate racial discrimination, it is still accurate to say that children's risk of entering foster care depends on their race.

The system's racial disparity also *inflicts* a group-based harm. The damage caused by the child welfare system is visited upon a disproportionate share of Black people. Those parents and children directly injured by child welfare authorities should have legal claims based on the violation of their family and civil rights—although current legal doctrines make it difficult for many to establish such a cause of action. But the harmful impact of a racist child welfare system is also felt by Blacks who are not directly involved in it. The negative consequences of disrupting large numbers of Black families and placing them under state supervision affects Black people's status and welfare as a group. I see this more as a political claim that calls for radical systemic change than as a legal claim to be redressed by the courts.

Explaining the racial injustice of the child welfare system is part of the inquiry into the role of group identity in conceptions of justice. Claims for recognition and respect by ethnic groups around the world have brought to light the inadequacy of protecting individual rights. The focus of liberal political theorists on the individual and the state has failed to account for the importance of membership in cultural groups. But how do groups fit within democratic political systems? As the philosopher Jurgen Habermas framed the broader questions: "Should citizens' identities as members of ethnic, cultural, or religious groups *publicly* matter, and if so, how can collective identities make a difference with the framework of constitutional democracy? Are collective identities and cultural membership politically relevant, and if so, how can they legitimately affect the distribution of rights and the recognition of legal claims?"[14]

The racially disparate state intervention in Black families inflicts political damage that gives rise to a group-based claim of racial injustice. I will explicate this claim in three parts. First, I argue that there is a connection between the welfare of individual Black children and parents and the welfare of Blacks as a group. Second, I discuss the power of state supervision of families to influence the political status of groups. Last, I present the specific ways in which the child welfare system inflicts group-based harms and address potential objections to this approach. In sum, I hope to show that the child welfare system's racial disparity has negative material and ideological consequences for Black families that affect the status of Blacks in America as a whole. This group-based harm can be redressed only by reversing the course of government destruction of Black families and redefining child welfare to generously support children in their homes.

Connecting Black Individual and Group Interests

Black Americans' welfare is determined not only by the atomistic decisions of each individual but also by the condition of the entire group. According to the American system of racial classification, individuals are born into racial categories that determine their status in society. By the eighteenth century, African chattel slavery constituted a perpetual, lifelong condition passed on to the next generation. Whites established a racial caste system that required a clear racial demarcation between slaves and their masters. An official rule of racial purity based on the natural separation of the races survived Emancipation and was not abolished until 1967 when the United States Supreme Court held antimiscegenation laws to be unconstitutional in *Loving v. Virginia*.[15]

America's racial hierarchy continues to accord automatic benefits and privileges to people who are born white and automatic disadvantages to others.[16] Powerful racist imagery portrays Black bodies, intellect, character, and culture as inherently inferior and vulgar.[17] Demeaning racial stereotypes judge African American individuals according to assumed group traits. The criminal behavior of a minority of individual Blacks makes all Blacks seem suspicious. This negative group treatment is exemplified by racial profiling, the routine use of race by police in deciding whom to stop and question, as well as actor Danny Glover's inability to catch a taxi.

Black Americans have been subjected to discrimination on the basis of their race in the political, economic, and social realms. Although racism is not as blatant or brutal as existed during the periods of slavery and Jim Crow laws, it continues through practices such as employment discrimination, neighborhood segregation, and police abuse. The eradication of overt barriers to equal opportunity have not equalized the condition of Black and white Americans. For example, past barriers to Black property accumulation have produced a huge racial gap in wealth generations later.[18] As University of Chicago political scientist Michael Dawson sums up, "in African Americans' historical experience, life chances have been linked to the ascriptive feature of race in all spheres of life."[19]

Most African Americans also self-identify as part of a group whose members are tied together by a common heritage, culture, and social experience.[20] By the turn of the twentieth century, Blacks had developed a race consciousness rooted in a sense of shared destiny, which laid the foundation for later civil rights struggles. "Black nationhood is not rooted in territoriality," writes John Gwaltney, "so much as it is in a profound belief in the fitness of core black culture and in the solidarity born of a transgenerational detestation of our subordination."[21] These bonds have produced a strong affiliation among Blacks and a set of distinctive styles, customs, and beliefs about social issues that are widely recognized, if not uniformly followed, by Black people.[22]

Black Americans' group identification is reflected in Black political behavior and cultural values. Michael Dawson highlights the critical role of racial group interests in explaining Black Americans' relatively unified political behavior.[23] Blacks' political beliefs and actions as *individuals* are strongly related to their sense of racial *group* interests. Black people have a strong belief in their "linked fate"; a defining aspect of the racial identity of African Americans, writes Dawson, is "the perceived link between one's own fate and that of the race." For example, a 1988 national survey of Black Americans found that 64 percent responded affirmatively to the question, "Do you think that whatever happens generally to the black people in this country will have something to do with what happens in your life?" Most African Americans are deeply aware that, whatever their individual character and efforts, their personal well-being and chances of success are inextricably tied to the advancement of African Americans as a group.

Scholars have identified a similar feature in Black culture. They argue that most Black Americans share a social orientation characterized by "communalism," which emphasizes the social interdependence of people. "Individuals view themselves as inextricably linked with others in their social milieu," explains Howard University professor A. Wade Boykin and his colleagues. "There exists an emphasis on social bonds and mutual interdependence such that the good of the individual is closely intertwined with the good of the group."[24] Some trace this collective conception of self back to traditional African customs and worldview. But this Afrocultural trait is manifested in contemporary African American life in the continued tradition of extended families and the superior performance of Black students in cooperative learning situations. It is also reflected in *Nguzo Saba* (the Seven Principles), a set of seven key values developed by Black nationalist Maulana Karenga to serve as a guide for Black community relations.[25] These principles are typically recited during the celebration of Kwanzaa, an Afrocentric holiday instituted by Karenga, which many Black Americans observe during the week following Christmas. For instance, the first principle, Umoja (Unity), exhorts Blacks to "strive for and maintain unity in the family, community, nation and race." The third principle, Ujima (Collective Work and Responsibility) means "to build and maintain our community together and make our sisters' and brothers' problems our problems and to solve them together."

What happens to individual parents and children in the child welfare system is closely related to the status of Black Americans as a whole. The fate of Jornell's, Devon's, and Valerie's children depends on the economic well-being of Black Americans and the public's view of Black family fitness. And the fate of Black children who may not come into contact with child protection authorities—their opportunity to flourish as equal human beings in this society—is affected by the child welfare system's treatment of Black families.

The Political Impact of Family Disintegration

Family disruption has historically served as a chief tool of group oppression. The racial bias in state interventions in the family clarifies the reasons for safeguarding family autonomy. Parents' freedom to raise their children is important not only to individuals but also to the welfare or even survival of ethnic, cultural, and religious groups. Weakening the parent-child bond and disintegrating families within a group are a means of subordinating the entire group. The individualized focus on preserving personal choice in the private sphere of family life fails to recognize the family's *political* role. Families are not only expressions of individual choices. The family is a social institution serving political ends.

The American regime of slavery reveals better than any other example the political function of repressing family autonomy. Slave law installed the white master as the head of an extended plantation family that included his slaves. The plantation family ruled by white men was considered the best institution to transmit moral values to uncivilized Africans.[26] Courts reasoned that the slave owner's moral authority over the family was ordained by divine imperative. Slaves, on the other hand, had no legal authority over their children. Naming a slave after his owner reinforced the child's ultimate subservience to his white master rather than to his parents.

In *Neglected Stories: The Constitution and Family Values,* Peggy Cooper Davis powerfully uncovers the antislavery origins of rights to family autonomy.[27] The legislators who drafted the Civil War Amendments understood the importance of protecting families because of slavery's destruction of families. "Abrogation of the parental bond was a hallmark of the civil death that United States slavery imposed," writes Professor Davis.[28] Slave masters' control of their slaves hinged on restricting slaves' capacity to educate and socialize their children. In this way, whites attempted to prevent slaves from constructing their own system of morals and from acting according to their own chosen values. Slaveholders proclaimed their moral authority by reinforcing the message of parental helplessness, frequently whipping adult slaves in front of their children. The sale of children apart from their parents was another brutal incarnation of this power. "These messages of parental vulnerability and subordination were repeatedly burned into the consciousness of slave parents and children,"

Davis explains, "undermining their sense of worth, diminishing the sense of family security and authority, eroding the parents' function as a model of adult agency and independence, and, most importantly for our purposes, kindling a determination that freedom would entail parental prerogatives."[29]

According to Davis, painful stories of family disruption told by former slaves motivated the Fourteenth Amendment rights guaranteeing family autonomy. The rights of family were central to the antislavery movement. In petitions to the government, slaves often based their claims for freedom on the natural right to family integrity. White abolitionists also focused their condemnation of slavery on its immoral destruction of families. Slavery's deprivation of family rights was a burning issue for the Reconstruction Congress as it drafted the Thirteenth Amendment prohibiting slavery and involuntary servitude and the Fourteenth Amendment protecting liberty. The legislators were "deeply affected by the widely publicized accounts of parental separations and fully responsive to the argument that rights of family are inalienable," writes Professor Davis. This is what inspired them to establish the constitutional rights "to maintain a parental relationship, to have a measure of liberty in child rearing, and some would argue, to expect a measure of public responsibility for children." Contemporary notions of family liberty, typically interpreted as individual rights, can trace their roots to the effort to eradicate racial oppression.

Professor Davis also finds the genesis of family rights in Black people's own meaning of freedom. After Emancipation, the first act of many newly freed Blacks was to claim their children.[30] White planters exploited the apprenticeship laws to maintain their control over Black children. Judges had the power to place Black children in the care and service of whites if they found the parents to be unfit and deemed placement to be "better for the habits and comfort of the child." Out of the 90,000 emancipated slaves in Maryland, 10,000 were re-enslaved under apprenticeship laws, generally to their former owners. Some Black parents succeeded in taking back their children, while others appealed to the courts for relief. Three hundred Black citizens sent a petition to President Andrew Johnson charging that "our homes are invaded and our little ones seized at the family fireside, and forcibly bound to masters who are by law expressly released from any obligation to educate them in secular or religious knowledge." Masters were required by law to educate their white, but not their Black, apprentices.

The ideology supporting the apprenticeship system adopted "one of the most insidious defenses of the slave system," notes Professor Davis. According to this ideology, "slavery provided protection and safe governance for a people unfit to live as free agents or to provide suitably for their children."[31] Whites, like Federick Eustis, a Georgia plantation superintendent, argued that Black children needed the supervision afforded by apprenticeship because the Black race "was not prepared for freedom yet." A key component of Blacks' presumed need for continued white supervision was a "theory of black parental incompetence." Whites contended that because slave children had been subject to their masters' authority, their parents were not able to discipline them properly after the family was emancipated.

Professor Davis contrasts the ideology justifying re-enslavement with Blacks' ideology of family freedom. Blacks located their family members still held by former slave masters and negotiated for their return. Establishing a family free from the sovereignty of slave masters formed the heart of Black self-determination. Emancipated parents, determined to recover their children, "shared a passionate commitment to the stability of family life as a badge of freedom," writes historian Eric Foner.[32] Blacks often faced brutal retaliation from ex-owners reluctant to give up the human chattel they still viewed as their property. "If any one has your children, go and get them," General John M. Palmer advised Black soldiers fighting in Kentucky in 1865. "If they will not give them to you, steal them out at night. I do not think you will be committing any crime, nor do I believe the Almighty Ruler of the Universe will think you have committed any." Countless mothers endured vicious beatings at the hands of whites when they demanded the return of their children. In a letter to his wife in 1864, a Union officer wrote that every day he was "visited by some poor woman who has walked perhaps ten or twenty miles to try to procure the release of her children taken forcibly away from her and held to all intents and purposes in slavery." For these mothers, having custody of their children was an integral part of freedom. "God help us, our condition is bettered but little; free ourselves, but deprived of our children, almost the only thing that would make us free and happy," Lucy Lee wrote in a petition to free her daughter. "It was on their account we desired to be free."

It is not surprising, then, that Malcolm X, the most penetrating critic of white supremacy, would see the parallels between the modern child welfare system and the institution of slavery. In his autobiography, Malcolm X compares the destruction of his own family by the child welfare agency to slavery.[33] His family's demise began with caseworkers' intrusion into their home after his father was murdered by the Ku Klux Klan. "When the state Welfare people began coming to our house," he writes, "they acted and looked at [my mother] and us, and around in our house, in a way that had about it the feeling—at least for me—that we were not people." He describes his mother as a proud woman who resisted the caseworkers' meddling in her family life. "But the monthly Welfare check was their pass. They acted as if they owned us, as if we were their private property. As much as my mother would have liked to, she couldn't keep them out."

The caseworkers' sights turned to removing Malcolm and his seven siblings from their mother's custody. "I think they felt that getting children in foster homes was a legitimate part of their function, and the result would be less troublesome, however they went about it." He blames the caseworkers for unnecessarily breaking up his family through their assault on his mother's spirit. "They were vicious as vultures. They had no feelings, understanding, compassion, or respect for my mother. They told us 'She's crazy for refusing food.' Right then was when our home, our unity, began to disintegrate. We were having a hard time, and I wasn't helping. But we could have made it, we could have stayed together." Using the same technique as white slaveholders, the caseworkers humiliated Malcolm X's mother in front of her children to send a message that they were in control.

The caseworkers finally got their way when Malcolm's mother was committed to a state mental hospital and the children were sent to foster care. "A Judge had authority over me and all my brothers and sisters. We were 'state children,' court wards; he had the full say-so over us. A white man in charge of a Black man's children! *Nothing but legal, modern slavery*—however kindly intentioned."

The Child Welfare System's Group-Based Harms

The political impact of family disruption, combined with the linked fate of all Black Americans, explains the child welfare system's racial harm. The disproportionate removal of individual Black children from their homes has a detrimental impact on the status of Blacks as a group. Excessive state interference in Black family life damages Black people's sense of personal and community identity. Family and community disintegration weakens Blacks' collective ability to overcome institutionalized discrimination and to work toward greater political and economic strength. The system's racial disparity also reinforces negative stereotypes about Black people's incapacity to govern themselves and need for state supervision.

Family integrity is crucial to group welfare because of the role parents and other relatives play in transmitting survival skills, values, and self-esteem to the next generation. Growing up in a family teaches children how to form healthy relationships with others in their immediate community and in the broader society. Families provide a base of support from which neighbors can join together to accomplish communal projects. Social theorists use the term "social capital" to describe this valuable function that families perform when they interact with other families and institutional networks through schools, social organizations, and religious institutions. Social capital is the intangible good produced by relationships among people, as distinguished from the tangible skills, resources, and knowledge that constitute human capital, "making possible the achievement of certain ends."[34]

Robert Putnam is credited with reviving the analysis of social capital in his 1993 book, *Making Democracy Work: Civic Traditions in Modern Italy,* which argued that Northern Italy's strong civic traditions, currently characterized by cooperatives, mutual aid societies, and neighborhood associations, were largely responsible for a healthy social and economic life. Relationships of mutual cooperation are especially critical in impoverished communities to gain access to scarce resources. "Social capital is best understood as a process that facilitates access to benefits, not as a concrete thing appropriated by individual or networks," explains sociologist Patricia Fernandez Kelly.[35] Although some conservative scholars have used this concept to advocate replacing social welfare programs with self-help measures, understanding the importance of social capital counsels in favor of public policies that strengthen struggling families.

Families are also a principal form of "oppositional enclaves" that are essential to democracy. Families, as well as other voluntary associations among citizens, help their members to collectively contest domination by the state and the forces that perpetuate racial, economic, and gender inequalities. "The goals of these counterpublics," writes Harvard political theorist Jane Mansbridge, "include understanding themselves better, forging bonds of solidarity, preserving the memories of past injustices, interpreting and reinterpreting the meanings of those injustices, working out alternative conceptions of self, community, of justice, of universality."[36] Sara Evans and Harry C. Boyte similarly identify "free spaces" as a source of democratic change. These contexts in which "people are able to learn a new self-respect, a deeper and more assertive group identity, public skills, and values of cooperation and civic virtue" are the seed beds of transformative political action.[37] There is mounting concern that the economic devastation of inner-city communities has eroded social networks that historically sustained Black civic life and social protest.[38] State destruction of family ties contributes to the gradual demise of Black civil society.

Just as whites have made family disruption a tool of racial oppression, so Blacks have made family solidarity a tool of resistance. For slaves, the family was a site of solace from white oppression.[39] Slaves' care for their families defied the expectation of total service to whites. Angela Davis observes that "slave women perform[ed] the only labor of the slave community which could not be directly and immediately claimed by the oppressor."[40] Although some slave mothers opposed slavery by abandoning or even killing their children, the vast majority defied bondage by caring for their children. Blacks have held a political interpretation of the home as a site of resistance against outside oppression.

The mother-child relationship continues to have a political significance for Black women. Black women historically have experienced motherhood as an empowering denial of the dominant society's denigration of their humanity. Alice Walker described her relationship with her child in terms of their political solidarity: "We are together, my child and I. Mother and child, yes, but *sisters* really, against whatever denied us all that we are."[41] Black women have seen their children as the source of motivation, courage, and insight to resist oppression. Concern for children has often served as the foundation for formal collective struggles among Black women, such as the Sisterhood of Black Single Mothers in Brooklyn and the Welfare Mothers' Movement. Black women often explain their involvement in social activism as an outgrowth of their experience as mothers and use their mothering skills in their political work.

Placing large numbers of children in state custody interferes with these critical functions served by families. It depletes a community's social capital, weakening the group's ability to form productive connections among its members and with people and institutions outside the community. It destroys oppositional enclaves, depriving the community of a central means of resisting injustice. The child welfare system undermines Black people's ability to struggle against the many forms of institutional discrimination that persist in this country and to improve the welfare of Black communities.

"We learn how to love and share in families," Dr. Maisha Hamilton-Bennett, an African American psychologist who treats families in Chicago's child welfare system, told me. "We learn how to trust by trusting our parents to take care of us no matter what. Many foster children feel abandoned by their parents because they can't understand why they are in foster care. Foster care prepares children for dependency." When children are removed from their parents and placed in the custody of the state, it disrupts their sense of security and self-determination. Certain practices in the foster care system reinforce the disruption in children's lives. Children are often moved from one foster home to another. Many are drugged with psychiatric medications to keep them docile.[42] They are stigmatized and made to feel inferior just by being involved in the system. One study of adolescents ages twelve to nineteen with at least two years experience in foster care found that it had a negative impact on identity development.[43] Children reported that they felt devalued both because of negative stereotypes about foster children and because of the institutional structure of foster care characterized by excessive restrictiveness, lack of respect, a focus on pathology, and discontinuity in caregiving. "The development of a stigmatized self-identity gives rise to several other interrelated consequences, including social isolation and lack of family connection," writes the study's author. "The abnormality and stigma associated with being a foster child often leave one socially ostracized and disconnected."

Social psychologists believe that individuals' evaluation of their self-efficacy—the "judgment of their capabilities to organize and execute courses of action required to attain designated types of performances"—is an important part of their concept of themselves.[44] Self-efficacy involves our beliefs about our own competence, power, and control, as well as our feelings of self-worth. Foster care seems almost calculated to destroy children's perception of self-efficacy because it disrupts all their sources of a sense of empowerment.

Family disintegration leads to community disintegration. The material impact of family disruption and supervision is intensified when the child welfare system's destruction is concentrated in inner-city neighborhoods. In Chicago, for example, almost all child protection cases are clustered in two zip code areas, which are almost exclusively African American. Most of the families in the city's Englewood neighborhood are involved with state protective services.[45] One in ten children in Central Harlem have been taken from their parents and placed in foster care. In 1997, 3,000 children in this single neighborhood were in the state's custody. "In Mott Haven and Hunts Point, Bed-Stuy and Brownsville," reports *City Limits* about the extent of child removals in New York City, "about 6 percent of all the neighborhood's kids have been uprooted and sent to a new home, which could be anywhere in the city or even outside of it."[46]

The publication of *The Truly Disadvantaged* by sociologist William Julius Wilson in 1987 spawned heightened interest in research testing Wilson's assertions about the social consequences of unemployment concentrated in isolated inner-city neighborhoods. Studies measuring "neighborhood effects" investigate how the spatial configuration of poverty and other socioeconomic factors influence individuals' behavior above and beyond individual sociodemographic characteristics.[47] In *American Apartheid*, Douglas Massey and Nancy Denton describe a damaging relationship between residential segregation and welfare receipt. "Because of racial segregation . . . the higher levels of welfare receipt were confined to a small number of isolated, all-black neighborhoods," they write. "By promoting the spatial concentration of welfare use, therefore, segregation created a residential environment within which welfare dependency was the norm, leading to the intergenerational transmission and broader perpetuation of urban poverty."[48]

Although this explanation for transmission of welfare dependency is controversial, it provides a useful way of understanding the impact of neighborhood characteristics on residents' handling of social problems. The spatial concentration of child welfare supervision similarly creates an environment in which state custody of children is a realistic expectation, if not the norm. Everyone in the neighborhood has either experienced state intrusion in their family or knows someone who has. Parents are either being monitored by case-workers or live with the fear that they may soon be investigated. Children have been traumatized by removal from their homes and placement in foster care or know that their parents are subject to the state's higher authority.

Social science research suggests further that neighborhood conditions can affect residents' sense of control over their lives. Perceived control is the belief that you are the master of your life, possessing the power to shape the events that determine your future. At the opposite end of the spectrum, perceived powerlessness describes the expectation that you are incapable of achieving desired ends and your fate is determined by forces outside your control. Two sociologists at Ohio State University found that people who live in disordered neighborhoods where social control has broken down have significantly higher levels of perceived powerlessness, in part because they have weak social ties to their neighbors.[49]

A 2000 University of Michigan study examined differential patterns of relationships between unfair treatment and psychological distress across high and low poverty census tracts in Detroit.[50] The findings suggested that individuals living in communities with higher poverty rates are more vulnerable to the effects of unfair treatment, perhaps because they have reduced access to problem-solving resources. The researchers concluded, "These results contribute to a growing body of evidence suggesting that 'race' effects operate through multiple pathways, including race-based residential segregation combined with economic disinvestment and unfair treatment at the interpersonal level."

Theories about the impact of neighborhood disorder on crime and social norms are the subject of intense scholarly debate. But it stands to reason that high rates of family disruption within neighborhoods negatively affect residents' sense of control over their lives and make it hard for neighbors to achieve collective goals.

The spatial concentration of state supervision of families also increases the level of family disruption caused by state supervision. There is an inevitable mismatch between the neighborhoods that produce most of the children in foster care and those that provide the most foster homes. The very poorest communities have the highest proportion of children who go to foster care, but are the least likely to have residents and housing that meet foster care licensing requirements. Many of the children removed from their parents are sent to foster homes in distant communities. This geographic dispersion adds to the disorientation foster children experience. "It disrupts their schooling, it disrupts their friendships," Anne Lown, a Brooklyn social services manager told *Child Welfare Watch*. "Everything they know in their lives is gone."[51] Children are shipped out of these communities for foster care and return bearing the marks of social isolation and state custody.

How can we measure the extent of community damage caused by the child welfare system? To my knowledge, no one has tried to do it. But we can look for guidance to the emerging literature on the collateral consequences of mass incarceration. Social scientists are just beginning to investigate the harm caused to Black communities by locking up the large portions of young Black men and women in the nation's prisons. A "Mass Incarceration Working Group" sponsored by the Russell Sage Foundation, composed of the preeminent scholars in the field, is evaluating "the consequences of incarcerating ever growing numbers of individuals, especially young, less-educated minority men." Its first task is to examine the possibility that this regime "reinforces the marginal position of these individuals in the labor market and larger political economy through a cycle of diminished employment opportunities, illicit work, and incarceration."[52] The working group plans to pursue diverse research strategies, including statistical analyses of large data sets, surveys of at-risk populations, and ethnographic studies.

Other social scientists have focused attention on the corrosive impact that high Black incarceration rates have on Black communities' civic life. In thirteen states, a felony conviction can result in lifetime denial of the right to vote. The Sentencing Project estimated in 1997 that 1.4 million African American men were currently or permanently disenfranchised from voting as a result of a felony conviction. Today the number has grown to more than 2 million. Almost a third of Black men in Alabama and Florida cannot vote. And in five other states—Iowa, Mississippi, New Mexico, Virginia, and Wyoming—one-quarter of Black men were disenfranchised because of felony convictions.[53] At this rate, according to *Chicago Tribune* columnist Salim Muwakkil, "experts predict that 30 to 40 percent of the next generation of black men can expect to lose their right to vote at some point in their lifetimes."[54] This startling dilution of Black voting strength affects the ability of

Blacks to shape political decision making. Felony convictions, then, cause a political harm to Blacks as a group.

Placing large numbers of children in state custody inflicts similar collateral damage on Black communities. Although child removals do not impose immediate disenfranchisement, they disrupt the family and community networks that prepare children to participate in future political life. Like mass incarceration, mass government supervision of children negatively affects the welfare of entire neighborhoods in addition to its deprivation of individuals' liberty. Evaluating a policy from a group perspective changes the calculus of the policy's costs and benefits. The reasons that justify incarcerating individual defendants may be outweighed by the collateral harms that mass incarceration causes to Blacks as a group and to society as a whole. Likewise, even if we could justify separating children from their parents in individual cases (and these decisions are often unwarranted), we must still contend with the collective harms that racially disparate state interventions in families produce.

So far I have described the internal harm that the child welfare system inflicts on Black families and communities. The system's racial disparity also has an external impact. The disproportionate shattering of Black family ties reinforces stereotypes that negatively affect the way others view group members. Negative stereotyping is one of the most common forms of group harm.[55] Negative stereotyping occurs when someone creates a mental model of a group from a composite of unfavorable characteristics of a few group members. Those holding the stereotype then perceive all members of the group according to the model without regard to whether individual group members actually fit the model. Negative stereotypes cause harm to groups when they form the basis of unfair treatment of group members. They are especially powerful when they are pervasive in a culture and apply to a group whose members are easily distinguishable.

All of these factors have made the negative stereotyping of Blacks an extremely effective means of perpetuating racial inequality in America. Racial stereotypes are part of a belief system deeply embedded in American culture that is premised on the superiority of whites and the inferiority of Blacks. A pattern of oppositional categories associates whites with positive characteristics (industrious, intelligent, responsible), while associating Blacks with the opposite aberrational qualities (lazy, ignorant, shiftless). Negative images of African Americans are displayed in the media and reinforced by institutions in which Blacks hold a position of disadvantage. So, for example, the stereotype that Black people are predisposed to law breaking and violence is broadcast in the media's preoccupation with stories involving Black criminals. The belief that most criminal activity is committed by Blacks is then reinforced by the mass incarceration of young Black men and women. Similarly, the stereotype that Black people are lazy and prefer being dependent on government handouts is perpetuated by the media's portrayal of welfare recipients as almost exclusively Black and by barriers to equal participation in the economy. These negative stereotypes, in turn, legitimate punitive policies that imprison and impoverish more Blacks, entrenching further their inferior social status. The images of Blacks as crime-prone and lazy affects more than those who are locked in prison or welfare reliant. These images redound on the perceived character and the opportunities of all Black people. They place Black individuals, regardless of their personal character, at greater risk of being stopped by the police and being turned down for a job.

The racial disparity in the child welfare system works the same way. A child welfare system that takes Black children from their parents at twice the rate of whites sends a negative message about Black families. It says that Black parents are unfit to raise their children and that Black children are better off in the state's custody. It reinforces long-held stereotypes about Black mothers' and fathers' irresponsibility and corrupting influence on their children. It replicates the notion created in chattel slavery that there is no such thing as a Black family. In fact, placing so many Black children in the state's custody implements the quintessential racist insult—that Black people are incapable of governing themselves and need white supervision.

In his pathbreaking article "The Id, the Ego, and Equal Protection," legal scholar Charles Lawrence III challenges equal protection doctrine that requires proof that government officials have a discriminatory purpose.[56] This standard was too restrictive, Lawrence argues, because many discriminatory policies result from unconscious racism. He proposed instead a "cultural meaning" test to determine the constitutionality of government policies that have a racially disparate impact. "This test would evaluate governmental conduct to see if it conveys a symbolic message to which the culture attaches racial significance."

The U.S. child welfare system passes the cultural meaning test for racial discrimination—it sends a well-recognized message of Black inferiority. The message that Black people need white supervision legitimates the most destructive incidents of racial injustice—the brutal regulation of Black communities by law enforcement, welfare reform, and child protective services. This message helps to perpetuate a degrading view of Black citizenship, that Blacks are less capable of both participating in the political economy and of governing themselves.

The political harm to Blacks that I outlined above can be distinguished from both traditional legal claims of individual discrimination and from claims based on an essential biological or cultural Black identity. Under the dominant individualistic model of justice, individuals bring lawsuits to enforce their rights and to redress the harm they suffered. Although the individual discrimination claims of many Black families have merit, this is not what I wish to argue here. My claim of group-based harm does not depend on evidence that decisions in individual cases were motivated by racial bigotry or would not have been made if the parents were white. Rather they rely on the group-wide damage that racial disparities in the child welfare system inflict on African Americans. This is a reason not just to compensate Black families for the disruption of their lives but to change the entire system of child welfare so that it stops inflicting its racially biased destruction of families.

Individual parents and children are harmed by discriminatory child welfare practices at the same time that this harm is tied inextricably to their group status. Political philosophers have explored the relationship between the moral claims of individuals and groups, and their work is helpful in explicating my argument. In *The Morality of Groups,* Larry May criticizes the dualistic conception of rights and justice that divides into two models—an individualistic model that sees only harms to individuals and a collectivist model that attaches rights to groups with individuals holding only derivative rights. Viewing groups as "individuals in relationships," he develops an intermediate category of group-based rights, which are rights the individual obtains by virtue of being a member of a group.[57] Carol Gould similarly characterizes social groups as entities composed of "individuals-in-relations." She argues that although individuals as agents exist prior to groups, "they stand in internal relations to each other such that they become the individuals they are in and through such social relations."[58]

Building on an understanding of individuals in relation to social groups, Jurgen Habermas dismisses any conflict between the principle of equal respect for individuals, regardless of gender, race, or ethnicity, and the demand for respect for disadvantaged groups. He argues that "private autonomy" is necessarily connected to "public autonomy" because private persons cannot achieve the enjoyment of equal individual liberties unless they jointly exercise their autonomy as citizens to participate in making the laws that govern them. "A correctly understood theory of rights," Habermas writes, "requires a politics of recognition that protects the integrity of the individual in the life contexts in which his or her identity is formed."[59] Respecting the rights of individuals to equality, then, requires equal treatment of the collectives that safeguard their identities.

These philosophical explorations of the importance of groups to individual identity and welfare arrive at the same conclusion that ordinary Black Americans have understood for centuries. Although Black individuals experience the effects of racial discrimination, the reason they become victims of discrimination and their prospects for ending it depend on the status of Black people as a group.

My argument also differs from the more familiar group-based characterization of the harm Black children suffer when they are placed in white adoptive homes. The most influential articulation of this claim is the controversial resolution opposing transracial adoption that was passed by the National Association of Black Social Workers in 1972. The 1960s had witnessed a dramatic rise in transracial adoptions as fewer unmarried white women gave up their babies. By the early 1970s, more than 15,000 white families had adopted Black children. Calling transracial adoptions a form of "genocide," the NABSW declared:

> Black children should be placed only with Black families whether in foster care or adoption. Black children belong physically, psychologically and culturally in Black families in order that they receive the total sense of themselves and develop a sound projection of their future. Human beings are products of their environment and develop their sense of values, attitudes, and self-concepts within their own family structure. Black children in white homes are cut off from the healthy development of themselves as Black people.[60]

Analysts have attributed the subsequent decline in transracial adoptions, from 2 percent of all adoptions in 1975 to 1 percent in 1987, to the NABSW's opposition.[61]

The Black social workers' position centered around a theory about Black children's socialization and sense of self. The organization asserted that a Black cultural environment was crucial for Black children to develop self-esteem and a healthy racial identity. Black children also need to learn specialized skills to survive in a racist society, something the organization argued white parents were not equipped to impart. The NABSW saw the "love conquers all" philosophy of transracial adoption supporters as hopelessly naive. Black children raised in white homes, argued NABSW President William Merritt, "often do not develop coping mechanisms necessary to function in a society that is inherently racist against African-Americans."[62]

Another aspect of the Black social workers' position emphasized transracial adoption's harm to Black cultural life. The organization argued that Black people were hurt as a political entity by the loss of such a large portion of its children. The position paper referred to "the necessity of self-determination from birth to death, of all Black people" and "the philosophy that we need our own to build a strong nation." As one expert explained it, "Blacks inculcated with white perspectives cannot contribute meaningfully to the African American community. The adoption of black children by white parents erodes the economic, political, and cultural bases of black social life."[63] This explanation of the harm caused by transracial adoption focuses on the impact on the Black community as a whole rather than the psychological well-being of individual children.

In recent years, the NABSW has softened its absolute race-matching policy. Their attention has shifted away from opposing adoption of Black children by whites toward supporting adoptions within the African American community. They point out that Blacks face numerous barriers to adopting; if agencies made a concerted effort to find Black adoptive parents, there would be no need for transracial adoption. The issue, then, isn't whether whites should be permitted to adopt Black children. "Why is it so commonly accepted that African-American families are not interested in adoption and that there is not a sufficient number of black families to adopt all of the African-American children who need families?" Toni Oliver, a NABSW spokesperson, says is the right question. "Why would people think that, in order for black children to escape the treachery of foster care, their salvation is to be placed with white families?"[64]

What appeared radical to many Americans in the NABSW's resolution was echoed in United Nations protections of endangered cultures. Human rights law supports the claim that transracial adoption may constitute cultural genocide. A number of international laws protect the rights of indigenous peoples and other minorities to preserve their distinct cultural identity. Children are a prominent focus of these laws because "one of the most important elements of cultural preservation or self-determination is transmission of indigenous culture to indigenous children."[65] The United Nations definition of genocide includes destroying "in part" a national, ethnic, racial or religious group by "measures intended to prevent births within the group" and "forcibly transferring children from one group to another group." Article 27 of the International Covenant on Civil and Political Rights guarantees the right of members of minority groups "to enjoy their own culture, to profess and to practice their own religion, [and] to use their own language." The Convention on the Rights of the Child extends these protections to children. This law also provides that, when the state places children in substitute care, "due regard shall be paid to the desirability of continuity in a child's upbringing and to the child's ethnic, religious, cultural, and linguistic background." Human rights experts interpret these protections of minority cultures to require that children should be cared for by families in their own group; that minority groups should participate in decisions relating to the care, custody, and placement of children in the group; and that decisions on child welfare should be made through the group's own institutions.[66]

With the recent legislation prohibiting race-matching, the federal government has definitively rejected this notion of Black cultural injury. Yet Congress recognized this type of claim when it passed the Indian Child Welfare Act in 1978. The federal lawmakers acknowledged a deliberate government campaign to wrongfully remove Indian children from their parents to place them in white homes and institutions. The practice was so rampant that it threatened to decimate some tribal cultures. In Senate hearings, Indians presented evidence that between one-quarter to one-third of all Indian children had been separated from their families. Official removal of Indian children from their parents dated back to 1860, when federal authorities promoted boarding schools designed to strip Indian children of their customs and assimilate them into white culture.[67] Adoption later became a central part of federal policy to uproot Indian children from reservations. The Bureau of Indian Affairs, in collaboration with the Child Welfare League of America, launched the Indian Adoption Project in 1958 to stimulate adoptions of Indian children nationwide. Huge numbers of Indian children were relocated from reservations to adoptive homes in distant white communities. In 1971, for example, nearly one in four Indian infants under age one in Minnesota was placed for adoption.[68]

The government's reason for the wide-scale transfer of Indian children was the familiar child-saving rationale. *Far from the Reservation,* a 1972 report by Columbia social work professor David Fanshel, explained the relocation program as a response to the "tragic plight" of Indians, marked by unsanitary housing, illiteracy, unemployment, and alcoholism.[69] "The children placed through the Indian Adoption Project," Fanshel wrote, "were those who, from the perspective of the social workers who intimately knew their situations, were doomed to lives of stark deprivation." Most of the Indian children Fanshel surveyed were removed because of their parents' alcoholism, "personality disorder," or neglect. Social workers alleged that Indian children suffered "social deprivation" or "emotional damage" by living with their parents. Fanshel also sought to justify the program with interviews of whites following the progress of Indian children they adopted. He concluded that "more than fifty percent of the children were rated as showing relatively problem-free adjustments . . . and another 25 percent were rated as showing adequate adjustments with strengths outweighing weaknesses." Subjective judgments about Indian parents' unfitness and Indian children's well-being helped to divert attention from the political implications of mass family destruction.

Congress rejected these excuses for taking Indian children from their homes. It condemned the culturally biased decisions of government social workers who judged Indian families based on "a white, middle-class standard which, in many cases, forecloses placement with [an] Indian family." The House Report noted that "in areas where rates of problem drinking among Indians and non-Indians are the same, it is rarely applied against non-Indian parents." The House Report also criticized social workers for removing Indian children on such vague grounds as "neglect" or "social deprivation." "Indian communities are often shocked to learn that parents they regard as excellent caregivers have been judged unfit by non-Indian social workers," the Report stated. The House Report highlighted caseworkers' misunderstanding of the role of the extended family in Indian culture. In the same way agencies used to view Black kin networks as evidence of neglect, "many social workers, untutored in the ways of Indian family life or assuming them to be socially irresponsible, consider leaving the child with persons outside the nuclear family as neglect and thus as grounds for terminating parental rights."

Congress identified a group harm as well as injury to individual Indian families. The United State Supreme Court noted that in addition to testimony that "focused on the harm to Indian parents and their children who were involuntarily separated by decisions of local welfare authorities," the Senate heard "considerable emphasis on the impact on the tribes themselves of the massive removal of their children."[70] The Tribal Chief of the Mississippi Band of Choctow Indians testified, "Culturally, the chances of Indian survival are significantly reduced if our children, the only real means for the transmission of the tribal heritage, are to be raised in non-Indian homes and denied exposure to the ways of their People." He pointed out the importance of family ties to tribal self-determination: "These practices seriously undercut the tribes' ability to continue as self-governing communities. Probably in no area is it more important that tribal sovereignty be respected than in an area as socially and culturally determinative as family relationships." Congress adopted this group-based approach to the removal of Indian children, expressly finding *"there is no resource that is more vital to the continued existence and integrity of Indian tribes than their children."*

Congress moved to redress the cultural injury that the adoption policy inflicted on Indian tribes. The Indian Child Welfare Act gives sovereign Indian tribes control over child welfare decisions involving tribal members. Tribal courts have exclusive jurisdiction over custody proceedings involving an Indian child who lives on a tribe's reservation. Congress essentially established a separate child welfare system geared specifically to the interests of Indian tribes. The act has generated jurisdictional contests with state court judges and Indian parents who disagree with tribal decisions, and it is ignored by local authorities in some parts of the country. But its recognition of "cultural genocide" and a group-based remedy for it are firmly established aspects of federal child welfare policy regarding Indian children.

In May 2001, Shay Bilchik, executive director of the Child Welfare League of America, apologized for the organization's role in the Indian Adoption Project at a gathering of Indian adoptees and child welfare experts in Anchorage, Alaska. "What we did may have been well-intentioned, but it was wrong, it was biased, it was hurtful," Bilchik said. "It is time to tell the truth—that our actions presupposed that Indian children would be better off with white families as opposed to staying in their own communities and tribes—and be reconciled."[71]

Aborigines in Australia have recently made a similar claim about the removal of indigenous children from their families.[72] From the turn of the twentieth century until the 1960s, Aboriginal children were systematically taken from their parents and placed in white-controlled institutions and foster care. This practice was part of a deliberate, government-sponsored attempt to absorb the indigenous population biologically into the white population as well as to assimilate them into the dominant culture. The Aborigines Act of 1905 mandated that the Aborigines Department provide for the custody, maintenance, and education of indigenous children. It empowered the Chief Protector to order any Aborigine to be moved from his or her home district to another, a prerogative soon extended to police officers and judges. In 1936, the Native Administration Act expanded state authority over indigenous children: it declared the Commissioner of Native Affairs the legal guardian of every Aboriginal and "half-caste" child, "notwithstanding that the child has a parent or other relative living."[73]

In *In re Marriage of B and R*, the Australian court acknowledged that the official removal policies were motivated by "the belief that the indigenous people of this country would die out, and their young children would be better served by occupying (lowly) places in a dominate white society."[74] A letter from the Commissioner of Native Affairs to a government bureaucrat stationed in Western Australia, dated July 21, 1944, explained why the Commissioner denied an Aboriginal mother's petition for her son's release from an orphanage. "Children placed with Sister Kate are never to be released to their parents. This would be a direct contradiction of the principle of their segregation from native persons, as they are placed with Sister Kate for this very reason," the Commissioner wrote. "I am James' legal guardian up to 21 years, notwithstanding that his mother is alive, and since the principal consideration is the lad's welfare I regret I am unable to accede to Mrs. Cadoux's request. If I did so I would be inundated with similar requests from other native mothers."[75] Australia's removal policy not only injured the displaced children, who today suffer from high rates of psychological and social problems, but also helped to destroy the Aboriginal culture. In its 1997 report on this policy, the Australian Human Rights and Equal Opportunity Commission recommends a number of measures to protect indigenous cultural rights and self-determination, including Aboriginal participation in legislating national standards for the welfare of indigenous children and the transfer of jurisdiction over Aboriginal child welfare matters to indigenous organizations.[76]

Claims of cultural genocide have been less persuasive in the case of Black children removed from their families by white-dominated child protective services. Black Americans don't constitute a sovereign entity like Indian tribes or a disappearing culture like the Australian Aborigines. It is harder for Americans to grasp the group harm to Blacks caused by child welfare agencies despite the remarkable parallels with the government policies and racial disparities in the other cases. Americans have largely subscribed to an assimilationist approach to ethnic differences and are unfamiliar with the global struggle for recognition and protection of minority cultures.[77] I once shared a panel with a professor from Australia at a child welfare conference at New York University. Before my presentation, the professor showed a documentary about the removal of indigenous children from their families in Australia. The opening scenes showed orphanages filled with dark-skinned, curly-haired children under the supervision of a white blond-haired staff. There were interviews with Aborigines who had been adopted into white homes painfully describing the loss they felt by being robbed of their cultural identity. The conference participants were palpably moved by the stories of family and cultural destruction. There was something disturbing about the sight of Aboriginal children in the custody of whites. No one raised the question whether some Aboriginal children might have been better off raised by white adoptive parents. Everyone understood that a racial injustice had taken place. When it was my turn to speak, I told the same audience that the juvenile court, group homes, and youth detention centers in Chicago look strikingly similar to the Australian institutions for Aborigines—except the children are almost all Black. But now the participants, immediately convinced that the Australian system was racist, weren't quite sure how to respond.

The cultural injury approach to the proper placement of Black children has been vehemently criticized as both factually unsound and as essentialist. Supporters of transracial adoption argue that white parents can be just as successful as Black parents at raising healthy Black children in American society. They point to studies showing that transracial parenting has not adversely affected adopted children. For example, a twenty-year study by Rita Simon and Howard Altstein found that Black adoptees raised in white homes are "aware of and comfortable with their racial identity."[78] Supporters of transracial adoption have also criticized the notion of an essential and uniform Black identity that must be transmitted to Black children. The harm to Black children caused by languishing in foster care, they argue, outweighs any disadvantage in being raised in a culturally unfamiliar but loving home.

It is important to note criticism of studies refuting transracial adoption's psychological harm. A recent review of the empirical research on transracial adoption highlights its methodological flaws, including a failure to use comparison groups and sampling problems.[79] Simon and Altstein, for example, used families who were members of two Midwestern organizations and lost a significant number of families over the course of their study. It is possible that their favorable conclusions about transracial adoptees were skewed because the organizations were not representative of white families who adopt Black children and because the families that disappeared were having problems with their adoptions. Furthermore, African American psychologists, who might develop more culturally sensitive research tools, have fewer resources to conduct and publish empirical studies than researchers who support transracial adoption.[80] The question of the impact of transracial adoption on Black children, then, is still open to investigation. Nevertheless, it seems unlikely that transracial adoption will perpetrate a literal decimation of Black culture, as was threatened in the case of indigenous peoples in the United States and Australia. Adoptions of Black children by white parents are still relatively rare (although they may increase with new federal incentives), and an increasing number of Black children are placed with kin when removed from their parents' care.

However, none of these criticisms negates the racial harm of child welfare interventions. My assertion of group-based harm does not posit an essential Black identity or way of raising children, nor does it warn of the total obliteration of Blacks as a cultural group. I argue instead that disproportionate state intervention in Black families reinforces the continued political subordination of Blacks as a group. This argument is closely related to claims for respect of Black Americans as a cultural group, like the NABSW statement on transracial adoption. As Habermas observes, "normally, of course, the failure of cultural recognition is connected with gross social discrimination, and the two reinforce each other."[81]

My claim does not seek to preserve a particular set of Black cultural values. Rather, it seeks to liberate Black families from state control so they may be free to form and pass on their own values. This, after all, is the role of families in a free society. "For children, civil freedom brings nothing less than the right to grow to moral autonomy," writes Peggy Cooper Davis, "because the child-citizen, like the child-slave, flowers to moral independence only under authority that is flexible in ways that states and masters cannot manage."[82] The greatest danger to Black children in the child welfare system is the destructive and degrading regulation of their families by the state. The American child welfare system is raising too many Black children with the dispiriting perspective that state authorities are in charge of them instead of their parents. As I discuss later, concerns about cultural transmission might be allayed if the state placed more Black children in Black foster or adoptive homes. But the political harms created by racially disparate family disruption and state supervision of children would remain.

What About Children's Rights?

Recognizing the child welfare system's racial impact does not necessarily establish that the system causes a net harm to Black people as a group. The state might be charged with racism if it failed to rescue Black children from dangerous parents. As a group of social work researchers noted, "in the absence of efforts to improve the lot of impoverished families, it might be justifiable cause for concern if the children of such families were *not* overrepresented in child welfare services caseloads."[83] Responding to my argument, philosopher and adoptive parent Larry May argues that Black children suffer a group-based harm different from the one I have described—"the insecurity of Black children who go back and forth between abusive or neglectful homes and unstable foster care."[84] This harm, May asserts, is also having a devastating impact on Black community life and might be abated through programs that free these children for adoption. "Some Black children are harmed much more by their own biological families and by the systemic deprivation they suffer by never having a stable, loving home life," May argues. "Black children are also harmed by the deterioration of Black communities that results from so many Black children remaining in unstable homes during their most formative years."

Elizabeth Bartholet makes a similar point in *Nobody's Children*. She recognizes that the emphasis on child removal has a racially imbalanced effect but sees family preservation as more damaging to Black children. "Keeping them in their families and their kinship and racial groups when they won't get decent care in those situations may alleviate guilt," Bartholet argues, "but it isn't going to do anything to promote racial and social justice. It isn't going to help groups who are at the bottom of the socioeconomic ladder to climb that ladder. It is simply going to victimize a new generation."[85]

Taking into account the serious individual and group injuries caused by child maltreatment, however, does not offset the harms caused by the racial disparity in the system. I do not argue that Black children who are abused and neglected should never be removed from their parents. Surely Black children deserve the same protection from injury as others. But acknowledging the problem of child maltreatment does not determine how the problem should be addressed. The racial disparity in the foster care population should cause us to reconsider the state's current response to child maltreatment. The enormity of the racial gap suggests that at least some significant portion of children are removed from their homes unnecessarily. As I demonstrated in Part One, compelling research confirms that Black children are taken from their parents in disproportionate numbers because of racial bias at all stages of child welfare decision making. There is also evidence of irrationality in the process, whose detrimental effects disproportionately hurt Black children.

Moreover, the state could address the group harms caused by both neglectful parents and the disruption of families by doing more to improve the material circumstances of families. The strategy of moving more Black children in foster care into adoptive homes, on the other hand, may improve the well-being of a fraction of the population, but it will not solve the group-based harm I have identified. Indeed, the adoption strategy bolsters the stereotype of Black family incompetence and may yield a net increase in the number of Black children with no legal ties to a family. I see the child welfare system's racial harms as a powerful argument in favor of policies that are more supportive of struggling families. The price of present policies that rely on child removal rather than family support falls unjustly on Black families.

The last chapter of *Nobody's Children* broaches the lurking issue of social injustice. Given the correlation between poverty and child maltreatment, Bartholet acknowledges that providing more generous support to families and creating a more egalitarian society would be the most effective child welfare strategy. But she hastens to add: "Sadly we can predict that profound social and economic reform is not on the horizon, and we can also predict that our society will continue to scrimp on the support services that it makes available to poor people, including those at risk for child maltreatment."[86] In the meantime, she argues, coercive intervention should be intensified to place children in nurturing homes. Although Bartholet sees publicly funded services as an impractical solution to child maltreatment, she proposes a system of massive government surveillance, including a mandatory home visitation program "covering children from the prenatal period through the preschool period."[87] And although she doubts that white Americans would be willing to support poor Black families any time soon, she calls on them to "begin to think of children born to other people, and to other racial groups . . . as in some sense 'ours'" for purposes of adoption.[88]

This brand of liberalism recognizes that poor Black families are victims of societal injustice but uses their victimization as an excuse to intervene in their families instead of a reason to work toward social change. Its recognition of social injustice is dangerously limited, for it sees injustice as the root of child maltreatment but not as the root of state intrusions into poor families. It appeals to whites only to pity Black parents involved in the child welfare system but not to respect their autonomy, their claims of discrimination, or their bonds with their children. This approach demands an especially pernicious type of white benevolence toward Black people—a benevolence that depends on loss of Black family integrity in favor of white supervision of their children.

It sets up adoption as the only realistic way to persuade whites to care for Black children. White compassion for Black children depends on Black children "belonging" to them, to use Bartholet's term. This, it seems to me, is a particularly selfish way to approach child welfare that perpetuates rather than challenges America's racial hierarchy.

The concept of children's rights is easily co-opted by powerful people to achieve their social objectives and maintain their social position. The federal adoption law was promoted as a children's rights initiative. But as I showed in Part Two, speedy termination of parental rights to free children for adoption does not further the interests of most children in foster care. What is advocated as benefiting children in foster care contradicts the traditional understanding of children's need to maintain a relationship with their parents. Most important, the shift in federal child welfare policy directs attention away from the chief injustice of the foster care system—the removal of hundreds of thousands of mostly poor, minority children from their homes. This, too, is a violation of children's rights.

Framing the assault on family preservation in terms of children's rights masks battles between other political interests. Children rarely speak for themselves, so the issue underlying a claim of children's rights frequently involves determining which adult will speak for them. These contests are often political struggles that are influenced by race, class, and gender inequalities. The tragic story chosen for broadcast on the evening news depends less on the amount of children's suffering than on the political interests at stake.

A notion of children's rights devoid of political context is based on an inaccurate description of children's welfare. Each child is embedded in a social network composed of her family, community, social groups, and society at large. The rights of Black children must be interpreted in the context of racial oppression. Individualized explanations of harm do not account for the particular injury inflicted on children by racially disparate state intervention in families. Without careful attention to social justice, rights tend to reinforce social hierarchies and benefit the most privileged members of society. To be just, children's rights must be part of a broader struggle to eradicate oppressive structures that ruin the fortunes of the least privileged children and to create a more egalitarian society that cherishes all children. Supporting families to prevent removal of children from their homes fits within this struggle.

Why Kinship Care Doesn't Solve the Problem

Some people believe that the increased use of kinship care by child welfare agencies cures the racial harm in the child welfare system. They think that racism is eliminated when Black children are placed with their own relatives, who are almost always Black. Kinship care would solve the problem if the problem were confined to moving Black children into white homes. But this is not the racial harm that I have described. Rather, the most serious injury inflicted by the child welfare system is the disintegration and control of Black family life. That injury occurs whether children are placed with white or Black families, even if those families are kin. In fact, understanding why kinship care does not negate racism in the child welfare system helps to clarify my argument.

Kinship care historically had a double-edged relationship to the child welfare system. Child rearing by relatives was often a response to poverty and other hardships that made it difficult for parents to raise children by themselves. Because Black families were excluded from the formal child welfare system, they relied heavily on extended family networks to take care of children whose parents were unable to meet their needs. Kinship care continued in more recent decades as an informal safety net for struggling Black families. By temporarily moving children to the care of kin, parents could avoid either voluntarily relinquishing them to the state or running the risk of coercive state intervention.[89] Kinship care, then, served as a family-preserving alternative to foster care.

On the other hand, kinship care also invited state intrusion. The Black community's cultural tradition of sharing parenting responsibilities among kin was often mistaken by child welfare authorities as parental neglect. Skyrocketing female incarceration rates, cutbacks in social services, the AIDS epidemic, and maternal substance abuse led to a resurgence in caregiving by relatives, especially grandmothers, in the late 1980s.[90] Between 1980 and 1990, the number of children living with grandparents increased by 44 percent. In 1994, nearly 4 million children lived in grandparent-headed households.[91] More than one-third of these children lived in homes with no parent present. Almost half of these children being raised by grandparents were Black.[92]

Although state child welfare agencies used to consider private kinship care neglectful, they increasingly turn to relatives to place neglected and abused children. Private kinship care is arranged by families without child welfare agency involvement; kinship foster care is provided to children who are in the legal custody of the state.[93] Just as private kinship care has been especially prevalent among Black families, most children placed in kinship foster care are Black.[94] This is both because of the overrepresentation of Black children in the foster care population and because agencies are more likely to turn to relatives in the case of Black children than other children. For example, a study of foster care in suburban Baltimore County, Maryland, found that 49 percent of relative caregivers were African American, whereas only 25 percent of nonrelative foster parents were.[95] Similarly, a California study reported that 43 percent of kin and 22 percent of nonkin foster parents were African American, whereas 34 percent of kin and 63 percent of nonkin foster parents were white.[96] Kinship care is the main type of out-of-home placement for Black children in New York City, Chicago, and Philadelphia.[97] In fact, almost all—90 percent—of relative caregivers in Chicago are Black.[98]

Kinship foster care is generally better for children than foster care with strangers. For most people, staying in the extended family is a benefit for children. Children are more likely to maintain contact with their parents and to stay with siblings if they are living with relatives than if they are placed in nonrelative foster care.[99] It is likely that children are already familiar with the kin caregiver, so the placement avoids the trauma of moving in with strangers. Kinship foster care usually allows children to stay in their communities and to continue the cultural traditions their parents observe. Kinship foster care is more stable: children living with relatives are less likely to be moved to multiple placements while in substitute care.[100] There is also evidence that children are better cared for by relatives than by strangers: more children in kinship foster care reported that they felt loved and happy, and fewer are abused while in state custody.[101]

Kinship foster care also provides financial support for relatives' caregiving. Public assistance is especially significant because kinship caregivers tend to have limited means and have substantially lower incomes than traditional foster parents.[102] A 1996 study of foster care in a southern county found that almost 60 percent of relative caregivers earned less than $10,000 annually whereas only 10 percent of nonrelative foster parents earned so little.[103] The median annual income of kin caregivers in Toledo is only $13,000.[104]

Although federal child welfare policy promotes kinship foster care, it gives states wide latitude in creating the system of financial support for kin caregivers.[105] The level of state support for kinship caregivers is directly correlated with the level of state intrusion into their lives. The higher the payment, the greater the intensity of state supervision. The two principal sources of public financial assistance for relatives are Temporary Assistance to Needy Families (TANF) and foster care benefits. All states offer TANF benefits to relatives caring for children as they do other needy families. Foster care stipends, however, are much larger than TANF benefits, and they are multiplied by each child in the home instead of the marginal increase per child under TANF. A relative caring for several children might receive two to four times as much in foster care payments as she would in welfare benefits. In the early 1990s, Illinois paid foster parents an average of $350 per child, whereas AFDC benefits were $102 for one child and less for each additional child.[106] A California foster parent of siblings ages eight and sixteen received a foster care stipend of $849 per month in 1996, compared to only $479 in AFDC benefits.[107]

This difference in levels of support reflects the government's perverse willingness to give more financial aid to children in state custody than to children in the custody of their parents. Relatives can take advantage of the higher benefit level of foster care only by becoming involved in the child protection system. As Jill Duerr Berrick, director of the Berkeley Center for Social Services Research, observes, "This disparity spawns concerns that the foster care payment system may act as an incentive for a troubled family to seek a formal agency-supervised placement with kin rather than sharing child-rearing informally with the same relatives."[108] In addition to a stipend, kin foster parents are entitled to Medicaid, clothing allowances, and other assistance to meet the children's needs. Child welfare agencies make available services that address the parents' problems, such as drug treatment, mental health counseling, and housing assistance, only to families under their supervision. Welfare reform makes foster care even more attractive for relative caretakers, despite the burdens it entails. The federal welfare law's policies, designed to modify the behavior of poor parents, exact a harsh penalty on kin who are forced to rely on TANF benefits to support the children in their care.

The amount of kinship foster care payments depends, in turn, on whether the kin caregiver is licensed by the state child welfare agency. Most states require that relatives must meet the same licensing requirements as nonrelative foster parents to receive foster care payments.[109] The licensing process involves another layer of intrusion into relatives' lives. The agency inspects relatives' homes, including sleeping arrangements, the number of bedrooms, and square footage, and investigates relatives' backgrounds to check for compliance with strict licensing standards. If relatives are not licensed, they are paid less than licensed foster parents. In some states, unlicensed kin caregivers receive only the TANF child-only benefit; in others, they receive a lower foster care payment. The Illinois Department of Children and Family Services, for example, pays licensed foster parents about $100 more per month than unlicensed relatives. The federal government recently issued new rules under the Adoption and Safe Families Act that mandate that relatives meet the foster care licensing standards in order for states to receive federal foster care reimbursement.

Families involved in kinship care must exchange a degree of autonomy and independence in child rearing that is in proportion to the amount of financial support they receive from the government. The price of the highest amount of aid—foster care benefits—is relinquishing custody of children to the state and submitting to foster care regulations and supervision by the child welfare system. Increasingly, Black families are paying the price of state supervision. The number of children in private kinship care has decreased since 1994, while the number in kinship foster care has increased.[110]

Making kinship care part of the child welfare system has a dramatic impact on the relationships of family members and on their relationship to the state. Foster care assistance is available only to state wards. The family must therefore hand over legal custody of the children to the state child welfare agency. In addition, relatives must be approved by the child welfare agency to care for children in its custody. The kin network is transformed from a "natural family" to a "foster family." In *Smith v. Organization of Foster Families for Equality and Reform,*[111] the United States Supreme Court upheld limitations on the rights of foster parents on the grounds that a foster family has "its source in state law and contractual arrangement." In the case of kinship care, the extended family exchanges its autonomy over child raising for financial support and services needed to raise its children.

Transferring custody to the state means losing control over important child rearing decisions. Kinship foster care also requires waiver of protections against state intrusion in family life. Although the children are cared for by kin, it is the state that has authority over them. The parents and kin caregivers must submit to surveillance by caseworkers and requirements that the agency prescribes. Kin foster parents must comply with agency rules specifying the type of home and care they provide, and they must allow periodic visits by caseworkers to check compliance. They must give the agency access to personal information and may have to undergo psychological evaluations. The child may be represented by a guardian ad litem, adding another outsider who has a say in family affairs. The family also runs the risk that the agency will move the children to another foster home if the relatives fail to comply with agency demands.

The transformation of kinship care from a private to a state-run arrangement suppresses the historical strengths of this family form. Social scientists have remarked at the success of Black kin networks in meeting the challenges of raising children under conditions of poverty and racial discrimination. Some have called for policy makers to "affirm a black family kinship system that was historically strong, intact, resilient and adaptive."[112] Yet research shows that many caseworkers devalue the important role that kin traditionally have had in helping to raise children. For example, a study of caseworkers serving children in kinship care in Illinois revealed that caseworkers failed to involve kin caregivers or the rest of the extended family in making long-term plans for the children.[113] According to the study's authors, "permanency plans appear to be made primarily by child welfare caseworkers, their supervisors, and other service providers rather than by the person who will have to live with the consequences of these decisions." They attributed the lack of involvement by kin both to the bureaucratic nature of child welfare practice and to caseworkers' lack of understanding of kin participation in child rearing as a cultural strength of African American families. To a large extent, the suppression of kin involvement in decision making is an inherent feature of foster care as it requires relinquishing legal custody of children.

I described in Part One how relative caregivers receive inferior services. Not only does kinship foster care give insufficient support to families, but it often affirmatively harms them. One of the most perplexing discoveries from recent empirical research is that children placed with relatives remain in state custody longer.[114] According to University of Chicago social work professor James P. Gleeson, "studies in several states have demonstrated lower return home and lower adoption rates for children in kinship foster care than for those in nonrelative care."[115] The increased time spent in foster care may result from the inadequacy of reunification and other services provided to families involved in kinship care. The incentives for families themselves to prefer children to remain longer with kin foster caregivers probably also plays a role in delaying reunification. Parents whose children are living with relatives rather than strangers may be less anxious to regain custody because the entire family is comfortable with the living arrangement and needs the higher level of financial support foster care affords. Total family income may drop precipitously if children leave grandmother's care to return home. In California, children in kinship homes receiving foster care benefits were half as likely to be reunited with their parents after four years as were children in kinship homes receiving lower welfare benefits.[116] This financial disparity appears to have the greatest impact on Black families: "African American children in kinship homes supported by the foster care subsidy remained in care approximately twice as long as all other children."[117] All of these reasons suggest that kinship foster care imposes powerful incentives on poor Black families and caseworkers to keep children in state custody. Even with inadequate services and loss of family autonomy, kinship foster care offers the only avenue for needed public support for many Black children.

Kinship care, which historically kept Black families together, sometimes disrupts family relationships when incorporated in the public child welfare system. Madeleine Kurtz, a clinical professor at New York University Law School, argues that because traditional foster care rules are based on the nuclear family model, they "frustrate the extent to which children might be maintained by extended family."[118] Kurtz examines two cases from the New York child welfare system to show that kinship foster care encourages the unnecessary severance of family ties. In one case, Marcus, the father of a girl living in kinship foster care with her great grandmother, did not realize his daughter was technically in foster care. Marcus visited and maintained a relationship with his daughter for several years without arranging the contacts through the agency. The agency sent letters to Marcus in care of his mother, but failed to make meaningful efforts to strengthen his relationship with his daughter. Marcus was taken by surprise when the agency petitioned to terminate his parental rights on grounds of abandonment. He thought that, because his daughter was living with family, he had satisfied his parental obligation to his daughter by keeping in touch with her. But the court treated the case as an ordinary foster care arrangement: it "held Marcus to the standard of behavior expected and required of a parent with a child in a traditional foster care setting, where a parent's failure to actively pursue custody is a critical failure indicative of inability or disinterest." The court suspended judgment, imposing a number of conditions on the family as well as continued court supervision. If this family had been able to maintain a private kinship care arrangement, Marcus's legal status as father would not have been jeopardized. Instead, by involving the state in their family life, writes Kurtz, "the legal and permanent dissolution of this family was and continues to be a very real possibility."

Marcus's experience of exclusion is typical of Black fathers with children in kinship foster care. A secondary analysis of the study of Illinois caseworkers mentioned earlier focused on casework with African American fathers.[119] Most of the fathers had not participated in a single case planning activity and only 5 percent of the fathers were receiving any services to assist them in playing a greater role in their children's lives. Caseworkers simply were not interested in what fathers could offer. In most cases, caseworkers had incomplete information that would be essential in assessing fathers' caregiving ability, and they reported no communication with fathers or with their supervisors about the fathers during the previous six months. "The extensive absence of and silence about fathers in these cases," the study's author concludes, "suggest systemic deterrence to paternal involvement."

It appears that the exclusion of fathers from kinship foster care results from "mutual avoidance between caseworkers and fathers." On the one hand, Black fathers tend to view child welfare agencies as demeaning and coercive institutions that have targeted them for child support enforcement without appreciating the obstacles they face in providing financially for their children.

Dealing with a caseworker only intensifies the emotional stress many poor and unemployed Black fathers experience about their inability to live up to the middle-class breadwinner ideal. On the other hand, caseworkers view Black fathers as a particularly hostile and perplexing clientele whom it is easiest to ignore. Whereas placing kinship care in the child welfare system diminishes the autonomy of Black mothers, aunts, and grandmothers, it erases the already limited role of Black fathers.

The second case Kurtz discusses involves a woman, Nora, who became the kinship foster caregiver for her infant granddaughter, Evelyn, who was born exposed to crack cocaine.[120] When Evelyn was three years old, the agency obtained an order terminating Nora's daughter's parental rights, and Evelyn became a ward of the state. Ending the mother's legal status meant that Nora had become simply a foster parent—an employee of the state hired to take care of Evelyn; she was no longer Evelyn's legal grandmother. The family lost all of the protections against state disruption that kinship bonds ordinarily afford. So when the agency determined that Nora had a drinking problem and was not an appropriate adoptive parent for Evelyn, it had virtually complete discretion to move Evelyn to a more suitable family. As Kurtz puts it, because Nora had broken the agency's rules, the agency was permitted to "fire a bad foster parent and find a better home for its foster child." No longer a grandmother or a foster parent, Nora—and the rest of Evelyn's family—lacked standing to challenge the agency's plan for Evelyn. As in the case of Marcus, transforming a private kinship care arrangement into a formal one put the family at a disadvantage in its relationship to the state. If Nora had never become a foster parent, her alleged drinking problem could not so easily have justified the destruction of her bonds with her granddaughter.

The ordeal that Devon and her nieces and nephews went through demonstrates even better the damage caused by putting family relationships in the control of state child welfare authorities. Devon became a licensed foster mother so she could take advantage of the benefits offered by the Department of Children and Family Services. But the monthly check and social services came at a steep cost: she and the children were completely separated from each other for a year and a half because the size of Devon's apartment failed to meet state licensing requirements. Because she was a foster mother, her family could be torn apart at the whim of a caseworker. The woman who raised her nieces and nephews from infancy was denied any say in their whereabouts or even the chance to communicate with them.

In September 2000, after the children had been in foster care for more than a year, Devon happened to run into two of them at a community center, accompanied by a new foster mother she had known nothing about. The foster mother told Devon that the children had been removed from the first foster home because they had been physically abused there. They were split up and placed in pairs in two different foster homes. The child welfare agency maintains that what happened to the children is confidential, but Devon says she saw a gash in one boy's head and another boy's ear was slit. Devon learned that her relentless complaints to the child welfare agency and her state representative had apparently triggered an internal investigation into the children's foster care placement. Soon after discovering the children's abuse and relocation, Devon received a call informing her that the children would be returned to her by Christmas.

"It was a happy time," Devon told me after she got the children back. "They were supposed to make a gradual transition from foster care, but they didn't want to leave me. The caseworker said the first time she took them back to the foster home she almost had a car accident because they were screaming so much." The children are overjoyed to be reunited with their aunt. But Devon now has to deal with the aftermath of their traumatic separation from her. The children are confused about why they were forced to live away from home for so long and why they were placed in the care of someone who ended up hurting them. Devon says the children were given potent mood-altering drugs to make them more manageable, and she is working on weaning them from the medication. Devon is also grappling with a devastating financial penalty. The private child welfare agency that licensed her—the same agency that placed the children in another foster home—revoked her foster care license. As a licensed foster mother, Devon used to receive $3,000 per month because all of the children require specialized care. As an unlicensed kin caregiver, her monthly grant was dropped to $192 and a food voucher. Only after months of wrangling with agency officials, Devon obtained an increase to $1,000 a month—an amount still inadequate to meet the children's special needs. The child welfare system is willing to give Devon the support she needs to care properly for her nieces and nephews only if she resubmits to a regulatory regime that nearly destroyed her family.

Kinship foster care, promoted as a way of keeping Black families together, exacts a high price for state assistance that may include tearing families apart. The child welfare system provides foster care only to state wards and higher benefits to foster parents, so families involved in kinship foster care must relinquish custody of children and submit to government supervision to receive needed support. The transformation of kinship care from a private family arrangement to a type of public foster care illustrates a deeper flaw in the philosophy underlying the child welfare system—the assumption that parents' inability to provide for their children warrants coercive state intervention. It also shows that placing Black foster children with relatives under the state's supervision does not erase the system's racial harm.

CONCLUSION:
CHILD WELFARE AND SOCIAL JUSTICE

RACE IS CRITICAL TO EXPLAINING why so many Black children are removed from their homes by child welfare authorities and placed in state custody. Race is also critical to explaining the harm that Black families suffer as a result. Given the disproportionate impact of state intervention on Black families and its role in maintaining Blacks' unequal status, race must move to the center of public debate about changing the child welfare system. Only by focusing on group-based racial injustice can we understand the damage inflicted by the system and take the right steps to address it. Trying to reform child protective services without attending to its racial harm will prove futile—or even more disastrous for Black families. We must first come to grips with racism in child welfare's philosophy, practices, and impact on families.

The racial disparity also suggests that we must do more than increasing the resources and improving the management of the present system. The very structure of child welfare is fundamentally flawed. Instead of targeting the systemic reasons for family hardship to prevent child maltreatment, it lays the blame on individual parents' failings after a crisis has already occurred. Instead of supporting families, it punishes them by taking children from their homes for placement in foster care. Redressing this racial harm requires placing greater control over child welfare services in Black communities, addressing the deprivation of poor and minority families, and eliminating the coercive function of a system that is supposed to serve them.

Recognizing the historical relationship between the child welfare system and institutionalized racism in this country should also temper our hopes for reform. We cannot expect that even the most radical modifications of the child welfare system will immunize it from the influence of racism and white privilege in the broader society. In the 1960s, for example, the welfare rights movement succeeded in toppling the welfare system's discriminatory regime of eligibility and procedural rules that excluded Blacks from receiving public assistance. Welfare activists secured entitlements to benefits, raised benefit levels, and increased availability of benefits to families headed by women. But as welfare became increasingly associated with Black mothers, it was transformed into an unpopular and stingy program geared at modifying the behavior of its vilified recipients. Nevertheless, we must work toward creating a child welfare system that takes better care of children and pays greater respect to Black families, strengthening the ability of Black communities to struggle for a more just society.

Social Support for Families

One way to preserve more families is to prevent child maltreatment. An overwhelming body of research on the negative effects of poverty on children tells us that generous public support of child welfare would drastically reduce cases of child abuse and neglect. More importantly, it would serve what should be the purpose of a child welfare system—to provide for the well-being of children. The ingredients for a strong child welfare program are clear and simple: first, reduce family poverty by increasing the minimum wage, instituting a guaranteed income, and enacting aggressive job creation policies; second, establish a system of national health insurance that covers everyone; third, provide high-quality subsidized child care, preschool education, and paid parental leaves for all families. Increasing the supply of affordable housing is also critical.

The difficulty, of course, is finding the political will to implement this program. Proposals for a more generous U.S. welfare state are often dismissed as utopian, naive, and anti-democratic. But this country's puny social programs and abysmal support for families are a glaring exception among Western democracies. The rate of child poverty in the United States is many times greater than in most European countries. And the poorest children in this country are much worse off than their European counterparts. The chief reason that so few children in countries like Sweden, Denmark, and France are poor is that, unlike the United States, they have decent national welfare programs.[121] The governments of these nations provide generous social services, income subsidies, and other family supports to their citizens as a matter of right.

The second excuse typically deployed to defeat adequate programs for families—that they cost too much—falls flat in the context of child welfare. Federal and state governments already spend more than $10 billion annually on the child welfare system. But most of the money goes to maintaining children in out-of-home care. Centering the system's services on family support and preservation would be a matter of shifting these funds from their current destructive purpose. A truly adequate social welfare system that includes universal income subsidies, health insurance, and child care would cost billions more. But the price is well worth the ultimate savings we will reap in healthier and more productive communities. "Where will the money to do this come from?" asks Elliot Currie after calling for social action to reduce the prison population. "In large part, it will come from reduced spending on welfare and unemployment insurance, prisons and foster care, emergency medical care and drug treatment."[122] This country can afford to spend far more on social welfare, but it squanders its wealth on prison construction, corporate tax breaks, the defense budget, and other programs that prop up its unequal social order.

The related objection that social welfare programs constitute "too much government" rings equally false in light of the child welfare system's enormous intervention in families. Generous social services and income subsidies would be a less intrusive alternative to the current regime of draconian child protection and law enforcement. Public support for families would help to relieve the poorest communities of a coercive government presence that threatens their participation in democratic and civic life.

Many people will still think a European-style system of family supports goes too far. The truth, though, is that this proposal is far too modest. Universal social welfare programs must be accompanied by two reforms in the child welfare system that more directly address its racial harm. The child welfare system must change the purpose of its services as well as the way they are administered.

By improving conditions for all families, especially poor families, universal social programs will reduce the need for state intervention in Black homes. Because Blacks are disproportionately poor, a more generous welfare state should, in theory, yield a disparately positive benefit for these families. Universal welfare programs also have the advantage of avoiding the political vulnerability of "targeted" welfare policies—programs that are means-tested or designed to benefit a disadvantaged group, such as Blacks. Targeted programs that have a high proportion of Black beneficiaries, such as subsidized housing, are easily plucked from the budget when opposed by white taxpayers. Some welfare rights theorists support programs that base eligibility on universal criteria as a way of building broad-based support. In fact, William Julius Wilson advocates deemphasizing the racial objectives of anti-poverty programs for this reason: "The hidden agenda is to improve the life chances of groups such as the ghetto underclass by emphasizing programs in which the more advantaged groups of all races can positively relate."[123] In his latest book, *Bridge over the Racial Divide,* Wilson promotes a strategy of multiracial coalition building that evades racial conflict by focusing on economic justice issues.[124] By obscuring welfare's benefits for poor Blacks, these universalists reason, an array of race-neutral programs will garner more support than the current welfare system, which the public associates with Blacks.

But it is a mistake to depend entirely on universal social programs to alleviate the child welfare system's racial harm. These programs constitute an improbable guarantee that Black families will receive sufficient benefits and services. They have a "trickle up" effect: programs designed to benefit all citizens, rich and poor, are likely to benefit rich citizens the most because they have greater political and economic resources to structure programs to their advantage. As University of Chicago political philosopher Iris Marion Young points out, "If a political movement wishes to address the problems of the truly disadvantaged, it must differentiate the needs and experiences of relatively disadvantaged social groups and persuade the relatively privileged—heterosexual men, white people, younger people, and the able bodied—to recognise the justice of the group-based claims of these oppressed people to specific needs and compensatory benefits."[125]

Nor do universal programs attempt to dismantle the institutionalized impediments to Blacks' full social and economic participation. By maneuvering around racism to become more palatable to white Americans, purely universal programs lose their power to contest the forces that make Black families especially vulnerable to state disruption. In opposition to the obfuscation of race is the growing call for reparations—the claim that Americans of African descent are entitled to compensation for the exploitation and social injury they have suffered as a result of centuries of oppression. In *The Debt: What America Owes to Blacks*, Randall Robinson declares, "Solutions to our racial problems are possible, but only if our society can be brought to face up to the massive crime of slavery and all that it has wrought."[126] As a matter of justice, this nation has an obligation to directly address the child welfare system's racial disparity, which stems from institutionalized discrimination against Black families.

Shifting Control to Black Communities

How can the child welfare system begin to confront the racial disparity in the population it serves? The most common response has been the implementation of "culturally competent" social work practice. The purpose of this approach is to make child welfare services more sensitive to the distinctive needs and customs of Black families. Learning to be culturally competent helps caseworkers to deliver services more effectively to a diverse clientele and to uncover unrecognized biases in their view of minority families. But there are serious limitations to this strategy for addressing the system's racism. Without changing the system's goals and structure, teaching caseworkers to be culturally sensitive is just as likely to help them regulate Black families more effectively. Social work scholars have noted that cultural sensitivity "increases client receptiveness to intervention."[127] Whether this is a good thing depends on the purpose of the intervention. This remedy might also convince caseworkers, administrators, and judges that they are acting fairly while they continue to dismantle Black families.

Tackling racism requires altering relationships of power. Changing the relationship between child welfare agencies and the communities they serve means giving the clients more say in the way the system operates. There are a number of avenues to increase client participation in child welfare policy and practice. *R.C. v. Hornsby*, a class action lawsuit against the Alabama child protection department for violating children's constitutional right to family integrity, sought remedies that focused on families' involvement in all aspects of services.[128] The consent decree implemented to reform the state system required that families be involved in the planning and delivery of services and instituted a philosophy of service delivery in home-based and community-based settings.

Another strategy is to make child welfare agencies more accountable to the communities where their clients live. Strengthening Black neighborhood institutions provides bases of power needed to advance Black people's distinct interests and to ensure that government programs actually benefit Black residents. The white-dominated welfare system has always administered its services in a way that reinforces Black subordination. As a result, Robert Allen contended in *Black Awakening in Capitalist America*, "if neocolonialism is to be avoided, it is essential that control over the use of any outside aid must rest completely in the hands of the black community."[129] In *Forsaking Our Children: Bureaucracy and Reform in the Child Welfare System*, John Hagedorn describes a program he implemented in 1988 as coordinator of Milwaukee County's "Youth Initiative" to empower client communities and strengthen social service institutions within poor neighborhoods.[130] The pilot project involved two steps centered on redirection of control and money. First, it decentralized the basic operation of the child welfare bureaucracy by creating neighborhood planning bodies. These neighborhood councils were made up of residents and service providers located in the community. Ideally, such neighborhood councils would include parents involved in the system. Then the project invested more funds into neighborhood-based agencies by giving councils the authority to develop neighborhood service delivery plans.

Unfortunately, Hagedorn reports that the Youth Initiative ended in failure. Never receiving the support they needed, the neighborhood councils were unable to remain independent of the child welfare department. "Milwaukee's public remained more concerned with punishing abusive parents than restructuring social services to be more supportive," Hagedorn writes.[131] Other cities have experienced similar frustration with experiments in neighborhood-based services. A number of initiatives to integrate New York City's child welfare services into local institutions have been attempted since the 1970s with little success. "There has never been the political will to make them work," says James Dumpson, who served as the head of the Bureau of Child Welfare under Mayor Wagner.[132] However, Hagedorn remains convinced that these reforms are attainable if there is enough pressure for community involvement.

But is community participation in public child welfare agencies sufficient to overcome the tendency of white-dominated institutions to reinforce racial inequality? In 1972, after reviewing the history of racial discrimination in the U.S. child welfare system, Andrew Billingsley and Jeanne Giovannoni proposed the creation of a Black system of child welfare services that was designed by and for Black communities. "The major sources of power and control over the distribution of child welfare services are white; but the resources themselves—the love, the nurturance, and the sustenance—are in Black families and Black people," they wrote in the tenor of the times. "It is time, we think, that control over the children's resources be turned over to their people."[133] They envisioned an association of child welfare agencies tied to some existing community structure such as the Urban League that made all the important policy decisions about staff and services to children. To maintain its autonomy, they recommended, the association should launch fund-raising within the Black community.

The burgeoning Black Power movement spurred on by the War on Poverty made proposals for Black self-determination seem feasible. A couple of years earlier, in 1970, the Congress of African Peoples meeting in Atlanta unanimously adopted a statement that called for the creation of alternative social institutions based on a Black ideology, including adoption agencies, welfare and health centers, and day care centers. When the National Association of Black Social Workers held its second annual convention that year at Howard University, each member was asked to pledge, "I will consciously use my skills, and my whole being, as an instrument for social change, with particular attention directed to the establishment of Black social institutions such as schools, hospitals and voluntary agencies."[134] Our challenge today is to develop institutions in communities that are more devastated than thirty years ago and in a political climate that has become more hostile to them.

Ending the System's Punitive Function

Addressing the racial harm caused by the child welfare system also requires eliminating the structural flaws that make Black families vulnerable to coercive state intervention. Chief among these flaws is the system's punitive function. Black communities have become targets of stigmatized services designed to investigate and punish deficient parents rather than preserve families. Leroy Pelton makes a compelling case that the elimination of the child welfare system's rescue mentality is as critical as expanded social welfare programs for restricting foster care's growth. Pelton observes that Western European countries with coercive, judgmental child protection systems like ours place children in foster care at similar rates as the United States, despite their substantially lower child poverty rates.[135] "When it is placed under the cover of benevolent intervention," Pelton explains, "a coercive system can take on a life of its own and expand independently of need." Lowering child poverty rates is an important goal, and there have been significant declines in the number of children removed from their homes in most Scandinavian countries, particularly in Denmark, in the past few decades.[136] Nevertheless, the history of child welfare policy in America supports Pelton's claim.

The fluctuations in America's own foster care population have historically been tied to the political interpretation of child maltreatment rather than its actual incidence. The excessive use of foster care will continue as long as the child welfare system retains its dysfunctional structure, pursuing the conflicting tasks of both providing services to help families and investigating families for the purpose of removing children from their homes. This structure, along with lopsided federal funding of foster care, encourages the rescue function to dominate even under a family preservation ideology.

Some child welfare advocates propose abolishing the child welfare system's coercive role. Pelton would do this by transferring the investigative and foster care functions of child welfare agencies to law enforcement and the civil court system, respectively, so that the child welfare system can be devoted to providing preventive services to families on a nonjudgmental, voluntary acceptance basis. Placing all child welfare investigations in the hands of police, however, is likely to increase rather than decrease the government's punitive presence in Black communities.

A solution might be to restrict the reach of law enforcement to carefully defined cases of child abuse and to decriminalize general child neglect. Duncan Lindsey and Wesley Hawkins argue that police and not child welfare agencies should be responsible for investigating severe physical and sexual assaults on children. "Preoccupation with this narrow aspect of child welfare has displaced our obligation to a much greater population of children," Lindsey and Hawkins write. "The mission of the child welfare system is not to protect children from criminal abuse, but to ensure the welfare of all children."[137] Jane Waldfogel of Columbia's Child Welfare Research Center proposes a "differential response system" within child welfare agencies that directs authoritative intervention at the small share of high-risk families, while the larger share of low-risk families would be served on a voluntary basis.[138] The key is to create a system that offers voluntary services, without threat or stigma, to the vast majority of its clients, shifting its philosophical orientation and resources away from foster care toward prevention and family preservation.

The child welfare system I've described would not eliminate state involvement with families but would radically change its nature. Take, for instance, home visiting, a component of the national health care systems of many European countries. Public health nurses or social workers stop by the homes of mothers and infants to check on their health, dispense parenting advice, and offer needed social services. In the current U.S. system, these home visitors would most likely be dispatched only to investigate new mothers suspected of mistreating their newborns, and mothers would most likely view them with suspicion. In a community-based, voluntary system supported by guaranteed health care, visiting nurses could be far more effective at preventing future harm to children. In Denmark, for example, home visiting programs are popular because they are "backed by a nationwide network of community maternal- and child-health clinics whose services are available to all families as a matter of right."[139] Imagine if a nurse based in a free community clinic, who was committed to family unity and linked to comprehensive services, had been available to help Jornell treat David's health problems. This family-supportive approach would have ensured David's health and security far better than the three-year ordeal of foster care and psychological therapies the family was put through. And it would have preserved far more the community networks that will help to ensure David's opportunity to participate fully in this society.

Why would Americans prefer a punitive system that needlessly separates thousands of children from their parents and consigns millions more to social exclusion and economic deprivation? Racism is at the heart of this tragic choice. Only by coming to terms with child welfare's racial injustice can we turn from the costly path of family destruction.

Notes

Notes to Part One

1. Andrew Billingsley and Jeanne M. Giovannoni, *Children of the Storm: Black Children and American Child Welfare* (New York: Harcourt Brace Jovanovich, 1972), pp. 34–38; David Rosner and Gerald Markowitz, "Race, Foster Care, and the Politics of Abandonment in New York City," *American Journal of Public Health* 87 (1997): 1844.

2. Billingsley and Giovannoni, *Children of the Storm,* p. 76.

3. Ibid., p. 80.

4. Ibid., pp. 77–79.

5. Rosner and Markowitz, "Race, Foster Care, and the Politics of Abandonment in New York City"; Nina Bernstein, *The Lost Children of* Wilder: *The Epic Struggle to Change Foster Care* (New York: Pantheon, 2001); Richard Wexler, *Wounded Innocents: The Real Victims of the War Against Child Abuse* (Buffalo, N.Y.: Prometheus Books, 1990, 1995), pp. 221–224.

6. Bernstein, *The Lost Children of* Wilder; "Foster Placement by Skin Shade Is Charged," *New York Times,* January 18, 1990, p. B1.

7. Billingsley and Giovannoni, *Children of the Storm,* p. 93.

8. U.S. Dept. of Health and Human Services, Administration for Children and Families, "The AFCARS Report: Current Estimates as of October 2000," p. 1, available at www.acf.dhhs.gov/programs/cb; Office of the Assistant Secretary for Planning Evaluation, U.S. Department of Health and Human Services, *Trends in the Well-Being of Children and Youth: 1996* (Washington, D.C.: U.S. Department of Health and Human Services, 1996), p. 2.

9. Robert Goerge, Fred Wulczyn, and Allen Harden, "New Comparative Insights into States and Their Foster Children," *Public Welfare* 54 (1996): 12, 15.

10. Select Committee on Children, Youth, and Families, *U.S. Children and Their Families: Current Conditions and Recent Trends* (Washington, D.C.: U.S. House of Representatives, 1989).

11. Administration for Children and Families, U.S. Department of Health and Human Services, "The AFCARS Report: Current Estimates as of October 2000," p. 2 (reporting that 42 percent of children in foster care are Black).

12. California, Legislative Analyst's Office, *Child Abuse and Neglect in California: A Review of the Child Welfare Services Program* (Sacramento: Legislative Analyst's Office, 1996).

13. Robert M. Goerge, Fred S. Wulczyn, and Allen Harden, *Foster Care Dynamics, 1983–1992: California, Illinois, Michigan, New York, and Texas—A First-Year Report from the Multi-State Foster Care Data Archive* (Chicago: Chapin Hall Center for Children, 1994).

14. Bong Joo Lee and Robert Goerge, "Poverty, Early Childbearing, and Child Maltreatment: A Multinomial Analysis," *Children and Youth Services Review* 21 (1999): 755.

15. Teresa Moore, "Social Worker's Hard Choices, Soft Heart," *San Francisco Chronicle,* March 8, 1995, p. A1.

16. Ann F. Garland et al., "Minority Populations in the Child Welfare System: The Visibility Hypothesis Reexamined," *American Journal of Orthopsychiatry* 68 (1998): 142.

17. Goerge, Wulczyn, and Allen, "New Comparative Insights into States and Their Foster Children," p. 15.

18. Natalie Pardo, "Losing Their Children," *Chicago Reporter* 28 (January 1999): 1, 7.

19. Martin Guggenheim, "Somebody's Children: Sustaining the Family's Place in Child Welfare Policy," *Harvard Law Review* 113 (2000): 1716, 1718. n. 11, citing New York City Administration for Children's Services, *Selected Child Welfare Trends* 81 (1998).

20. Ibid.; Center for an Urban Future, "Race, Bias, and Power in Child Welfare," *Child Welfare Watch* (Spring/Summer 1998): 1.

21. Ann F. Garland et al., "Minority Populations in the Child Welfare System: The Visibility Hypothesis Reexamined," *American Journal of Orthopsychiatry* 68 (1998): 142, 143; Shirley Jenkins and Beverly Diamond, "Ethnicity and Foster Care: Census Data as Predictors of Placement Variables," *American Journal of Orthopsychiatry* 55 (1985): 267.

22. Garland et al., "Minority Populations in the Child Welfare System," p. 145.

23. Leroy H. Pelton, *For Reasons of Poverty: A Critical Analysis of the Public Child Welfare System in the United States* (New York: Praeger, 1989), p. 20.

24. William I. Trattner, *From Poor Law to Welfare State: A History of Social Welfare in America* (New York: Free Press, 1989), pp. 110–139.

25. Barbara J. Nelson, *Making an Issue of Child Abuse: Political Agenda Setting for Social Problems* (Chicago: University of Chicago Press, 1984).

26. Alvin Schorr, "The Bleak Prospect for Public Child Welfare," *Social Service Review 74* (2000): 124.

27. Duncan Lindsey, *The Welfare of Children* (New York: Oxford University Press, 1994), pp. 89–126.

28. U.S. Department of Health and Human Services, Children's Bureau, *National Study of Protective, Preventive, and Reunification Services Delivered to Children and Their Families* (Washington, D.C.: U.S. Government Printing Office, 1997).

29. Ibid.

30. Legislative Analyst's Office, *Child Abuse and Neglect in California.*

31. Dorothy Roberts, *Killing the Black Body: Race, Reproduction, and the Meaning of Liberty* (New York: Pantheon, 1997), pp. 203–209.

32. Jill Quadagno, *The Color of Welfare: How Racism Undermined the War on Poverty* (New York: Oxford University Press, 1994).

33. Ibid.

34. U.S. Department of Health and Human Services, *National Study,* Executive Summary, Finding 4, p. 3 (emphasis added).

35. Richard Wexler, "Geisinger Case Badly Mishandled; Early Intervention Leads to Much Better Solutions in Child Endangerment Cases," *Portland Press Herald,* May 4, 2000, p. 11.

36. Seth Farber, "The Real Abuse," *National Review,* April 12, 1993, p. 47.

37. U.S. Department of Health and Human Services, *National Study.*

38. Mark E. Courtney and Vin-Ling Irene Wong, "Comparing the Timing of Exits from Substitute Care," *Children and Youth Services Review* 18 (1996): 307, 320.

39. Edward V. Mech, "Public Social Services to Minority Children and Their Families," in *Children in Need of Roots,* ed. R. O. Washington and Joan Boros-Van Hull (Davis, Calif.: International Dialogue Press, 1985), pp. 161, 164.

40. Ibid.

41. U.S. Department of Health and Human Services, *National Study.*

42. Goerge et al., *Foster Care Dynamics, 1983–1992.*

43. Kathleen Wells and Shenyang Guo, "Reunification and Reentry of Foster Children," *Children and Youth Services Review* 21 (1999): 273, 289.

44. Jenkins and Diamond, "Ethnicity and Foster Care."

45. Charles Glisson, James W. Bailey, and James A. Post, "Predicting the Time Children Spend in State Custody," *Social Service Review* 74 (2000): 253, 273.

46. Ibid.; Mary M. Close, "Child Welfare and People of Color: Denial of Equal Access," *Social Work Research and Abstracts* (1983): 13; and Ketayun H. Gould, "Limiting Damage Is Not Enough: A Minority Perspective on Child Welfare Issues," in *Child Welfare: An Africentric Perspective,* ed. Joyce E. Everett, Sandra S. Chipungu, and Bogart R. Leashore (New Brunswick, N.J.: Rutgers University Press, 1991), pp. 58, 59.

47. Robert L. Pierce and Lois H. Pierce, "Toward Cultural Competence in the Child Welfare System," *Children and Youth Services Review* 18 (1996): 713, 714.

48. Wells and Guo, "Reunification and Reentry of Foster Children," p. 290; Mark Courtney, "Reentry to Foster Care of Children Returned to Their Families," *Social Services Review* 69 (1995): 228.

49. Loring P. Jones, "Social Class, Ethnicity, and Child Welfare," *Journal of Multicultural Social Work* 6 (1997): 123, 128, citing National Black Child Development Institute, *The Black Child in Foster Care* (Washington, D.C.: National Black Child Development Institute, 1989).

50. U.S. Department of Health and Human Services, *National Study.*

51. Close, "Child Welfare and People of Color"; Sandra M. Stehno, "The Elusive Continuum of Child Welfare Services: Implications for Minority Children and Youth," *Child Welfare* 69 (1990): 551.

52. Close, "Child Welfare and People of Color," p. 19.

53. Erin Hallissy, "Foster Care Criticized by Grand Jury; System Assailed as Unfair to Minority Children," *San Francisco Chronicle,* June 1, 1995, p. A13.

54. R. Hough, A. F. Garland, and B. Reynolds, "Race/Ethnic Differences in the Use of Mental Health Services Among Children in Foster Care," presented at the Mental Health Services Research Conference, National Institutes of Mental Health, Bethesda, Md., September 1995; Ann F. Garland and Bridgett A. Besinger, "Racial/Ethnic Differences in Court Referred Pathways to Mental Health Services for Children in Foster Care," *Children and Youth Services Review* 19 (1997): 651.

55. Garland and Besinger, "Racial/Ethnic Differences in Court Referred Pathways to Mental Health Services for Children in Foster Care," p. 663.

56. Mary Davidson and Gary Anderson, "Child Welfare and Title VI," *Social Work* (March 1982): 147, 150 n. 10.

57. Mark E. Courtney, "Correlates of Social Worker Decisions to Seek Treatment-Oriented Out-of-Home Care," *Children and Youth Services Review* 20 (1998): 281.

58. Courtney and Wong, "Comparing the Timing of Exits from Substitute Care," p. 328.

59. Richard P. Barth, "Effects of Age and Race on the Odds of Adoption versus Remaining in Long-Term Out-of-Home Care," *Child Welfare* 76 (1997): 285.

60. S. McMurtry and G. Lie, "Differential Exit Rates of Minority Children in Foster Care," *Social Work Research and Abstracts* 28 (1992): 42.

61. Administration for Children and Families, U.S. Department of Health and Human Services, "The AFCARS Report: Current Estimates as of October 2000," p. 3.

62. Annie Woodley Brown and Barbara Bailey-Etta, "An Out-of-Home Care System in Crisis: Implications for African American Children in the Child Welfare System," *Child Welfare* 76 (1997): 76.

63. James Gleeson, "Kinship Care as a Child Welfare Service: The Policy Debate in an Era of Welfare Reform," *Child Welfare* 75 (1996): 419, 429.

64. James P. Gleeson et al., "Understanding the Complexity of Practice in Kinship Foster Care," *Child Welfare* 76 (1997): 801, 802.

65. Rob Geen, "In the Interest of Children: Rethinking Federal and State Policies Affecting Kinship Care," *Policy and Practice* (March 2000): 19, 21; Jill Duerr Berrick, "When Children Cannot Remain Home: Foster Family Care and Kinship Care," *Future of Children* 8 (1998): 72, 74.

66. Madeleine L. Kurtz, "The Purchase of Families into Foster Care: Two Case Studies and the Lessons They Teach," *Connecticut Law Review* 26 (1994): 1453, 1454; Geen, "In the Interest of Children," pp. 21–22; Gleeson, "Kinship Care as a Child Welfare Service," p. 425.

67. 440 U.S. 125 (1979).

68. Kurtz, "The Purchase of Families into Foster Care," p. 1472.

69. Timothy Gebel, "Kinship Care and Nonrelative Family Foster Care: A Comparison of Caregiver Attributes and Attitudes," *Child Welfare* 75 (1996): 5; Jill D. Berrick et al., "A Comparison of Kinship Foster Homes and Foster Family Homes: Implications for Kinship Foster Care as Family Preservation," *Children and Youth Services Review* 16 (1994): 33; Gleeson et al., "Understanding the Complexity of Practice in Kinship Foster Care," p. 803.

70. Maria Scannapieco et al., "Kinship Care and Foster Care: A Comparison of Characteristics and Outcomes," *Families in Society* 78 (1997): 480, 487.

71. Marla Gottlieb Zwas, "Kinship Foster Care: A Relatively Permanent Solution," *Fordham Urban Law Journal* 20 (1993): 343, 355–356.

72. "Foster Care: Health Needs of Many Young Children Are Unknown and Unmet," Letter Report Number HEHS–95–114 (Washington, D.C.: Government Accounting Office), March 26, 1995.

73. S. Gennaro, "Vulnerable Infants: Kinship Care and Health," *Pediatric Nursing* 24 (1998): 119.

74. Gleeson, "Kinship Care as a Child Welfare Service," p. 442; Gleeson et al., "Understanding the Complexity of Practice in Kinship Foster Care," p. 803; Berrick et al., "A Comparison of Kinship Foster Homes and Foster Family Homes," pp. 36, 57.

75. Ramona Denby and Nolan Rindfleisch, "African Americans' Foster Parenting Experiences: Research Findings and Implications for Policy and Practice," *Children and Youth Services Review* 18 (1996): 544, 547.

76. Judith Areen, "Intervention between Parent and Child: A Reappraisal of the State's Role in Child Neglect and Abuse Cases," *Georgia Law Journal* 63 (1975): 887, 899.

77. Pelton, *For Reasons of Poverty*, pp. 2–3.

78. Linda Gordon, *The Great Arizona Orphan Abduction* (Cambridge: Harvard University, 1999), p. 309.

79. Pelton, *For Reasons of Poverty.*

80. Goerge et al., "New Comparative Insights into States and Their Foster Children"; Duncan Lindsey, "Adequacy of Income and the Foster Care Placement Decision: Using an Odds Ratio Approach to Examine Client Variables," *Social Work Research and Abstracts* 28 (1992): 29; G. Zellman, "The Impact of Case Characteristics on Child Abuse Reporting Decisions," *Child Abuse and Neglect* 16 (1992): 57; Robert Hampton, "Race, Class, and Child Maltreatment," *Journal of Comparative Family Studies* 18 (1987): 113; Jenkins and Diamond, "Ethnicity and Foster Care."

81. Lindsey, "Adequacy of Income and the Foster Care Placement Decision."

82. Rachel L. Swarns, "Baby Starves and Mother Is Accused of Homicide," *New York Times,* May 29, 1998, p. B3.

83. Nina Bernstein, "State Faults Hospital in Death of Baby Who Was Denied Care," *New York Times,* October 26, 1998, p. A21.

84. Roberts, *Killing the Black Body,* pp. 8–19.

85. Kristine E. Nelson, Edward J. Saunders, and Miriam J. Landsman, "Chronic Child Neglect in Perspective," *Social Work* 38 (1993): 661; Richard J. Gelles, "Child Abuse and Violence in Single-Parent Families: Parent Absence and Economic Deprivation," *American Journal of Orthopsychiatry* 59 (1988): 492; Leroy H. Pelton, "Child Abuse and Neglect: The Myth of Classlessness," *American Journal of Orthopsychiatry* 48 (1978): 608; Elizabeth D. Jones and Karen McCurdy, "The Links Between Types of Maltreatment and Demographic Characteristics of Children," *Child Abuse and Neglect* 16 (1992): 201; Leroy Pelton, "The Role of Material Factors in Child Abuse and Neglect," in *Protecting Children from Abuse and Neglect,* ed. Gary Melton and Frank Barry (New York: Guilford Press, 1994); Isabel Wolock and Bernard Horowitz, "Child Maltreatment and Material Deprivation Among AFDC-Recipient Families," *Social Service Review* 53 (1981): 175.

86. A. J. Sedlak and D. D. Broadhurst, *Third National Incidence Study of Child Abuse and Neglect, Final Report* (Washington, D.C.: U.S. Department of Health and Human Services, 1996).

87. Howard I. Bath and David A. Haapala, "Intensive Family Preservation Services with Abused and Neglected Children: An Examination of Group Differences," *Child Abuse and Neglect* 17 (1993): 213.

88. Joint Center for Poverty Research, *Congressional Research Briefing: Child Maltreatment and Policy Issues,* Chicago, October 2000, available at http://www.jcpr.org/conferences/child-abuse_briefing.html.

89. Brett Drake and Shanta Pandey, "Understanding the Relationship Between Neighborhood Poverty and Specific Types of Child Maltreatment," *Child Abuse and Neglect* 22 (1998): 79, 88.

90. Goerge et al., "New Comparative Insights into States and Their Foster Children"; Bath and Haapala, "Intensive Family Preservation Services with Abused and Neglected Children."

91. Lindsey, *The Welfare of Children*; Christina Paxson and Jane Waldfogel, "Work, Welfare, and Child Maltreatment" (Cambridge, Mass.: National Bureau of Economic Research, 2000), available at http://nber.org/papers/w7343; Kristen Shook, "Assessing the Consequences of Welfare Reform for Child Welfare," *Poverty Research News* 2 (Winter 1998): 1, available at http://www.jcpr.org/winter98/article2.html.

92. Pelton, "Child Abuse and Neglect," pp. 608–616.

93. William J. Bennett, John J. DiIulio Jr., and James P. Walters, *Body Count: Moral Poverty and How to Win America's War Against Crime and Drugs* (New York: Simon & Schuster, 1996).

94. See, for example, Pelton, "Child Abuse and Neglect," pp. 614–15; Robert L. Hampton, "Child Abuse in the African American Community," in *Child Welfare: An Africentric Perspective*, ed. Joyce E. Everett, Sandra S. Chipungu, and Bogart R. Leashore (New Brunswick, N.J.: Rutgers University Press, 1991), pp. 220, 230.

95. Hampton, "Child Abuse in the African American Community," p. 230.

96. Alan Booth, *Urban Crowding and Its Consequences* (New York: Praeger, 1976).

97. Bill Hewitt, "A Day in the Life," *People,* December 15, 1997, pp. 48, 49.

98. B. Needle et al., "Transitions from AFDC to Child Welfare in California," *Children and Youth Services Review* 21 (1999): 815; Vonnie C. McLoyd, "The Impact of Economic Hardship on Black Families and Children: Psychological Distress, Parenting, and Socioemotional Development," *Child Development* 61 (1990): 311.

99. Sheila Zedlewski, "Work Activity and Obstacles to Work Among TANF Recipients," *New Federalism: National Survey of America's Families,* Series B, No. B-2 (Washington, D.C.: Urban Institute, 1999).

100. R. Conger et al., "Economic Stress, Coercive Family Process, and Developmental Problems of Adolescents," *Child Development* 65 (1994): 541.

101. Jeanne Brooks-Gunn, Greg J. Duncan, and J. Lawrence Aber, eds., *Neighborhood Poverty* (New York: Russell Sage, 1997); McLoyd, "The Impact of Economic Hardship on Black Families and Children."

102. Vonnie McLoyd et al., "Unemployment and Work Interruptions Among African American Single Mothers: Effects on Parenting and Adolescent Socioemotional Functioning," *Child Development* 65 (1994): 563.

103. Renny Golden, *Disposable Children: America's Child Welfare System* (Belmont, Calif.: Wadsworth, 1997), p. 74.

104. Annette R. Appell, "Protecting Children or Punishing Mothers: Gender, Race, and Class in the Child Protection System," *South Carolina Law Review* 48 (1997): 577, 584.

105. Legislative Analyst's Office, *Child Abuse and Neglect in California* (January 1996), http://www.lao.ca.gov/cw11096toc.html.

106. Administration for Children and Families, U.S. Department of Health and Human Services, *Child Maltreatment 1998: Reports from the States to the National Child Abuse and Neglect Data System* (Washington, D.C.: U.S. Government Printing Office, 2000).

107. J. Green, *Cultural Awareness in Human Services* (New York: Prentice-Hall, 1991).

108. Pelton, *For Reasons of Poverty.*

109. Committee on Ways and Means, Subcommittee on Human Resources, *President Clinton's Budget Proposal for New Funding for Child Welfare Services Targeted for Family Support and Preservation Services,* testimony of Peter Digre, U.S. House of Representatives, April 21, 1993, pp. 87–88.

110. Legislative Analyst's Office, *Child Abuse and Neglect in California* (1996).

111. Lindsey, *The Welfare of Children,* pp. 139–154; Joyce E. Everett, Sandra S. Chipungu, and Bogart R. Leashore, eds., *Child Welfare: An Africentric Perspective* (New Brunswick, N.J.: Rutgers University Press, 1991), p. 184.

112. Lindsey, *The Welfare of Children,* p. 155 (emphasis added).

113. U.S. Department of Health and Human Services, *National Study.*

114. Guggenheim, "Somebody's Children," p. 1724. See, for example, Janita Poe and Peter Kendall, "Cases of Neglect May Be Only Poverty in Disguise," *Chicago Tribune,* December 24, 1995, sec. 1, p. 1; Tamar Lewin, "Child Welfare Is Slow to Improve Despite Court Order," *New York Times,* December 30, 1995, p. A6.

115. Pelton, *For Reasons of Poverty,* p. 146.

116. Wexler, *Wounded Innocents,* p. 48.

117. Hewitt, "A Day in the Life."

118. *In re N.M.W.,* 461 N.W. 2d 478 (Iowa Ct. App. 1990).

119. Pelton, "Child Abuse and Neglect," p. 615.

120. Akka Gordon, "Taking Liberties," *City Limits,* December 2000, p.18.

121. Hampton, "Child Abuse in the African American Community," p. 222.

122. Mitchell H. Katz, Robert L. Hampton, Eli H. Newberger, Roy T. Bowles, and Jane C. Snyder, "Returning Children Home: Clinical Decision Making in Cases of Child Abuse and Neglect," *American Journal of Orthopsychiatry* 56 (1986): 253.

123. *In re Juvenile Appeal* (83-CD), 455A2d 1313 (Conn. 1983).

124. 1992–1993 Santa Clara County Grand Jury, "Final Report: Investigation of the Department of Family and Children's Services" (June 1993).

125. *In re P.F. and E.F.,* 638 N.E.2d 716 (Ill. App. 1994).

126. Nina Bernstein, "Suit Charges That Boy Was Illegally Kept in Foster Care as Mother Sought Return," *New York Times,* August 31, 2000, p. B4.

127. Michael C. Dawson, *Behind the Mule: Race and Class in African-American Politics* (Princeton: Princeton University Press, 1994), pp. 15–34.

128. Office of the Assistant Secretary for Planning Evaluation, U.S. Department of Health and Human Services, *Trends in the Well-Being of America's Children and Youth,* p. 36.

129. U.S. Census Bureau, Current Population Reports, Series P60-209, *Money Income in the United States: 1999* (Washington, D.C.: U.S. Government Printing Office, 2000); Tamar Lewin, "Children's Well-Being Improves, Report Says," *New York Times,* July 19, 2001, p. A14; Neil G. Bennett, "Child Poverty in the States: Levels and Trends from 1979 to 1998" (Washington, D.C.: National Center for Children in Poverty, 2000); Dale Russakoff, "Report Paints Brighter Picture of Children's Lives," *Washington Post,* July 14, 2000, p. A1; Don Terry, "U.S. Child Poverty Rate Fell as Economy Grew, but Is Above 1979 Level," *New York Times,* August 11, 2000, p. A10.

130. Joseph Dalaker and Bernadette D. Proctor, U.S. Census Bureau, Current Population Reports, Series P60-210, *Poverty in the United States: 1999* (Washington, D.C.: U.S. Government Printing Office, 2000).

131. Children Defense Fund, "Extreme Child Poverty Rises More Than 400,000 in One Year, New Analysis Shows," Washington, D.C., August 22, 1999.

132. Dalaker and Proctor, U.S. Census Bureau, Current Population Reports, Series P60-210, *Poverty in the United States: 1999.*

133. Office of the Assistant Secretary for Planning Evaluation, "Trends in the Well-Being of America's Children and Youth," citing calculations by Greg J. Duncan, based on data from the Panel Study of Income Dynamics (PSID), Survey Research Center, University of Michigan.

134. Mark R. Rank, "The Racial Injustice of Poverty," *Washington University Journal of Law and Policy* 1 (1999): 95, 96.

135. Office of the Assistant Secretary for Planning Evaluation, U.S. Department of Health and Human Services, *Trends in the Well-Being of America's Children and Youth*, p. 49, Figure E S1.5.B, Percent of Children in Poverty by Number of Years in Poverty by Race, for Cohort Age 18 in 1988–1990.

136. Office of the Assistant Secretary for Planning Evaluation, U.S. Department of Health and Human Services, *Trends in the Well-Being of America's Children and Youth*, p. 30.

137. William Julius Wilson, quoted in Carl Husemoller Nightengale, *On the Edge: A History of Poor Black Children and Their American Dreams* (New York: Basic Books, 1993), p. 64.

138. Jeanne Brooks-Gunn, Greg Duncan, P. Klebanov, and N. Sealand, "Do Neighborhoods Influence Child Adolescent Behavior?" *American Journal of Sociology* 99 (1994): 353. See, generally, Brooks-Gunn, Duncan, and Aber, eds., *Neighborhood Poverty*.

139. Bill Gillham et al., "Unemployment Rates, Single Parent Density, and Indices of Child Poverty: Their Relationship to Different Categories of Child Abuse and Neglect," *Child Abuse and Neglect* 22 (1998): 79, 88.

140. Mark E. Courtney et al., "Race and Child Welfare Services: Past Research and Future Directions," *Child Welfare* 75 (1998): 99, 102.

141. Murray Levine et al., "African-American Families and Child Protection," *Children and Youth Services Review* 18 (1996): 693.

142. Susan Zuravin and Diane DePanfilis, "Predictors of Child Protective Service Intake Decisions: Case Closure, Referral to Continuing Services, or Foster Care Placement," in *The Foster Care Crisis: Translating Research into Policy and Practice,* ed. Patrick A. Curtis, Grady Dale Jr., and Joshua C. Kendall (Lincoln: University of Nebraska Press, 1999), p. 63.

143. U.S. Census Bureau, Current Population Reports, Series P60-209, *Money Income in the United States: 1999.*

144. Garland et al., "Minority Populations in the Child Welfare System," pp. 145–146.

145. Thomas D. Morton, "The Increasing Colorization of America's Child Welfare System," *Policy and Practice* (December 1999): 23, 25.

146. U.S. Census Bureau, Current Population Reports, Series P20-515, *Household and Family Characteristics: March 1998* (Washington, D.C.: U.S. Government Printing Office, 1998).

147. Morton, "The Increasing Colorization of America's Child Welfare System," pp. 25–26.

148. Toshio Tatara, "Overview of Child Abuse and Neglect," in *Child Welfare: An Africentric Perspective,* ed. Joyce E. Everett, Sandra S. Chipungu, and Bogart R. Leashore (New Brunswick, N.J.: Rutgers University Press, 1991), pp. 187, 190.

149. A. J. Sedlak and D. D. Broadhurst, *Third National Incidence Study of Child Abuse and Neglect,* Final Report, pp. 4–28.

150. U.S. Department of Health and Human Services, *National Study.*

151. Hampton, "Child Abuse in the African American Community," 222; Robert L. Hampton, "Race, Ethnicity, and Child Maltreatment: An Analysis of Cases Recognized and Reported by Hospitals," in *The Black Family: Essays and Studies,* 3rd ed., ed. Robert R. Staples (Belmont, Calif.: Wadsworth, 1986), p. 172.

152. R. Hampton and E. Newberger, "Child Abuse Reporting: Significance of Severity, Class, and Race," *American Journal of Public Health* 75 (1985): 56; R. Hampton, "Race, Ethnicity, and Child Maltreatment and Analysis of Cases Recognized and Reported by Hospitals,"

in *The Black Family: Essays and Studies,* ed. R. Hampton (Belmont, Calif.: Wadsworth, 1991), p. 172.

153. Richard J. Gelles and Claire P. Cornell, *Intimate Violence in Families* (Beverly Hills, Calif.: Sage, 1985), p. 56.

154. Carole Jenny et al., "Analysis of Missed Cases of Abusive Head Trauma," *Journal of the American Medical Association* 281 (1999): 621.

155. Ira J. Chasnoff, Harvey J. Landress, and Mark E. Barrett, "The Prevalence of Illicit-Drug or Alcohol Use During Pregnancy and Discrepancies in Mandatory Reporting in Pinellas County, Florida," *New England Journal of Medicine* 322 (1990): 1202, 1204.

156. Daniel R. Neuspiel and Terry Martin Zingman, "Custody of Cocaine-Exposed Newborns: Determinants of Discharge Decisions," *American Journal of Public Health* 83 (1993): 1726.

157. J. Eckenrode, J. Powers, J. Doris, J. Munsch, and N. Bolger, "Substantiation of Child Abuse and Neglect Reports," *Journal of Consulting and Clinical Psychology* 38 (1988): 9.

158. U.S. Department of Health and Human Services, *National Study.*

159. Norma Harris, "Dealing with Diverse Cultures in Child Welfare," *Protecting Children* (Fall 1990): 6, 7.

160. Morton, "The Increasing Colorization of America's Child Welfare System," p. 28.

161. Ibid.

162. Edward Mech, "Decision Analysis in Foster Care Practice," in *Foster Care in Question,* ed. H. D. Stone (New York: Child Welfare League of America, 1970), p. 26.

163. M. H. Phillips, B. L. Haring, and A. W. Shyne, *A Model for Intake Decisions in Child Welfare* (New York: Child Welfare League of America, 1972).

164. Lindsey, *The Welfare of Children,* pp. 136–138.

165. Ibid., p. 138.

166. Guggenheim, "Somebody's Children," pp. 1725–1726.

167. Ibid.

168. National Association of Public Child Welfare Administrators, *Guidelines for a Model System of Child Protective Services for Abused and Neglected Children and Their Families* (Washington, D.C.: American Public Welfare Association, 1988), p. 23.

169. Julie Deardorff, "Judge Rules Boy, 6, Faces Nursing 'Harm,'" *Chicago Tribune,* December 12, 2000, sec. 1, p. 1.

170. Carol C. Williams, "Expanding the Options in the Quest for Permanence," in *Child Welfare: An Africentric Perspective,* ed. Joyce E. Everett, Sandra S. Chipungu, and Bogart R. Leashore (New Brunswick, N.J.: Rutgers University Press, 1991), pp. 266, 273.

171. Alyssa Katz, "Court Says City Too Quick to Pull Kids from Parents," *City Limits,* October 18, 1999; *Tenenbaum v. Williams,* 193 F. 3d 581, 591 (2d Cir. 1999).

172. Lehrer and Redleaf, Background Briefing on *Dupuy v. McDonald,* press briefing, Chicago, 2001.

173. Robert L. Pierce and Lois H. Pierce, "Moving Toward Cultural Competence in the Child Welfare System," *Children and Youth Services Review* 18 (1996): 713, 724.

174. Brown and Bailey-Etta, "An Out-of-Home Care System in Crisis," pp. 65, 69.

175. Larry Bivins, "Foster Care System a 'Tragedy' for Blacks," *Detroit News,* June 2, 1997, p. A1.

176. Caitlin Liu, "Grand Jury Finds Foster Care System in Disarray," *Los Angeles Times,* July 1, 2000, p. B1.

177. Susan J. Rose, "Reaching Consensus on Child Neglect: African American Mothers and Child Welfare Workers," *Children and Youth Services Review* 21 (1999): 463, 467; Michael Wald, "State Intervention on Behalf of 'Neglected' Children: A Search for Realistic Standards," *Stanford Law Review* 27 (1975): 985.

178. Amy Sinden, "Why Won't Mom Cooperate?: A Critique of Informality in Child Welfare Proceedings," *Yale Journal of Law and Feminism* 11 (1999): 339, 380.

179. T. McDonald and J. Marks, "A Review of Risk Factors Assessed in Child Protective," *Social Service Review* 65 (1991): 112; Michael S. Wald and Maria Woolverton, "Risk Assessment: The Emperor's New Clothes?" *Child Welfare* 69 (1990): 483.

180. Quoted in Lindsey, *The Welfare of Children,* p. 117.

181. Howard J. Doueck et al., "Decision-Making in Child Protective Services: A Comparison of Selected Risk-Assessment Systems," *Child Welfare* 72 (1993): 441, 449.

182. Wald and Woolverton, "Risk Assessment: The Emperor's New Clothes?" p. 484

183. Hewitt, "A Day in the Life."

184. Ibid., p. 56.

185. R. Bruce Dold, "Kids Suffer Under DCFS Reform Efforts," *Chicago Tribune,* September 22, 1995, p. 19.

186. Pelton, *For Reasons of Poverty,* p. 67.

187. Appell, "Protecting Children or Punishing Mothers"; Tonya Plank, "How Would the Criminal Law Treat Sethe: Reflections on Patriarchy, Child Abuse, and the Use of Narrative to Re-Imagine Motherhood," *Wisconsin Law Journal* 12 (1997): 83. See also Ann Shalleck, "Child Custody and Child Neglect: Parenthood in Legal Practice and Culture," in *Mothers in Law: Feminist Theory and the Legal Regulation of Motherhood,* ed. Martha Albertson Fineman and Isabel Karpin (New York: Columbia University Press, 1995), pp. 308–309: "A Black woman raising her children with her mother as they faced the challenges of their daily lives did not fit within the vision of parenting dominant within child custody law."

188. Minnesota Supreme Court Task Force on Racial Bias in the Judicial System, "Symposium on Racial Bias in the Judicial System," *Hamline Law Review* 16 (1993): 624, 631.

189. Carol Stack, "Cultural Perspectives on Child Welfare," *New York University Review of Law and Social Change* 12 (1983–1984): 539, 541.

190. E. P. Martin and J. M. Martin, *The Black Extended Family* (Chicago: University of Chicago Press, 1978).

191. Carol B. Stack, *All Our Kin: Strategies for Survival in a Black Community* (New York: Harper & Row, 1974).

192. Appell, "Protecting Children or Punishing Mothers," p. 586.

193. Harold W. Neighbors et al., "Psychiatric Diagnosis of African Americans: Diagnostic Divergence in Clinician-Structured and Semistructured Interviewing Conditions," *Journal of the National Medical Association* 91 (1999): 601.

194. "Race, Bias, and Power in Child Welfare," p. 4.

195. bell hooks, *Ain't I a Woman: Black Women and Feminism* (Boston: South End Press, 1981), pp. 84–85. See also Deborah Gray White, *Ar'n't I a Woman?: Female Slaves in the Plantation South* (New York: Norton, 1985), pp. 46–61.

196. Michael P. Johnson, "Smothered Slave Infants: Were Slave Mothers at Fault?" *Journal of Social History* (1981): 493.

197. Ibid., p. 493 (quoting South Carolina Mortality Schedules, 1850, Abbeville District).

198. Quoted in Beverly Guy-Sheftall, *Daughters of Sorrow: Attitudes Toward Black Women, 1880–1920* (Brooklyn, N.Y.: Carlson, 1990), p. 44.

199. Jacqueline Jones, *Labor of Love, Labor of Sorrow: Black Women, Work, and the Family from Slavery to the Present* (New York: Vintage, 1986).

200. Roberts, *Killing the Black Body,* pp. 154–159.

201. See, for example, Cathy Trost, "Born to Lose: Babies of Crack Users Crowd Hospitals, Break Everybody's Heart," *Wall Street Journal,* July 18, 1989, p. A1.

202. Office of Planning and Policy Research, U.S. Department of Labor, *The Negro Family: The Case for National Action* (Washington, D.C.: U.S. Dept. of Labor, 1965).

203. Carrie Teegardin, "Single with Children," *Atlanta Journal & Constitution,* May 7, 1995, p. G6.

204. Tamar Lewin, "Creating Fathers out of Men with Children," *New York Times,* June 18, 1995, p. A1.

205. Charles Murray, "The Coming White Underclass," *Wall Street Journal,* October 29, 1993, p. A14.

206. William Julius Wilson, *The Truly Disadvantaged: The Inner City, the Underclass, and Public Policy* (Chicago: University of Chicago Press, 1987).

207. Kathryn Edin, "How Low-Income Single Mothers Talk About Marriage," *Social Problems* 47 (2000): 112; Kathryn Edin, "Few Good Men: Why Low-Income Single Mothers Don't Get Married," *American Prospect* 11 (2000): 26.

208. Stephanie Coontz, *The Way We Never Were* (New York: Basic Books, 1992), p. 250.

209. Charles Murray, *Losing Ground: American Social Policy, 1950–1980* (New York: Basic Books, 1984): 154–166.

210. Dorothy E. Roberts, "Irrationality and Sacrifice in the Welfare Reform Consensus," *Virginia Law Review* 81 (1995).

211. U.S. Census Bureau, *Mothers Who Receive AFDC Payments,* Statistical Brief, March 1995.

212. In *Wyman v. James,* 400 U.S. 309 (1971), for example, the U.S. Supreme Court held that the Fourth Amendment does not protect welfare recipients from mandatory, unannounced home inspections by government caseworkers.

213. *United States v. Clary,* 846 F. Supp. 768, 780–781 (E.D. Mo. 1994).

214. *United States v. Clary,* 34 F. 3d 709 (8th Cir. 1994).

215. Ruth Lawrence Karski, "Key Decisions in Child Protective Services: Report Investigation and Court Referral," *Children and Youth Services Review* 21 (1999): 643.

216. Coontz, *The Way We Never Were.*

217. "Race, Bias, and Power in Child Welfare," p. 5.

218. "Troubled Children Flood Ill-Prepared Foster Care System," *New York Times,* September 8, 1992, p. A1.

219. Leslie Jones McCloud, "Tina Olison Case Heats Up," *Chicago Defender,* October 19, 1999, p. 1.

220. Cornelia Grumman, "Parents Give Advice on Reforming DCFS," *Chicago Tribune,* April 13, 1999, sec. 2, p. 3.

221. "Race, Bias, and Power in Child Welfare," p. 2.

222. Carol Marbin Miller, "Fostering Change," *Broward Daily Business Review,* March 10, 1999, pp. A1, A2.

223. Lindsey, *The Welfare of Children,* p. 98.

224. Somini Sengupta, "Child Welfare Turns Nightmare," *New York Times*, May 31, 2000, p. A27.

225. Morgan Ward Doran and Dorothy E. Roberts, *The Impact of Welfare Reform on Families Involved in Child Protective Services: Parents' Perceptions and Experiences* (Chicago: Children and Family Research Center, 2001).

226. Somini Sengupta, "Tough Justice: Taking a Child When One Parent Is Battered," *New York Times*, July 8, 2000, pp. A1, A11.

227. Mike Claffey, "Testimony by Mother Rips ACS," *Daily News*, July 17, 2001, news section, p. 24.

228. *In re Farley*, 469 N.W. 2d 295 (Mich. 1991)

229. Sengupta, "Child Welfare Turns Nightmare." See also William D. Diorio, "Parental Perceptions of Authority of Public Child Welfare Caseworkers," *Families in Society* (April 1992): 222 (describing parents' perceptions of intimidation and other unfair treatment by caseworkers).

230. Alison B. Vreelans, "The Criminalization of Child Welfare in New York City: Sparing the Child or Spoiling the Family," *Fordham Urban Law Journal* 27 (2000): 1053, n. 6.

231. Joanne Wasserman, "More Kids Left Alone, State Says," *New York Daily News*, July 27, 1997, p. 4.

232. Rachel L. Swarms, "In a Policy Shift, More Parents Are Arrested for Child Neglect," *New York Times*, October 25, 1997, p. A1.

233. Blaine Harden, "A Baby Alone Lands Parents in N.Y. Jail; Pair Arrested for Parking Stroller Outside Cafe," *Washington Post*, May 14, 1997, p. A1.

234. "Mom of 6 Charged with Endangerment," *Chicago Tribune*, February 24, 1995, Chicagoland section, p. 3.

235. "Mom Convicted of Endangerment," *Cincinnati Enquirer*, July 12, 1995, p. C3.

236. Swarms, "In a Policy Shift, More Parents Are Arrested for Child Neglect."

237. L. Gustafson and D. Allen, "A New Management Model for Child Welfare," *Public Welfare* 52 (1994): 31.

238. "Accountability with Foster Care," *Child Welfare Watch* (Summer 1999), available at http://www.afscme.org/publications/child/research/htm.

239. Sinden, "Why Won't Mom Cooperate?: A Critique of Informality in Child Welfare Proceedings," pp. 382–383.

240. Ibid., p. 383.

241. Sheila B. Kamerman and Alfred J. Kahn, "If CPS Is Driving Child Welfare—Where Do We Go from Here?" *Public Welfare* (Winter 1993): 41.

242. David L. Lewis, "Tidal Wave of Needy Teens," *New York Daily News*, July 19, 1998, p. 18.

243. Somini Sengupta, "Many Frustrated Parents Turn to Foster Care as Their Only Option," *New York Times*, September 1, 2000, p. B1.

244. *In the Interest of Micah Alyn R.*, 202 W.Va. 400, 504 S.E. 2d 635 (1998).

245. Mary Giliberti and Rhoda Schulzinger, *Relinquishing Custody: The Tragic Result of Failure to Meet Children's Mental Health Needs* (Washington, D.C.: Bazelon Center for Mental Health Law, 2000), p. 8.

246. Ibid., p. 1.

247. Kelly Blankenship, Michael Pullman, and Barbara J. Friesen, *Keeping Families Together: Implementation of an Oregon Law Abolishing the Custody Relinquishment Requirement*

(Portland, Ore.: Research and Training Center on Family Support and Children's Mental Health, 1999).

248. Giliberti and Schulzinger, *Relinquishing Custody,* p. 9.

249. Ibid., p. 14.

250. Katherine C. Pearson, "Cooperate or We'll Take Your Child: The Parents' Fictional Voluntary Separation Decision and a Proposal for Change," *Tennessee Law Review* 65 (1998): 835.

251. Nancy Goldhill, *Families at Risk: The Need for Foster Care Reform, Report on Foster Care Placement in New Jersey* (New Brunswick, N.J.: Legal Services of New Jersey, 1994).

252. Lewis, "Tidal Wave of Needy Teens."

253. Sinden, "Why Won't Mom Cooperate?: A Critique of Informality in Child Welfare Proceedings," p. 385.

254. Billingsley and Giovannoni, *Children of the Storm,* p. 4.

255. Martha A. Fineman, *The Neutered Mother, The Sexual Family, and Other Twentieth-Century Tragedies* (New York: Routledge, 1995); Gwendolyn Mink, *Welfare's End* (Ithaca: Cornell University Press, 1998).

256. Billingsley and Giovannoni, *Children of the Storm,* p. viii.

257. Lindsey, *The Welfare of Children,* pp. 4–5; see also Billingsley and Giovannoni, *Children of the Storm,* p. 5.

258. Carol B. Stack, "Social Policy and Practice," in *Empowering the Black Family: A Roundtable Discussion with Ann Hartman, James Leigh, Jacquelynn Moffett, Elaine Pinderhughes, Barbara Solomon, and Carol Stack,* ed. Sylvia Sims Gray, Ann Hartman, and Ellen S. Saalberg (Ann Arbor, Mich.: National Child Welfare Training Center 1985), pp. 21, 26 (comments of Ann Hartman).

259. The United State Supreme Court recognized similarities between proceedings to terminate parental rights and criminal trials. See *Lassiter v. Dep't. of Social Services,* 452 U.S. 18 (1981) (holding that parents have a due process right to counsel in complex proceedings to terminate parental rights); *Santosky v. Kramer,* 455 U.S. 745 (1982) (holding that termination of parental rights must be justified by clear and convincing evidence).

260. Susan J. Wells, "Child Protective Services: Research for the Future," *Child Welfare* 73 (1974): 431, 444.

261. Billingsley and Giovannoni, *Children of the Storm,*, p. 215.

262. "Race, Bias, and Power in Child Welfare," p. 2.

263. Ibid., p. 5.

264. Randall Kennedy, "Suspect Policy," *New Republic,* September 13 and 20, 1999, pp. 30, 32–33.

265. Ibid., p. 33.

266. Courtney et al., "Race and Child Welfare Services: Past Research and Future Directions," p. 130.

267. Rank, "The Racial Injustice of Poverty," p. 97.

268. William Darity Jr. and Samuel Myers Jr., *Persistent Disparity: Race and Economic Inequality in the United States Since 1945* (Cheltenham, U.K.: Edward Elgar, 1998); Douglas S. Massey and Nancy A. Denton, *American Apartheid: Segregation and the Making of the Underclass* (Cambridge: Harvard University Press, 1993); William Julius Wilson, *The Truly Disadvantaged: The Inner City, the Underclass, and Public Policy* (Chicago: University of Chicago, 1987); William

Julius Wilson, *When Work Disappears: The World of the New Urban Poor* (New York: Vintage, 1996).

269. Dalton Conley, *Being Black, Living in the Red: Race, Wealth, and Social Policy in America* 152 (Berkeley: University of California Press, 1999), p. 152.

270. William Darity Jr., "History, Discrimination, and Racial Inequality," in *The State of Black America 1999: The Impact of Color-Consciousness in the United States* (New York: National Urban League, 1999), pp. 153, 161–162.

271. David T. Wellman, *Portraits of White Racism,* 2nd ed. (Cambridge: Cambridge University Press, 1993), p. 55 (emphasis added).

272. Levine et al., "African-American Families and Child Protection," pp. 707–708.

273. Administration for Children and Families, U.S. Department of Health and Human Services, *Child Maltreatment 1998: Reports from the States to the National Child Abuse and Neglect Data System* (Washington, D.C.: U.S. Government Printing Office, 2000).

274. Jeanne M. Giovannoni, "Reports of Child Maltreatment from Mandated and Non-Mandated Reporters," *Children and Youth Services Review* 17 (1995): 487.

275. S. J. Rose and W. Meezan, "Child Neglect: A Study of the Perceptions of Mothers and Child Welfare Workers," *Children and Youth Services Review* 17 (1995): 471.

276. Rose, "Reaching Consensus on Child Neglect."

277. Jeanne Giovannoni and William Meezan, "Rethinking Supply and Demand in Child Welfare," *Children and Youth Services Review* 17 (1995): 465, 467.

278. For a study of the complexity of institutional racism in another bureaucratic context, see Simon Halliday, "Institutional Racism in Bureaucratic Decision-Making: A Case Study in the Administration of Homelessness Law," *Journal of Law and Society* 27 (2000): 449.

279. Pelton, *For Reasons of Poverty,* p. 60.

280. Melvin Thomas, "Anything But Race: The Social Science Retreat From Racism," *African American Research Perspectives* 6 (Winter 2000): 79, 90.

281. Billingsley and Giovannoni, *Children of the Storm,* p. vii.

NOTES TO PART TWO

1. Peggy J. Farber, "Broken Homepage," *Harper's Magazine,* April 2001, p. 76.

2. Richard Krugman, "The Politics," *Child Abuse and Neglect* 23 (1999): 963.

3. See, for example, Robert H. Mnookin, "Foster Care: In Whose Best Interest?" *Harvard Education Review* 43 (1973): 599; Michael S. Wald, "State Intervention on Behalf of 'Neglected' Children: Standards for Removal of Children from Their Homes, Monitoring the Status of Children in Foster Care, and Termination of Parental Rights," *Stanford Law Review* 28 (1976): 623.

4. Martin Guggenheim, "The Foster Care Dilemma and What to Do About It: Is the Problem That Too Many Children Are Not Being Adopted out of Foster Care or That Too Many Children Are Entering Foster Care?" *University of Pennsylvania Journal of Constitutional Law* 2 (1999): 141.

5. Wald, "State Intervention on Behalf of 'Neglected' Children," 679.

6. *Adoption and Safe Families Act of 1997,* Public Law 105–189, 111 Stat. 2115 (1997) (codified in scattered sections of *U.S. Code,* vol. 42).

7. Alison Mitchell, "President Tells Government to Promote More Adoptions," *New York Times*, December 15, 1996, p. 34.

8. Joseph Goldstein et al., *Beyond the Best Interests of the Child* (New York: Free Press, 1973); Henry S. Maas and Richard E. Engler Jr., *Children in Need of Parents* (New York: Columbia University Press, 1959).

9. Matthew B. Johnson, "Examining Risks to Children in the Context of Parental Rights Termination Proceedings," *New York University Review of Law and Social Change* 22 (1996): 397.

10. For an excellent study and critique of judicial opinions adopting psychological parent principles, see Peggy C. Davis, "'There Is a Book Out . . . ': An Analysis of Judicial Absorption of Legislative Facts," *Harvard Law Review* 100 (1987): 1539.

11. Jennifer Ayres Hand, "Note, Preventing Undue Terminations: A Critical Evaluation of the Length-of-Time-Out-of-Custody Ground for Termination of Parental Rights," *New York University Law Review* 71 (1996): 1251.

12. *Congressional Record,* 143d Cong., H10776–05, H10789, daily ed., Nov. 13, 1997.

13. "From Foster Care to Adoption," *Washington Post,* May 10, 1997, p. A24.

14. Jeff Katz, "Finally the Law Puts These Kids' Interests First," *Milwaukee Journal Sentinel,* December 28, 1997, p. 1.

15. Richard J. Gelles, *The Book of David: How Preserving Families Can Cost Children's Lives* (New York: Basic Books, 1996), pp. 152, 143.

16. Amanda Spake, "The Little Boy Who Didn't Have to Die," *McCall's,* November 1994, p. 142.

17. Michael Quinn, "Family Preservation: It Can Kill," *Newsday* (New York), January 11, 1996, p. A33.

18. *Congressional Record,* 143d Cong., H2012–06, H2017, daily ed., April 30, 1997.

19. *Congressional Record,* 143d Cong., S12526–02, S12526, daily ed., Nov., 13, 1997.

20. See, for example, Renny Golden, *Disposable Children: America's Child Welfare System* (Belmont, Calif.: Wadsworth, 1997), pp. 152–155; Cornel West and Sylvia Ann Hewlett, *The War Against Parents: What We Can Do for America's Beleaguered Moms and Dads* (Boston: Houghton Mifflin, 1998); Marsha Garrison, "Why Terminate Parental Rights?" *Stanford Law Review* 35 (1983): 423.

21. Golden, *Disposable Children,* p. 153.

22. Akhil Reed Amar and Daniel Widawsky, "Child Abuse as Slavery: A Thirteenth Amendment Response to DeShaney," *Harvard Law Review* 105 (1992): 1359.

23. Madelyn Freundlich, *Expedited Termination of Parental Rights: Risks and Benefits* (The Evan B. Donaldson Adoption Institute, February 9, 1999), available at http://www.adoptioninstitute.org/policy/polexp.html.

24. *Congressional Record,* 143d Cong., H10776–05, H10787, daily ed., Nov. 13, 1997 (statement of Rep. Kennelly).

25. *Santosky v. Kramer,* 455 U.S. 745, 749 (1982).

26. United States General Accounting Office, *Foster Care: States' Early Experiences Implementing the Adoption and Safe Families Act* (December 1999), p. 2.

27. Elizabeth Bartholet, *Nobody's Children* (Boston: Beacon Press), p. 190.

28. *Adoption Promotion Act of 1997,* 105th Cong., H.R. 867, Hearing Before the Subcommittee on Human Resources of the House Committee on Ways and Means, *Congressional Record* 73 (1997) (statement of Child Welfare League of America).

29. Barbara Vobejda, "Doing What's Best for the Children," *Washington Post*, May 3, 1999, p. 30.

30. Sarah Karp, "Adoption Surge: DCFS Policy Spells Pressure for Black Families," *Chicago Reporter*, October 1999.

31. Timothy Roche, "The Crisis of Foster Care," *Time*, November 13, 2000, pp. 74, 82.

32. LeRoy H. Pelton, *For Reasons of Poverty: A Critical Analysis of the Public Child Welfare System in the United States* (New York: Praeger, 1989), pp. 118–125.

33. Leslie Doty Hollingsworth, "Adoption Policy in the United States: A Word of Caution," *Social Work* 45 (March 1, 2000): 185.

34. "In re Catholic Child Care Society of Diocese of Brooklyn (New York Family Court, December 22, 1991)," *New York Law Journal* (December 23, 1991): 21.

35. See Children's Defense Fund, *The State of America's Children* (Washington, D.C.: Children's Defense Fund, 1998), p. 66.

36. *Congressional Record*, 143d Cong., H10776–05, H10789, daily ed., Nov. 13, 1997 (statement of Rep. Pomeroy).

37. *Congressional Record*, 143d Cong., S12526–02, S12526, daily ed., Nov. 13, 1997.

38. *Congressional Record*, 143d Cong., H10776–05, H10788, daily ed., Nov. 13, 1997.

39. Mary McGrory, "Adopt a Sense of Outrage," *Washington Post*, May 12, 1996, p. C1.

40. "Abused Children," *Talk of the Nation*, November 18, 1997.

41. Cheryl Wetzstein, "President Signs Foster Care Reforms; Law Will Make Adoption Easier," *Washington Times*, November 20, 1997, p. A3.

42. Peter Baker, "Clinton Signs Law to Speed Adoption Process for Children in Foster Care," *Washington Post*, November 20, 1997, p. A17.

43. Alison Mitchell, "Bush Proposes Move to Promote Adoptions," *New York Times*, July 12, 2000, p. A16; Bob Kemper, "Bush Bares $2.3 Billion Plan Aimed at Getting More Foster Kids Adopted," *Chicago Tribune*, July 12, 2000, sec. 1, p. 6; Jill Zuckman, "Bush Offers Plan on Adoption, Says Changes Would Promote Speedier System," *Boston Globe*, July 12, 2000, p. A24; R. G. Ratcliffe and Bennett Roth, "Bush Outlines $2.3 Billion Plan to Spur Adoptions," *Houston Chronicle*, July 12, 2000, p. 6.

44. Bartholet, *Nobody's Children*, p. 195.

45. Ibid., p. 196.

46. Council on Civil Society, *A Call to Civil Society: Why Democracy Needs Moral Truths* (New York: Institute for American Values, 1998), p. 23.

47. Ibid., p. 26; National Commission on Civic Renewal, *A Nation of Spectators: How Civic Disengagement Weakens America and What We Can Do About It* (College Park, Md.: University of Maryland Press, 1998), p. 13. An article in the Heritage Foundation's Policy Review discusses other organizations that promote adoption, including the Fund for the American Family, founded by former Pennsylvania governor Robert Casey, Institute for Children, and National Council for Adoption. See Charmaine Crouse Yoest, "A Solution Waiting to Be Adopted," *Policy Review*, September 19, 1996, p. 8.

48. Elizabeth Bartholet, *Family Bonds: Adoption and the Politics of Parenting* (Boston: Beacon Press, 1993), pp. 30–38.

49. *Congressional Record*, 143d Cong., H10776–05, H10789, daily ed., Nov. 13, 1997 (emphasis added).

50. *Congressional Record*, 143d Cong., H10776–05, H10790, daily ed., Nov. 13, 1997.

51. *Congressional Record*, 142d Cong., S5710–01, S5710, daily ed., June 4, 1996.

52. Marsha Garrison, "Parents' Rights vs. Children's Interests: The Case of the Foster Child," *N.Y.U. Review of Law and Social Change* 22 (1996): 371, 373.

53. Ibid., pp. 373–374.

54. Ibid., p. 386.

55. Judith S. Wallerstein and Joan Berlin Kelly, *Surviving the Breakup: How Children and Parents Cope with Divorce* (New York: Basic Books, 1980), p. 253.

56. Jacquelynn A. Moffett, "Practice with Black Families," in *Empowering the Black Family: A Roundtable Discussion with Ann Hartman, James Leigh, Jacquelynn Moffett, Elaine Pinderhughes, Barbara Solomon, and Carol Stack*, ed. Sylvia Sims Gray et al. (Ann Arbor, Mich.: National Child Welfare Training Center, University of Michigan, School of Social Work, 1985), pp. 57, 58.

57. *Congressional Record,* 143d Cong., S12668–03, S12672, daily edition, November 13, 1997.

58. *Adoption Promotion Act of 1997,* 105th Cong., H.R. 867, Hearing Before the Subcommittee on Human Resources of the House Committee on Ways and Means, *Congressional Record* 24 (1997) (prepared testimony of Olivia A. Golden, Ph.D., Acting Assistant Secretary, Children and Families, U.S. Department of Health and Human Services).

59. Robert Pear, "House Passes Bill to Encourage Adoptions of Abused Children," *New York Times,* May 1, 1997, p. A22.

60. Associated Press, "Adoption Reform Bill Passed," *Newsday,* November 15, 1997, p. A17.

61. Bartholet, *Nobody's Children,* pp. 8–15.

62. Ibid., p. 9.

63. Duncan Lindsey, *The Welfare of Children* (New York: Oxford University Press, 1994), pp. 136–137; Peggy Cooper Davis and Guatam Barua, "Custodial Choices for Children at Risk: Bias, Sequentiality, and the Law," *University of Chicago Law School Roundtable* 2 (1995): 139.

64. Lisa Snell, *Child Welfare Reform and the Role of Privatization,* Policy Study No. 271 (Washington, D.C.: Reason Public Policy Institute, 2000).

65. National Coalition for Child Protection Reform, "Financial Incentives," Issue Paper 11 of *Family Preservation,* available at http://www.nccpr.org.

66. Bruce Boyer and Steven Lubet, "The Kidnapping of Edgardo Mortara: Contemporary Lessons in the Child Welfare Wars," *Villanova Law Review* 45 (2000): 245.

67. Davis, "'There Is a Book Out . . . ,'" p. 1585.

68. Marjorie Beggs, *In a Day's Work: Four Child Welfare Workers in California* (San Francisco: Study Center Press, 1996), p. 54.

69. Akka Gordon, "Taking Liberties," *City Limits,* December 2000, p. 18.

70. Ibid.

71. Patrick Murphy, "Family Preservation and Its Victims," *New York Times,* June 19, 1993, p. 21.

72. Clark M. Peters and Shiela M. Merry, *Child Abuse and Neglect Proceedings in Illinois Jurisdictions Outside Cook County,* Chapin Hall Center for Children at the University of Chicago, December 1997.

73. Johnson, "Examining Risks to Children."

74. Jody Adams, "A Daily Disaster for Children," *New York Times,* February 19, 2001, p. 21.

75. Ibid.

76. Johnson, "Examining Risks to Children."

77. Ronald G. Silikovitz and Philip H. Witt, "The Role of the Psychologist in Guardianship Proceedings," *New Jersey Psychologist* 42 (1992): 39.

78. Davis, "'There's a Book Out,'" pp. 1539, 1556.

79. *In re J.C.,* 608 A.2d 1312 (N.J. 1992).

80. Naomi R. Cahn, "Children's Interests in a Familial Context: Poverty, Foster Care, and Adoption," *Ohio State Law Journal* 60 (1999): 1189, 1202.

81. Roche, "The Crisis of Foster Care."

82. Letters, *Time,* December 4, 2000, p. 14.

83. Nina Bernstein, "Plight of 2 Boys Exposes a Long Odyssey of Abuse," *New York Times,* February 2, 2001, p. A1.

84. Nina Bernstein, "Family Loyalty and Distrust of System Helped Hide Abuse of 2 Boys," *New York Times,* February 3, 2001, p. A10.

85. Shawn Raymond, "Where Are the Reasonable Efforts to Enforce the Reasonable Efforts Requirement?: Monitoring State Compliance under the Adoption Assistance and Child Welfare Act of 1980," *Texas Law Review* 77 (1999): 1235.

86. *Suter v. Artist M,* 503 U.S. 347 (1992).

87. *Foster Care, Child Welfare, and Adoption Reforms, 1988,* Joint Hearings Before the Subcommittee on Public Assistance and Unemployment Compensation of the House of Representatives Committee on Ways and Means and the Select Committee on Children, Youth, and Families, 100th Cong., 2d Sess. (1988), p. 252.

88. Alice C. Shotton, "Making Reasonable Efforts in Child Abuse and Neglect Cases: Ten Years Later," *California Welfare Law Review* 26 (1989–1990): 223, 227.

89. *Foster Care, Child Welfare, and Adoption Reforms,* p. 231.

90. Hand, "Note, Preventing Undue Terminations," p. 1278, n. 146.

91. Marcia Lowery, "Foster Care and Adoption Reform Legislation: Implementing the Adoption and Safe Families Act of 1997," *St. John's Journal of Legal Commentary* 14 (2000): 447, 450.

92. United States General Accounting Office, *Foster Care: States' Early Experiences Implementing the Adoption and Safe Families Act,* p. 9.

93. Richard Wexler, *The Lengthening Shadow: How Florida's Continuing Foster Care Panic Endangers Children* (Washington, D.C.: National Coalition for Child Protection Reform, February 2001), p. 13.

94. Marianne Berry, *The Family at Risk: Issues and Trends in Family Preservation Services* (Columbia: University of South Carolina Press, 1997), p. xi.

95. For a description of family preservation service models, see ibid., pp. 71–88.

96. Snell, *Child Welfare Reform and the Role of Privatization,* p. 15, Table 4.

97. John R. Schuerman, Tina L. Rzepnicki, and Julia H. Littell, *Putting Families First: An Experiment in Family Preservation* (New York: Aldine de Gruyter, 1994), p. 107.

98. Ibid.

99. Snell, *Child Welfare Reform and the Role of Privatization,* p. 15, Table 4.

100. Ibid., p. 13.

101. Mary I. Benedict and Susan Zuravin, *Factors Associated with Child Maltreatment by Family Foster Care Providers* (Baltimore: Johns Hopkins University School of Hygiene and Public Health, June 30, 1992).

102. U.S. Department of Health and Human Services, Administration on Children, Youth, and Families, *Child Maltreatment 1999* (Washington, D.C.: U.S. Government Printing Office, 2001), p. viii.

103. Kristine E. Nelson, "Do Services to Preserve the Family Place Children at Unnecessary Risk?: No," in *Controversial Issues in Child Welfare,* ed. Eileen Gambrill and Theodore J. Stein (Needham Heights, Mass.: Allyn & Bacon, 1993), p. 67.

104. Ibid., p. 69.

105. Catherine A. Faver, Sharon L. Crawford, and Terri Combs-Orne, "Services for Child Maltreatment: Challenges for Research and Practice," *Children and Youth Services Review* 21 (1999): 89.

106. United States General Accounting Office, *Child Welfare: States' Progress in Implementing Family Preservation and Support Services,* Report No. HHS–97–34, 1997, p. 3.

107. Mark E. Courtney, "Factors Associated with the Reunification of Foster Children with Their Families," *Social Services Review* 68 (1994): 81.

108. Richard P. Barth and Marianne Berry, "Implications of Research on the Welfare of Children Under Permanency Planning," *Child Welfare Research Review* 1 (1994): 323, 325.

109. Bartholet, *Nobody's Children,* p. 195.

110. Susan Kelly and Betty J. Blythe, "Family Preservation: A Potential Not Yet Realized," *Child Welfare* 79 (2000): 29.

111. "Too Fast for Families: Washington's Get-Tough Adoption Law Hits Home," *Child Welfare Watch* (Winter 2000).

112. Mary Ann Jones, *Parental Lack of Supervision: Nature and Consequence of a Major Child Neglect Problem* (Washington, D.C.: Child Welfare League of America, 1987).

113. Loring Jones, "The Social and Family Correlates of Successful Reunification of Children in Foster Care," *Children and Youth Services Review* 20 (1998): 305.

114. Leroy H. Pelton and E. Fuccello, *An Evaluation of the Use of an Emergency Cash Fund in Child Protective Services* (Trenton: New Jersey Division of Youth and Family Services, 1978).

115. Mark Fraser and David Haapala, "Home-Based Family Treatment: A Quantitative-Qualitative Assessment," *Journal of Applied Social Science* 12 (1987–1988): 1.

116. Marianne Berry, "An Evaluation of Family Preservation Services: Fitting Agency Services to Family Needs," *Social Work* 37 (1992): 314, 320.

117. *Washington State Coalition for the Homeless v. Department of Social and Health Services,* 949 P.2d 1291 (Wash. 1997).

118. Edith Fein and Anthony N. Maluccio, "Permanency Planning: Another Remedy in Jeopardy?" *Social Services Review* 66 (1992): 335, 339.

119. Brenda G. McGowan and Elaine M. Walsh, "Policy Challenges for Child Welfare in the New Century," *Child Welfare* 79 (2000): 11, 14; P. Adams, "Marketing Social Change: The Case of Family Preservation," *Children and Youth Services Review* 16 (1994): 417.

120. Marianne Berry, *Keeping Families Together* (New York: Garland, 1994), p. 4.

121. Richard P. Barth et al., *From Child Abuse to Permanency Planning: Child Welfare Services Pathways and Placements* (Hawthorne, N.Y.: Aldine de Gruyter, 1994), p. 265.

122. Ann Hartman, "Family Preservation Under Attack," *Social Work* 38 (1993): 509, 511.

123. Berry, *Keeping Families Together,* p. 4.

124. National Center on Addiction and Substance Abuse at Columbia University (CASA), "No Safe Haven: Children of Substance-Abusing Parents" (New York: January 1999), p. 5.

125. U.S. Department of Health and Human Services, *Blending Perspectives and Building Common Ground, a Report to Congress on Substance Abuse and Child Protection,* available at http://www.aspe.hss.gov/hsp/subabuse99/subabuse.htm.

126. CASA, "No Safe Haven," p. 34.

127. Stephen Magura and Alexandre B. Laudet, "Parental Substance Abuse and Child Maltreatment: Review and Implications for Intervention," *Child and Youth Services Review* 19 (1996): 193; Douglas J. Besharov, "Looking Beyond 30, 60, and 90 Days," *Child and Youth Services Review* 16 (1994): 445.

128. "Review Recommends Intensive Services to Improve Outcomes for Pregnant Addicts," *Alcoholism and Drug Abuse Weekly* 10 (June 29, 1998): 1.

129. CASA, "No Safe Haven," p. 80.

130. Ibid. See, for example, Alma J. Carten, "Mothers in Recovery: Rebuilding Families in the Aftermath of Addiction," *Social Work* 41 (1996): 214.

131. James Willwerth, "Should We Take Away Their Kids? Often the Best Way to Save the Child Is to Save the Mother as Well," *Time,* May 13, 1991, p. 62; CASA, "No Safe Haven," p. 24 (noting several reasons why "[i]t is essential to provide treatment for substance abusing parents").

132. Kathleen Wobie et al., "To Have and to Hold: A Descriptive Study of Custody Status Following Prenatal Exposure to Cocaine," paper presented at joint annual meeting of the American Pediatric Society and the Society for Pediatric Research, May 3, 1998.

133. Sandra M. Stehno, "The Elusive Continuum of Child Welfare Services: Implications for Minority Children and Youths," *Child Welfare* 69 (1990): 551. On targeting family preservation services to children of color, see Ramona Denby et al., "Family Preservation Services and Special Populations: The Invisible Target," *Families in Society: Journal of Contemporary Human Services* 79 (1998): 3.

134. Stehno, "The Elusive Continuum of Child Welfare Services," p. 554.

135. Hand, "Note, Preventing Undue Terminations," p. 1280.

136. "Too Fast for Families: Washington's Tough Adoption Law Hits Home."

137. McAdams, "The Parent in the Shadows," *Child Welfare* 51 (1972): 51, 52.

138. Pelton, *For Reasons of Poverty,* p. 61.

139. "Too Fast for Families: Washington's Get-Tough Adoption Law Hits Home."

140. Leroy H. Pelton, "Has Permanency Planning Been Successful? No," in *Controversial Issues in Child Welfare,* ed. Eileen Gambrill and Theodore J. Stein (Needham Heights, Mass.: Allyn & Bacon, 1993), pp. 268–271.

141. General Accounting Office, "Child Welfare: Complex Needs Strain Capacity to Provide Services," Letter Report, 9/26/95, GAO/HEHS–95–208.

142. Mark E. Courtney, "The Costs of Child Protection in the Context of Welfare Reform," *Future of Children* 8 (Spring 1998): 88, 93.

143. General Accounting Office, "Child Welfare: Complex Needs Strain Capacity to Provide Services."

144. Ibid.

145. Faver, Crawford, and Combs-Orne, "Services for Child Maltreatment," p. 93.

146. Guggenheim, "The Foster Care Dilemma," p. 143.

147. Staff of House Select Committee on Children, Youth, and Families, *No Place to Call Home: Discarded Children in America* 6, 101st Cong. (Comm. Print 1989).

148. Marianne Berry, "Has Permanency Planning Been Successful?: Rejoinder to Dr. Pelton," in *Controversial Issues in Child Welfare*," ed. Eileen Gambrill and Theodore J. Stein (Needham Heights, Mass.: Allyn & Bacon, 1993), pp. 272, 273.

149. Associated Press, "Adoption Reform Bill Passed," *Newsday*, November 15, 1997, p. A17.

150. Kelly and Blythe, "Family Preservation: A Potential Not Yet Realized."

151. U.S. Department of Health and Human Services, Administration on Children, Youth, and Families, *Child Maltreatment 1999* (Washington, D.C.: U.S. Government Printing Office, 2001).

152. See, for example, "Are Intensive Family Preservation Services Effective?" in *Controversial Issues in Child Welfare*, ed. Eileen Gambrill and Theodore J. Stein (Needham Heights, Mass.: Allyn & Bacon, 1993), p. 290; Richard P. Barth and Marianne Berry, "Implications of Research on the Welfare of Children Under Permanency Planning," in *Child Welfare Research Review*, vol. 1, ed. Richard Barth, Jill Duerr Berrick, and Neil Gilbert (New York: Columbia University Press, 1994), p. 321; Julia H. Littell and John Schuerman, *A Synthesis of Research on Family Preservation and Family Reunification Programs* (Westat, Inc., in association with James Bell Associates, and the Chapin Hall Center for Children at the University of Chicago, 1995).

153. Schuerman, Rzepnicki, and Littell, *Putting Families First*, pp. 199–216.

154. Ibid., p. 29.

155. Littell and Schuerman, *A Synthesis of Research on Family Preservation*, p. 10.

156. William M. Epstein, "Social Science, Child Welfare, and Family Preservation: A Failure of Rationality in Public Policy," *Children and Youth Services Review* 19 (1997): 41, 56.

157. Gary Cameron and Jim Vanderwoerd, *Protecting Children and Supporting Families: Promising Programs and Organizational Realities* (New York: Aldine De Gruyter, 1997), pp. 195–222.

158. Ibid., p. 213.

159. G. Halper and M. A. Jones, *Serving Families at Risk of Dissolution: Public Preventive Services in New York City*, Grant #90-C–1269 (New York: Children's Bureau of the Administration for Children, Youth and Families, Department of Health and Human Services, 1981).

160. Cameron and Vanderwoerd, *Protecting Children and Supporting Families*, p. 203.

161. C. Berquist, D. Szwejda, and G. Pope, *Evaluation of Michigan's Families First Program: Summary Report* (Lansing, Mich.: University Associates, 1993).

162. Littell and Schuerman, *A Synthesis of Research on Family Preservation*, p. 13.

163. Ibid., p. 14.

164. Mark W. Fraser et al., "An Experiment in Family Reunification: Correlates of Outcomes at One-Year Follow-Up," *Children and Youth Services Review* 18 (1996): 335. For additional studies evaluating family preservation programs, see Kathleen Wells and David E. Biegel, eds., *Family Preservation Services: Research and Evaluation* (Newbury Park, Calif.: Sage Publications, 1991); Berry, *The Family at Risk*, pp. 91–105.

165. Barth and Berry, "Implications of Research on the Welfare of Children Under Permanency Planning," pp. 333–334.

166. Schuerman, Rzepnicki, and Littell, *Putting Families First*, p. 29.

167. Ibid., p. 229.

168. Richard Wexler, "There Is No Child Protection Without Family Preservation," *Tampa Tribune*, October 29, 1997, p. 15.

169. Peter Kendall and Terry Wilson, "Boy's Death Casts Shadow on Foster Care," *Chicago Tribune,* February 28, 1995, p. 11.

170. Schuerman, Rzepnicki, and Littell, *Putting Families First,* p. 240.

171. Pelton, "Has Permanency Planning Been Successful?" p. 271.

172. Joseph M. Lauria, Letter to the Editor, *New York Times,* March 5, 2001, p. A22.

173. Heath Foster, "Move Toward Permanent Homes Is on a Faster Track," *Seattle Post-Intelligencer,* June 18, 1998, p. A10.

174. Farber, "Broken Homepage."

175. United States General Accounting Office, *Foster Care: States' Early Experiences Implementing the Adoption and Safe Families Act,* p. 7.

176. "Too Fast for Families: Washington's Get-Tough Adoption Law Hits Home"; Joanne Wasserman, "Cutoff of Parental Rights Climbs," *New York Daily News,* January 19, 2000, p. 10.

177. Natalie Pardo, "Losing Their Children: As State Cracks Down on Parents, Black Families Splinter," *Chicago Reporter,* January 1999.

178. *In re J. M.,* 574 N.W. 2d 717 (Minn. 1998).

179. *Matter of S. Children* (Kings County Family Court), *New York Law Journal,* February 2, 2001.

180. *In the Interest of H. G.,* Gen. No. JAK 96 41 (Ill. Cir. Ct., January 27, 2000).

181. Cornelia Grumman, "Parents Give Advice on Reforming DCFS; Agency Criticized at Panel Hearings," *Chicago Tribune,* April 13, 1999, Metro Chicago, p. 3.

182. Hand, "Note, Preventing Undue Terminations," p. 1292.

183. CASA, "No Safe Haven," p. 39.

184. Joseph A. Califano, "The Least Among Us: Children of Substance-Abusing Parents," *America* 180 (1999): 10, 12.

185. CASA, "No Safe Haven," p. 8.

186. Deborah Elman, Paul Wise et al., "National Survey of the States: Policies and Practices Regarding Drug-Using Pregnant Women," *American Journal of Public Health* 88 (1998): 117.

187. *Whitner v. South Carolina,* 328 S.C. 1, 492 S.E. 2d 777 (Sup. Ct. 1997), cert. denied, 523 U.S. 1145 (1998).

188. 579 N.W. 2d 338 (Iowa Ct. App. 1998).

189. 75 Cal. Rptr. 2d 851 (Cal. Ct. App. 1998).

190. Somini Sengupta, "Completing a Family with the Children Others Avoid," *New York Times,* September 23, 2000, p. A13.

191. Ibid.

192. Vobejda, "Doing What's Best for the Children," p. 30.

193. Martin Guggenheim, "The Effects of Recent Trends to Accelerate the Termination of Parental Rights of Children in Foster Care: An Empirical Analysis in Two States," *Family Law Quarterly* 29 (1995): 121.

194. Ibid., p. 131.

195. Snell, *Child Welfare Reform and the Role of Privatization,* p. 1.

196. Quoted in Richard Wexler, "Spies in the Living Room," unpublished manuscript, 1999, p. 13.

197. Penny Ruff Johnson et al., "Family Foster Care Placement: The Child's Perspective," *Child Welfare* 74 (1995): 959.

198. Malcolm Bush and Andrew C. Gordon, "The Case for Involving Children in Child Welfare Decisions," *Social Work* 27 (1982): 309, 310.

199. Johnson, "Examining Risks to Children in the Context of Parental Rights Termination Proceedings."

200. Robert Borgman, "Antecedents and Consequences of Parental Rights Termination for Abused and Neglected Children," *Child Welfare* 60 (1981): 391.

201. Ibid.

202. National Coalition for Child Protection Reform, *Family Preservation and Adoption*, Issue Paper 13, citing "Adoption: What to Do When Love Is Not Enough," *Deseret News*, April 15, 1999, p. C1; "Nobody's a Winner When Adoption Fails," *Arizona Republic*, March 9, 1999, p. B1; "Number of Children in DHS Care to Grow," *Sunday Oklahoman*, July 19, 1998, p. 1. See also Barth and Berry, "Implications of Research on the Welfare of Children Under Permanency Planning," pp. 337–339.

203. Guggenheim, "The Effects of Recent Trends to Accelerate the Termination of Parental Rights of Children in Foster Care," p. 134.

204. See, for example, D. Fanshel and E. Shinn, *Children in Foster Care* (New York: Columbia University Press, 1978), pp. 486–488; Rosemary J. Avery, "Identifying Obstacles to Adoption in New York State's Out-of-Home Care System," *Child Welfare* 78 (1999): 653; Arthus R. Cantos et al., "Behavioral Correlates of Parental Visiting During Family Foster Care," *Child Welfare* 76 (1997): 309; Ner Littner, "The Importance of the Natural Parents to the Child in Placement," *Child Welfare* 54 (1975): 175.

205. See, for example, Patrick R. Tamilia, "A Response to Elimination of the Reasonable Efforts Required Prior to Termination of Parental Rights Status," *University of Pittsburgh Law Review* 54 (1992): 211, 217; Marsha Garrison, "Why Terminate Parental Rights?" *Stanford Law Review* 35 (1983): 423; Michael S. Wald, "State Intervention on Behalf of 'Neglected' Children: Standards for Removal of Children from Their Homes, Monitoring the Status of Children in Foster Care, and Termination of Parental Rights," *Stanford Law Review* 28 (1976): 623, 691, 696–699, 706.

206. Susan L. Brooks, "Permanency Through the Eyes of a Child: A Critique of the Adoption and Safe Families Act," *Children's Legal Rights Journal* 19 (1999): 3.

207. Ibid., p. 4. See also Nell Bernstein, "Kids' Interests Lose in Adoption Option," *Newsday*, May 30, 1999, p. B6.

208. *Adoption Promotion Act of 1997*, 105th Cong., H.R. 867, Hearings Before the Subcommittee on Human Resources of the House Committee on Ways and Means, *Congressional Record* 37 (1997) (statement of Jess McDonald, Director, Illinois Department of Children and Family Services).

209. Barth et al., *From Child Abuse to Permanency Planning*, pp. 213–214.

210. Jesse L. Thornton, "Permanency Planning for Children in Kinship Foster Homes," *Child Welfare* 70 (1991): 593, 597.

211. Gail Vida Hamburg, "An Act of Compassion May Require Some Decisive Action to Make It Work," *Chicago Tribune*, January 4, 1998, Woman News section, p. 1.

212. Meryl Schwartz, "Reinventing Guardianship: Subsidized Guardianship, Foster Care, and Child Welfare," *New York University Review of Law and Social Change* 22 (1996): 442.

213. Garrison, "Parents' Rights vs. Children's Interests," p. 379.

214. Sarah Karp, "Adoption Surge: DCFS Policy Spells Pressure for Black Families," *Chicago Reporter*, October 1999.

215. *Congressional Record*, 144th Cong., S12452–01, S12452, daily ed., Oct. 13, 1998 (statement of Sen. DeWine).

216. Larry May, "Adoption, Race, and Group-Based Harm," *Washington University Journal of Law and Policy* 1 (1999): 77.

217. Bartholet, *Nobody's Children,* p. 188.

218. Dorothy E. Roberts, "The Genetic Tie," *University of Chicago Law Review* 62 (1995): 209.

219. Garrison, "Parents' Rights vs. Children's Interests," p. 376 (citing Alfred Kadushin and Judith A. Martin, *Child Welfare Services,* 4th ed. (New York: Macmillan, 1988), pp. 535–540.

220. Erva Zuckerman, *Child Welfare* (New York: Free Press, 1983), pp. 119–120.

221. Rita James Simon and Howard Alstein, *Transracial Adoption* (New York: Wiley, 1977), p. 9.

222. R. Richard Banks, "The Color of Desire: Fulfilling Adoptive Parents' Racial Preferences Through Discriminatory State Action," *Yale Law Journal* 107 (1998): 875.

223. Ruth Arlene Howe, "Adoption Laws and Practices in 2000: Serving Whose Interests?" *Family Law Quarterly* 33 (1999): 677.

224. Amanda Spake, "Adoption Gridlock," *U.S. News and World Report,* June 22, 1998, p. 30.

225. Bartholet, *Nobody's Children,* p. 13.

226. Ibid., p. 4.

227. Ibid., p. 93.

228. Walter I. Trattner, *From Poor Law to Welfare State: A History of Social Welfare in America* (New York: Free Press, 1974), p. 118.

229. Stephen Lassonde, "Family Values, 1904 Version," *New York Times Book Review,* January 9, 2000, p. 7, reviewing Linda Gordon, *The Great Arizona Orphan Abduction* (Cambridge: Harvard University Press, 1999).

230. Bartholet, *Nobody's Children,* p. 26.

231. Ibid., pp. 3, 91.

232. Ibid., p. 26.

233. See, for example, Bonnie Miller Rubin and Robert Becker, "Will Clout Decide Battle for 'Baby T'?: Powerful Burkes Contend with Mother for Custody," *Chicago Tribune,* June 7, 1998, p. 1; Bonnie Miller Rubin and Robert Becker, "Baby T's Mom Ruled Fit in Fight for Toddler; Judge Rejects State's Case, All but Dooming Burkes' Adoption Bid," *Chicago Tribune,* November 5, 1998, p. 1; Robert Becker and Bonnie Miller Rubin, "Burkes Lose Key Adoption Supporter; Public Guardian Backs Mother, Blasts DCFS in Custody Dispute," *Chicago Tribune,* October 3, 1998, p. 1; Robert Becker and Bonnie Miller Rubin, "Mom Could Win Battle but Lose War; Tina Olison May Be Ruled Fit and Still Not Regain Her Child," *Chicago Tribune,* October 26, 1998, p. 1.

234. Bartholet, *Family Bonds,* p. 105.

235. Spake, "Adoption Gridlock"; Tamar Lewin, "At Core of Adoption Dispute Is Crazy Quilt of State Laws," *New York Times,* January 19, 2001, p. A12.

236. Madelyn Freundlich, *The Future of Adoption for Children in Foster Care: Demographics in a Changing Socio-Political Environment* (The Evan B. Donaldson Adoption Institute, 1999)(available at http://www.adoptioninstitute.org).

237. Sengupta, "Completing a Family," p. A13.

238. Eric Schmitt, "Children Adopted Abroad Win Automatic Citizenship," *New York Times,* February 27, 2001, p. A12.

239. Ibid.

240. Mary Jo McConahay, "The Baby Trade: Where There Is Poverty in the Third World and a Baby Shortage in the First, Children Become a Commodity," *Los Angeles Times Magazine,* December 16, 1990, p. 12.

241. Spake, "Adoption Gridlock."

242. Nina Bernstein, *The Lost Children of Wilder: The Epic Struggle to Change Foster Care* (New York: Pantheon, 2001), p. xii.

243. Martha Matthews, "Assessing the Effect of Welfare Reform on Child Welfare," *Clearinghouse Review* 32 (January-February 1999): 395, 397.

244. Matthews, "Assessing the Effect of Welfare Reform on Child Welfare"; Mark E. Courtney, "The Costs of Child Protection in the Context of Welfare Reform," *Future of Children* (Spring 1998): 88, 95–97; Kristen Shook, "Assessing the Consequences of Welfare Reform for Child Welfare," *Poverty Research News* 2 (Winter 1998): 8.

245. Courtney, "The Costs of Child Protection in the Context of Welfare Reform," p. 100.

246. Theda Skocpol, *Protecting Soldiers and Mothers: The Political Origins of Social Policy in the United States* (Cambridge: Belknap Press of Harvard University, 1992); Linda Gordon, *Pitied But Not Entitled: Single Mothers and the History of Welfare* (New York: Free Press, 1994).

247. Gordon, *Pitied But Not Entitled,* p. 38.

248. Ibid., p. 304; Gwendolyn Mink, *The Wages of Motherhood: Inequality in the Welfare State, 1917–1942* (Ithaca: Cornell University Press, 1995).

249. Leroy H. Pelton, "Welfare Discrimination and Child Welfare," *Ohio State Law Review* 60 (1999): 1479, 1480.

250. Gordon, *Pitied But Not Entitled,* p. 48.

251. Claudia Lawrence-Webb, "African American Children in the Modern Child Welfare System: A Legacy of the Flemming Rule," in *Serving African American Children,* ed. Sondra Jackson and Sheryl Brissett-Chapman (New Brunswick: Transaction Publishers, 1999), p. 9.

252. Gordon, *Pitied But Not Entitled,* p. 276.

253. L. Frame, "Suitable Homes Revisited: An Historical Look at Child Protection and Welfare Reform," *Children and Youth Services Review* 21 (1999): 719.

254. Charles Murray, "The Coming White Underclass," *Wall Street Journal,* October 29, 1993, p. A14.

255. "GOP Welfare Plan Would Take Cash from Unwed Mothers to Aid Adoptions," *Chicago Tribune,* November 14, 1994, p. 7.

256. Bernstein, *The Lost Children of Wilder,* p. xiii.

257. Mark Petix, "Is Adoption an Option?" *Press Enterprise,* January 27, 1997, p. A1.

258. Nina Bernstein, "New York City to Make Homeless Work," *New York Times,* October 26, 1999, p. A1.

259. Pelton, "Welfare Discrimination and Child Welfare," p. 1480.

260. Nancy Fraser, *Unruly Practices: Power, Discourse, and Gender in Contemporary Social Theory* (Minneapolis: University of Minnesota Press, 1989), pp. 144, 151–153.

261. Ann Crittenden, *The Price of Motherhood: Why the Most Important Job in the World Is Still the Least Valued* (New York: Metropolitan Books, 2001).

262. Ibid., p. 88.

263. Jill Quadagno, *The Color of Welfare: How Racism Undermined the War on Poverty* (New York: Oxford, 1995), pp. 20–22.

264. Gordon, *Pitied But Not Entitled,* p. 275.

265. Quoted by Judith Olans Brown et al., "The Mythogenesis of Gender: Judicial Images of Women in Paid and Unpaid Labor," *UCLA Women's Law Journal* 6 (1996): 457, 487, n. 134.

266. Quadagno, *The Color of Welfare,* p. 130.

267. "Wasserman's View," *Boston Globe,* September 25, 1995, p. 10.

268. Kathryn Edin and Laura Lein, *Making Ends Meet: How Single Mothers Survive Welfare and Low-Wage Work* (New York: Russell Sage Foundation, 1997), p. 6.

269. Robert Goerge et al., "New Comparative Insights into States and Their Foster Children," *Public Welfare* (Summer 1996): 12.

270. Duncan Lindsey, *The Welfare of Children* (New York: Oxford University Press, 1994); Leroy Pelton, "The Role of Material Factors in Child Abuse and Neglect," in *Protecting Children from Abuse and Neglect,* ed. Gary Melton and Frank Barry (New York: Guilford Press, 1994).

271. Shook, "Assessing the Consequences of Welfare Reform for Child Welfare," p. 1.

272. "From Welfare to Worsefare?" *Business Week,* October 9, 2000, p. 103.

273. Rob Geen, Lynn Fender, and Jacob Leos-Urbel, *Welfare Reform's Effect on Child Welfare Caseloads* (Washington, D.C.: Urban Institute, 2001).

274. Patrick T. Murphy, "A Trap of Welfare and Child Abuse," *New York Times,* August 11, 2000, p. A21.

275. Ron Haskins, Isabel Sawhill, and Kent Weaver, *Welfare Reform Reauthorization: An Overview of Problems and Issues* (Washington, D.C.: Brookings Institution, January 2001), p. 4.

276. Somini Sengupta, "71,400 Poor Families Nearing Limit on Federal Benefits," *New York Times,* February 10, 2001, p. A14.

277. Barbara Ehrenreich, *Nickel and Dimed: On (Not) Getting By in America* (New York: Metropolitan Books/Henry Holt, 2001).

278. Wendy Chavkin et al. "State Welfare Reform Policies and Declines in Health Insurance," *American Journal of Public Health* 89 (2000): 900, 903.

279. Women's Committee of One Hundred, "Open Letter," available at http://www.welfare2002.org or through gmink@mochamail.com.

280. Nina Bernstein, "Shelter Population Reaches Highest Level Since 1980s," *New York Times,* February 8, 2001, p. A27.

281. "From Welfare to Worsefare?"

282. Haskins, Sawhill, and Weaver, *Welfare Reform,* p. 4.

283. Ibid.

284. Joel F. Handler, "Low-Wage Work 'As We Know It,'" in *Hard Labor: Women and Work in the Post-Welfare Era,* ed. Joel F. Handler and Lucie White (Armonk, N.Y.: M. E. Sharpe, 1999), p. 4.

285. Laura Meckler, "Despite Welfare Overhaul, Racial Imbalance Escalates," *Times Union,* March 30, 1999, p. A1.

286. Sarah Karp, "Minorities Off Welfare Get Few Jobs," *Chicago Reporter,* January 2000.

287. Ibid.; Meckler, "Despite Welfare Overhaul, Racial Imbalance Escalates."

288. Peter T. Kilborn, "In New Orleans, Recession Could Hurt Past Welfare Recipients," *New York Times,* March 5, 2001, p. A11.

289. Peter Edelman, "Why Welfare? Better to Ask, Why Poverty?" *Times Union,* May 12, 1997, p. A7.

290. Jason DeParle, "Welfare Law Weighs Heavily on Delta, Where Jobs Are Few," *New York Times*, October 16, 1997, p. A14.

291. Women's Committee of One Hundred, "Open Letter."

292. Sengupta, "71,400 Poor Families Nearing Limit on Federal Benefits," p. A14.

293. Ann Collins and J. Lawrence Aber, *How Welfare Reform Can Help or Hurt Children*, Children and Welfare Reform Issue Brief 1 (New York: National Center for Children in Poverty, Columbia School of Public Health, 1997), p. 7.

294. Kristen Shook, "Does the Loss of Welfare Income Increase the Risk of Child Welfare Involvement Among Families Receiving Welfare?" (unpublished dissertation, University of Chicago, 1999).

295. Lindsey, *The Welfare of Children*, p. 151.

296. Collins and Aber, *How Welfare Reform Can Help or Hurt Children*.

297. Pelton, "Welfare Discrimination and Child Welfare," p. 1484.

298. Pamela Morris et al., *How Welfare and Work Policies Affect Children: A Synthesis of Research* (New York: Manpower Demonstration Research Corporation, January 2001), pp. 1–4.

299. Jason DeParle, "Wisconsin Welfare Overhaul Justifies Hope and Some Fear," *New York Times*, January 15, 1999, p. A1.

300. Personal communication with Martha Matthews, Staff Attorney, National Center for Youth Law, Los Angeles, CA. (January 1998).

301. Matthews, "Assessing the Effect of Welfare Reform on Child Welfare," p. 398.

302. Christina Paxson and Jane Waldfogel, "Welfare Reforms, Family Resources, and Child Maltreatment" (Chicago: Joint Center for Poverty Research, 2000), available at http://www.jcpr.org/book/pdf/IncentivesWaldPB.pdf.

303. Carol Kleiman, "Child-Care Dilemma: Pushed Off Welfare, Into Off Hours," *Chicago Tribune*, August 5, 1997, sec. 3, p. 2.

304. Jo Ann C. Gong, "Child Care in the Wake of the Federal Welfare Act," *Clearinghouse Review* 30 (January-February 1997), p. 1044.

305. Mark Courtney, "Welfare Reform and Child Welfare Services," in *Child Welfare in the Context of Welfare "Reform,"* ed. S. Kamerman and A. Kahn (New York: Columbia University School of Social Work, 1997), p. 1.

306. "How to Reform Welfare Sensibly and Humanely," *Washington Times*, March 23, 1995, p. A18.

307. Andrew Mollison, "Feds Go Back to the Drawing Board for Welfare Reform," *Austin American-Statesman*, January 7, 1995, A19.

308. Gong, "Child Care in the Wake of the Federal Welfare Act," p. 1044; Tamar Lewin, "From Welfare Roll to Child Care Worker," *New York Times*, April 29, 1998, p. A14.

309. Lewin, "From Welfare Roll to Child Care Worker."

310. Elizabeth Becker, "Millions Eligible for Food Stamps Aren't Applying," *New York Times*, February 26, 2001, p. A1; Ron Haskins, Isabel Sawhill, and Kent Weaver, *Welfare Reform Reauthorization: An Overview of Problems and Issues*, (Washington, D.C.: Brookings Institution, January 2001), p. 4; Robert Pear, "Poor Workers Lose Medicaid Coverage Despite Eligibility," *New York Times*, April 12, 1999, p. A1.

311. Nina Bernstein, "Medicaid to Be Restored for Thousands," *New York Times*, July 12, 2001, p. A23.

312. Howard Ires, Letter to the Editor, *New York Times*, February 27, 2001, p. A26.

313. Faith Mullen, "Welcome to Procrustes' House: Welfare Reform and Grandparents Raising Grandchildren," *Clearinghouse Review* 30 (1996): 511, 516; "Note, The Policy of Penalty in Kinship Care," *Harvard Law Review* 112 (199910: 1059.

314. DeParle, "Welfare Law Weighs Heavily on Delta, Where Jobs Are Few," p. A1.

315. Mark Hardin, "Sizing Up the Welfare Act's Impact on Child Protection," *Clearinghouse Review* 30 (1996): 1061, 1066.

316. Rob Geen and Shelley Waters, "The Impact of Welfare Reform on Child Welfare Financing," in *New Federalism: Issues and Options for States*, No. A–16 (Washington, D.C.: Urban Institute, 1997).

317. Hardin, "Sizing Up the Welfare Act's Impact on Child Protection," p. 1061.

318. Jean Tepperman, "Foster Care: The Last Entitlement," *Children's Advocate* (November-December 1998): 4.

319. Hardin, "Sizing Up the Welfare Act's Impact on Child Protection," p. 1065.

320. Bartholet, *Nobody's Children*, p. 87.

321. Courtney, "The Costs of Child Protection in the Context of Welfare Reform," p. 93.

322. Jennifer Pokempner and Dorothy E. Roberts, "Poverty, Welfare Reform, and the Meaning of Disability," *Ohio State Law Journal* 62 (2001): 425.

323. Christopher M. Wright, *SSI: The Black Hole of Welfare*, State Policy Analysis No. 224 (Washington, D.C.: Cato Institute, April 27, 1995); House Committee on Ways and Means, *Supplemental Security Income Fraud Involving Middlemen: Hearing Before the Subcommittee on Oversight*, 103d Cong., 1994, 223–227 (statement of Christopher M. Wright).

324. Jane Knitzer and Stanley Bernard, *The New Welfare Law and Vulnerable Families: Implications for Child Welfare/Child Protection Systems*, Children and Welfare Reform Issue Brief 3 (Washington, D.C.: National Center for Children in Poverty, 1997), pp. 4, 12.

325. Gwendolyn Mink, *Welfare's End* (Ithaca: Cornell University Press, 1998), p. 4.

326. Mimi Abramovitz, *Under Attack, Fighting Back: Women and Welfare in the United States* (New York: Monthly Review Press, 1996), pp. 33–34; Tonya L. Brito, "The Welfarization of Family Law," *University of Kansas Law Review* 48 (2000): 229, 233–237.

327. Dorothy Roberts, *Killing the Black Body: Race, Reproduction, and the Meaning of Liberty* (New York: Pantheon, 1997), pp. 209–213.

328. Noel A. Cazenave and Kenneth J. Neubeck, "Fighting Welfare Racism," *Poverty and Race* 10 (March-April 2001): 1.

329. Karp, "Minorities Off Welfare Get Few Jobs."

330. Stephanie A. Limoncelli, "The Politics of Motherhood and Paid Work: Gender, Class, Race, and the Construction of Need in a Welfare-to-Work Program," unpublished paper, March 31, 2000.

331. Nancy Gibbs, "The Vicious Cycle," *Time*, June 20, 1994, p. 24.

332. Mink, *Welfare's End*, p. 113.

333. Katherine Teghtsoonian, "The Work of Caring for Children: Contradictory Themes in American Child Care Policy Debates," *Women and Politics* 17 (1997): 77.

334. Courtney, "The Costs of Child Protection in the Context of Welfare Reform," p. 101.

335. Limoncelli, "The Politics of Motherhood and Paid Work."

336. Edin and Lein, *Making Ends Meet*, p. 7.

337. Ellen K. Scott et al., "Welfare Reform and the Work-Family Tradeoff," *Poverty Research News* 4 (July-August 2000): 9, 10.

338. DeParle, "Welfare Law Weighs Heavily on Delta, Where Jobs Are Few."

339. Brito, "Welfarization of Family Law," p. 246.

340. Knitzer and Bernard, *The New Welfare Law and Vulnerable Families*, p. 5.

341. Naomi Cahn, "Pragmatic Questions About Parental Liability Statutes," *Wisconsin Law Review* (1996): 399; Paul W. Schmidt, "Note, Dangerous Children and the Regulated Family: The Shifting Focus of Parental Responsibility Laws," *New York University Law Review* 73 (1998): 667.

342. See Daan Braveman and Sarah Ramsey, "When Welfare Ends: Removing Children from the Home for Poverty Alone," *Temple Law Review* 70 (1997): 447.

343. Marc Mauer, *Race to Incarcerate* (New York: New Press, 1999).

344. Fox Butterfield, "Number in Prison Grows Despite Crime Reduction," *New York Times,* August 10, 2000, p. A10.

345. Marc Mauer, *The Sentencing Project, Intended and Unintended Consequences: State Racial Disparities in Imprisonment* (Washington, D.C.: Sentencing Project, 1997), available at http://www.sentencingproject.org.

346. Jerome Miller, *Search and Destroy: African-American Males in the Criminal Justice System* (New York: Cambridge University Press, 1996), p. 5.

347. Elliot Currie, *Crime and Punishment in America* (New York: Henry, Holt, 1998), p. 4.

348. Anne L. Stahl, Office of Juvenile Justice and Delinquency Prevention, "Delinquency Cases in Juvenile Courts, 1997," *OJJDP Fact Sheet* (Washington, D.C.: U.S. Department of Justice, March 2000).

349. Charles M. Puzzanchera, Office of Juvenile Justice and Delinquency Prevention, "Juvenile Court Placement of Adjudicated Youth, 1988–1997," *OJJDP Fact Sheet* (Washington, D.C.: U.S. Department of Justice, October 2000).

350. Gillian Porter, Office of Juvenile Justice and Delinquency Prevention, "Detention in Delinquency Cases, 1988–1997," *OJJDP Fact Sheet* (Washington, D.C.: U.S. Department of Justice, November 2000).

351. Child Welfare League of America, *Responding to Alcohol and Other Drug Problems in Child Welfare* (Washington, D.C.: CWLA Press, 1998).

352. Cathy Spatz Wisdom, *The Cycle of Violence* (Washington, D.C.: U.S. Department of Justice, 1992).

353. Beverly Rivera and Cathy Spatz Wisdom, "Childhood Victimization and Violent Offending," *Violence and Victims* 5 (1990): 19.

354. M. L. Armstrong, *Adolescent Pathways: Exploring the Intersection Between Child Welfare and Juvenile Justice, PINS, and Mental Health* (New York: Vera Institute of Justice, May 1998).

355. J. William Spencer and Dean D. Knudsen, "Out of Home Maltreatment: An Analysis of Risk in Various Settings for Children," *Children and Youth Services Review* 14 (1992): 485.

356. James Rainey, "Grand Jury Cites Abuses in Group Foster Homes," *Los Angeles Times,* April 9, 1997, p. A1.

357. Nina Bernstein, "Probe of Foster Care Nightmares," *New York Newsday,* May 2, 1990, p. 16.

358. Ruth Teichroeb, "Judge's Choice: Lock Up the Kids or Put Them Out on the Street," *Seattle Post-Intelligencer,* September 23, 1999, p. A1.

359. Susan Vivian Mangold, "Extending Non-Exclusive Parenting and the Right to Protection for Older Foster Children: Creating Third Options in Permanency Planning," *Boston Law Review* 48 (Fall 2000): 835.

360. H.R. 3443, 106th Cong., 1999.

361. Westat, Inc., *A National Evaluation of Title IV-E Foster Care Independent Living Programs for Youth: Phase 2, Final Report* (Rockville, Md.: Westat 1991). Other studies of youth who aged out of foster care found similar results. See Mark E. Courtney and Irving Piliavin, *Transitions from and Returns to Out-of-Home Care* (Madison: University of Wisconsin–Madison, Institute for Research on Poverty, 1998); Richard P. Barth, "On Their Own: The Experiences of Youth After Foster Care," *Child and Adolescent Social Work* 7 (1990): 419.

362. Barth, "On Their Own."

363. Fred Bayles and Sharon Cohen, "Chaos Often the Only Parent for Abused or Neglected Children," *Los Angeles Times,* April 30, 1995, p. 1.

364. Beth Azar, "Foster Care Has a Bleak History, *APA Monitor* (November 1995).

365. Currie, *Crime and Punishment in America,* pp. 32–33.

366. Mauer, *The Sentencing Project,* p. 9.

367. Michael Tonry, *Malign Neglect* (New York: Oxford University Press, 1995), p. 30, Tables 1–3.

368. See Jonathan Simon, *Poor Discipline: Parole and the Social Control of the Underclass, 1890–1990* (Chicago: University of Chicago Press, 1993).

369. Mauer, *Race to Incarcerate,* p. 12.

370. See Christopher J. Mumola, Bureau of Justice Statistics, *Special Report: Incarcerated Parents and Their Children* (Washington, D.C.: U.S. Justice Dept., 2000).

371. John Hagan and Ronit Dinovitzer, "Collateral Consequences of Imprisonment for Children, Communities, and Prisoners" in *Crime and Justice: Prisons,* vol. 26, ed. Michael Tonry and Joan Petersilia (Chicago: University of Chicago Press, 1999),pp. 121, 124; Justin Brooks and Kimberly Bahna, "It's a Family Affair—The Incarceration of the American Family: Confronting Legal and Social Issues," *University of San Francisco Law Review* 28 (1994): 271, 272.

372. Denise Johnston, "Effects of Parental Incarceration" in *Children of Incarcerated Parents,* ed. Katherine Gabel and Denise Johnston (New York: Lexington Books, 1995), p. 59; Christina Jose Kampfner, "Post-Traumatic Stress Reactions in Children of Imprisoned Mothers," in *Children of Incarcerated Parents,* ed. Katherine Gabel and Denise Johnston (New York: Lexington Books, 1995), p. 89; W. H. Sack, "Children of Imprisoned Fathers," *Psychiatry* 40 (1977): 163.

373. Kampfner, "Post-traumatic Stress Reactions of Children of Imprisoned Mothers," p. 89.

374. See Mumola, *Special Report: Incarcerated Parents and Their Children,* p. 5.

375. Ibid., p. 2.

376. Hagan and Dinovitzer, "Collateral Consequences of Imprisonment," p. 139.

377. Jeffrey Fagan and Richard Freeman, "Crime and Work," *Crime and Justice: A Review of Research* 25 (1999): 225.

378. Ibid.; John H. Laub and Robert J. Sampson, "Long-Term Effect of Punitive Discipline," in *Coercion and Punishment in Long-Term Perspective,* ed. J. McCord (Cambridge: Cambridge University Press, 1995).

379. Peter T. Kilborn, "Ex-Convicts Seen Straining U.S. Labor Force," *New York Times,* March 15, 2001, p. A16.

380. See Robert Sampson and John Laub, *Crime in the Making* (Cambridge: Harvard University Press, 1993).

381. Kilborn, "Ex-Convicts Seen Straining U.S. Labor Force."

382. See Mumola, *Special Report: Incarcerated Parents and Their Children,* p. 3, Table 3 (7.4 percent of state prisoners and 6.8 percent of federal prisoners are mothers).

383. Mauer, *Race to Incarcerate,* p. 125.

384. Mumola, *Special Report: Incarcerated Parents and Their Children;* Barbara Bloom, "Imprisoned Mothers," in *Children of Incarcerated Parents,* ed. Katherine Gabel and Denise Johnston (New York: Lexington Books, 1995), p. 21.

385. Hagan and Dinovitzer, "Collateral Consequences of Imprisonment," p. 143; Diane S. Young and Carrie Jefferson Smith, "When Moms Are Incarcerated: The Needs of Children, Mothers, and Caregivers," *Families in Society* 81 (March 1, 2000); Denise Johnston, "The Care and Placement of Prisoners' Children," in *Children of Incarcerated Parents,* ed. Katherine Gabel and Denise Johnston (New York: Lexington Books, 1995), p. 103.

386. Philip M. Genty, "Procedural Due Process Rights of Incarcerated Parents in Termination of Parental Rights Proceedings: A Fifty-State Analysis," *Journal of Family Law* 30 (1991–1992): 757; Zachary R. Dowdy, "Moms Behind Bars as Female Prison Population Grows, Kids Get Left in the Wake," *Chicago Tribune,* October 6, 1999, p. 9.

387. Mumola, *Special Report: Incarcerated Parents and Their Children,* p. 4.

388. *Santosky v. Kramer,* 455 U.S. 745, 753 (1982).

389. See, for example, David Cole, *No Equal Justice: Race and Class in the American Criminal Justice System* (New York: New Press, 1998).

390. Ibid., pp. 34–41; David Cole and John Lamberth, "The Fallacy of Racial Profiling," *New York Times,* May 13, 2001, sec. 4, p. 13.

391. Jeff Brazil and Steve Berry, "Color of Driver Is Key to Stops in I-95 Videos," *Orlando Sentinel,* August 23, 1992, p. A1; Henry Pierson, "Statistics Show Pattern of Discrimination," *Orlando Sentinel,* August 23, 1992, p. A11.

392. Iver Peterson, "Whitman Concedes Troopers Used Race in Stopping Drivers," *New York Times,* April 21, 1999, p. A1.

393. *United States v. Leviner,* 31 F. Supp. 2d 23 (D. Mass. 1998); Fox Butterfield, "Bias Cited in Reducing Sentence of Black Man," *New York Times,* December 17, 1998, p. A22.

394. David B. Mustard, "Racial, Ethnic, and Gender Disparities in Sentencing: Evidence from the U.S. Federal Courts," *Journal of Law and Economics* 44 (2001): 285.

395. Marc Mauer and Tracy Huling, The Sentencing Project, *Young Black Americans and the Criminal Justice System: Five Years Later* (Washington, D.C.: Sentencing Project, 1995), p. 12.

396. Jeffrey Goldberg, "The Color of Suspicion," *New York Times Magazine,* June 20, 1999, pp. 51, 87.

397. Madeline Wordes, Timothy S. Bynum, and Charles J. Corley, "Locking Up Youth: The Impact of Race on Detention Decisions," *Journal of Research in Crime and Delinquency* 31 (1994): 149; Edmund F. McGarrell, "Trends in Racial Disproportionality in Juvenile Court Processing: 1985–1989," *Crime and Delinquency* 39 (1993): 29.

398. Katherine Hunt Federle and Meda Chesney-Lind, "Special Issues in Juvenile Justice: Gender, Race, and Ethnicity," in *Juvenile Justice and Public Policy: Toward a National Agenda,* ed. Ira Schwartz (New York: Lexington Books, 1992), p. 179.

399. Mike Males and Dan Macallair, *The Color of Justice: An Analysis of Juvenile Adult Transfers in California* (San Francisco: Justice Policy Institute, 2000), p. 4, citing Donna Ham-

parian and Michael Leiber, *Disproportionate Confinement of Minority Juveniles in Secure Facilities: 1996 National Report* (Washington, D.C.: Office of Juvenile Justice and Delinquency Prevention, 1997), p. 9.

400. See, for example, Kimberly Kempf Leonard, Carl E. Pope, and William H. Feyerherm, eds., *Minorities in Juvenile Justice* (Thousand Oaks, Calif.: Sage Publications, 1995); McGarrell, "Trends in Racial Disproportionality," p. 29; George S. Bridges and Sara Steen, "Racial Disparities in Official Assessments of Juvenile Offenders: Attributional Stereotypes as Mediating Mechanisms," *American Sociological Review* 63 (1998): 554; Jeffrey Fagan et al., "Blind Justice? The Impact of Race on the Juvenile Justice System," *Crime and Delinquency* 33 (1987): 224; Belinda McCarthy and Brent L. Smith, "The Conceptualization of Discrimination in the Juvenile Justice Process: The Impact of Administrative Factors and Screening Decisions on Juvenile Court Dispositions," *Criminology* 24 (1986): 41.

401. Wordes, Bynum, and Corley, "Locking Up Youth."

402. Miller, *Search and Destroy*, p. 71, citing Kimberly L. Kempf, *The Role of Race in Juvenile Justice Processing in Pennsylvania*, Study Grant #89–90/J/01/3615, Pennsylvania Commission on Crime and Delinquency, August 1992.

403. Miller, *Search and Destroy*, p. 78.

404. Donna M. Bishop and Charles E. Frazier, "Race Effects in Juvenile Justice Decision-Making: Findings of a Statewide Analysis," *Journal of Criminal Law and Criminology* 86 (1996): 392, 400.

405. "Teenage Population in Prisons Soaring," *Chicago Tribune,* February 28, 2000, sec. 1, p. 5.

406. Frankin E. Zimring, "Notes Toward a Jurisprudence of Waiver," in *Major Issues in Juvenile Justice Information and Training: Readings in Public Policy* (Washington, D.C.: U.S. Department of Justice, National Institute for Juvenile Justice and Delinquency Prevention, 1981), pp. 193, 195.

407. See, for example, Jeffrey Fagan and Elizabeth Piper Deschenes, "Determinants of Judicial Waiver Decisions for Violent Juvenile Offenders," *Journal of Criminal Law and Criminology* 81 (1990): 314; Barry C. Feld, "Bad Law Makes Hard Cases: Reflections on Teen-Aged Axe-Murderers, Judicial Activism, and Legislative Default," *Law and Inequality Journal* 8 (1990): 1, 41–46.

408. Jeffrey Fagan, Martin Forst, and T. Scott Vivona, "Racial Determinants of the Judicial Transfer Decision: Prosecuting Violent Youth in Criminal Court," *Crime and Delinquency* 33 (1987): 259; Robert J. Sampson and John H. Laub, "Structural Variations in Juvenile Court Processing: Inequality, the Underclass, and Social Control," *Law and Society Review* 27 (1993): 285.

409. U.S. General Accounting Office, *Juvenile Justice: Juveniles Processed in Criminal Court and Case Dispositions* (Washington, D.C.: USGAO, 1995), p. 59.

410. Charles M. Puzzanchera, U.S. Department of Justice, "Delinquency Cases Waived to Criminal Court" (2000), available at http://www.ncjrs.org/pdffiles1/ojjdp/fs200002.pdf.

411. *In re M.E.P.,* 523 N.W. 2d 913 (1994), aff'd, 528 N.W. 2d 240 (Minn. 1995).

412. Males and Macallair, *The Color of Justice,* pp. 5–9.

413. Bishop and Frazier, "Race Effects in Juvenile Justice Decision-Making," pp. 407–408.

NOTES TO PART THREE

1. Cheryl Wetzstein, "Case Studies Expose Failings of Foster Care; Writer Champions Better Chance for 'Orphans of Living,'" *Washington Times,* May 13, 1997, p. A2.

2. "Protecting Bad Foster Parents," *Chicago Tribune,* March 1, 2001, sec. 1, p. 12.

3. Nina Bernstein, *The Lost Children of Wilder: The Epic Struggle to Change Foster Care* (New York: Pantheon, 2001), p. 373.

4. 262 U.S. 400 (1923).

5. See *Pierce v. Society of Sisters,* 268 U.S. 510, 534 (1925).

6. Peggy Cooper Davis, *Neglected Stories: The Constitution and Family Values* (New York: Hill & Wang, 1997), pp. 83–90; Martha Minow, "We, the Family: Constitutional Rights and American Families," *Journal of American History* 74 (1987): 959.

7. 321 U.S. 158 (1944).

8. Barbara Bennett Woodhouse, "Who Owns the Child? *Meyer* and *Pierce* and the Child as Property," *William and Mary Law Review* 33 (1992): 995.

9. William Galston, "Parents, Government, and Children: Authority over Education in the Liberal Democratic State," paper presented at the 44th Annual Meeting of the American Society for Political and Legal Philosophy, September 2, 1999.

10. *Santosky v. Kramer,* 455 U.S. 745, 753 (1982).

11. Bruce A. Boyer and Steven Lubet, "The Kidnapping of Edgardo Mortara: Contemporary Lessons in the Child Welfare Wars," *Villanova Law Review* 45 (2000): 245, 253.

12. Peggy Cooper Davis and Gautum Barua, "Custodial Choices for Children at Risk: Bias, Sequentiality, and the Law," *University of Chicago Law School Roundtable* 2 (1995): 139, 141–142.

13. Boyer and Lubet, "The Kidnapping of Edgardo Mortara," p. 254.

14. Jurgen Habermas, "Multiculturalism and the Liberal State," *Stanford Law Review* 47 (1995): 849.

15. 388 U.S. 1 (1967). See A. Leon Higginbotham Jr. and Barbara K. Kopytoff, "Racial Purity and Interracial Sex in the Law of Colonial and Antebellum Virginia," *Georgetown Law Journal* 77 (1989), p. 1967.

16. See Cheryl Harris, "Whiteness as Property," *Harvard Law Review* 106 (1993): 1707 (detailing the evolution of the concept of whiteness as a valuable property interest).

17. Cornel West, *Race Matters* (Boston: Beacon 1993), pp. 85–86.

18. Dalton Conley, *Being Black, Living in the Red: Race, Wealth, and Social Policy in America* (Berkeley: University of California Press, 1999).

19. Michael C. Dawson, *Behind the Mule: Race and Class in African-American Politics* (Princeton: Princeton University Press, 1994), p. 56.

20. See, generally, Gerald Early, ed., *Lure and Loathing: Essays on Race, Identity, and the Ambivalence of Assimilation* (New York: Allen Lane, 1994) (a collection of essays by twenty Black intellectuals pondering the shaping of Black Americans' identity).

21. John L. Gwaltney, *Drylongso: A Self-Portrait of Black America* (New York: New Press, 1980), p. xxvii.

22. David B. Wilkins, "Introduction: The Context of Race," in *Color Conscious: The Political Morality of Race,* ed. K. Anthony Appiah and Amy Gutmann (Princeton: Princeton University Press, 1996), pp. 3, 23.

23. Dawson, *Behind the Mule,* pp. 45–68.

24. A. Wade Boykin et al., "Communalism: Conceptualization and Measurement of an Afrocultural Social Orientation," *Journal of Black Studies* 27 (1997): 409, 410. See also Richard L. Allen and Richard P. Bagozzi, "Consequences of the Black Sense of Self," *Journal of Black Psychology* 27 (2001): 3.

25. Maulana Karenga, *Kwanzaa: Origin, Concepts, Practice* (San Diego, Calif.: Kawaida Publications, 1977).

26. Orlando Patterson, *Slavery and Social Death: A Comparative Study* (Cambridge, Harvard University Press, 1982), pp. 189–190.

27. Davis, *Neglected Stories,* pp. 81–166.

28. Peggy Cooper Davis, "'So Tall Within': The Legacy of Sojourner Truth," *Cardozo Law Review* 18 (1996): 451, 452.

29. Davis, *Neglected Stories,* p. 98.

30. Davis, "'So Tall Within,'" pp. 454–459.

31. Ibid., p. 460.

32. Eric Foner, *Reconstruction: America's Unfinished Revolution* (New York: Harper & Row, 1988), p. 88.

33. Malcolm X and Alex Haley, *The Autobiography of Malcolm X* (New York: Ballantine Books, 1965), pp. 12–22.

34. James S. Coleman, *Foundations of Social Theory* (Cambridge: Belknap Press of Harvard University Press, 1990), p. 98. See also Pierre Bourdieu and Loic Wacquant, *Invitation to Reflexive Sociology* (Cambridge: Polity Press, 1992), p. 119.

35. M. Patricia Fernandez Kelly, "Towanda's Triumph: Social and Cultural Capital in the Transition to Adulthood in the Urban Ghetto," *International Journal of Urban and Regional Research* 18 (March 1994): 88, 98–99.

36. Jane Mansbridge, "Using Power/Fighting Power: The Polity," in *Democracy and Difference: Contesting the Boundaries of the Political,* ed. Seyla Benhabib (Princeton: Princeton University Press, 1996), pp. 46, 58.

37. Sara Evans and Harry C. Boyte, *Free Spaces: The Sources of Democratic Change in America* (New York: Harper & Row, 1986).

38. Frederick C. Harris, "Will the Circle Be Unbroken? The Erosion and Transformation of African American Civic Life," in *Civil Society, Democracy, and Civic Renewal,* ed. Robert K Fullinwider (Lanham, Md.: Rowman & Littlefield, 1999), p. 320; Walter Stafford, "Black Civil Society: Fighting for a Seat at the Table," *Social Policy* (Winter 1996): 11; Lisa Y. Sullivan, "The Demise of Black Civil Society: Once Upon a Time When We Were Colored Meets the Hip-Hop Generation," *Social Policy* (Winter 1996): 6.

39. Jacqueline Jones, *Labor of Love, Labor of Sorrow: Black Women, Work, and the Family from Slavery to the Present* (New York: Vintage, 1986), pp. 12–13.

40. Angela Y. Davis, *Women, Race and Class* (New York: Vintage, 1983), p. 17, quoting Angela Y. Davis, "The Black Woman's Role in the Community of Slaves," *Black Scholar* 3 (December 1971). Davis amended this statement to acknowledge that men also performed domestic tasks important to the slave community.

41. Alice Walker, "One Child of One's Own: A Meaningful Digression Within the Work(s)," *Ms.,* August 1979, pp. 47, 75.

42. Tracy Weber, "Chemical Straightjackets Given to Kids Under State Care," *San Francisco Examiner,* May 17, 1998, p. A11.

43. Susan M. Kools, "Adolescent Identity Development in Foster Care," *Family Relations* 46 (1997): 263.

44. Jason Boardman and Stephanie A. Robert, "Neighborhood Socioeconomic Status and Perceptions of Self-Efficacy," *Sociological Perspectives* 43 (2000): 117.

45. Presentation by Maisha Hamilton Bennett, Seminar on Current Controversies in Child Welfare Policy, Northwestern University School of Law, Chicago, September 7, 1999.

46. Alyssa Katz, "Mommy Nearest," *City Limits,* June 2000, p. 18.

47. Jason D. Boardman and Stephanie A. Robert, "Neighborhood Socioeconomic Status and Perceptions of Self-Efficacy," *Sociological Perspectives* 43 (2000): 117, 122.

48. Douglas S. Massey and Nancy A. Denton, *American Apartheid: Segregation and the Making of the Underclass* (Cambridge: Harvard University Press, 1993), p. 9.

49. Karlyn J. Geis and Catherine E. Ross, "A New Look at Urban Alienation: The Effect of Neighborhood Disorder on Perceived Powerlessness," *Social Psychology Quarterly* 61 (1998): 232.

50. Amy Schulz et al., "Unfair Treatment, Neighborhood Effects, and Mental Health in the Detroit Metropolitan Area," *Journal of Health and Social Behavior* 41 (2000): 314.

51. "Restoring the Community Connection," *Child Welfare Watch* (Winter 1997).

52. "Mass Incarceration Working Group," available at http://www.russ . . . ams/proj_reviews/incarceration.html.

53. The Sentencing Project and Human Rights Watch, *Losing the Vote: The Impact of Felony Disenfranchisement Laws in the United States* (Washington, D.C.: Human Rights Watch, October 1998); Somini Sengupta, "Felony Costs Voting Rights for a Lifetime in 9 States," *New York Times,* November 3, 2000, p. A18.

54. Salim Muwakkil, "Racist Roots," *Chicago Tribune,* October 2, 2000, sec. 1, p. 11.

55. Larry May, *The Morality of Groups: Collective Responsibility, Group-Based Harm, and Corporate Rights* (Notre Dame, Ind.: University of Notre Dame Press, 1987), p. 136.

56. Charles R. Lawrence III, "The Id, the Ego, and Equal Protection: Reckoning with Unconscious Racism," *Stanford Law Review* 39 (1987): 317.

57. May, *The Morality of Groups.*

58. Carol C. Gould, "Group Rights and Social Ontology," *Philosophical Forum* 28 (Fall-Winter 1996–1997): 73, 74.

59. Jurgen Habermas, "Struggles for Recognition in the Democratic Constitutional State," in *Multiculturalism: Examining the Politics of Recognition,* ed. Amy Gutman (Princeton: Princeton University Press, 1994), pp. 107, 113.

60. National Association of Black Social Workers, "Position Paper Developed from Workshops Concerning Transracial Adoption," reprinted in Rita J. Simon and Howard Alstein, *Transracial Adoption* (New York: John Wiley & Sons, 1977), p. 50. See also National Black Heritage Child Welfare Act proposed in 1986 as amendment to Indian Child Welfare Act of 1978.

61. James S. Bowen, "Cultural Convergences and Divergences: The Nexus Between Putative Afro-American Family Values and the Best Interests of the Child," *Journal of Family Law* 26 (1988): 487, 511.

62. Senate Committee on Labor and Human Resources, *Barriers to Adoption 1985,* Hearings on S. 99–288, 99th Cong. 1st Sess., 1985 (testimony of William Merritt, President, National Association of Black Social Workers), p. 217.

63. Anita Allen, "Responses to 'Where Do Black Children Belong?'" *Reconstruction* 1 (1992): 47.

64. Toni Oliver, "Options for Adoption," *Health Quest,* December 30 ,1997, p. 8. See also Leslie Doty Hollingsworth, "Symbolic Interactionism, African American Families, and the Transracial Adoption Controversy," *Social Work* 44 (September 1, 1999): 443.

65. Catherine J. Iorns Magallanes, "A New Zealand Case Study: Child Welfare" in *Recognizing the Rights of Indigenous Peoples,* ed. Alison Quentin-Baxter (Wellington, New Zealand: Institute of Policy Studies, 1998), pp. 132, 133.

66. Iorns Magallanes, "A New Zealand Case Study," pp. 133–34.

67. Judith Graham, "Adoption Apology Too Late for Indians," *Chicago Tribune,* May 7, 2001, sec. 1, p. 1.

68. *Mississippi Band of Choctow Indians v. Holyfield,* 490 U.S. 30, 33 (1989).

69. Boyer and Lubet, "The Kidnapping of Edgardo Mortara," pp. 245, 269–270, citing David Fanshel, *Far from the Reservation: The Transracial Adoption of American Indian Children* (Metuchen, N.J.: Scarecrow Press, 1972).

70. *Mississippi Band of Choctow Indians,* 490 U.S., p. 33.

71. Graham, "Adoption Apology Too Late for Indians," p. 13.

72. Commonwealth of Australia, Human Rights and Equal Opportunity Commission, *Bringing Them Home: Report of the National Inquiry into the Separation of Aboriginal and Torres Strait Islander Children from their Families* (Canberra: AGPS, 1997); Tony Buti, "Removal of Indigenous Children from Their Families in Australia: The History," paper presented at the conference "Families in an Open Society: A Proposal to Develop the Theoretical Foundations," New York University, May 7, 1999; Philip Shenon, "Bitter Aborigines Are Suing for Stolen Childhoods," *New York Times,* July 20, 1995, p. A4.

73. Buti, "Removal of Indigenous Children from Their Families."

74. 19 Fam. L.R. 594, 602 (1995).

75. Quoted in Buti, "Removal of Indigenous Children from Their Families."

76. Commonwealth of Australia, Human Rights and Equal Opportunity Commission, *Bringing Them Home.*

77. See, generally, Will Kymlicka, ed., *The Rights of Minority Cultures* (New York: Oxford University Press, 1995); Ian Shapiro and Will Kymlicka, eds., *Ethnicity and Group Rights* (New York: New York University Press, 1997); Charles Taylor, "The Politics of Recognition," in *Multiculturalism: Examining the Politics of Recognition,* ed. Amy Gutman (Princeton: Princeton University Press, 1994), p. 25.

78. Rita J. Simon and Howard Altstein, *Transracial Adoptees and Their Families: A Study of Identity and Commitment* (1987).

79. Rudolph Alexander Jr. and Carla M. Curtis, "A Review of Empirical Research Involving the Transracial Adoption of African American Children," *Journal of Black Psychology* 22 (May 1996): 223.

80. Sekai Turner and Jerome Taylor, "Underexplored Issues in Transracial Adoption," *Journal of Black Psychology* 22 (May 1996): 262.

81. Habermas, "Struggles for Recognition," p. 110.

82. Peggy Cooper Davis, "Contested Images of Family Values: The Role of the State," *Harvard Law Review* 107 (1994): 1348, 1371–1372.

83. Mark Courtney et al., "Race and Child Welfare Services: Past Research and Future Directions," *Child Welfare* 75 (1996): 130.

84. Larry May, "Adoption, Race, and Group-Based Harm," *Washington University Journal of Law and Policy* 1 (1999): 77, 82. This essay is a response to my presentation, "Poverty, Race,

and New Directions in Child Welfare Policy," *Washington University Journal of Law and Policy* 1 (1999): 63.

85. Elizabeth Bartholet, *Nobody's Children* (Boston: Beacon Press, 1999), p. 6.

86. Ibid., p. 238.

87. Ibid., p. 240.

88. Ibid., p. 3.

89. Maria Scannapieco and Sondra Jackson, "Kinship Care: The African American Response to Family Preservation," *Social Work* 41 (1996): 190.

90. Rob Geen, "In the Interest of Children: Rethinking Federal and State Policies Affecting Kinship Care," *Policy and Practice* (March 2000): 19, 21; Beth Witrogen McLeod, "The Second Time Around," *San Francisco Examiner*, August 12, 1997, p. C1.

91. U.S. Bureau of the Census, *Marital Status and Living Arrangements: March 1994* (Washington, D.C.: U.S. Government Printing Office, 1994).

92. Charlisse Nelson, "The New Nuclear Family: Grandparenting in the Nineties," *Black Child*, July 31, 1997, p. 9.

93. Marianne Takas, *Kinship Care and Family Preservation: A Guide for States in Legal and Policy Development* (Washington, D.C.: American Bar Ass'n. Ctr. for Children and the Law, 1993), p. 3.

94. Scannapieco and Jackson, "Kinship Care," p. 193.

95. Maria Scannapieco et al., "Kinship Care and Foster Care: A Comparison of Characteristics and Outcomes," *Families in Society* 78 (1997): 480.

96. Jill Duerr Berrick, "When Children Cannot Remain Home: Foster Family Care and Kinship Care," *Future of Children, Protecting Children from Abuse and Neglect* 8 (Spring 1998): 72, 78, Table 2.

97. Scannapieco and Jackson, "Kinship Care," p. 193; Sarah Karp, "Adoption Surge: DCFS Policy Spells Pressure for Black Families," *Chicago Reporter*, October 1999, pp. 1, 10.

98. Karp, "Adoption Surge," pp. 1, 10. See also Mark Testa et al., "Permanency Planning Options for Children in Formal Kinship Care," *Child Welfare* 75 (1996): 451.

99. Mark Testa, "Kinship Foster Care in Illinois," in *Child Welfare Research Review*, vol. 2, ed. Richard Barth, Jill D. Berrick, and Neil Gilbert (New York: Columbia University Press, 1997), pp. 101, 114.; Jill D. Berrick et al., "A Comparison of Kinship Foster Homes and Foster Family Homes: Implications for Kinship Care as Family Preservation," *Children and Youth Services Review* 16 (1994): 33; Marla Gottlieb Zwas, "Kinship Foster Care: A Relatively Permanent Solution," *Fordham Urban Law Journal* 20 (1993): 343, 354.

100. Berrick et al., "A Comparison of Kinship Foster Homes and Foster Family Homes"; Mark Courtney and Barbara Needell, "Outcomes of Kinship Care: Lessons from California," in *Child Welfare Research Review*, vol. 2, ed. Richard Barth, Jill D. Berrick, and Neil Gilbert (New York: Columbia University Press, 1997), p. 130; Alfreda P. Inglehart, "Kinship Foster Care: Placement, Service, and Outcome Issues," *Children and Youth Services Review* 16 (1994): 107.

101. Susan J. Zuravin, "Child Maltreatment in Family Foster Care: Foster Home Correlates," in *Child Welfare Research Review*, vol. 2, ed. Jill D. Berrick, Richard P. Barth, and Neil Gildber (New York: Columbia University Press, 1997), p. 189; Berrick, "When Children Cannot Remain Home," p. 80.

102. Berrick, "When Children Cannot Remain Home," pp. 77, 78, Table 2.

103. T. Gebel, "Kinship Care and Non-Relative Family Foster Care: A Comparison of Caregiver Attributes and Attitudes," *Child Welfare* 75 (1996): 5.

104. B. Davidson, "Service Needs of Relative Caregivers: A Qualitative Analysis," *Families in Society* 78 (1997): 502.

105. Geen, "In the Interest of Children," p. 21.

106. James P. Gleeson et al., "Understanding the Complexity of Practice in Kinship Foster Care," *Child Welfare* 76 (1997): 801, 814.

107. Berrick, "When Children Cannot Remain Home," p. 75.

108. Ibid., pp. 75–76.

109. Geen, "In the Interest of Children," p. 23; Rob Geen, "Final Ruling for ASFA and Kinship Care," *Public Welfare* 58 (June 1, 2000): 5.

110. Geen, "In the Interest of Children," p. 21.

111. 431 U.S. 816 (1977).

112. Scannapieco and Jackson, "Kinship Care," p. 194, quoting Sadye M. L. Logan et al., *Social Work Practice with Black Families* (New York: Longman, 1990). See also Ramona Denby and Nolan Rindfleisch, "African Americans' Foster Parenting Experiences: Research Findings and Implications for Policy and Practice," *Children and Youth Services Review* 18 (1996): 523, 545 (documenting the importance of building on African American foster parents' strengths, including family orientation, religious obligation, community responsibility, and interconnection of family, religion, and community).

113. See Gleeson et al., "Understanding the Complexity of Practice in Kinship Foster Care," p. 819.

114. See, for example, Berrick et al., "A Comparison of Kinship Foster Homes and Foster Family Homes"; Scannapieco et al., "Kinship Care and Foster Care"; Courtney and Needell, "Outcomes of Kinship Care"; Testa, "Kinship Foster Care in Illinois."

115. Gleeson et al., "Understanding the Complexity of Practice in Kinship Foster Care," p. 430.

116. Berrick et al., "A Comparison of Kinship Foster Homes and Foster Family Homes," p. 75.

117. Berrick, "When Children Cannot Remain Home," p. 82.

118. Madeline L. Kurtz, "The Purchase of Families into Foster Care: Two Case Studies and the Lessons They Teach," *Connecticut Law Review* 25 (1994): 1457. For a similar argument that the foster care system was not designed to meet the needs of kinship caregivers, see Randi Mandelbaum, "Trying to Fit Square Pegs into Round Holes: The Need for a New Funding Scheme for Kinship Caregivers," *Fordham Urban Law Journal* 22 (Summer 1995): 907.

119. See John M. O'Donnell, "Involvement of African American Fathers in Kinship Care Services," *Social Work* 44 (1999): 428.

120. Kurtz, "The Purchase of Families into Foster Care," pp. 1499–1500.

121. Ruth Sidel, *Keeping Women and Children Last: America's War on the Poor* (New York: Penguin Books, 1996), pp. 180–182.

122. Elliot Currie, *Crime and Punishment in America* (New York: Henry Holt, 1998), pp. 156–157.

123. William Julius Wilson, *The Truly Disadvantaged: The Inner City, The Underclass, and Public Policy* (Chicago: University of Chicago Press, 1987), p. 120.

124. William Julius Wilson, *The Bridge over the Racial Divide: Rising Inequality and Coalition Politics* (Berkeley: University of California Press, 1999).

125. Iris Marion Young, "Together in Difference: Transforming the Logic of Group Political Conflict" in *The Rights of Minority Cultures,* ed. Will Kymlicka (New York: Oxford University Press, 1995), pp. 155, 156.

126. Randall Robinson, *The Debt: What America Owes to Blacks* (New York: Dutton, 2000), p. 7.

127. Margaret S. Sherraden and Uma A. Segal, "Multicultural Issues in Child Welfare," *Children and Youth Services Review* 18 (1996): 497, 502.

128. Bazelon Center for Mental Health Law, *Making Child Welfare Work: How the R.C. Lawsuit Forged New Partnerships to Protect Children and Sustain Families* (Washington, D.C.: Judge David L. Bazelon Center for Mental Health Law, May 1998).

129. Robert Allen, *Black Awakening in Capitalist America,* 2nd ed. (Garden City, N.Y.: Anchor Books, 1970), pp. 233–234.

130. John M. Hagedorn, *Forsaking Our Children: Bureaucracy and Reform in the Child Welfare System* (Chicago: Lake View Press, 1995), pp. 130–137.

131. Ibid., p. 137.

132. "Restoring the Community Connection," *Child Welfare Watch* (Winter 1997), available at http://www.nycfuture.org/child_welfare/cww_02.htm.

133. Andrew Billingsley and Jeanne M. Giovannoni, *Children of the Storm: Black Children and American Child Welfare* (New York: Harcourt Brace Jovanovich, 1972), p. 215.

134. Ibid., pp. 216–217.

135. Leroy H. Pelton, "Child Welfare Policy and Practice: The Myth of Family Preservation," *American Journal of Orthopsychiatry* 67 (1997): 545, 551–552; LeRoy H. Pelton, "Commentary," *Future of Children* (Spring 1998): 126, 128.

136. Keith Pringle, *Children and Social Welfare in Europe* (Buckingham, England: Open University Press, 1998), p. 103.

137. Duncan Lindsey and Wesley E. Hawkins, "Should the Police Have Greater Authority in Investigating Cases of Suspected Child Abuse? Yes," in *Controversial Issues in Child Welfare,* ed. Eileen Gambrill and Theodore J. Stein (Boston: Allyn and Bacon, 1994), pp. 73, 82–83.

138. Jane Waldfogel, *The Future of Child Protection: How to Break the Cycle of Abuse and Neglect* (Cambridge: Harvard University Press, 1998), p. 212.

139. Currie, *Crime and Punishment in America,* p. 99.

Acknowledgments

DURING THE FOUR YEARS I worked on *Shattered Bonds*, I was fortunate to collaborate with a number of organizations and individuals dedicated to reforming the child welfare system: the Children and Family Justice Center at Northwestern University School of Law, Mothers Organizing Systems for Equal Services (MOSES), the National Coalition for Child Protection Reform, the Women's Committee of One Hundred, Annette Appell, Bruce Boyer, Bernardine Dohrn, Steven Drizin, Cheryl Graves, Martin Guggenheim, Carolyn Kubitschek, Diane Redleaf, Ora Schub, and Richard Wexler. This book benefited enormously from the information and inspiration they gave me. I am especially grateful to Jornell, the founder of MOSES, and Devon for telling me their stories, for providing me with voluminous documentation about child protective services, and for putting me in contact with other mothers involved in the child welfare system. *Shattered Bonds* pays homage to their courage and determination.

I completed most of the research for *Shattered Bonds* after I joined the faculty of Northwestern University School of Law in 1998. Dean David Van Zandt generously provided financial support for my work, including grants from the Elyse H. Zenoff Research Fund. My joint appointment as a faculty fellow at the Institute for Policy Research, directed by Fay Lomax Cook, was a godsend. My fellowship at IPR put me in touch with the nation's best child welfare researchers and gave me more time to write. Greg Duncan, Dan Lewis, and Kristen Shook were especially helpful in introducing me to the social science literature on child welfare and child protective services. Mark Courtney, Director of the Chapin Hall Center for Children at the University of Chicago, was also extremely helpful, through both his excellent research on child welfare issues and personal conversations. The Children and Family Research Center at the University of Illinois provided funding for a study that I conducted with

Northwestern graduate student Morgan Ward Doran in 1999–2001, "The Impact of Welfare Reform on Families Involved in Child Protective Services," which informed my understanding of the child welfare system.

I presented papers that contributed to this book at the American Bar Foundation, the Center for Families in an Open Society at New York University Law School, the Institute for Policy Research, University of California–Davis School of Law, UCLA Law School, University of Chicago Law School, Fordham University School of Law, University of Georgia School of Law, University of Maryland Law and Health Care Program, Northwestern University School of Law, University of Pennsylvania School of Law, St. Thomas University School of Law, Washington University School of Law, University of Wisconsin School of Law, Yale Law School, UCLA Sociology Department, University of Maryland Women's Studies Department, Ohio State University English Department, University of Toledo Africana Studies Department, American Society for Political and Legal Philosophy, Association of Northwestern University Women, Charles H. Revson Fellows Program on the Future of the City of New York, Child Welfare League of America, and Family Resource Coalition of America. I greatly appreciate the invitations to share my works in progress, as well as the comments of professors, students, practitioners, and activists too numerous to name who attended. Conversations with Maisha Hamilton Bennett, Bonnie Honig, Anita Rivkin-Carothers, and Iris Marion Young were especially helpful. I owe a special debt of gratitude to Peggy Cooper Davis, whose brilliant scholarship on slavery and family rights and critique of the contemporary child welfare system greatly influenced my argument in *Shattered Bonds*.

I could not have completed this book without the superb research assistance of several Northwestern law students. Donyelle Gray, Sarah Mervine, Monica Neuman, and Faiza Shirazi conducted research for papers that contributed to the book. As I prepared to write *Shattered Bonds*, Carolyn Frazier did a remarkable job of organizing, updating, and completing mountains of files. Her energy and dedication to this project exceeded my highest expectations. At the final stage, Candace Chambliss tirelessly tracked down needed information under a tight deadline. Jennifer Pokempner, a University of Pennsylvania graduate, also volunteered to help with research out of her sincere devotion to changing the system. I am most grateful to these wonderful students for their commitment and friendship. I wish to thank Shirley Scott for her excellent administrative assistance throughout the years and the staff of the Pritzker Legal Research Center, directed by Christopher Simoni, especially Nancy Armstrong, Lesliediana Jones, Lynn Kincade, and Steven Miller, for providing every source I ever requested. I am also grateful to David Halpern of the Robbins Office and Vanessa Mobley of Basic Books for their encouragement and advice and to Felicity Tucker of Basic Books for her production assistance.

Finally, I am indebted to my husband, children, sisters, and parents for their love and devotion. In September 2000, in the midst of writing *Shattered Bonds,* I gave birth to my fourth child, Dessalines. The whole family pitched in to care for the new baby so I could simultaneously perform the exquisite tasks of mothering and writing. Later, Percis Golding and Rahat Kahn opened their hearts and homes to Dessalines while I was at work. My friends at Sherman United Methodist Church also offered their prayers and support. May Dessalines grow up in a society that cares for all its children with equity and justice.

Some of the material in this book is adapted from the following articles: "Criminal Justice and Black Families: The Collateral Damage of Overenforcement," *U.C. Davis Law Review* 34 (2001): 1005; "Kinship Care and the Price of State Support for Children," *Chicago-Kent Law Review* 76 (2001): 101; "Is There Justice in Children's Rights? A Critique of Federal Family Preservation Policy," *University of Pennsylvania Journal of Constitutional Law* 2 (2000): 112; "The Ethics of Punishing Indigent Parents," in *From Social Justice to Criminal Justice: Poverty and the Administration of Criminal Law,* ed. William C. Heffernan and John Kleinig (New York: Oxford University Press 2000), p. 161; "The Challenge of Substance Abuse for Family Preservation Policy," *Journal of Health Care Law and Policy* 3 (1999): 72; "Welfare's Ban on Poor Motherhood," in *Whose Welfare?* edited by Gwendolyn Mink (Ithaca: Cornell University Press, 1999), p. 152; "Welfare and the Problem of Black Citizenship," *Yale Law Journal* 105 (1996): 1563.

Index

ABC bill. *See* Act for Better Child Care Services

ABC Evening News, 172

Aber, J. Lawrence, 186

Aborigines, 251–252

Aborigines Act (Australia), 251

Abusive head trauma (AHT), 50

Accountability, 79, 272–273

Act for Better Child Care Services (ABC bill), 195, 196

Adams, Jody, 36–37, 126

ADC. *See* Aid to Dependent Children

Administration for Children's Services (New York City), 38, 70, 76, 79, 93, 124–125, 130–131, 152, 203–204

Adolescent Pathways (Vera Institute), 203

Adolescents

"aging out" of foster care, 205

chronic runaways, 204–205

conditions in group homes, 204

overlapping involvement in child welfare and juvenile justice systems, 202–207

See also Black children; Children; Juvenile delinquency; Juvenile justice system

Adoption

alternatives to, 162–163

by Black Americans, 172, 247–248

compared to family preservation services, 147

"concurrent permanency planning" and, 111–112

costs to children, 159–162

current federal policies toward, 105–113, 149

decline in numbers of, 167

defects in current federal policies, 149–150, 163–165

disparagement of biological parents and, 117–121

fast-track policies, 149

federal Indian policy and, 249–251

impact on foster care population, 157–159

increase in numbers of, 158

increasing numbers of "legal orphans" and, 158–159

international, 172

notions of civil society revival and, 116–117

popular support for federal policies, 114–117

"pre-adoptive" placements, 112

race-matching policies, 166

racial disparity in, 23–24

rates of disruption in, 160

shortage of white babies and, 166–167

supply and demand relationship with foster care, 166

tax credit legislation, 165

termination of parental rights and, 150–154

web sites, 103

welfare reform and, 173–174

by white parents, 171–172

See also Adoption and Safe Families Act; Foster care; Transracial adoption

Adoption and Safe Families Act (ASFA)

attacks on family preservation, 105–113, 121

Elizabeth Bartholet's criticism of reunification "loopholes," 115–116

Adoption and Safe Families Act (continued)
  "concurrent permanency planning" and,
     111–112
  disparagement of biological parents, 113,
     115–116, 120–121
  financial incentives to increase adoption,
     110–111
  focus on acceleration of adoption process,
     105, 109–111
  funding of family preservation services
     and, 143
  goal of permanency, 106
  licensing of kinship caregivers and, 261
  limits on reasonable efforts to return
     children, 108–109, 131–133
  passage of, 105
  termination of parental rights and,
     109–110, 128, 151, 163
  transracial adoption and, 165, 167
  welfare reform and, 173–174
Adoption Assistance and Child Welfare Act,
     27, 105, 106, 142, 143, 158
Adoption Saturday, 149
African American Child Welfare Act
     (Illinois), 70
AHT. *See* Abusive head trauma
AIDS, 86
Aid to Dependent Children (ADC), 16, 176
Aid to Families with Dependent Children
     (AFDC), 173, 174, 176, 180, 182,
     186, 188, 191, 260
Alabama, 155, 272
Alcohol, 155
Allen, Robert, 272
Altstein, Howard, 253
Alwysh, Sourette, 78
Amar, Akhil, 109
American Apartheid (Massey & Denton),
     240
American Bar Association, 110, 150
American Indians, 248–251
Andrea L. v. Superior Court, 156–157
Angel Guardian Home, 152
Antimiscegenation laws, 230
"Anything but race" theories, 97–98
Appell, Annette, 32

Apprenticeship laws, 234–235
Areen, Judith, 26–27
Arizona, 23
Arkansas, 128
ASFA. *See* Adoption and Safe Families Act
     (ASFA)
Asian American children, 8
Australia, Aboriginal policy, 251–252
Australian Human Rights and Equal
     Opportunity Commission, 252

Baby T case, 69, 169–171
Baltimore, 24, 48, 134, 207
Banks, Richard, 167
Barth, Richard, 136, 205
Bartholet, Elizabeth, 115–116, 121–122,
     136, 164, 168, 169, 171, 255,
     256–257
Battered women, 76
Bazelon Center for Mental Health Law,
     86–87
Bennett, Homer, 129
Bennett, William, 31, 116
Bernstein, Nina, 44, 130–131, 173, 177,
     223–224
Berrick, Jill Duerr, 260
Berry, Halle, 68
Berry, Marianne, 136, 137–138, 143
Beyond the Best Interests of the Child
     (Goldstein, Freud, & Solnit), 106, 123
Bilchik, Shay, 251
Billingsley, Andrew, 89, 273
Bishop, Donna, 220
Black Americans
  adoption of Black children, 247–248
  American racial hierarchy and, 230–231
  apprenticeship laws and, 234–235
  family rights and, 234–235
  incarceration and, 207–213
  interrelationship of self- and group-
     identity, 231–232
  negative stereotyping, 60–65, 194,
     219–220, 243–244
  racial disparity in incarceration, 201
  See also Black children; Black
     communities; Black families; Black

men/fathers; Black parents; Black
women/mothers; Group-based harm

Black Awakening in Capitalist America
(Allen), 272

Black children
consequences of being imprisoned,
209
disproportionate representation in child
welfare system, 6, 7–10
group-based racial harm and, 223–225,
254–257
incarceration of parents and, 207–208,
209–211, 212–213
inferior treatment in child welfare system,
10–25
juvenile detention and, 213–220
negative effects of adoption and foster
care, 17–19, 159–162, 239–240
overlapping involvement in child welfare
and juvenile justice systems, 200,
202–207
poverty and, 44–46
psychological evaluations of, 43–44
transracial adoption, 165–172, 248–249,
252–253
visibility hypothesis and, 9–10
See also Adoption; Child abuse; Child
maltreatment; Child neglect; Child
removal; Child welfare system; Foster
care; Juvenile delinquency; Juvenile
justice system; Transracial adoption

Black communities
control of Black child services and,
273
group-based racial harm of welfare system
and, 236–254
increasing accountability of child welfare
agencies to, 272–273
nonmandated reporting of child
maltreatment, 96
supervisory roles of child welfare and
juvenile justice systems, 206–207
See also Black families

Black families
apprenticeship laws and, 234–235
Black civil society and, 238

collateral damage from incarceration of
parents, 207–208, 209–211, 212–213
collateral damage from juvenile detention,
213, 218–219
cultural prejudice and, 59–60
efforts to reunite during the Civil War,
235
group-based harm of child welfare system,
236–254
impediments to economic equality, 94–95
kinship care and, 24–25, 258–267
kinship system and, 262
myth of absent fathers, 64
myth of the Black matriarch, 63
parenting services and, 21
political impact of disruption, 233–236
portrayed as abandoning children in
foster care, 67–68
public's perceptions of, 120
single motherhood and, 63–64
slavery and, 233–234
solidarity and, 238
stereotyping by juvenile justice system,
219–220
visibility hypothesis and, 9–10
See also Black children; Black
communities; Black men/fathers; Black
parents; Black women/mothers;
Parental rights, termination of

Black foster parents, 25. *See also* Kinship care

Black men/fathers, 64
disenfranchisement and, 242–243
exclusion from kinship foster care,
263–265
incarceration and, 207–209, 210–213,
242–243
See also Black families; Black parents

Black parents
efforts to reform child welfare system,
68–74
incarceration and, 207–213
portrayed as abandoning children in
foster care, 67–68
See also Black families; Black men/fathers;
Black women/mothers; Parental rights,
termination of

Black Power movement, 273
Black women/mothers
  adoption of Black foster children, 172
  Black family solidarity and, 238
  communal child-care, 59–60
  exclusion from Progressive Era welfare,
    175–176
  image of pregnant crack addict, 62–63
  incarceration and, 208, 209–210
  public devaluation of caregiving work,
    179, 180
  racial bias in drug testing and, 50–51, 72,
    155
  rating of neglectful behaviors toward
    children, 96
  relationship with caseworkers, 66–67
  stereotypes of maternal unfitness, 28,
    60–67, 194
  welfare reform and, 184
  See also Black families; Black parents;
    Parental rights, termination of; Single
    mothers; Teen mothers; Welfare
    mothers
Blakeslee, Sandra, 118
"Bonding evaluations," 127
Book of David, The (Gelles), 107
Boston, 111
Boston Globe (newspaper), 180
Bowling Alone (Putnam), 116
Boyer, Bruce, 108, 123, 227–228
Boykin, A. Wade, 232
Boyte, Harry C., 238
Brace, Charles Loring, 168
Brawka, Judith, 154, 171
Breast feeding, 55
Bridge over the Racial Divide (Wilson),
  270
Brooks, Susan, 161, 162
Brown, Curley, 190
Bureau of Indian Affairs, 249
Bureau of Justice Statistics, 207
Burke, Anne, 169, 171
Burke, Edward, 169
Burton, Dan, 121
Bush, George, 201
Bush, George W., 114

Bush, Vernon, 81–82
Byers, Joy, 31

Califano, Joseph, 155
California
  biasing of psychological evaluators, 42
  child maltreatment and foster care
    placement, 34–35
  definition of child neglect, 33
  family preservation services in, 137
  financial assistance to kinship caregivers,
    260
  foster care and public aid payments, 191
  job readiness classes, 194
  length of time children remain in kinship
    care, 263
  parent liability for child delinquency, 199
  racial disparities in foster care, 8–9, 19, 23
  racial disparity in juvenile detention, 214
  racial disparity in kinship care, 259
  racial disparity in service provision, 22,
    23
  transfer of Black children to adult courts,
    216
  unavailability of family preservation
    services in, 136
  welfare reform and child maltreatment,
    177, 185, 186
Call to Civil Society, A (Council on Civil
  Society), 116
Cameron, Gary, 145
Camp, David, 114
Caregiving. *See* Child care
CASA. *See* National Center on Addiction
  and Substance Abuse
Caseworkers
  biasing of psychological evaluations,
    41–43
  child removal on "emergency" basis,
    55–56
  community perceptions of, 74–75
  "concurrent permanency planning" and,
    111
  criticism of decision making by, 53–59
  exclusion of Black fathers from kinship
    care, 264, 265

family preservation services and,
133–134, 135
financial incentives to remove children,
125
funds spent on individual families, 134
interference in family reunification,
140–141
lack of adequate training and supervision,
56
misinterpretation of Black cultural
traditions, 59
pressures for child removal, 122–123,
124–125
presumptions of white family fitness, 67
racial bias in service provision, 21–22
rescue approach to child welfare and, 90
unreasonable service plans and, 80–82
visitations and, 141
working with Black mothers, 66–67
Catholic charities, 224
Cato Institute, 192
Cazenave, Noel, 194
Chafee, John, 108, 113, 121, 150
Cheeks, Tatiana, 27–28, 89
Chicago
Baby T case, 69, 169–171
biased psychological evaluations, 42–43
Black parents and efforts to reform child
welfare services, 68–70
child endangerment arrests, 78
children's deaths in foster care, 223
Devon's case, 10–13, 18, 35, 265–267
geographical overlap in child
maltreatment, poverty and Black
families, 44–45, 240
job readiness classes, 194
Jornell's case, 3–6, 40–41, 43–44, 88, 90,
127
overlap between child welfare and juvenile
justice systems, 202
racial disparity in child protection
involvement, 75
racial disparity in foster care, 9
racial disparity in kinship foster care, 259
scrutiny of parents in child welfare
system, 39–41

See also Department of Children and
Family Services; Illinois
Chicago Reporter (newspaper), 151, 184
Chicago Tribune (newspaper), 58, 170–171,
223, 242
Child abuse
in foster care, 129, 134
laws linking to prenatal drug/alcohol use,
155
medical model of, 14–15
nationwide statistics, 34
pernicious effects of child protection
philosophy and, 130–131
racial bias in reporting, 49–51
termination of family preservation
services and, 147–148
welfare income level and, 186
See also Child maltreatment; Child
neglect
"Child Abuse and Neglect" (Pelton), 30
Child Abuse Prevention and Treatment Act,
14, 143
Child care
communal, 59–60
welfare reform and, 187–189
Child care workers, 188–189
Child delinquency. *See* Juvenile delinquency
Child endangerment arrests, 77–79
Child exclusion laws, 65
Child homicide, 30, 129
Child maltreatment
child removal on "emergency" basis,
55–56
definitions of, 55
family structure and, 48–49
heightened monitoring of poor families
and, 32–33
juvenile delinquency and, 202–203
laws linking to prenatal drug/alcohol use,
155
misdemeanor arrests for, 77–79
nationwide statistics, 34
parental income and, 49, 186
poverty and, 29–44
racial bias in reporting, 49–51, 53
repeated abuse or neglect, 144

Child maltreatment (continued)
reporting behavior of mandated and
nonmandated reporters, 96
universal social welfare and, 268–271
welfare reform and, 185–186, 187
Child neglect
defined by poverty, 33–44
definitions of, 33, 37–38
income level and, 186
leaving children unattended, 36
misdemeanor arrests for, 77–79
nationwide statistics, 34
See also Child abuse; Child maltreatment
Child poverty, 44–46, 184
Child protective services
adversarial relationship with parents,
88–89
community perceptions of, 74–75
criticism of underlying presumptions in,
89–91
failure of, 130–131
impact on community and family life,
75–76
punitive nature of, 90–91
racial disparity in child welfare system
and, 74
requirement for parents to confess to
unfitness, 85
service plans, 79–82
See also Child welfare system; Foster
care
Child removal
Australian Aboriginal policy and,
251–252
consequences of, 17–19
on "emergency" basis, 55–56
family rights and, 225–228
federal Indian policy and, 248–251
financial incentives to caseworkers, 125
group-based racial harm and, 243,
254–257
parental income as indicator, 35, 185
pressures on caseworkers and agencies to
perform, 122–123, 124–125
racial bias in, 51–52
for reasons of housing, 21, 35

for reasons of poverty, 34–35
welfare reform and, 177–178, 186–187,
189–192
See also Adoption; Foster care; Parental
rights, termination of; Transracial
adoption
Children
interests in family integrity, 108
negative effects of adoption and foster
care, 17–19, 159–162, 239–240
psychological evaluations of, 43–44
See also Adoption; Black children; Child
abuse; Child maltreatment; Child
neglect; Child removal; Child welfare
system; Foster care; Juvenile
delinquency; Juvenile justice system;
Transracial adoption
Children in Need of Parents (Mass &
Engler), 106
Children of the Storm, 99
Children's Defense Fund, 182
Children's rights, issues of group-based harm
and racial oppression, 254–257
Children's Rights agency, 44
Children's Welfare League of America, 110
Child safety, 104–105
Child welfare
medical model of abuse and, 14–15
"residual approach," 90
social reform movement and, 14
See also Child welfare system
Child Welfare Act. See Adoption Assistance
and Child Welfare Act
Child Welfare Institute, 48, 58
Child Welfare League of America, 56, 133,
136, 138, 249, 251
Child welfare policy
"concurrent permanency planning,"
111–112
creation of "legal orphans" and, 158–159
current trends in, 103–104
federal adoption laws and attacks on
family preservation, 105–113,
121–122
historical trends in family preservation
and child safety objectives, 104–105

increasing client participation in, 272
popular support for adoption and
    disparagement of biological parents,
    113–121
termination of parents' rights to children,
    106–107, 109–110, 113, 119, 120,
    128, 150–154
See also Adoption and Safe Families Act
Child welfare system
    accountability and, 79, 272–273
    annual costs of, 269
    Black parents' efforts to reform, 68–74
    community-based, voluntary, 275
    compared to slavery by Malcolm X,
        235–236
    concentration in inner-city
        neighborhoods, 240
    criticism of underlying presumptions,
        89–91
    cultural sensitivity and, 271
    decline in family services, 15
    dual legal system based on wealth, 26–27
    federal funding, 142–144
    fundamental flaws in, 267–268
    group-based racial harm and, 223–225,
        228–230, 236–267
    history of, 7–9, 14–16
    inferior treatment of Black children,
        10–25
    interference in family reunification,
        140–141
    interrelationship with Black children and
        the juvenile justice system, 200,
        202–207
    irrationality of decision making in, 53–55
    kinship care and, 258–259
    neighborhood effects and, 240–241
    pressures for child removal, 122–123,
        124–125
    presumptions of white family fitness, 67
    Progressive Era origins, 174
    proposed changes: to end punitive
        functions, 274–276; to provide social
        support for families, 268–271; to shift
        control to Black communities,
        271–273

psychological evaluations, 40–44
racial disparity in, 6, 7–10; group-based
    racial harms, 223–225, 228–230,
    236–267; inferior treatment of Black
    children, 10–25; philosophy of child
    protection as cause, 74–92; poverty
    and, 25–46; racism as cause, 47–74
as racist institution, 92–99
regulation of mother's behavior
    and, 193
scrutiny of parents in, 39–41
service plans, 79–82
social justice and, 267–276
supervisory role in Black communities,
    206–207
welfare reform and, 173–174, 177–178,
    181–182, 193–200
See also Caseworkers; Child protective
    services; Foster care
Child Welfare Watch, 67, 70, 79, 136,
    140–141, 242
Choctow Indians, 250
Cincinnati, 78–79
City Limits, 240
Civil rights movement
    welfare system and, 15–16, 176
Civil society, 116–117
Civil War, 235
Clinton, Bill, 105
Clinton, Hillary Rodham, 114
Collective Work, 232
Collins, Ann, 186
"Colored orphan asylums," 7
Color of Justice, The, 217–218
Color of Welfare, The (Quadagno), 16
Communal child-care, 59–60
Communalism, 232
Comprehensive support programs, 145
"Concurrent permanency planning,"
    111–112
Congregate care, 204
Congress, U.S.
    Adoption and Safe Families Act, 105,
        108, 109, 113, 121
    Adoption Assistance and
        Child Welfare Act, 105

Congress, U.S. (continued)
 federal Indian policy and, 248, 249–251
 misidentification of problem of foster
  care, 163–164
 transracial adoption policies, 166
 welfare reform and child removal, 178
Congressional Budget Office, 188, 192
Congress of African Peoples, 273
Conley, Dalton, 94–95
Connecticut, 38–39, 205
Constitution, U.S., 225
"Contract with America," 177
Cook County (Illinois), 70–71
Cook County Hospital, 72
Coontz, Stephanie, 64, 67
Council on Civil Society, 116
Courtney, Mark, 135–136, 142, 174, 196
Courts. *See* Custody hearings; Family courts;
 Judges
Crack addicts
 image of Black women as, 62–63, 155
 media portrayals of, 68
Criminality, incarceration and, 209
Criminal justice system
 prison industrial complex, 206
 racial discrimination in, 211–212
 racial disparity in incarceration, 200, 201
 transfer of Black children to adult courts,
  216–218
 U.S. prison population, 201
 See also Incarceration; Juvenile justice
  system
Crittenden, Ann, 178–179
Cultural genocide
 Australian Aboriginal policy and,
  251–252
 federal Indian policy and, 248–251
 transracial adoption of Black children as,
  246, 248, 252–253
Cultural prejudice, 59–60
Cultural sensitivity, 271
"Culture of dependency," 194
Currie, Elliot, 206, 209, 269
Custody hearings
 foster parents and, 120–121
 See also Family courts; Judges

Cycle of Violence, The (U.S. Justice
 Department), 202

Darity, William, Jr., 95
Davis, Angela, 238
Davis, Ernestine, 73
Davis, Peggy Cooper, 123, 233–234, 235,
 254
Dawson, Michael, 231
DCFS. *See* Department of Children and
 Family Services
Debt, The (Robinson), 271
Delahunt, Bill, 172
Democracy, families and, 237–238
Denmark, 274, 275
Denton, Nancy, 240
DeParle, Jason, 183, 198
Department of Children and Family
 Services (Illinois), 75, 111, 127
 Baby T case, 69, 169–171
 biasing of psychological evaluations, 42–43
 children's deaths in foster care, 223
 class action suit against, 70–74
 design of service plans with apparent
  intent of ensuring failure, 81–82
 Devon's case, 10–13, 18, 35, 265–267
 efforts to reform, 70
 Jornell's case, 4–6, 40–41, 43–44, 88, 90,
  127
 mapping of child maltreatment, poverty
  and Black families in Chicago, 44–45
 payments to kinship caregivers, 261
 "reasonable efforts" policy and, 131
 relationship with private child services
  agencies, 71–72, 73
 Valerie's case, 82–85
Department of Health and Human Services
 (U.S.), 19, 21, 29, 35, 103, 131
Department of Health and Rehabilitative
 Services (Florida), 218–219
Dependency court, 6
Devon (Black woman), 10–13, 18, 35,
 265–267
DeWine, Mike, 118
Digre, Peter, 34
DiIulio, John, 31

Disenfranchisement, 242–243
Disposable Children (Golden), 32
District of Columbia, 35
Divorce, 118–120
Domestic violence, 76
Drug testing, racial bias in administering, 50–51, 72
Dumpson, James, 273
Duncan, Greg, 45

Economic equality, Black families and, 94–95
Economic recession, welfare-to-work programs and, 184–185
Edelman, Peter, 185
Edin, Kathryn, 64, 180, 194–195, 197–198
Ehrenreich, Barbara, 182–183
Elshtain, Jean Bethke, 116
Engesser, Eve, 178
Engler, Richard E., Jr., 106
Eubanks, Bobby, 209
Eunick, Tiffany, 213
European social welfare, 269
Eustis, Frederick, 235
Evans, Sara, 238
Extreme poverty, 45, 184

Families
    divorce and, 118–120
    group welfare and, 237
    significance to democratic society, 237–238
    welfare reform goals and family size, 193
    See also Black families; Family disruption;
        Family preservation;
        Family preservation services;
        Family reunification;
        Family rights
Families First programs, 134, 144, 146, 147–148
Family Assistance Plan, 179–180
Family Bonds (Bartholet), 171
"Family caps," 193
Family courts
    bias against biological parents, 125–128
    psychological experts and, 127

"reasonable efforts" policy and, 131–133
    substance-abusing parents and, 156–157
    termination of parental rights and, 151–154, 156–157
    See also Custody hearings; Judges
Family day care providers, 188–189
Family disruption
    impact on neighborhoods, 241
    political impact, 233–236
    See also Child removal; Parental rights, termination of
Family integrity, group welfare and, 237
Family Law (television show), 68
Family preservation
    bias against biological parents in family courts, 125–128
    children's interest in, 108
    federal policy attacks on, 105–113, 121–122
    historical trends in child welfare policy, 104–105
    issues of children's rights and racial oppression, 254–257
    meanings of, 133
    media attacks on, 107–108, 114
    popular support for adoption and disparagement of biological parents, 113–121
    pressures for child removal, 122–125
    "reasonable efforts" policy and, 105, 108–109, 131–133
    transracial adoption policies and, 165, 166, 167–168
    See also Family preservation services
Family Preservation and Support Services Program, 142
Family preservation services
    child welfare system and, 148–149
    compared to adoption, 147
    comprehensive support programs, 145
    decline in, 15
    effects of terminating, 147–148
    evidence for effectiveness of, 144–148
    factors limiting success of, 135–144
    failure of states to provide, 135–136

Family preservation services (continued)
    failure to address needs of families,
        136–140
    inadequate funding of, 142–144
    interference in family reunification,
        140–141
    measures of success, 134–135
    overview of, 133–134
    problems with short duration of,
        137–140
Family reunification
    Elizabeth Bartholet's criticism of
        Adoption and Safe Families Act,
        115–116
    Black families' efforts to reunite during
        the Civil War, 235
    family preservation services and, 146–147
    interference by caseworkers and agencies
        in, 140–141
    racial disparity in, 19–20, 23–24
    visitation issues and, 141
    See also Service plans
Family rights
    Black American history and, 234–235
    constitutional protection, 225–228
    slavery and, 233–234
    See also Parental rights, termination of
Fanshel, David, 248
Farber, Peggy, 103
Farber, Seth, 18
Far from the Reservation (Fanshel), 248
Federal adoption law. *See* Adoption and Safe
    Families Act
Federation of Protestant Welfare Agencies,
    61
Federle, Katherine Hunt, 213
Fillmore, Kendra, 134
Finding Fish (Fisher), 224
Fisher, Antwone Quenton, 224
Florida
    community perception of child
        protection agency, 75
    conviction of Lionel Tate, 213
    Kayla McKean Child Protection Act, 123
    laws linking drug use and child abuse,
        155

prenatal substance abuse, 51
racial disparity in juvenile detention,
    218–220
"reasonable efforts" policy and, 132–133
termination of parental rights and, 151
Foner, Eric, 235
Food stamps, 189
Forsaking Our Children (Hagedorn),
    272–273
"Fost-adopt" placements, 112
Foster care
    "aging out" of, 205
    Black parents portrayed as abandoning
        children to, 67–68
    child involvement in juvenile justice
        system and, 200, 205–206
    crisis in, 223
    expansion under welfare reform,
        186–187, 190–191
    federal policy and legislation, 105–113
    financial incentives to keep children in,
        123
    geographic dispersion of children,
        241–242
    group-based racial harm and, 223–224,
        243
    income insecurity as predictor of
        placement, 185
    increasing numbers of children in, 15,
        143, 159
    misidentifying problem with, 163–165
    negative effects on children, 17–19,
        159–162, 239–240
    physical abuse and, 129, 134
    "pre-adoptive" placements, 112
    provision of inferior services to Black
        children, 20–23
    psychological evaluations and, 40–44
    public perceptions of, 128–130
    public sympathy for, 123
    racial disparity in family reunification,
        19–20, 23–24
    racial disparity in placements, 8, 16–19,
        51–52
    reentry rates of Black children, 20–21
    reform efforts by Black parents, 68–74

supply and demand relationship with adoption, 166
termination of parental rights and, 151–154
Title IV and Title IV-E funding, 176
visibility hypothesis and, 9–10
visitations and, 141
"voluntary" placements, 82–89
See also Adoption; Child protective services; Child removal; Child welfare system; Kinship care
Foster Care Independence Act, 205
Foster parents
advantageous comparisons with biological parents, 112–113
federal policy on custody hearings and, 120–121
lack of involvement in juvenile justice, 204
public sympathy for, 123
treatment by family courts, 127–128
Fourteenth Amendment, 225, 234
Fourth Amendment, 287(n212)
Frazier, Charles, 220
Freud, Anna, 106, 123
Furman v. Georgia, 216

Galston, William, 116, 227
Garrison, Marsha, 118, 119, 163
Gelles, Richard, 50, 107
General Accounting Office, U.S., 132, 135, 142, 217
Genetic relatedness, 164–165
"Genetic Tie, The" (Roberts), 164–165
Genocide, 248. *See also* Cultural genocide
Georgia, 198
Gertner, Nancy, 212
Gingrich, Newt, 177
Giovannoni, Jeanne, 89, 96, 273
Giuliani, Rudolph, 78, 125, 177–178
Gleeson, James P., 263
Glover, Danny, 231
Goldberg, Jeffrey, 212
Golden, Renny, 32
Goldstein, Joseph, 106, 123
Gordon, Linda, 27, 175

Gould, Carol, 245
Grandparents, kinship care and, 258
Grandparents Helping Grandparents, 69–70
Green, Sabrina, 108
Group-based harm
Australian Aboriginal policy and, 251–252
child welfare system and, 223–225, 228–230, 236–267
federal Indian policy and, 248–251
interrelationship of individuals and social groups, 245–246
issues of children's rights and, 254–257
kinship foster care and, 258–267
political impact of family disintegration, 233–236
Group homes, juvenile delinquency and, 204
Group identity, of Black Americans, 231–232
Group welfare, family integrity and, 237
Guardians
ad litem, 125–126
kinship care and, 163
"standby," 86
Guggenheim, Martin, 54, 158, 161
Guthrie, William Dameron, 227
Gwaltney, John, 231

Habermas, Jurgen, 230, 246, 254
Hagedorn, John, 272–273
Hamilton-Bennett, Maisha, 239
Hampton, Robert, 31, 49–50
Handler, Joel, 184
Hardin, Mark, 190
Harley, Linda, 130–131
Harris, Norma, 52
Hartman, Ann, 90, 137
Hawkins, Wesley, 275
Head Start, 187
Health care, 25. *See also* Mental health care
Healthy Family Intervention Team (Mt. Sinai Hospital, Chicago), 3
Henry, Anisha, 88
Hispanic women, 96

Hochman, Gloria, 172
Homebuilders program, 140
Homeless, 177–178, 183
Home visiting, 275
Homicide. *See* Child homicide
Hospitals, racial bias in reporting child
    abuse, 50–51, 72
Housing problems, as reason for child
    removal, 21, 35
Housing services, racial disparity in
    provision of, 21
Howard, Connie, 70
Howell, Frank, 185
Human rights law, 248

"Id, the Ego, and Equal Protection, The"
    (Lawrence), 244
Illinois
    African American Child Welfare Act, 70
    bias against biological parents in family
        court, 126
    definitions of child neglect and
        maltreatment, 33, 55
    Family First program, 144, 147–148
    financial assistance to kinship caregivers,
        260
    increasing rates of kinship care in, 24
    Jornell's case, 3–6, 40–41, 43–44, 88, 90,
        127
    laws linking drug use and child abuse,
        155
    racial disparities in foster care, 8, 19
    termination of parental rights and, 128,
        151, 153–154
    welfare reform and, 182, 184
    youths involved in foster care and
        juvenile justice, 205
    See also Chicago; Department of Children
        and Family Services
Illinois Adoption Act, 153–154
Immigrant women, 175
Immigration laws, 172
"Incarcerated Parents and Their Children"
    (Bureau of Justice Statistics), 207
Incarceration
    of Black children, 209

    Black disenfranchisement and, 242–243
    of Black women, 208, 209–210
    impact on Black community civic life,
        242–243
    negative effects on Black children and
        families, 207–208, 209–211, 212–213
    racial discrimination and, 211–212
    racial disparity in, 200, 201, 207
Income
    child abuse and, 186
    as indicator for child removal, 35, 185
    as indicator of child maltreatment, 49, 186
Indiana, 204
Indian Adoption Project, 249, 251
Indian Child Welfare Act, 248, 250–251
Individual Responsibility Agreements
    (IRAs), 198–199
Infants, drug-affected, racial bias in
    reporting, 50–51, 72
In re J.C., 127–128
In re Marriage of B and R, 251
Institutional racism, 92–99
"Intensive Family-Centered Crisis Services,"
    133
International adoption, 172
International Covenant on Civil and
    Political Rights, 248
In the Interest of H.G., 153–154
In the Interest of N.F. and C.H., 156
IRAs. *See* Individual Responsibility
    Agreements
Izquierdo, Elisa, 54, 77

Jeffers, Geraldine, 78–79
Jewish charities, 224
Johnson, Andrew, 234
Johnson, Beverly, 72
Johnson, Madie, 69–70
Johnson, Matthew, 126, 127–128
Jornell (Black woman), 3–6, 40–41, 43–44,
    88, 90, 127
Journal of the American Medical Association,
    50
Judges
    acknowledgement of unconscious racism,
        65–66

guardians and, 126
irrational decision making, 53–55
"reasonable efforts" policy and, 131–133
sympathy for foster parents, 123
See also Criminal justice system; Custody
  hearings; Family courts; Juvenile justice
  system
Juvenile delinquency, 23, 202–203, 204
Juvenile detention, 202, 213–220
Juvenile justice system
  child involvement in foster care system
    and, 200, 205–206
  interrelationship with Black children and
    the child welfare system, 200,
    202–207
  overrepresentation of Black children in,
    202
  parental involvement and, 203–204
  racial disparity in detention, 202,
    213–220
  stereotyping of Black families and,
    219–220
  supervisory role in Black communities,
    206–207
  transfer of Black children to adult courts,
    216–218
  See also Criminal justice system;
    Incarceration

Kahn, Alfred, 85
Kalfus, Allen, 223
Kamerman, Sheila, 85
Karenga, Maulana, 232
Kayla McKean Child Protection Act
  (Florida), 123
Kelly, Patricia Fernandez, 237
Kempf, Kimberly L., 214
Kennedy, Randall, 93
Kennelly, Barbara, 108
Kilborn, Peter, 185, 209
Killing the Black Body (Roberts), 60–61
Kinship care
  as alternative to foster care, 162–163, 258
  Elizabeth Bartholet on, 169
  benefits of, 259–260
  Devon's case, 10–13, 18, 35, 265–267

disruption of family relationships,
  263–267
family loss of autonomy over child
  raising, 261–262
incarceration of parents and, 210
inferior services provided to Black
  families, 24–25
length of time children remain in,
  263
levels of financial support for caregivers,
  260–261
licensing requirements, 261
overrepresentation of Black children in,
  259
private, 258, 259, 261
relationship to child welfare system,
  258–259
waiver of protections against state
  intrusion in family life, 262
welfare reform and, 190
Ku Klux Klan, 236
Kurtz, Madeleine, 263–264, 265
Kwanzaa, 232

Lange, Jessica, 68
Latino children, 8, 9, 23, 48–49
Lauria, Joseph, 149
Law enforcement, child welfare investigation
  and, 274–275
Lawrence, Charles, III, 244
Lee, Lucy, 235
Legal Aid Society, 24
Legal orphans, 24, 158–159
Legal Services of New Jersey, 87
Lein, Laura, 180, 194–195, 197–198
Lewis, Julia, 118
Limoncelli, Stephani, 196
Lind, Meda Chesney, 213
Lindsey, Duncan, 15, 35, 54, 75, 90, 275
Littell, Julia, 146
Long, Russell, 179
Los Angeles, 34, 56, 201, 204, 217–218
Los Angeles Times (newspaper), 172
Losing Isaiah (film), 68
Lost Children of Wilder, The (Bernstein),
  223–224

Loving v. Virginia, 230
Lowery, Marcia, 132, 224
Lown, Anne, 242
Lubet, Steven, 123, 227–228

Maas, Henry S., 106
Making an Issue of Child Abuse (Nelson), 14
Making Democracy Work (Putnam), 237
Making Ends Meet (Edin & Lein), 64, 180, 194–195, 197–198
Malcolm X, 235–236
Maluccio, Anthony, 141
Mansbridge, Jane, 238
Marquez, Cynthia, 76
Maryland, 259
Massachusetts, 215
Massey, Douglas, 240
"Mass Incarceration Working Group," 242
Maternal unfitness, racial stereotypes of, 28, 60–65, 194
Mathematics Policy Research Group, 139
Matter of S. Children, 152–153
Matthews, Martha, 186–187
Mauer, Mark, 206, 207
May, Larry, 164, 245, 255
McCall's (magazine), 108
McConahay, Mary Jo, 172
McDonald, Jess, 110, 154
McKean, Kayla, 123
McLaughlin, Megan, 61
Mead, Lawrence, 93
Mech, Edmund, 53
Media
    attacks on family preservation, 107–108, 114
    portrayal of Black parents and foster care, 67–68
Medicaid, 86, 139, 189
Medina, Luis, 141
Meezan, William, 96
Mental health care, 22–23, 86–87
Mental illness, 60
MEPA. *See* Multiethnic Placement Act
Merritt, William, 247
Mexican Americans, 22
Meyer v. Nebraska, 225, 226, 227

Michigan, 57–58, 134, 146
Miller, Jerome, 215
Miller v. Youakim, 24
Milwaukee, 183, 185, 272–273
Mink, Gwendolyn, 192, 195
Minnesota, 151, 217
Minorities, visibility hypothesis and, 9–10
Minority rights, 226
Miscegenation, 230
Mississippi, 190, 198
Mississippi Delta, 185
Moffett, Jacquelynn, 120
Moffett, Lashonya, 71–72
Mondale, Walter, 14
Morality of Groups, The (May), 245
Morton, Thomas, 48, 53
Mothers. *See* Black women/mothers; Single mothers; Teen mothers; Welfare mothers
Mother's aid, 174–176
Mothers Organizing Systems for Equal Services (Operation MOSES), 69
Mt. Sinai Hospital (Chicago), 3
Moynihan, Daniel Patrick, 63
Mullen, Faith, 190
Multiethnic Placement Act (MEPA), 166, 169
Munchausen's syndrome by proxy, 5
Murphy, Patrick, 126, 170, 182
Murray, Charles, 63–64, 177, 193
Mustard, David, 212
Muwakkil, Salim, 242

NABSW. *See* National Association of Black Social Workers
National Adoption Center, 172
National Association of Black Social Workers (NABSW), 246–248, 273
National Black Child Development Institute, 21
National Center on Addiction and Substance Abuse (CASA), 138, 155
National Center on Child Abuse and Neglect, 48
National Child Welfare Leadership Center, 52

National Coalition for Child Protection
 Reform, 18, 123
National Committee to Prevent Child
 Abuse, 31
National Council on Civil Renewal, 116
National Governors Association, 188
National Incidence Study of Child Abuse
 and Neglect, 31, 49, 91
National Opinion Research Center Survey,
 194
National Public Radio, 114
Nation of Spectators, A (National Council
 on Civil Renewal), 116
Native Administration Act (Australia), 251
Nebraska, 225, 226
Negative stereotyping, 243–244
 of Black families, 219–220
 of Black maternal unfitness, 28, 60–65,
 194
Neglected Stories (Davis), 233–234, 235
Negro Family, The (Moynihan), 63
Neighborhood effects, 240–241
Neighborhoods
 effects on residents, 240–241
 impact of family disruption in, 241
Nelson, Barbara, 14
Nelson, Kristine, 135
Neubeck, Kenneth, 194
Nevada, 110
Newberger, Eli, 49–50
New Deal, 176
New England Journal of Medicine, 51
New Haven, 38–39
New Jersey
 bias against biological parents in family
 court, 126, 127–128
 family preservation services in, 137
 racial profiling by police, 211–212
 "voluntary" foster care placements, 87
New York Children's Aid Society, 168
New York City
 Administration for Children's Services,
 38, 70, 76, 79, 93, 124–125,
 130–131, 152, 203–204
 bias against biological parents in family
 court, 126

biasing of psychological evaluations, 44
child endangerment arrests, 77–78
child protective services and, 75, 76–78,
 79, 130–131
concentration of child welfare services in
 inner-city neighborhoods, 240
effect of high publicity cases on child
 welfare practice, 54
efforts to integrate local institutions with
 child welfare services, 273
failure to provide family preservation
 services, 136
fast-track agency adoption, 149
inferior treatment of children in kinship
 care, 24–25
pressures on caseworkers to remove
 children, 124–125
presumptions of white family fitness,
 67
racial bias in child removal, 51
racial disparity in foster care, 9
Special Services for Children, 145–146
teenager involvement with welfare and
 juvenile justice systems, 203–204
termination of parental rights and,
 151–153
variation in performance of child service
 agencies, 140–141
voluntary foster care placements, 85,
 87–88
welfare reform and, 177–178, 183
New York City Family Court, 149
New York Civil Liberties Union, 7
New York Daily News (newspaper), 87
New York Newsday (newspaper), 108
New York State
 conditions in group homes for children,
 204
 definition of child neglect, 37–38
 increase in numbers of unadopted state
 wards, 158
 kinship care and disruption of family ties,
 263–264, 265
 Safety Net program, 185
 studies on racial bias in child welfare
 system, 48

termination of parental rights and
parental incarceration, 211
visitation requirements, 141
welfare reform and the working poor,
182, 185
New York Times (newspaper), 76, 126,
130–131, 149, 178, 183, 186, 189
Nguzo Saba, 232
Nice, Julie, 194
Nicholson, Sharwline, 76
Nickel and Dimed (Ehrenreich), 183
Nobody's Children (Bartholet), 115–116,
168, 255, 256–257
Norplant, 193
North Dakota, 128
Norwood, D. J., 152–153

Ohio, 19, 25, 214
Olison, Tina, 69, 70, 71, 169–170
Olison v. Ryan, 71
Oliver, Toni, 247–248
Operation MOSES, 69
"Oppositional enclaves," 237
Oregon, 226
Orlando Sentinel (newspaper), 211
Orphan asylums, "colored," 7
Orphans, legal, 24, 158–159
Orphans of the Living (Toth), 223
Out-of-home placements, 202. *See also*
Foster care

Pacific Islanders, 8
Page, Alan, 217
Palmer, John M., 235
Parental rights, termination of
Adoption and Safe Families Act and,
109–110, 128, 151, 163
in cases of divorce, 119
costs to children, 160–162
creation of "legal orphans" and, 158,
159
in current child welfare policy, 150–151
economic incentives for, 119
incarceration of parents and, 211
increasing occurrence of, 150–151
judicial questioning of, 151–154

permanency planning and, 106–107,
110, 113, 150, 154–157
public depreciation of poor and Black
families and, 120
state laws aiding, 128
statutory limits on foster care and, 107,
109, 110, 151–154
substance-abusing parents and, 154–157
Supreme Court high standard for,
227–228
transracial adoption and, 167, 169–171
Parenting services, 21
Parents
adversarial relationship with child
protective services, 88–89
bias against in family courts, 125–128
disadvantageous comparisons with foster
parents, 112–113
involvement in juvenile justice and,
203–204
liability for child delinquency, 199
poverty-related stress and child
maltreatment, 27–28, 29–32
"voluntary" foster care placements and,
82–88
See also Black parents; Foster parents;
Parental rights, termination of
Paxson, Christina, 187
Pelton, Leroy, 30, 36–37, 58, 97, 175, 274
People (magazine), 58
Permanency planning
"concurrent," 111–112
costs to children, 161–162
in current federal policy, 106
limits on reasonable efforts to return
children, 106
termination of parents' rights and,
106–107, 113, 150, 154–157
See also Service plans
Personal Responsibility and Work
Opportunity Reconciliation Act, 173
Peterson, Terrell, 129
Peton, Leroy, 148–149, 178
Philadelphia, 79–80
Pierce v. Society of Sisters, 225–226, 227
Pitied But Not Entitled (Gordon), 175

Platt, Stacy, 162–163
Police
    child welfare investigation and, 274–275
    racial profiling, 211–212
Poor Laws, 26
Poverty
    Black children and, 44–46
    child maltreatment and, 29–44
    child welfare system and, 26–29
    extreme, 45, 184
    welfare reform and, 181, 182, 183, 184
Pre-adoptive parents, 120–121. *See also*
    Foster parents
Pre-adoptive placements, 112
Prejudice, cultural, 59–60
Press. *See* Media
Presser, Harriet, 187
Price of Motherhood, The (Crittenden),
    178–179
Prince v. Massachusetts, 226
Prison industrial complex, 206
Private kinship care, 258, 259, 261
Pro bono attorneys, 126
Progressive Era, welfare policies in,
    174–176
Protecting Children and Supporting Families
    (Cameron & Vanderwoerd), 145
Pryce, Deborah, 107, 118
Psychiatry, 23, 60. *See also* Mental health
    care
Psychological evaluations
    of children in foster care, 43–44
    of parents in child welfare system, 40–41
    potential for bias in, 41–43
"Psychological parent" theory, 106, 123
Psychologists
    biasing of psychological evaluations,
        41–43
    as experts in family court, 127
Public aid
    Progressive Era policies, 174–176
    See also Welfare system
Public radio, 114, 115
Putnam, Robert, 116, 237

Quadagno, Jill, 16

Racial discrimination
    child welfare system and, 244–245
    criminal justice system and, 211–212
    juvenile justice system and, 213–220
    religious charities and, 7
    See also Child welfare system, racial
        disparity in; Racial injustice; Racism
Racial injustice
    child welfare system and, 223–225,
        228–230
    issues of children's rights and racial
        oppression, 256–257
    political impact of family disintegration,
        233–236
    See also Group-based harm
Racial profiling, 211–212, 231
Racism
    American racial hierarchy, 230–231
    "anything but race" arguments, 97–98
    conditions promoting racial bias, 55–59
    "cultural meaning" test for, 244–245
    cultural prejudice, 59–60
    definitions of, 95
    evidence of racial bias, 47–55
    institutional, 92–99
    judicial acknowledgement of unconscious
        racism, 65–66
    juvenile justice system and, 213–220
    negative stereotyping and, 28, 60–65,
        194, 219–220, 243–244
    presumptions of white family fitness, 67
    See also Child welfare system, racial
        disparity in; Racial discrimination;
        Racial injustice
Radio. *See* Public radio
Rainbow/Push Coalition, 69
Rank, Mark, 45–46, 94
R.C. v. Hornsby, 272
Reagan, Ronald, 201
"Reasonable efforts" policy
    ASFA limits on, 108–109, 131–133
    legislation entailing, 105
    permanency planning limits on, 106
Redleaf, Diane, 55–56
Relapse, in drug recovery, 156–157
Religious charities, 7, 224

Responsibility, Black Americans and, 232
Reunification plans. *See* Service plans
Risk assessment instruments, 57
Rivkin-Carothers, Anita, 70–71, 72–74
Robinson, Randall, 271
Rodriquez, April, 76
Roxbury, 111
Runaway children, 204–205
Russell Sage Foundation, 242
Ryan, George, 70

Safety Net program (New York), 185
Safir, Howard, 78
St. Christopher's, Inc., 141
Sampson, Rev. Al, 69, 70
San Diego, 8–9, 48, 81, 136
San Francisco, 8
Santosky v. Kramer, 210–211, 227
Scandinavia, 274
Schizophrenia, 60
Schuerman, John, 146
Scoppetta, Nicholas, 93, 158
Seattle Post-Intelligencer (newspaper), 150
Self-efficacy, 239–240
Sengupta, Solmini, 76–77
Sentencing Project, 206, 242
Service plans
    with apparent intent of ensuring failure,
        81–82
    lack of parental input, 79–80
    unreasonable expectations of parental
        compliance, 80–81
    See also Permanency planning
Seven Principles. *See* Nguzo Saba
Shaw, E. Clay, Jr., 118
Simon, Rita, 253
Sinden, Amy, 79–80, 88
Single mothers, 63–64
    welfare reform and, 178–179, 180–181,
        184
Sisterhood of Black Single Mothers, 238
Slavery
    American racial hierarchy and, 230
    Black family solidarity and, 238
    child welfare system compared to by
        Malcolm X, 235–236

myth of careless Black mother and,
    61–62
repression of Black family autonomy,
    233–234
Social capital, 237
Social injustice
    issues of children's rights and racial
        oppression, 256–257
    See also Racial injustice
Social insurance, 176
Social reform movement, 14
Social Security Act, 142, 176
Social Security Income (SSI), 191–192
Social welfare programs, 268–271
Solnit, Albert, 106, 123
Sorenson, Annette, 78
South Carolina, 54, 62, 155
South Dakota, 33
Special Services for Children
    (New York City), 145–146
SSI. *See* Social Security Income
Stack, Carol, 60
"Standby guardians," 86
Starvation, 27–28
Stehno, Sandra, 140
Stewart, Cathryn, 126
Suarez, Ray, 114
Substance-abusing parents
    need for long-term treatment programs,
        138–140
    termination of parental rights and,
        154–157
Supreme Court, U.S., 24, 131, 250,
    287(n212), 289(n259)
    constitutional protection of family rights,
        225–228
    constitutional protection of parent-child
        relationship, 210–211
    on transfer of children to adult courts,
        216
    upholding of antimiscegenation laws, 230
Suter v. Artist M, 131

Talk of the Nation (radio show), 114
TANF. *See* Temporary Assistance to Needy
    Families

"Targeted" welfare policies, 270
Tate, Lionel, 213
Tayleur, Eleanor, 62
Taylor, Carole, 78
Teenagers. *See* Adolescents
Teen mothers, welfare reform and, 191
Teghtsoonian, Katherine, 195–196
Television. *See* Media
Temporary Assistance to Needy Families
 (TANF), 139, 173, 180, 181, 188,
 189, 190, 191, 192, 193, 197,
 198–199, 260
Tennessee, 19
Tepperman, Jean, 191
"Termination Barriers Project," 110, 150
Texas, 115, 214
Thirteenth Amendment, 109, 234
Thomas, Melvin, 97, 98
Thompson, Tommy, 183
Time (magazine), 129
Title IV (IV-E, IV-B), 142, 176
Toth, Jennifer, 223
Transracial adoption, 117
 Baby T case, 169–171
 as cultural genocide, 246, 248–253
 federal Indian policy and, 248–251
 impact studies, 253
 position of the NABSW against, 246–247
 racial politics of, 165–172
 termination of parental rights and, 167,
 169–171
Trattner, Walter, 168
Treatment foster care, 23
Troxel v. Granville, 228
Truly Disadvantaged, The (Wilson), 240

Ujima, 232
Umoja, 232
Unconscious racism
 "cultural meaning" test for, 244–245
 judicial acknowledgment of, 65–66
Unemployment insurance, 176
Unexpected Legacy of Divorce, The
 (Wallerstein, Lewis, & Blakeslee), 118
Unisys, 57–58
United Nations, 248

Unity, Black Americans and, 232
Universal social welfare, 268–271
University of Chicago, 144
University of Florida, 139
Unwed mothers. *See* Single mothers
U.S. News & World Report (magazine), 167
Utah Family Reunification Services program,
 146–147

Valerie (Black woman), 82–85
Vanderwoerd, Jim, 145
Venegas, Laura, 79
Vera Institute of Justice, 203, 204
Visibility hypothesis, 9–10
Visitation, 141
"Voluntary" foster care placements
 coercion of parents into, 87–88
 reasons for, 85–87
 recent increases in, 85
 Valerie's case, 82–85
Voluntary services, 275

Wald, Michael, 105
Waldfogel, Jane, 187, 275
Walker, Alice, 238
Wallace, Gilbreania, 129
Wallace, Joseph, 54, 147–148
Wallerstein, Judith, 118, 119
Wall Street Journal (newspaper), 63
War on Poverty, 16, 273
Washington, Claudette, 58
Washington, Harold, 170
Washington Post (newspaper), 107
Washington State, 29, 140, 186
Washington State Coalition for the
 Homeless, 137
Washington Times (newspaper), 188
Wasserman, Dan, 180
Way We Never Were, The (Coontz), 67
Web sites, on adoption, 103
Weinrich, David, 124
Weinstein, Jack, 76
Welfare mothers
 attitudes toward leaving welfare for work,
 197–198
 child care services and, 187–189

Welfare mothers (continued)
  "childfirst philosophy" among, 196–197
  conflicting requirements from welfare
    reform and child welfare services,
    193–199
  devaluation of caregiving work by,
    178–179, 180, 195–197
  economic consequences of welfare
    reform, 173–174, 180–185
  Individual Responsibility Agreements
    and, 198–199
  liability for child delinquency, 199
  welfare reform objectives for, 178,
    192–193
  welfare reform work requirements and,
    181, 184, 194–195
  See also Black women/mothers; Teen
    mothers, 193–199
Welfare Mothers' Movement, 238
Welfare queens, 64–65, 194
Welfare reform
  child care services and, 187–189
  child maltreatment and, 185–186, 187
  child removal and, 177–178, 186–187,
    189–192
  child welfare system and, 173–174,
    177–178, 181–182, 193–200
  conflicting requirements for welfare
    mothers, 193–199
  "culture of dependency" and, 194
  devaluation of caregiving work and,
    178–179, 180, 195–197
  disruption of families and, 189–192
  economic recession and, 184–185
  expansion of foster care and, 186–187,
    190–191
  impact on welfare mothers and families,
    173–174, 180–185
  objectives with regard to welfare mothers,
    178, 192–193
  pressure to limit family size, 193
  sanctions for non-compliance, 181
  services for children lost by working poor,
    189
  Social Security Income and, 191–192

substance-abusing parents and, 139
teen mothers and, 191
welfare queen myth, 65, 194
work requirements and, 181, 183–184,
    194–195
Welfare system
  Black menial labor and mandatory work
    provisions, 179–180
  civil rights movement and, 15–16, 176
  cultural sensitivity and, 271
  exclusion of Black women from, 175–176
  impact of growing numbers of Blacks in,
    16, 176–177
  Individual Responsibility Agreements,
    198
  myth of the Black welfare queen, 64–65,
    194
  New Deal regime, 176
  Progressive Era policies, 174–176
  See also Child welfare system; Welfare
    reform
Welfare-to-work programs
  devaluation of caregiving work, 196–197
  economic recession and, 184–185
  impact on mothers and children,
    173–174
  job readiness preparation and, 194
  See also Welfare reform
Westat, Inc., 205
Western, Bruce, 209
West Virginia, 86, 120
Wexler, Richard, 18, 36, 132
White, LaBrenda, 42, 43
White House Conferences on Children, 174
Whitman, Christine Todd, 211–212
Wilder v. Sugarman, 7, 224
Williams, Rev. Anthony, 69
Wilson, Pete, 177
Wilson, William Julius, 46, 64, 94, 240,
    270
Winston, Tina, 223
Wisconsin, 183, 185, 186
Women
  battered, 76
  immigrant, 175

See also Black women/mothers; Single
  mothers; Teen mothers; Welfare
  mothers
Woodhouse, Barbara Bennett, 226–227
Working poor
  economic consequences of welfare reform,
    180–181, 182–185
  loss of services for children, 189

Wright, Christopher, 192
Wyoming, 199
Young, Iris Marion, 270
Youth Initiative project (Milwaukee),
  272–273

Zimring, Frank, 216
Zuniga, Sidelina, 78